Right to Food

Right to Food

Dr. Devendra Prasad Pandey

ADHYAYAN

ADHYAYAN PUBLISHERS & DISTRIBUTORS
New Delhi-110002

Published by
ADHYAYAN PUBLISHERS & DISTRIBUTORS
4378/4B, 105, J.M.D. House, Murari Lal Street
Ansari Road Darya Ganj, New Delhi - 110002
Ph.: 011-23263018, 011-23277156, Fax: 23280028
Email: adhyayanpublishers@yahoo.com

Right to Food

Edition 2010
ISBN 978-81-8435-204-4

Printed in India

Published by Harish Chandra Yadav for Adhyayan Publishers & Distributors, Delhi. Laser Typesetting at V. M. Graphics and Printed at Tarun Offset Printers, Delhi

Preface

Every day 799 million people in developing countries about 18% of the world's population go hungry. India is a home to the largest number of hungry people (233 million.) Around 852 million people, out of 6.35 billion in the world are undernourished due to extreme poverty. The World Food Summit held in 1996 has an important objective of reducing hunger by 2015 but the goal seems to be difficult to achieve. The malnutrition in India has fallen from 11.1% in 1991-92 to 6.4% in 2002. As estimated by the National Commission on Population, the country's population is expected to touch 1.33 billion by 2020-2021 and the demand for foodgrains will be around 280 million tonne. India's domestic production of foodgrains has averaged 211.4 million tonnes and has become stagnant over the last five years (2003-04 to 2007-08).

Hunger is more than just lack of available food. According to Food and Agriculture Organisation (2002), the concept of food security implies, "a situation that exists when all people, at all times, have physical, social and economic access to sufficient, safe and nutritious food that meets their dietary needs and food preferences for an active and healthy life." The food security becomes a reality only at the household level. The entitlement theory of Amartya Sen which posits relationship between endowments of the households and their entitlement, definitely provide rich insight in understanding food insecurity—once the concept is widened to include not only legally enforceable entitlements, but also the market induced and civil society bestowed entitlements. More than three quarters of hungry people are in rural areas. About half live in farm households on marginal lands. Landlessness is rising in most rural region because of higher farming density and unequal distribution. The situation in districts like Sidhi is grim. The villages are far away and most of the land is owned by forest department. The book lament on the poverty alleviation through initiatives like Right to Food programme being organised by Gram Sudhar Samiti (GSS).

Countries like Bolivia, Cameroon, Egypt, Senegal and Uzbekistan have recently witnessed riots and violent demonstrations as people have gone on the rampage to protest against the scarcity of food and the inevitable consequence of scarcity—rising food prices. Price of pulse reached to Rs. 100 per kg. in various parts of the country. A person living below or just above the poverty line will find it impossible to purchase pulses which makes vegetarian to fulfill minimum calories requirement. It is sure that such high prices will force majority of the people living in rural areas towards malnutrition.

While participating in a press conference at New Delhi on 8 July, 2009 Nobel laureate Amartya Sen advocated Right to Food in India because availability of food prevents many diseases caused by malnutrition. India is well placed in meeting the challange of food security. It is one of the largest producers of food grains in the world, feeding 17 percent of the world's population on only 3 percent of the world's arable land. In 2007-08, foodgrain production took a quantum jump to 230.8 million tonnes as a result of series of measures and good monsoon. However, due to late onset of monsoon in 2009, the foodgrain production in 2009-10 is predicted at 229.9 million tonnes. Our foodgrain buffer stock is enough to feed our people for 13 months. In the beginning of this year, there was 180.6 lakh tonnes of wheat in the Central Government's pool, which is more than twice the buffer stock requirement of 82 lakh tonnes. But the rising food prices of food grain specially pulses is threat to food security. It is true that poor will be out of net to purchase pulses, sugar, vegetables which forms nutritious diet.

The book contains hououurable Supreme Court's orders in the Right to Food case and reports of the Commissioners of the Supreme Court. It also include eight report in detail i.e. "A special report on the most vulnerable social groups and their access to food." I am highly indebted to these resources, authors and the organisations.

During my association with the 'Right to information movement", I realised the importance of an enactment to check hunger death. Though hunger death is lesser reported and government deny such reports but it is a grim picture of today's society. Government's claim of having buffer stock of foodgrain and world's largest network of cheap ration shops under public distribution system is working in the country but people suffer from malnutrition and hunger.

I first worked on right to food campaign in 2005 and realised that it needs doing. My association with NGOs working on rights based movements and the most viable system should it be rights mode school of though which ensures transparent and efficient delivery mechanism in favour of poor community or livelihood systems school of thought which ensures availability of employment, etc. It was a great pleasure for me to be associated with Right to Food programme being organised by Gram Sudhar Samiti with support from Sir Dorabji Tata Trust. I participated in many activities including training of staff on leadership in which I found volunteers full of zeal and courage to work against corruption and in favour of dalits and scheduled tribe community.

I wrote articles on right to food and received appreciation from all quarters specially from activists who are working on like issues. The constant linkage with right to food programme motivated me to write a book on "Right to Food". The book has a chapter on strategic intervention on right to food programme by Gram Sudhar Samiti.

I am grateful to volunteers of Gram Sudhar Samiti, Sidhi for providing valuable data and organising field visits.

I acknowledge my gratitude to all authors and agencies whose resource materials are included in this book. I am indebted to my family members whose constant inspiration motivated me to work on this subject. I acknowledge my sincere gratitude to officials of Nehru Gram Bharti University to relieve me to write this book. Suggestions for the improvement in the book will be highly appreciated.

(Dr. Devendra Prasad Pandey)
Director
Rajiv Gandhi Institute of
Professional Management
Nehru Gram Bharti University
Kotwa-Jamunipur, Allahabad.

Contents

	Preface	v
1.	Hunger, Malnutrition and Food Security	1
2.	Connecting Indian Agriculture : Problems and Prospects	54
3.	The Right to Food	74
4.	Social Capital as Basis of Rights	105
5.	The Programme Partners	116
6.	Strategic Intervention by Gram Sudhar Samiti on Right to Food	153
7.	Management of Right to Food Programme	176
	Annexures	198
	Index	437

1

Hunger, Malnutrition and Food Security

Hunger, malnutrition and unemployment symbolise poverty – these are loyal companions. The situation in respect of all the three components has been turning grimmer day by day.

According to one estimate, one-third of the world's estimated 860 million people go to bed hungry in India in times of plenty. Prof P.N. Srivastava, the noted scientist and a former Member, Planning Commission, expressed the view that more than 200 million people, nearly 25 per cent of our population, were not having two square meals a day, adding that wastage of food amounted to Rs. 25,000 crores per annum at different levels in products, transportation and handling. Yet another expert, Madhura Swaminathan, who teaches at the Indian Statistical Institute, Kolkata, quoting from "State of Food Insecurity" of the FAO, told a seminar in July 2004 that India was home to 29 per cent of the world's chronically hungry. She, however, opined that this was an underestimate.

We have referred above to widespread poverty. One estimate says that India has one-third of the world's absolute poor. According to another assessment, more than 50 per cent of people in India subsist on less than $ 1 a day. The abject poverty is fraught with disastrous consequences. There were reports of babies being sold for paltry sums, in some cases for merely Rs. 10 per baby. There was a chilling report of the killing of his three minor daughters by a person by throwing them into the Narmada river in Gujarat on February 5, 2004. His wife in her complaint said her husband had been under mental stress due to paucity of money and the "thought of bringing up five daughters kept on worrying him". And what a pity to see a photograph in *The Hindu* of August 30, 2004 wherein a child (half naked), aged three, was shown breaking stones on the banks of the Mahananda, one among several hundred thousand children working as labourers.

Turning to the sister problem of malnutrition, the second National Family Health Survey reveals that about half of all the children below the age of three are undernourished and, according to the latest *Human Development Report,* India has the highest levels of child under-nutrition in the world, along with Bangladesh and Nepal. An item in *Mainstream* of April 10, 2004 indicated that 40 million of the Indian population is under-nourished due to lack of 'effective purchasing power'. A recent report of the FAO stated that India was among 17 countries where the number of the under-nourished increased substantially in the second half of the 1990s. (Arora 2004)

Government of India in order to ensure food security in the country has launched the **National Food Security Mission**. The NFSM scheme has been launched by the Central Government from 2007-08 to increase the production of rice by 10 million tones, wheat by 8 million tonnes and pulses by 2 million tonnes by the end of 11th five year plan (2011-12). The approach is to bridge the yield gap in respect of these crops through dissemination of improved technologies and farm management practices was really needed at this hour. NFSM - Rice, NFSM - Wheat and NFSM - Pulses will be implemented in 133, 138 and 168 identified districts of different States, respectively. The targets set for the mission are indeed crucial given the frequent shortfall of grains in the recent years for the food security buffer and welfare schemes as well as for open market consumption. The mission set is definitely of top priority for the government and can play an important role to give boost to the food grain production. Non-treasury mode of fund transfer for speedy availability of funds, awards for best performing district etc. are some of the approaches in the mission plan that should be appreciated. Department of Food and Public Distribution is responsible for the management of the food economy of the country. It maintains a buffer stock of food grains in order to meet any emergencies like drought/failures of crop, as well as to enable open market intervention in case of price rise. The minimum stocks that should be available in the Central Pool at the beginning of the four quarters of a year are as follows :

(With effect from April 2005) in Lakh Tonnes

Date	*Rice*	*Wheat*	*Total*
1st April	122.0	40.0	162.0
1st July	98.0	171.0	269.0
1st Oct.	52.01	10.0	162.0
1st Jan.	118.0	82.0	200.0

Source: Department of Food and Public Distribution, GOI (Bardoloi & Sarmah 2008)

Population and Per Capita Per Day Net Availability of Food Grains

Year	*Population (in Million)*	*Per Capita net availablility per day (in grams)*		
		Cereals	*Pulses*	*Total*
1952	369.2	325.4	59.1	384.5
1962	452.2	398.9	62.2	460.9
1972	563.9	419.1	47.0	466.1

Year	*Population (in Million)*	*Per Capita net availablility per day (in grams)*		
		Cereals	*Pulses*	*Total*
1982	703.8	415.6	39.2	454.8
1992	867.8	434.5	34.3	468.8
2002	1050.6	458.7	35.4	494.1
2003	1068.2	408.5	29.1	437.6
2004	1085.6	426.9	35.8	462.7
2005	1102.8	390.9	31.5	422.4

Source: Economic Survey, Government of India, 2007-08.

Policy on Food Security and Management

India has set three pronged objectives for its food management initiatives viz., procurement of food grains from farmers at remunerative prices, distribution of foodgrains to the consumers particularly the vulnerable sections of the society and maintaining a buffer stock of food grains to ensure food security in the country through Minimum Support Prices (MSP). This initiative tries to ensure remunerative prices to the poor farmers by procuring food grains and through the Central Issue Price (CIP) mechanism, it distributes food grains with a view to ensuring stability in food prices. Being the nodal agency, FCI is responsible for procurement, distribution and storage of food grains.

The years 2001-03 witnessed high levels of stock build up. The food grain stocks available with the FCI stood at an all time high of 64.7 million tonnes against an annual requirement of around 20 million tonnes for ensuring food security in June 2002. After the year 2002, there has been a steady decline in the food stocks because of relatively lower procurement of rice and wheat, reduction in the growth of agriculture sector, relatively high off-take of cereals. The stock position of food grains as on January 1, 2008 was 19.2 million tonnes against a buffer stock norm of 20 million tonnes comprising 11.5 tonnes of rice and 7.7 million tonnes of wheat. The reduced buffer stock of wheat has led to the government for resorting to import of wheat from abroad to meet the demand as committed towards targeted public distribution system and other welfare programmes for the poor. Since the world food price is at a peak now, the domestic prices of wheat after the projected import is not expected to see a downward trend.

Further, the enhancement in MSP of food grain over the years has given rise to an increase in the economic cost and the distribution cost of the food grains. While the distribution cost of wheat and rice was Rs. 165.3 per quintal in 2003-04 the same rose to Rs. 286.7 in 2007-08. During the same period the economic cost of wheat and rice was Rs. 928.7 and 1371.3 per quintal. The Government's steps in price stability in food commodities for poor have not really benefited the poor farmers. Steps to insulate the poorer section of the society from price rise by distribution of essential food items through fair price shops, allocating food grains to Below Poverty Line (BPL) and Antyodaya Anna Yojana beneficiaries, and maintaining CIP of wheat and rice at July 2002 level could not ensure the availability of sufficient food grains to the poor due to inflationary situation and price rise in food articles. Further, there has been a huge gap between the MSP and CIP for BPL people under Targeted Public Distribution System (TPDS). This gap has encouraged the unscrupulous Fair Price Shop owners to divert the food grains to open market (Tripathy 2008).

The recent crisis in financial markets around the world has figured prominently in the media. Despite the severity of the global financial crisis and its potential adverse impact on world growth rates, the current food crisis threatens to have a significantly more serious impact on people's lives, particularly in developing countries. The crisis has been developing for some time now, and should have been anticipated. Unfortunately, the media and, perhaps more important, governments across the world seem to have realized the magnitude of this crisis relatively recently.

World food prices have increased on an average by almost 40 per cent during the course of the last year, while the prices of staple food items have increased by 80 per cent over three years. The United Nation's World Food Programme seems to have woken up to the severity of the crisis, and has launched an appeal to increase its aid budget from $2.9 billion to $3.4 billion in order to meet its target of feeding 73 million people across the world at the higher prices prevailing today. The World Bank president has also appealed to the rich countries to provide funds to feed the poorer country (Dutta 2009).

Address by Amartya Sen titled, "Hunger in India": at a public hearing on hunger and right to food in Delhi University on 10 Janaury 2003: When India achieved independence, more than fifty years ago, the people of the country were much afflicted by endemic hunger. They still are. Since India is often considered to be one of the great success stories in tackling the food problem. the belief in success has to be scrutinized in the light of the grim reality that we can observe.

The positive perception is not, however, entirely mistaken. Certain things have been achieved and it is important to see what has been accomplished and what remains to be done. Some positive things have certainly occurred. First, pre-independence India had a stagnating agriculture and this has been firmly replaced by an imposing expansion of the production possibilities in Indian agriculture, through innovative departures. The technological limits have been widely expanded. What holds up Indian food consumption today is not any operational inability to produce more food but a far-reaching failure to make the poor of the country able to afford enough food.

Second, substantial famines that so plagued India until independence has been effectively eliminated : the last sizeable famine occurred in 1943. And yet this creditable record in famine prevention has not been matched by a similar success in eliminating the pervasive presence of endemic hunger that plights the lives of hundreds of millions of people in this country.

Indeed, India has not, it should be absolutely clear, done well in tackling the pervasive presence of persistent hunger. Not only are there persistent recurrences of severe hunger and starvation in particular regions, but there is also prevalence of endemic hunger across much of India. Indeed, India does much worse in this respect than even Sub-Saharan Africa. Estimates of general undernourishment - what is sometimes called "protein-energy malnutrition" - are nearly twice as high in India as in Sub-Saharan Africa. It is astonishing that despite the intermittent occurrence of famine in Africa, it too manages to ensure a much higher level of regular nourishment than does India. About half of all Indian children are, it appears, chronically undernourished and more than half of all adult women suffer from anaemia. In maternal undernourishment as well as the incidence of underweight babies and also in the frequency of cardiovascular diseases in later life (to which adults are particularly prone if nutritionally deprived in the womb). India's record is among the very worst in the world.

What then, should we do, indeed what can we do? People have to go hungry if they do not have the means to put enough food. Hunger is primarily a problem of general poverty and thus overall economic growth and its distributional pattern cannot but be important in solving the hunger problem. It is particularly critical to pay attention to employment opportunities, other ways of acquiring economic means and also food prices, which influence people's ability to buy food and thus affect the food entitlements they effectively enjoy. It is also crucial to use the means of specialized delivery of food that particularly helps poor children, such as more extensive use of feeding in the school. This can not only increase the incentive of children to go to school but also actually make them healthier and less undernourished. The Supreme Court has been judicious in emphasizing thc importance of this right.

Further, since undernourishment is not only a cause of

ill health, but can also result from it, attention has to be paid to health care, in general and to the prevention of endemic diseases that prevent absorption of nutrients, in particular. There is also plenty of evidence to indicate that lack of basic education too contributes to undernourishment, partly because knowledge and communication are important, but also because the ability to secure jobs and incomes are influenced by the level of education.

Indeed, low incomes, relatively higher prices, bad health care and neglect of basic education are all influential in causing and sustaining the extraordinary levels of undernutrition in India. There are also more complex connections. Recent medical research has brought out the long-run effects of maternal undernourishment, which not only ruins the health of the mothers, but can also cause serious health problems for the children who are born with low birth weight, since they are more prone to children's diseases and later on in life also to adult diseases. Indeed, low birth weight substantially increases the incidence of cardiovascular diseases later in life.

What about food policy, and in particular food prices policy? Why is it the case that the large expenditure on food subsidy in India does not achieve more in reducing undernourishment ? Part of the answer lies in the fact that the subsidy is mainly geared to keep food prices high for the sellers of food - farmers in general rather than to make food prices low for the buyers of food. The high incentive to produce more food while giving little help to the poorer people to buy food has produced the massive stocks of food grains that we find in India today.

In 1998, stocks of food grains in the central government's reserve were around 18 million tonnes - close to the official "buffer stock" norms needed to take care of possible fluctuations of production and supply. Since then, it has climbed and climbed, firmly surpassing the 50 million mark, and while it has had some ups and some downs, the total stock is still extraordinarily large. To take Jean Dreze's graphic description, if all the stock of grain were laid up in a row, this would stretch more than one million kilometres, taking us to the moon and back.

The public expense of the programme of subsidies (estimated, not long ago, at a staggering Rs. 21,000 crores a year) is mainly used to add to the market food prices to raise the incomes of the farmers. We are evidently determined to maintain, at heavy cost, India's unenviable combination of having the worst of undernourishment in the world and the largest of unused food stocks on the globe. Indeed, a regime of high prices in general (despite a gap between procurement prices and consumers retail prices) both expands procurement and depresses the affordability of food. The bonanza for food producers and sellers is matched by the privation of the consumers. Since the biological need for food is not the same thing as the economic entitlement to food (that is, what people can afford to buy given their economic circumstances and the prices). The large stocks procured are hard to get rid of, despite rampant undernourishment across the country. The very price system that generates a massive supply keeps the hands and the mouths of the poorer consumers away from food.

In fact, much of the subsidy goes into the cost of maintaining a massively large stock of food grains, with a mammoth and unwieldy food administration. Also, since the cutting edge of the price subsidy is to pay farmers to produce more and earn more, rather than to sell existing stocks to consumers at lower prices (that too happens, but only to a limited extent and to restricted groups), the overall effect of food subsidy is more spectacular in transferring money to farmers than in transferring food to the undernourished Indian consumers.

Of course, those who want high producer prices of food include some who are not affluent, in particular the small farmer or peasant who sells a part of the crop. The interest of this group is mixed up with those of big farmers and this produces a lethal confounding of food politics. While the powerful lobby of privileged farmers presses for higher procurement prices and for public funds to be spent to keep these prices high, the interests of poorer farmers, who too benefit from the high prices, are championed by political groups that represent these non-affluent beneficiaries. Stories of hardship of these people play a powerful part not only in the rhetoric in favour of high food prices, but also in the genuine conviction of many equity-oriented activists that this would help some very badly off people. And so it would, but of course it would help the rich farmers much more and cater to their pressure groups, while the vital interests of the much larger number of people who have to buy food rather than sell it are thoroughly sacrificed.

There is need for more explicit analysis of the effects of public policies on the different classes and in particular on the extreme underdogs of society who, along with their other deprivations (particularly low income, bad health care, inadequate opportunities of schooling), are also remarkably underfed and undernourished. For casual labourers, slum dwellers, poor urban employees, migrant workers, rural artisans, rural non-farm workers, even farm workers who are paid cash wages, high food prices bite into what they can eat. The overall effect of the high food prices is to hit many of the worst off members of the society extremely hard. And while it does help some of the farm-based poor, the net effect is quite regressive on distribution. There is, of course, relentless political pressure in the direction of high food prices coming from farmers' lobbies and the slightly muddied picture of benefitting some farm-based poor makes the policy issues sufficiently befuddled to encourage the confused belief that high food prices constitute a pro-poor stance, when in overall effect it is very far from that.

Given our democratic system, nothing is as important as clear-headed public discussions of the causes of deprivation and the possibility of successful public intervention. Public action includes not only what is done for the public by the state, but also what is done by the public for itself. It includes what people can do by demanding remedial action and through making governments accountable. That is exactly why we are gathered here today. The lives and well-being of hundreds of millions of people will depend on the extent to which our public discussion can be broadened and be made more informed. I hope we manage to have some impact." (Sen 2003)

The then Prime Minister, Atal Bihari Vajpayee, had said in his inaugural address to a national consultation on "Towards a Hunger Free India" in the last week of April 2001, in New Delhi : "Democracy and hunger cannot go together. A hungry stomach questions and censures the system's failure to meet what is a basic biological need of every human being. There can be no place for hunger and poverty in a modern world in which science and technology have created conditions for abundance and equitable development."

Now it is challenge for Indian government to make India hunger free. The Congress party, in its election manifesto, has already expresses desire to implement Food Security Act an enactment on Right to Food.

Exclusion of Destitutes

Destitute people are those who almost completely lack the resources (financial and material), the employment, assets, access to credit and social family support and networks which are required to secure the means for dignified survival.

Karl Marx wrote evocatively of the exclusion of destitute population from what he described as "political economy": "political economy does not recognise the unoccupied worker.... the begger, the unemployed, the starving [and] the destitute are figures which exist not for it, but only for the eyes of doctors, judges, gravediggers and beadles. Nebulous... political economy." Incidently, Marx was right about their exclusion, but not about their being "unoccupied workers." On the contrary, we have found that the destitute are forced to labour in ardous, low-paid, undignified work in order even to stay barely alive as each new day dawns. (Mander 2009)

Towards Zero Hunger

While launching "Hunger Zero" programme, Lula da

Silva, President of Republic of Brazil said, "we will make it possible for people in our country to eat three square meal a day, every day, with no need for hand outs from any one Brazil can not go on living with so much inequality. We must overcome hunger, extreme poverty and social exclusion. Our war is not to kill any one. It is to save lives."

There have been earlier attempts at 'fighting hunger. Brazil's Zero Hunger programme launched by President Lula in 2003, for instance, was the result of a year of inputs from various stake-holders, and is still far away from alleviating hunger. It was launched with the objective of providing three square meals a day to an estimated 46 million people living in hunger and extreme poverty.

By 2005, Brazil had invested US $12 billion in the Zero Hunger programme, although President Lula was not satisfied and later criticised the programme for being riddled with mistakes. Drawing inspiration from the Brazilian programme, Egypt also launched a US $2 billion programme for a food insecure population. The sub-title of Brazil's food security policy was equally iridescent. "Brazilians who eat helping those who do not." (Mander 2009)

There are further lessons to be drawn from Mexico's *Progresa-oportunidades* human development programme launched in 1997, which took one year to research and roughly two years to plan. The programme serves 4.2 million households, and costs almost US $1 billion every year.

Even in the United States, which invests heavily in food stamp programmes, hunger is on the rise. More than 31.6 million people, or one in every 10 Americans, are either a beneficiary of the food stamp programme or takes part in the Supplemental Nutrition Assistance programme.

At present, the Government of India provides 35 kg. of food grains, including wheat and rice, to 65.2 million families classified as living below the poverty line (BPL). These subsidised rations are made available at a price of Rs. 4.15 per kg. for wheat, and Rs. 5.65 per kg. for rice. For the 24.3 million families classified under the *Antyodaya scheme* (also part of the BPL category), the price of grains is reduced to Rs. 2 for wheat and Rs. 3 for rice.

In other words, India's Public Distribution Scheme technically caters to 316 million people. These are the poorest of the poor, and the way the BPL line has been drawn the PDS should provide them with their minimal daily food intake. If the PDS had been even partially effective, I see no reason why India should be saddled with the largest population of hungry in the world. There is no reason why Punjab, for example, the best performing state in terms of hunger, should be ranked below Gabon, Honduras and Vietnam in the Global Hunger Index.

Any programme aimed at providing food-for-all on a long-term basis has to look beyond food stamps and public distribution schemes. India must move to a Zero Hunger programme by attacking the structural causes of poverty and hunger.

Creating adequate employment opportunities and promoting sustainable livelihoods by involving the village communities has to be woven into any long-term food security plan. Better health care facilities, access to safe drinking water and sufficient micro-nutrient intake will ensure that food is properly absorbed.

An empty stomach cannot wait. With the passage of time it will inevitably lead to social upheavals, and the repercussions could be still more damaging to society at large. It is so painful to see that while the government is trying to fight the growing menace of *naxalism* on the one hand, on the other it is actually perpetuating the conditions that help promote extremism. Agriculture is being sacrificed for the sake of industry, mining and exports, and land acquisitions are divesting Indian farmers of their only form of economic security by forcing them to quit agriculture.

The proposed National Food Security Act cannot be a stand-alone activity. It has to be integrated with various other programmes and policy initiatives to ensure that hunger becomes history. To achieve this objective, the food security plan should essentially aim at adopting a five-point approach:

- *Public Policies for Zero Hunger*: A combination of structural policies aimed at the real causes of hunger and poverty, specific policies to meet the household needs for long-term access to food and nutrition, and local policies based on local needs that keep the concept of sustainable livelihoods in focus. For instance, all policies should be aimed at reversing the rural-urban migration. The more migration escalates, the more urban centres will be chocked, and the greater the burden on government support for fighting hunger. Agriculture and rural development remains the best defence against the growing threat of naxalism.
- *Sustainable livelihoods:* In a country where agriculture is the mainstay of the economy, all efforts must be directed towards strengthening low external input sustainable agricultural practices. There is an urgent need to revitalise the natural resource base, restore groundwater levels, and provide higher incomes to farmers. A monthly take-home income package based on land holdings has to be worked out for farmers. The NREGA has to be integrated with agriculture, and the interest on micro-credit for the poorest of the poor has to be brought down to 4 per cent from the existing 20-48 per cent.
- *Public Distribution System*: There is an urgent need to dismantle the PDS except for the *Antyodaya* families (those identified by the Indian Government as the poorest of the poor who should receive state-provided wheat and rice). The present classification of BPL and APL ('below poverty levels' and 'above poverty levels') needs to be done away with. The recommendation of the National Commission on Enterprise in the Unorganised Sector (NCEUS), which states that 836 million people in India spend less than Rs. 20 (40 US cents) a day, should be the criteria for a meaningful food-for-all programme. The average ration per family at 25 kg. also needs to be revised

upwards, and there is a need to expand the food basket by including coarse cereals and pulses.

- *Foodgrain Banks:* The dismantling of the Public Distribution System has to be followed by the setting up of foodgrain banks at the village and block level. Any long-term food security plan cannot remain sustainable unless the poor and hungry become partners in the fight against hunger. There are ample examples of successful models of traditional grain banks (for instance, the famed *gola* system in Bihar), which need to be replicated through a nationwide programme involving self-help groups and NGOs. Programmes and projects must be drawn up to make foodgrain banks sustainable over the long-term and viable without government support in a couple of years, involving charitable institutions, religious bodies, self-help groups (SHGs) and the non-profit organizations to ensure speedy implementation.
- *International Commitments:* Global commitments and neoliberal economic policies should not be allowed to interfere with the food security plan. The World Trade Organisation (WTO) agreements, the Free Trade Agreements (FTAs) and various bilateral trade deals should not be allowed to displace farming communities and play havoc with national food security. For instance, India cannot compromise agriculture in the ongoing Doha Round of negotiations in the WTO which will allow cheaper and subsidised imports. Importing food for a country like India is like importing unemployment, thereby increasing the number of hungry. (Sharma, Devinder)

From Malnutrition to Nutrition

Overall, significant progress has been made in the reduction at child malnutntion, with underweight prevalence declining from 33 to 28% in the developing world as a whole. The largest decline was achieved in East Asia and the Pacific where underweight levels decreased by a third (from 25% to 17%). This regional decline is driven primarily by improvements in China, where underweight prevalence declined by nearly 50% during the 1990s. However, underweight prevalence for other countries in the region did not decline at the same level. Substantial improvements were also made in the Latin America and the Caribbean region where rates fell from 11% to 7%, although overall levels were already relatively low to begin with South Asia also expenenced declines over the decade (from 53% to 47%). However, the region continues to suffer from staggeringly high levels of child malnutrition with close to half of all under five children being underweight. The underweight prevalence rates for the Middle East and North Africa region remained roughly the same. Similarly, in Sub-Saharan Africa there has been little or no change over the decade and nearly a third of all under five remain underweight.

When we try to understand what any of the commonly used terms such as progress, economic growth and development mean to average Indians, it is clear that it is being able to provide a better life for their children. Unfortunately, we have an astonishingly bad record of child and infant care. In India, one million children die within the first 28 days of life – that's a quarter of such deaths worldwide. Of the ones that are lucky enough to survive, 8.3 million are babies born underweight. The situation worsens as these babies grow older. Every third child who is underweight, and under five, in the world is an Indian.

Malnutrition is the underlying cause of as many as half the deaths of children under five. About 25 per cent of children under age five in the world are underweight. In India the underweight prevalence rate is 43 per cent.

We all take pride in being a country with one of the youngest populations in the world. But collectively, as a nation, we seem to have turned our face away from the millions of children who continue to remain hungry, malnourished and sick in our country.

The states with the highest number of underweight

children are Madhya Pradesh, Jharkhand and Bihar. They are followed by Gujarat, Orissa, Chhattisgarh, Uttar Pradesh and Meghalaya. India also has the largest pool of children who have never been immunised in the world. And pneumonia and diarrhoea are still the biggest killers.

Ours is a country of contrasts. The contrasts between the rich and the poor, the urban and the rural have always existed. But nowhere is this contrast more appalling than between the overweight children we see in our metros and cities who are battling obesity and the scrawny stick-legged children playing in the fields in our villages.

How serious are we in making sure that our young ones have at least minimum nutrition and basic health care so that they have a fighting chance of survival? The time for old debates—whether the blame lies with the state governments or the central government – is gone. It's time we got our act together and approached the problem with fresh perspectives. With about half of our children under five years of age being either malnourished or undernourished according to the National Family Health Survey - we have no time to waste.

We all —governments, bureaucrats, media, NGOs, civil society – have to work together and with focus to ensure that all our children are fed, vaccinated and educated. Much of our effort fails to get translated into tangible help on the ground for our children. There are numerous policies and programmes that have been in place for years. But how many of them have achieved even partial success? What makes all of this even more frustrating is the fact that audit reports, appraisals and feedback on the effectiveness of these programmes are also questionable.

The Integrated Child Development Scheme has been in place since 1975. Then there are other programmes like the Mid-day Meal Scheme and Supplementary Nutrition Programme. However, they will be a success only when they cover every needy child.

We have to be able to replicate some of the success stories in certain states in the underperforming areas. But we also have to assess the failures and see what we can learn from those experiences. In the last two or three decades our budget outlays have not been a problem, though one hopes for an unprecedented increase in funds in the 11th five-year plan for the social sector.

I have found, while touring the country, that simple things can help bring about a positive change. Like educating young mothers to overcome cultural biases, generating awareness about hygiene, providing information about post-natal care and dispelling myths. These are some of the ways in which people in the rural parts of our country can be helped to create a safer, better and healthier tomorrow for future generations. (Pilot, 2008)

Food : A Political Weapon and Commercial Enterprise

Nobel laureate Amartya Sen, in his well known theory of entitlements, challenged the then prevailing economic ratianale that people died in famines due to scarcity of food. His theory was partly based upon the study of the decisions made by the colonial masters when food was diverted for commercial purposes during the Bengal famine of 1943. In the last 60 years or so, following the great human tragedy of the Bengal famine, food aid has been conveniently used as a political weapon. But what is arguably one of the most blatantly anti-humanitarian and morally repugnant acts was the decision of the United States Agency for International Development (USAID) to offer US $50 millian in food aid to famine-stricken Zimbabwe an the proviso that it was used to purchase genetically modified (GM) maize. Food aid, therefore, is no longer just an instrument of foreign policy. It has now become a major commercial activity, even if it means exploiting famine victims and the starving millions.

An estimated 13 millian people in Zambia, Zimbabwe, Lesotho, Mozambique and Malawi were faced with severe hunger in 2002 and lived under the spectre of an expected famine, following two years of draught and floods.

For the genetically modified GM food industry, reeling

under a growing rejection of its untested and harmful food products, there was money in hunger, starvation and death. Spearheaded by USAID, the industry swung into action making it abundantly clear that it had only genetically modified maize to offer which it was not willing to segregate. The World Food Programme, which over the past few decades has for all practical purposes become an extension of USAID, was quick to add its rubber stamp. It had earlier helped the United States to reduce its grain surpluses by taking its genetically modified food for a mid-day meal programme for school children in Africa.

President Mugabe was not able to hold out for long. He had earlier told Zimbabwe's Parliament on July 23, 2004; "We fight the present drought with our eyes clearly set on the future of the agricultural sector, which is the mainstay of our economy. We dare not endanger its future through misplaced decisions based on acts of either desperation or expediency." But then, the biotechnology industry used all its financial power to break down African resistance. Once GM food was accepted as humanitarian aid, it would be politically difficult for African Governments to oppose the corporate take-over of Africa's agricultural economy. For the industry, Africa provides a huge and emotionally symbolic market.

Then Zambian President Levy Mwanawasa said that his people would rather die than eat toxic food. Although Malawi said it had no choice but to accept GM maize, newspaper reports cited Mozambique, across which Malawi's food aid had to pass, as asking the WFP to cover it with plastic sheeting to avoid spillage while in transit.

Malawi incidentally was faced with famine after it was forced to sell maize to earn dollars for debt servicing. One of Malawi's key commercial creditors needed to have their debt repaid, according to Malawi's President, who in a BBC interview said "the government had been forced (to sell maize) in order to repay commercial loans taken out to buy surplus maize in previous years." President Muluzi said the IMF and the World Bank "insisted that, since Malawi had a surplus and the (government's) National Food Reserve Agency had this huge loan, they had to sell the maize to repay the commercial banks." So Malawi duly sold 28,000 tonnes of maize to Kenya. Under pressure from her creditors, led by the World Bank and the IMF, Malawi exchanged maize—her people's staple diet—for dollars.

And then, it got another loan to purchase genetically modified food from the United States. A market for genetically modified food industry is being created in connivance with the powers that be.

Ironically, the country which was laden with overflowing grain silos and an unmanageable grain reserves is the one to have come to the rescue of a famine-stricken Ireland in the nineteenth century. The first shipload of grain that came for the starving Irish was from India. And more recently, India had provided food on a 'humanitarian' basis to the war-torn Iraqis. And soon after Bin Laden and his associates were forced out, India had stepped in to fight immediate hunger in Afghanistan. Earlier too, India had come to the rescue of Ethiopia at the height of the Ethiopian famine in the mid-1980s.

With 60 million tonnes of foodgrains stockpiled in the open, and that too of non-genetically modified grain, India was the right choice for food supply. Even the European Union had ample stocks of non-genetically modified corn and there were significant surpluses available for purchase in other parts of Africa.

At the height of the 1974 famine in the newly born Bangladesh, the US withheld 2.2 million tonnes of food aid to 'ensure that it abandoned plans to try Pakistani war criminals'. And a year later, when Bangladesh was faced with severe monsoons and imminent floods, the then US Ambassador to Bangladesh made it abundantly clear that the US probably could not commit food aid because of Bangladesh's policy of exporting jute to Cuba. And by the time Bangladesh succumbed to the American pressure, and stopped jute exports to Cuba, the food aid in transit was 'too late for famine victims. (Sharma 2004)

In India, few members of parliament submitted a memorandum to make arrangement for distribution of packaged biscuits under mid-day meal scheme in the country. Scores of social activists and academicians opposed the move and blamed commercial benefits behind the move.

After the announcement by President that legislating a Right to Food Act was among the new government's highest priority, the Ministry of Food and Civil Supplies circulated a proposal which tried to restrict the legal obligations of governments under the proposed law only to supplying 25 kilograms a month of rice and wheat at three rupees a kg. This would cost too heavy a burden on the state treasury. But shortly after, the chairperson of the UPA, Sonia Gandhi, seized the initiative by writing her first letter to the Prime Minister since the installation of this government, proposing a bill that much more comprehensively guarantees adequate food to people who live with hunger.

Understanding Food Security

FAO at its World Food Summit reaffirmed "the right of everyone to have access to safe and nutritious food, consistent with the right to adequate food and the fundamental right of everyone to be free of hunger". Further, as per the Rome Declaration "Food Security exists when all people, at all times, have physical and economic access to sufficient, safe and nutritious food to meet their dietary needs and food preferences for an active and healthy life." Also there was a pledge of political will and commitments to eradicate hunger in all countries with an immediate view to reducing the number of undernourished people by half their present level not later than 2015.

Food Security is basically understood in terms of food availability, stability and accessibility. Ensuring availability of food implies efficient domestic production and internal trade to make enough food available for the entire population. It calls for taking appropriate preemptive measures to ensure stability during harmful, seasonal and inter-annual instability of food supplies. However, despite food being abundantly available, it may not be within easy access to certain sections of society. Hence, enhancing people's purchasing power to buy food where it is not produced or making it available at subsidised rates through the public distribution system and employment programmes provides a safety-net and ensures accessibility to adequate and safe food. Given the ironical situation in India, food security needs to be understood also in terms of vulnerability of certain sections of society who are physically and mentally preoccupied with getting the next meal. It entails intervening sensitively to make opportunities available to such sections so that they can overcome exploitation, injustice and discrimination and gain access to the basic necessities of human existence with dignity.

There are several reasons why people face hunger and are unable to exercise their right to food. These are powerlessness and politics, violence and militarism, poverty, rapid growth of population exerting strain on environment, over-consumption and gender discrimination, vulnerability and age. A programme to overcome hunger and food insecurity must include among other things, measures for enhancement of economic growth, expansion of employment, diversification of production, enhancement of medical health care, management of special eccess to food on the part of poor people and spread of basic education and literacy, strengthening democracy, media focus on hunger and reduction in gender based inequality.

The TPDS introduced in 1997 to focus more on poor has also several deficiencies. The CAG report (1999-2000) indicated that inefficient targeting affected targeted PDS and in majority of states identification process was not completed and ration cards were not provided to a significant number of people. (Jena, Rani & Ramachandran 2004)

The Concept of Hunger

Hunger has been variously defined. According to

Mukherjee (2002), a nation or a community or a household is considered to be free from hunger if six conditions are met :

(a) *Food is available at all times.* That is, there is enough food in the system. In the absence of enough food in the system at all times, people can not access food and must, therefore, go hungry.

(b) *Food that is systemically available is also culturally acceptable.* People will not eat food, which is not acceptable culturally (in the broad sense). A Hindu may not eat beef, even when it is available. A Muslim may not eat pork, even if Pork goes abegging.

(c) *People have economic access to food.* That is, people have the purchasing power to buy food. Even if culturally acceptable food is available in the system, people will go hungry if they have no purchasing power to buy that food, or what is called economic access. In the great Bengal famine of the early 1940s, people were dying outside granaries full of food grains, because, inter alia, they had no purchasing power to buy the food (Sen, 1986).

(d) *People have physical access to food.* That is, people can buy food if they have the purchasing power. There must be a place where people can buy food, which is culturally acceptable and if they had the purchasing power to do so.

(e) *Food that people consume has the requisite nutritional value for a healthy life.* Food that people can access must have nutritional value. Consumption of food, which has no nutritional value will leave people without energy for a healthy life and hence hungry.

(f) *People have access to potable water, for absorption of food by the body.* Unsafe drinking water will prevent absorption of nutrition from food into the body, because unsafe drinking water leads to diseases and other forms of attrition.

Whenever any of these conditions or some combination thereof are violated, food security is jeopardized, and hunger sets in symptomatically when none is undernourished and no one faces absence of access to food, we have absence of hunger.

Food and Public Action

For long the Government believed that the food produced in the country did not reach certain sections of the population. The Government of India, therefore, made two interventions. One, it set up the Public Distribution System (PDS) and two, it established the system of price incentives to farmers, to grow more food and sell them to the Government for feeding into the PDS. Started in early 1960s, PDS entails supplying to the vulnerable sections of society essential commodities, notably food grains, at subsidized prices, to shield the poor from the volatility of prices and fluctuations in the supply of essential commodities." In the macro-micro terminology, the PDS in India is intended to translate the macro level self-sufficiency in foodgrain production to micro level food security by ensuring access to food and other essential commodities, to poor families. Many noted commentators, including Sen (1998) maintains that India could avoid large scale famines and saved millions of lives because of the PDS, something that other countries which did not have such a system, such as China, failed to prevent.

The PDS That Does Not Work

The PDS failed to reach the poor effectively due to urban bias and lack of transparency and accountability. Although the PDS is a centrally sponsored program, its implementation is dependent on the State Government. In States with appropriate political and administrative and infrastructural facilities, the public distribution system has worked; in most it has floundered.

Due to poor targeting the system is being used (misused) by all irrespective of the standard of living. Of the food provided through the PDS, 36 per cent of wheat, 31 per cent of rice and 23 per cent of sugar are diverted away from the PDS. Diversion of rice is 64 per cent in Bihar and Assam. Diversion in wheat is 69 per cent in Punjab and 100 per cent in Nagaland. Excepting for sugar, jowar and standard cloth, there is virtually no variation in the utilization of items supplied according to levels of living. The objective of resources transfer has not been achieved. (Mukherjee 2002)

The leakage from the system and other wastes associated with PDS is proverbial. The inefficiency of the entire bureaucracy of food is questioned. Significant number of observers believe that the PDS has served the interest of the big farmers only, who had surplus to sell to the State (NCAER, 2000). Consequently no attempt has been made to extend the coverage of PDS to other crops and the required back up R&D have not come about.

The Average Indian is Hungry

Indeed it is an even harsher reality that the average Indian is hungry. Despite the impressive output of food grain, our current availability of cereals per capita is only 435 grams per day. The per capita availability of pulses is about 31.2 grams per day. Thus the per capita net availability of cereals and pulses is only 466 grams per day. Nutritionally for a healthy life per 'capita availability of cereals and pulses per day should be at least 510 grams per day. There are some recent estimates that the per capita availability of food is 494 gm. per day. Even if this is accepted, the sad fact remains that hundreds of million of Indians have much less than 494 gm. per day, for that is only the average. The per capita availability of cereals and pulses for the Indians is, therefore, below the acceptable level for a healthy life. And hence, the average Indian is hungry because she or he does not have food which gives her or him the required nutrition.

The picture becomes worse, if we take a differentiated look. On an average daily food consumption should provide us about 2400 K. Cals per person. But for the poorest 30 %

of the people, their food intake provides them with only about 1600 K. Cals. About 60% of India's children suffer from malnutrition. Over 74 per cent of all children under 3 years of age suffer from anaemia, with the percentage going as high as 84 per cent in Haryana. As many as 53 per cent of India's children under the age of five are malnourished, as compared to 32 per cent in Sub-Saharan Africa. Nearly 52 per cent of married women in India between the age of 15-45 are anemic, as compared to only 20 per cent in sub-Saharan Africa (The Hunger Project, 2001). Calculations of general undernourishment - what is sometimes called "protein-energy malnutrition"- is nearly twice as high in India as is in Sub-Saharan Africa on an average. Judged in terms of usual standards of retardation in weight for age, the proportion of undernourished children in Africa is 20 to 40 per cent, whereas the percentage of undernourished Indian children is a gigantic 40-60 per cent. (Scrimshaw, 1998). While Indians, therefore, live longer than Africans, nevertheless there are many more undernourished children in India, in both absolute terms and as proportion of all children, than in Africa. Thus Sen (1995) pointed out, these stark figures confront us with the fact that the forces of normal mortality - unprevented by good nutrition and healthcare - kill more people every four or five years in India, than the death toll of the world's largest recorded famines.

Reports of hunger starvation poured regularly from Kalahandi and Kashipur region of Orissa. Kalahandi is a fertile tract and has traditionally been a basket of food. So much so that is 1943, at the time of the Bengal famine, Kalahandi had come to the rescue of the famine sticken Bengal. Kalahandi was the biggest contributor of surplus rice to the central food reserves. Between 1996 and 2001, Kalahandi provided some 50,000 tonnes of rice surplus on an average to the food reserves of the Government of India. The reason why people died of starvation and hunger is not because there is not enough food but because they cannot afford to buy the food they produce. (Sharma 2004)

Food Security Challenge

The world is grappling with the crisis of food security. Global recession, climate change, conversion of foodgrains to bio-fuels and rising prices of foodgrains are the major contributing factors for the crisis.

The G-8 leaders' announcement to raise US $ 20 billion in L'Aquila, Italy, for food, and agricultural aid to the most impoverished countries is a major step forward to improve the world food security. This will particularly help the poor nations where people are more vulnerable to such crisis.

Food crisis was brought to the forefront of the glogal development agenda when representatives from 181 countries including 43 heads of state and government and over 100 ministers participated in the high-power conference on world food security from June 3-5, 2008 at Rome.

Agriculture has to be able to double global food production by 2050, when the current population of the globe now stands at 6 billion, will reach 9 billion. According to the Food and Agricultural Organisation (FAO), rising prices have plunged an additional 75 million people below the hunger threshold, bringing the estimated number of undernourished people worldwide to 923 million in 2007. FAO estimates reveal that at least 37 countries reeling under food crisis presently require external assistance. Of these, 21 countries are in Africa, 10 in Asia, five in Latin America and one in Europe. After many years of stability, world food prices have increased by 83 per cent since 2005, prompting concerns of a food crisis in many countries, especially in Sub-Saharan Africa and South Asia, where the majority of the world's poor people are found. Food prices are expected to remain high through 2010 and then decline as supply and demand respond to high prices.

However, for most food crops, they are likely to remain above 2004 levels through 2015. Current high food prices are a short-term emergency for millions of people, specially the poor, but they also signal longer-term failures in the functioning of the world food system.

Similarly, there was 173.4 lakh tonnes of rice, which is far more according to the buffer stock requirement of 118 lakh tonnes. The total foodgrain stock stood at 354 lakh tonnes which is way above the buffer stock requirement of 200 lakh tonnes. The Central Government needs to procure 40 lakh tonnes each of rice and wheat to maintain the Central foodgrain buffer but the procurement was more than 50 lakh tonnes of each.

As regards sugar stock, the country had a carryover stock of 100 lakh tonnes at the start of the 2008-09 season and the production was 155 lakh tonnes. The total sugar stock is 255 lakh tonnes and the domestic consumption is 220 lakh tonnes.

The target for agriculture credit has been raised to Rs. 3,25,000 crore in 2009-10. The Centre has also provided an additional allocation of Rs. 1,000 crore for accelerated irrigation projects which will help bring sustainability to the food security. The FAP plans a World Food Summit of Heads of State and Government in November to try and reach a broad consensus on eradicating hunger, better governance of the international agricultural system and on ways to ensure world food security. (Gautam 2009)

Various Aspects of Food Security

Voice to enact the Right to Food law is raised by different quarters including political parties. The Congress manifesto pledged to, "enact a Right to Food Law that guarantees access to sufficient food for all people particularly the most vulnerable sectors of Society." Father of Green Revolution and M.P. Rajya Sabha Dr. M.S. Swaminathan high-lighted various issues in his article titled "Synergy between Food Security Act and NREGA" in the Hindu.

The successful implementation of the NREGA and the Right to Information Act indicates that the climate is conducive for a far-reaching, rights-based legislation to eliminate hunger and deprivation. Supreme Court rulings reinforce the view that the right to food is basic to achieving the right to life enshrined in Article 21 of the Constitution. One of the terms of reference the UPA government set in 2004 for the National

Commission on Farmers was to "work out a comprehensive medium-term strategy for food and nutrition security in the country in order to move towards the goal of universal food security over time." The NCF held consultations all over India on the pathways to a nutrition-secure India. Its report was submitted on October 4, 2006.

By definition, food security involves every individual gaining physical, economic, social and environmental access to a balanced diet that includes the necessary macro- and micro-nutrients, safe drinking water, sanitation, environmental hygiene, primary health care and education so as to lead a healthy and productive life. The food should originate from efficient and environmentally benign production technologies that conserve and enhance the natural resource base of crops, farm animals, forestry, inland and marine fisheries.

Such a holistic definition requires concurrent attention to the following aspects, too:

Food availability : This is a function of home production or, where absolutely essential, imports.

Food access : This is a function of livelihood opportunities and purchasing power. (As early as in 1859, a Famine Commission appointed by the colonial government said: "Indian famines are not famines of food, but of works; where there is work there is money and where there is money there is food." This is why Mahatma Gandhi said in 1946 at Noakhali. "To a people famishing and idle, the only acceptable form in which God can dare appear is work and promise of food as wages."

Food absorption : The utilisation of food in the body will depend on non-food factors such as safe drinking water, environmental hygiene, primary healthcare and access to toilets. Therefore, while developing legislation for food security, food and non-food; factors will have to be considered together on the following lines.

Food availability : The government has initiated programmes to increase food production, such as the Rashtriya Krishi Vikas Yojana, the Food Security Mission, and the National Horticulture Mission. Food availability should relate to macro-

and micro-nutrients. In addition to protein calorie undernutrition, there is severe micro-nutrient malnutrition, as for example, of iron, iodine, vitamin A, vitamin B12 and zinc, leading to hidden hunger. The National Horticulture Mission provides an opportunity to introduce horticultural remedies to nutritional maladies. All that is needed is mainstreaming the nutritional dimension in designing the horticulture programme in each agroclimatic area.

The other areas which will need attention are : widening the food basket by including local grain varieties like ragi, jowar and millets in the public distribution system; the promotion of community gene, seed, food and water banks in each village, and the establishment of community kitchens modelled on the Indira Gandhi Community Kitchen organised years ago in Pune. These are particularly effective in combating malnutrition in urban areas. The widening of the food basket by including millets, legumes and tubers, which have greater tolerance to adverse conditions, is important in the context of climate change.

Food access : The Congress manifesto has said 25 kg. of rice or wheat would be provided each month to economically underprivileged families at Rs. 3 a kg. With the initiation of the National Rural Employment Guarantee Act (NREGA), the minimum purchasing power for food security is being created in families living below the poverty line.

By adopting the support price policy recommended by the NCF, that is, C2 (total cost of production) plus 50 per cent as has been done in the case of wheat this year, the purchasing power of small and marginal farmers can be improved. Universalisation of the PDS is an idea whose time has come, since there are adequate grain stocks.

Food absorption : Here, the schemes dealing with drinking water, sanitation, environmental hygiene and so on should be brought together. The Total Sanitation programme and the Rajiv Gandhi Drinking Water Mission, if implemented with community participation through panchayats and nagarpalikas, will make a difference in promoting effective absorption of food in the body, particularly among children.

With such a holistic approach, chronic hidden and transient hunger can be addressed in a cost effective and meaningful manner. To provide political oversight and to foster a pan-political approach in matters relating to food security, the NCF recommended the establishment of a National Food Security and Sovereignty Board under the chairmanship of the Prime Minister and with members drawn from different political parties, Union Ministers and Chief Ministers. Such a political support and oversight body should become an integral part of the legislation. (Swaminthan 2009)

Prime Minister Worried of Drought

The deepening shadow of a drought in the wake of a wayward monsoon saw Prime Minister Manmohan Singh asking states to immediately commence relief operations while operationalizing contingency plans for crops, drinking water and human and animal health.

He warned that shortfall in kharif sowing was bound to increase inflationary pressure on prices and states needed, in tandem with the Centre, to keep a sharp eye on availability of foodgrains and essential commodities. "The need is for us to act promptly, collectively and efficiently," he said.

The PM offered his assessment at a meeting of chief secretaries convened by the Cabinet secretary which he addressed in what is seen a protocol break as he would normally have spoken at a meeting of chief ministers. His intervention is seen to reflect the sense of urgency in government as the next week also offers a bleak monsoon forecast. Putting matters bluntly, Singh said the deficit in paddy sowing was more than six million hectares with rice being the worst affected crop.

Pointing out that high procurement over the past two years has provided a sufficient buffer to enable provision of foodgrains in drought-affected areas, Singh said both the Centre and states should not hesitate in intervening in the market if so required.

The PM said efforts will have to be made to maximize production in areas that have received adequate rainfall and implement alternate crop plans in regions that got scanty or deficient precipitation. He also underlined the need for planning for the rabi season to increase production.

Singh's reference to rising prices of pulses, sugar and some vegetables points to a concern that apart from ensuring proper functioning of the public distribution system, the general availability at retail points needs to be monitored. This may need, as PM suggested, strong action against hoarders and black marketeers. He said as many as 141 districts have been declared drought affected. With both the PM and agriculture minister Sharad Pawar addressing the meeting, the Centre is close to considering the more dire projections in terms of rainfall. The monsoon has dried up after a somewhat decent spell in the last week of July and thereafter till August 5 the departure from the long-term average was minus 64% at the all-India level and as much as minus 76% and minus 93% in north-west and central India. (Times News Network)

Drought : Danger to Food Security

Observing that the country was facing a "difficult situation" following delayed and deficient rainfall, Prime Minister Manmohan Singh said the Centre has adequate foodgrains and would not hesitate to take strong measures and intervene in the market if the need arose.

"Agricultural operations have been adversely affected in several parts of the country causing distress to farmers. A deficit of more than 6 million hectares has been reported in paddy, which is the worst affected crop," he said addressing the Conference of Chief Secretaries on the monsoon situation in New Delhi.

The Government has enough cushion on account of bumper production the previous two years, Singh said.

"We are in a position to ensure adequate availability of foodgrains in drought affected areas. We should not hesitate to take-strong measures and intervene in the market if the need were to rise," Singh said in the presence of Agriculture Minister Sharad Pawar on 7 August, 2009.

Cautioning that the reduced production of Kharif crop in the current year may have an inflationary impact on prices of food items in the coming months, Singh said the Centre and states will have to work together and activise the public distribution system (PDS).

"We will also have to ensure effective enforcement of stock holding limits and strong action against hoarders and black marketeers," Singh said, observing that of late, the country has witnessed rising trend in prices of pulses, sugar and some vegetables. On immediate concerns over monsoon, Singh urged states to commence relief operations wherever there was a need. "In case the Contingency Relief Fund available with the States is not sufficient, they (States) should quickly prepare a detailed memorandum for assistance under the National Calamity Contingency Fund," he said.

Singh regretted that no state government has so far sent memorandum seeking assistance for drought affected districts, even though 141 districts of the country have been declared drought-affected.

"In short, the contingency plans for crops, drinking water, human and animal health and fodder should be brought into operation without delay and a close watch kept on availability of foodgrains and prices of essential commodities," he said.

Singh said the Centre has recently decided to reimburse 50 per cent of the cost that states would incur in providing diesel subsidy to the affected farmers and provided additional power from central pool to few states.

He said the Power Minister has been asked to extend similar support to other states, which should ensure that the additional availability should be used only for agricultural operations.

To mitigate the adverse affect of inadequate rain, Singh suggested the farmers should look for alternate crop in those areas where paddy cannot be sown and maximise production in traditional crop in those areas which had adequate rainfall.

Asking states to meticulously plan for the availability of seeds, fertilisers and other inputs to farmers for coming Rabi season, he said : "Since the country is deficit in pulses and oilseeds production, this may be a good opportunity to utilise available land by diversifying in Rabi pulses and oilseeds".

Expressing concern over non-utilisation of funds by few states from Rashtriya Krishi Vikas Yojna and National Food Security Mission, the two major schemes for the agriculture sector launched by the Centre, he said the funds meant for the farmers should not be left unutilised due to procedural constraints.

On the food front, Singh said the major challenge was to ensure proper management and distribution of food stocks. He asked states to intervene in procurement process to supplement the efforts of Centre. (NIP, August 9, 2009)

India to Import More

Last year, a hike of 70% had taken place in wheat futures in Europe as soon as India bought nearly 8 lakh tonnes of wheat, and wanted to buy more.

All this means that the government will have very limited options—either it buys sugar at higher prices and sells lower in India by subsidizing it, or it continues to allow free entry to imported sugar and lets the consumers pay through their noses for it.

In India, by far the world's largest consumer of pulses, production has stagnated between 13 and 15 million tonnes, causing a decline in availability from 60.7 grams per person in 1961 to 35.5 grams in 2007. In a largely vegetarian country, pulses used to be the main source of protein but they are increasingly getting priced out of the common man's reach.

India has been importing pulses for several years now, as farmers have cut down on cultivating it. Last year, 25 lakh tonnes were imported. This year; orders for about 4 lakh tonnes import have been placed, but 1.8 lakh tonnes has been delivered according to the Pulse Importers Association of India.

Oils and fats could also see a further jump in prices as India, again one of the top three consumers is expected to import about 7.5 million tonnes in the current year, as per FAO forecasts. (Varma 2009)

Consumption : Top Three

Pulses		*Sugar*		*Oils & Fats*	
World	57	World	162.2	World	161.6
India	20	India	25.3	China	29.2
Brazil	3.2	China	16.6	India	17.3
China	2.4	USA	9.6	USA	16.9

FAO 2008-09 est. (million tonnes)

Expected Imports by India

Wheat	0.5
Rice	0.1
Oils & Fats	7.5
Sugar	3.0
Pulses	2.5

FAO 2008-09 est. (million tonnes)

Report of the Working Group on Integrating Nutrition with Health for the XI Five Year Plan (2007-2012)

1.1 Nutrition and Health are two sides of the same coin and are, therefore, inseparable. While good health is the ultimate objective of nutrition, nutrition is the vital component of health. Nutrition is increasingly being recognized as an important indicator of development at national and international levels. Nutritional well being of the population is considered as an economic asset and a pre-requisite for national development.

1.2 India has progressed dramatically in various fields but the levels of malnutrition in the country are not showing desired reduction rates. As a result the magnitude of the problem of malnutrition and poor health indicators like infant mortality rate, under 5 mortality rate and maternal mortality rate in the country are higher than some of the developing countries of the South East Asia. Malnutrition, therefore, continues to be a cause for concern. Malnutrition being a multifaceted problem requires inputs from various sectors like health, women & child development, agriculture, food, education, rural development etc. The health sector assumes greater significance as many of the nutrition related activities fall under the purview of this sector.

1.3 Malnutrition contributes to 60% of the 10 million deaths globally that occur every year among children under five years of age. Its contribution to child deaths is even higher during first six months of life, when mortality is highest. Breastfeeding can avoid this within one hour, and exclusive breastfeedlng during first six months.

. There has been a **conquest of nutritional deficiencies** — Florid Nutritional Deficiency Syndromes like Pellagra, Beri Beri, Scurvy, Kwashiorkar have disappeared, famines are no more, severe malnutrition among preschoolers has reduced appreciably and nutritional status of adults has improved significantly. But still the high level of malnutrition continue to influence morbidity and mortality rates in the country.

2.1 The **Challenge** that still remains include -

- High Malnutrition Level particularly in Women and Children
- Undernutrition
- Micro-nutrient Malnutrition
- Emerging diet related diseases,
- High Mortality Rates-IMR, U5MR and MMR
- Inadequate Access to Health Care, Immunization etc.

2.3 **Undernutrition** is defined as the outcome of insufficient food intake (hunger) and repeated infectious diseases. Undernutrition includes underweight (being underweight for ones age), stunted (being too short for ones age), wasted (being dangerously thin), and micro-nutrient malnutrition (being deficient in vitamins and minerals). As per NFHS 2 (1998-99) 47% of children under three years are **underweight,** 455% **stunted** and 15.5% **wasted.** India fares poorly even among the South East Asian countries, occupying the third place from the bottom with only Nepal and Bangladesh faring worse than India. The prevalence **of low birth weight** continues to be about 30% for last three decades. Low birth weight babies are more likely to die because of neonatal infections and under nutrition **Chronic Energy Deficiency** in adults is 39% in females and 37% in males (NNMB 2002).

2.4 Iron Deficiency Anaemia prevalence continues to be high particularly among the high risk groups like children under 5 years, adolescent girls, pregnant and lactating women. About 68-78 per cent of these population groups suffer from anaemia (NNMB 2003)

2.5 **Vitamin A Deficiency** continues to be a problem of. public health significance among pre-school children with prevalence of Bitot spots, an objective sign of vitamin A deficiency being equal to or more than WHO cut off level of 0.5%. The stagnant prevalence of vitamin A deficiency (Bitot Spots) ranging from 0.7% to 1.1 % during the period 1988-90 to 2003 requires a comprehensive approach for its prevention and control.

2.6 No state in India is free from Iodine Deficiency Disorders. The total goiter rate (TGR) in 260 districts out of 321 districts surveyed is reported to be more than 10%, a prevalence more than the WHO recommended cut off level of 5%, indicating endemicity of 100.

2.7 Infant Mortality Rate is still very high, i.e., 58 per thousand live births (as per SRS 2006 for the year 2004). The plateau in IMR observed since 1990 can only be removed by addressing malnutrition in mother-child dyad. Under 5 Mortality Rate and Maternal Mortality Rate are also unacceptably high.

2.8 Under-five mortality rate is also high. About 11 million children under the age of five die each year, 98% of them in developing countries. Almost 40% of these deaths occur in the first 28 days after birth, the neonatal period. Infections account for 36% of these deaths. Malnutrition is closely linked to child mortality; a malnourished child faces a much greater risk of death compared to a well nourished child. More than half of these child deaths are preventable if a set of do-able interventions and practices were to be applied on a large scale. These relatively simple but highly effective interventions and practices include timely and adequate infant feeding (early and exclusive breastfeeding) practices, treatment of diarrhea, immunization, keeping a newborn baby warm, and others.

2.9 **Infant and young child feeding practices** in India are far from optimal. According to NFHS-2, exclusive breastfeeding falls rapidly from 72% at one month to 20% at six months. Only about 16% babies in India start breastfeeding within one hour. Other indicators are also disappointing. For instance, complementary feeding practices are very poor : only 33% of children aged between 6-9 months are given solid mushy foods (NFHS-2). Comparison with NFHS-1 highlights that we are able to stop the decline in breastfeeding. However, achieving the national goals will require massive action and resources. Results from a recent study from 49 districts (2003), with data for about 9000 mothers, also show a dismal picture. This is where malnutrition begins as young baby are dependent on parents or other caregivers for their food intake.

2.9.1 Age wise distribution of prevalence of underweight in children reveals that malnutrition peaks during the first two years of life. From 11.9% prevalence among 0-6 month old infants, it reaches 58.5% in 12-23 months old children. This steep rise in malnutrition during the first two years is mainly due to poor infant feeding practices.

2.10 Maternal mortality also continues to be high in many parts of the world, especially in Sub-Saharan Africa and some of the countries in Asia. It is estimated that worldwide more than 500,000 women die each year while giving birth. In Sub-Saharan Africa the rate is 940 deaths per 100,000 live births, while in South Asia it is 560. The main causes are depicted in the graph below and include severe bleeding, infection, unsafe abortion and eclampsia. More than 20 percent of maternal deaths are caused by diseases such as malaria, anaemia, TB, and HIV/AIDS that are aggravated by pregnancy. Adolescents are at increased risk of dying during pregnancy and childbirth. They are twice as likely to die as women in their twenties and teens younger than 15 are five times as likely to die of complications. As with child mortality, high rates of maternal mortality can also be brought down drastically through a combination of do-able interventions. The chances of survival are greatly increased by availability and access to emergency obstetrical care.

Initiatives to Fight with Hunger and Mulnutrition

Case-1. Nandi Foundation

There is nothing quite as transfixing as watching a hungry child down a hot meal. Today, at the Government Upper Primary School in Addagutta, a Secunderabad slum, it's boiled egg day, and I watch fascinated as hundreds of tiny fingers work in unison to remove the shells. Most students here are children of domestic helps, rickshaw pullers, masons and daily wage labourers, and for nine out of ten kids, this is the first meal of the day. Most came to school with only a cup of tea warming their insides. After school, many will get by on the leftovers their parents bring home from the houses they work in.

No wonder, then, that as soon as the lunch bell goes off, the nearly 400 children who eat-here come pouring into the courtyard and eagerly stand in line. I ask them what they like best, and hundreds of voices cry out, 'Pulihora'. This is tamarind rice, a favourite dish with Telugus.

Sunita, a class V student, says she loves the peanuts in the pulihora seasoning. T. Rohit, a student of class II, pipes up with a question : Can papad be included in the menu? His friend K. Krishna wants Boost with milk once a week.

Manjula of class III shyly voices a preference for upma. Headmistress K. Radha smiles indulgently as we talk about food. Government schemes evoke so much cynicism that when you come across one that functions with clockwork precision, you feel a sense of disbelief. But this public-private partnership between the NGO Naandi Foundation, and the Andhra Pradesh government is an invitation to suspend scepticism. Thanks to this scheme, which may just be one of the best implemented mid-day meal programmes in the country. 1,30,000 children in Hyderabad, Secunderabad eat at least one healthy, tasty and hygienically prepared meal every school day.

Launched in February 2003, in response to the Supreme Court order for the universalisation of the mid-day meal scheme, Naandi's centralised kitchen serves 868 government schools, non-residential bridge schools and madrassas in the twin cities. The day begins early—at 3.30 a.m. to be precise—at the huge modernised kitchen at Uppal in Hyderabad, spread over two acres, with a built-up area of 18,000 sq. feet. The kitchen runs to impressive standards of efficiency, hygiene and safety. Most operations are hands-free and the meals are high on quality. The state government supplies free rice to Naandi, and pays it Rs. 2 for every meal it serves. Naandi spends anywhere between 10 and 50 paise extra on each meal, says CEO Manoj Kumar.

Inside the kitchen, stones, glass and, yes, nails are removed from rice with a destoning machine and then washed. About five tonnes of vegetables are cooked here everyday. The Supreme Court has specified that each meal should contain 450 calories and 8 to 12 gm. of protein. In the Hyderabad model, that translates into rice and sambhar or dal mixed with lots of vegetables, tomato rice, jeera rice with mixed vegetables and pulihora. These dishes are rotated—like all children, they too won't eat the same food everyday Naandi has also begun serving eggs or bananas (for vegetarians) and iron-fortified biscuits once a week to make the meal more nutritious. It also "tricks" AP kids, who like potatoes, tomatoes and brinjals but not carrots, into eating their carrots by grating them and mixing them with rice.

Manoj Kumar recounts the small joys of being a provider of meals to young children—how their eyes light up, for instance, when they see a truck; driving in with cardboard boxes full of biscuits. Each child four biscuits once a week.

Pickles are a new addition in the menu, to cater to the need of South Indian children for something spicy to pep up the meal. All masalas and pickles are produced in-house. This leads to good quality, but also a higher nutrition value—peanuts and jaggery are added to masalas to raise their protein and iron content. Naandi is also working with the Geneva based Global Alliance for Improved Nutrition to develop a nutrition supplement of iron, zinc and folic acid that can be added to curries or dal without ruining the taste for children.

By 8.30 a.m., the food is cooked and ready to be transported to various schools. Packed and sealed in plastic and steel containers, it is opened only when the lunch bell rings, to prevent contamination. Naandi employs 250 staffers and 52 trucks for its mid-day meal operations. Meals are generally served between 11 a.m. to 1 p.m. because some schools have three shifts. Currently, the scheme is capped at class V, but the state is planning to provide free lunches to older children too.

It is amazing to see what one wholesome meal a day can do to a child's life. Enrolment in state-run schools in the twin cities has gone up by 25 to 30 per cent since the mid-day meal scheme began, says Una Joseph, programme head of the Naandi mid-day meal scheme. A large number of the newly enrolled are girls. There is 10 to 20 per cent improvement in children's health and malnutrition levels, too, have fallen similarly. Hearteningly, attendance rates in the schools, where absenteeism has been rampant, have gone up by 10 to 20 per cent. Teachers say children concentrate better in class once they have eaten.

The centralised Naandi model has a lot going for it. Its costs are tower than that of the self-help groups (SHGs) normally employed in rural areas to serve mid-day meals at schools, since its operations are on large scale. Beside these groups cook at school. That doesn't work for urban schools, which function in congested structure. Fire hazards are also a coming danger, as was recently found in Tamil Nadu. Government agencies also find it easier to monitor a centralised kitchen instead of trooping from school to school to supervise the work of SHGs and anganwadis.

For all these reasons, the Naandi model has found favour with the Madhya Pradesh and Rajasthan Governments as well Naandi works in Udaipur, Bhilwara, Chittorgarh, Ajmer, and Jhalawar in Rajasthan. In MP, it provides mid-day meals in Bhopal, Jabalpur and Indore. In AP, it has another unit in Vizag which caters to about 40,600 children. Its hot lunches find their way to 4,000 schools everyday-food for the body, mind and soul. (Tata 2008)

Case 2: Alternative PDS

"Physically and fiscally unsustainable" is how the Central Government's Department of Food and Public Distribution describes the tottering Public Distribution System (PDS).

The Indian PDS, perhaps the largest welfare measure anywhere in the world, amounts to a food subsidy bill of Rs. 23,828 crore (2006-07). The subsidy stood at Rs. 2,850 crore in 1991-92. Despite the size of the outlay, however, a large number of the 180 million families targeted by the system do not receive their share of foodgrains.

N.C. Saxena, Commissioner of the Supreme Court on Food Security, considers the prevailing state of affairs a mockery of the entire governmental exercise in securing food and nutrition for millions of Indians living below the poverty line (BPL). The PDS requires over 75 million tonnes of foodgrain, at 35 kg. per family per month. The entitlement, however, is only on paper. In reality, the PDS gets only 25 million.

Of this, too, diversions and leakages take away a bulk. At the national level, the average leakage amounts to around 36.4% of the off-take of the BPL quota. Bihar had recorded a high of around 81.5 % in diversions and leakages. Alarmed by the state's inability to shore up food security, policymakers have been contemplating a number of measures. "It will be good idea to look at direct transfers or just giving cash to the poor," says Saxena.

A New Approach

While the governmental machinery battles the issue. Deccan Development Society (DDS), an NGO in Medak district of Andhra Pradesh, has demonstrated a viable and sustainable alternative public distribution system (APDS), where foodgrain production, procurement, storage and distribution is carried out at the village level. Interestingly, the entire system is managed by women, mostly dalit, grouped as *sanghams.*

The alternative PDS goes beyond 'food security' to a more refined concept of 'food sovereignty.' "It's not enough to empower communities to access food. They should also grow and consume what they want to," says P.V. Satheesh, Director, DDS.

The system, which embraces coarse cereals and a variety of millets, the traditional food of the region, has ensured food, nutrition, fodder and livelihood security to communities who participate in the programme. It has been proven across 50 villages, over 2,000 hectares, in the semi-arid, south-western parts of Andhra Pradesh.

DDS believes that the rice- and wheat-driven PDS and the continued neglect of coarse grains has serious implications for both dry-land farming and food security in the country. "The government has spent all its resources in marginalising the most nutritive millets that people have grown on their rainfed lands and driven it out of people's food systems," he says.

The APDS rests on an elaborate system to bring fallows under cultivation. The DDS extends a loan to each member, based on the cost of low-input and organic cultivation, and the money required to convert fallows into productive land.

This amount is to be repaid in the form of grain and cash over a period of five years, in pre-fixed quantities and pre-fixed rates. For instance, in the first year, a farmer will have to repay 150 kg. of sorghum (jowar) and Rs. 125 cash.

The grain component thus collected goes into a community grain store. Women of the *sangham,* through participatory approaches of wealth ranking, rate households in the village on a scale of four. The destitute black card holders receive the maximum monthly entitlement of jowar at a subsidised rate. Accordingly, entitlements are apportioned—the landless poor (red card holders), marginal farmers (green card) and the small farmer (yellow). The money received from the sale of foodgrain is deposited in a bank as the Community Grain Fund (CGF), which is utilised year after year to reclaim more fallows.

Far-reaching Impact

The result of the initiative has been remarkable. In 2002, when India faced one of the most severe droughts in recent times, none of the APDS villages were in stress. "In fact, some of the villages had more than they needed," says Satheesh.

Again, in 2003, when Andhra Pradesh announced subsidised seeds for farmers, there was a mad rush to buy them. Police had to a fire on farmers at a block near Hyderabad. In Zaheerabad, where much of the DDS work has been undertaken, scores of villages were sitting on gene banks, huge quantities of dozens of varieties of seeds. Women *sanghams,* over the years, have even retrieved over 80 seed varieties on the brink.

The 50 APDS villages produce an extra 1.5 million kg. of jowar every year, which translates into 3 million extra meals per year over 1,000 extra meals for every participating family. The fodder produced by the newly cultivated fields sustains over 10,000 head of cattle and, in each village, 2,500 extra wages have been created per year.

The APDS has now been expanded to the Telangana and

Rayalseema regions, and also in two districts of coastal Andhra Pradesh.

The system has established the viability of a robust community-driven PDS. All that is required is a one-time investment that can banish or reduce to a great extent the mounting food subsidies every year.

"Even in harsh dryland conditions, every village community can be self-sufficient in food production and ensure its own food security. But it must have access to resources and credit. Once it is made available, there can be vibrant food-producing, food-secure communities in this country," says Satheesh.

And now for the denouement : In the mainstream PDS, for every Rs. 7 that is spent on the programme, only Rs. 1 reaches the ultimate consumer; while in the APDS, out of every Rs. 1.60 spent on the programme, Rs. 1 reaches the ultimate consumer. (Karunakaran 2008)

Case 3

Food Security at Micro-Level : The Gram Sudhar Samiti (GSS) Way

Introduction

Food security and elimination of hunger is an issue that requires a concerted national attention and effort. In ensuring food security, the perception of the communities which suffer from the pains of hunger (poor communities, small and marginal farmers, women, poor people, landless labourers and the tenants) have to be examined in order to know the factors that cause hunger and evolve strategies to mitigate the pains of hunger.

The views of the communities are critical both in understanding problem of food insecurity and hunger and in working out the policies and strategies most appropriate to solve the problem. It is widely known that even in a vast country like India, decisions which affect the lives of millions are often taken at central location without consulting them. There is no institutional mechanism to consult the people on this vital matter PRIs as local institutions can play a major role in this regard. But PRIs are not provided with functions and resources to become an effective instrument of the state. Perspectives of the community on livelihood, hunger and food security together with the perspectives of the policy makers on hunger and food insecurity should be in conformity with the felt needs of the community.

The role of civil societies and NGOs perspective on hunger needs also to be taken seriously as they are better placed to know the reasons for people's food insecurity and access to food. This will help in planning for micro-level food security involving poor people themselves which is beneficial for the rural poor.

The grain banks experiment that are implemented in the tribal areas of the country is a good example and in some states, some NGOs are experimenting on ensuring food security to the poor.

Setting up of a community grain bank through local production is a new idea and experiments across the country have been carried out over last few years. The Government of India, in order to prevent malnutrition and starvation deaths in the remote tribal areas, lauched a village grain bank scheme since 1996-97.

Considering the role played by grain banks in the country, GSS started a grain bank in village Khair and based on success, the experiment was applied in other villages. Now, these banks are torch bearers in food security. With this successful experiment, villagers are free from hunger and starvation.

In addition, these groups are also encouraging local seed and gene banks for the purpose. Besides, they are also promoting organic farming, coarse cereal cultivation and bio-diversity for the purpose of ensuring community-oriented food security system at the grass-roots level.

The GSS model grain bank is operational in 17 villages in Majhauli and Kusumi blocks. The total membership of grain bank is 830. GSS is undertaking waterhed development programme and right to food programme in these villages.

The programme is meant for both tribal and non-tribal groups who face lean season scarcity. Tribals of Dubri Kala, Khaira, Chingawah and Kharwar shown path to other villagers in making whole village a food secure village.

The process of women's participation in the grain bank programme is significant because they utilise this forum to address issues of common concern in the village. The grain collected during repayment by owmen are found to be cleaner and of better quality. Women generally do not relax or change rules in the case of deserted widowed destitute women in the village grain banks. But members are known to help deprived women in other ways.

Problems Encountered

In the process of forming grain banks, most of the problems are encountered in the first stage and the last one. While introducing the concept of grain banks, one has to deal with people's doubts and apprehensions with patience. Influential leader in the village whose vested interests could be threatened due to grain banks could intimidate or threaten villagers and thus dissuade them from taking it up. Political dynamics also tend to surface at this point. There are rival political groups in almost every village, but GSS observed that if people have a fundamental need that is being addressed, then political issues do not cause hindrance. Villagers themselves make it a point not to organise meetings in villages around elections when political dynamics are at their peak. Moreover, once villagers realise that the agency is not involved in any political activities, they ensure that political issues in the village do not interfere with the grain bank programme.

Conflicts also arise at the time of repayment, especially when the grain bank is new. Members are alert about getting cheated and have a keen eye on the amount and type of grain being given to them. Those collecting their quota towards the end, usually complain of too much chaff in their share. It becomes essential to satisfy such complaints right then. Leadership conflicts are also common, especially when there is a generation gap. (Zena 2004, NIRD)

Food Security Issues in a Tribal Region

Tribal communities in Sidhi district face food shortages for three to four months in a year. Lack of adequate food has an adverse effect on the health and well being of tribals. Women and children are the worst affected.

Livelihoods of tribals are woven around hunting/ gathering and subsistence farming. Forests provide a wide range of food (uncultivated vegetables, fruits, tubers/ rhizomes, fish, crabs, animals, birds etc.) and are an important part of the food security of tribals. However, availability of forest produce declined considerably due to widespread deforestation. Foodgrain yields from substinence based farming are low and cannot meet the food needs of the family for the whole year. Tribal familites thus face shortages of food for 3-4 months in a year. The periodic cycle of food shortage represents the "lean period" for tribal families. This is a period of starvation and hardships for tribals.

State schemes like the PDS, ICDS, etc. which are aimed at providing food security to the poor and needy, do not work satisfactorily. As a result, tribal families do not have access to food during the lean period. They have been traditionally borrowing foodgrains from *Sahukars* or moneylenders to tide over the periodic food scarcity. Moneylenders charge an exorbitant interest rate on the grain loan and force tribals to work on their fields as bonded labour. The fields of tribal people get neglected in the process: resulting in lower yields, further marginalisation and a continuing cycle of exploitation.

The explicit thrust of the GSS grain programme is to encourage food security at the community level in tribal villages by ensuring timely availability of grains to the socio-economically weak, small and marginal farmers, agricultural labourers and the landless people. Any village interested in setting up a grain bank is given a certain quantity of grain in the form of loan by GSS on the basis of household requirement of members. Each member repays this loan over a period of four years. The repaid grain is used as revolving fund to extend the programme to other villages, desirous of initiating a grain bank. At the end of four years, the village would have repaid 100 per cent of its loan to GSS and the village then fully owns the stock of grain in their grain bank. From fifth year onwards, interest repayment from members adds to the grain buffer stock of the village. At the implicit level, the objective is to overcome the exploitation of the local moneylenders.

Philosophy

Empowerment of the powerless should facilitate democratic decentralisation of power and resource sharing, so that they are enabled to overcome their basic reoccupation with food security and actively participate in the governance of their communities.

Principles

* Democratic decentralisation should pervade every level of society.
* People's participation should achieve broad basing of social economic and political power sharing.
* Basic food security concerns should be addressed through mutual help to enable participation of every section of society in its development process.

Objectives

* Promote food security of tribal and other backward communities by setting up decentralised and self-sufficient village-level grain banks.
* Enable poor households to themselves from the clutches of moneylenders.

* Facilitate a process of participation and mutual cooperation among participating members.

Strategies

* Organise groups of men and women at the village level to facilitate participation and mutual cooperation.
* Build capacities of groups and their leaders for resource management and decision-making.
* Network among village grain banks for exchange and resource sharing.
* Federate for decentralised monitoring, pressure groups and conflict rcsolution.

Structure

Members

* Members are individuals who represent their household in the village grain bank
* Membership is guided by rules and regulations laid down by GSS while forming the grain bank, all representatives do a basic screening in terms of the member's ability/readiness to abide by rules and regulations of the grain bank.

Process

Any village interested in setting up a grain bank can get involved by first enroling members. A representative from each family seeking membership is a member of the grain bank. Members select the Committee and the Committee then puts in a formal request to GSS for a grain loan based on the requirement of individual members. Members decide the quantity and quality or type of foodgrain required. GSS provides grain loan to the village during April-May. The grain is then redistributed to individual members. Members repay the loan with 25 per cent interest to the grain bank immediately after the harvesting season, which is between October-November. The 25 per cent interest paid by each member goes back to GSS while the capital amount remains within the village. The capital amount is redistributed to members every year in the month of May and recollected after the loan to GSS over a period of four years. This grain is used by GSS as revolving fund to extend the programme to other needy villages. From the fifth year onwards, the grain bank is self-sufficient.

Economic Impact

The successful experiment of GSS has multiplier economic impact. The grain banks have combined stock of grains available in the 17 grain banks is 107 quintals.

The surplus grain stock is often sold to other villagers and the return from such sale builds into the village cash fund. The cash fund is utilised to meet credit needs of the members, to building community assets and to meet food requirements of members in case of crop failures. This has ensured economic viability of grain banks.

Grain banks also cushion the blow of frequent price rise. The barter system proves effective in countering market and political forces that influence agricultural pricing as well as other limitations of centralised agricultural marketing in the form of agents and middlemen. Economic empowerment is achieved as the villagers develop their asset base in their communities in the form of grain stocks and village fund.

An indirect impact of the grain bank programme has been the enhancement in people's negotiating power. The grain stock in the village provides a sense of security that translates into greater bargaining power. It was observed that generally in villages where grain banks were operating, the wage rates for agricultural labourers went up dramatically. People had a newfound confidence that helped them bargain for higher wages. Forced labour as part of debt repayment was curbed. People could use their labour in their own fields to enhance its productivity. The uncompromising factor of loan repayment, has also proved to be a push factor for members to invest their labour in their own land. Landless members have adopted share cropping and tenancy farming instead of casual labour. (Zena, Rani & Ramachandran 2004).

Although, the above two are also exploitative, are definitely better options than migrating as casual labourers for daily wages.

Social Impact

Self-sufficiency in meeting basic food needs gives a sense of dignity, which in itself is empowering. Overcoming the feeling of helplessness and dependence on the moneylender and countering the exploilation is encouraging. The model accommodates those in the lowest socio-economic strata. Hence, the landless labourers and the women in the community are not only the beneficiaries of the programme, but they also become active participants in the decision-making and resource management processes.

Incorporating of traditional cereals in the grain banks, replaces the sense of embarrassment in consuming them with a sense of respect and acceptance towards their cultural practices.

Political Impact

Grain banks facilitate periodic meetings and informal discussions within the village, a process that has not been a deliberate and conscious exercise. This process fosters a spirit of oneness and self-reliance among the villagers and promotes mechanisms for sorting out their differences and working towards community development.

The process of operating grain banks under this model ensures participation of people in developing the infrastructure for storage and distribution and gradually transfers the power to them as they manage grain banks at village level.

References

Arora, B.N. (2004): "Human Right Day is celebrated, but Right to Food continues to be denied," Economic and Political Weekly, December 11.

Tata, Madhavi (2008): "Round, Square & Oval," Northern India Patrika, October 11.

Karunakaran, Naren (2008): "New System throws up some food for thought," Outlook Business, May 3.

Tripathy, K.K. (2008), "Food Security and Food Management in India: A Review," Kurukshetra, Vol. 56 No. 8.

Bordoloi, Bedanga & Sarmah, Etali (2008): "Food Security and the way forward," Kurukshetra, June, 2008.

Dutta, Bhaskar (2009): "What has caused the current global food crisis," Northern India Patrika, May 7.

Sharma, Devinder (2009): "When Hunger Kills", Times of India, 24 January.

– "We will not allow any Indian to go hungary: PM," Northern India Patrika, August 9, 2009.

Mukherjee, Amitava (2002): "Hunger in Contemporary India," in Globalisation and the destruction of food security," Navdanya Publication.

Mander, Harsh (2009): "The silent tragedy of hunger," The Hindu, April 5.

Sharma Devinder (2004): "GM Food and Hunger," Forum for Biotechnology and Food Security, New Delhi.

Gautam, Harender Raj (2009): "Meeting the Challenge of Food Security," Northern India Patrika, August 10.

Verma, Subodh (2009): "Consumption : Top three," Times Insight Group," Times of India, August 10.

Swaminathan, M.S. (2009): "Synergy between Food Security Act & NREGA," The Hindu, June 1.

Jena, J.C., Rani, Ch. Radhika, Ramachandran, G. (2004): "Micro-level experiments in food security – a study across states," Research report series-74, NIRD, Hyderabad.

Sarkar, Anirbaran (2007): "Right to food as Human Right", Legal Service of India.com.

Mander, Harsh (2009): "Fixing hunger from every home," The Hindu, July 5.

Sen, Amartya (1981): "Poverty and Famines: An Essay on entitlements and deprivation," Clarendon Press, Oxford.

Sen, Amartya (2003): "Address at a public hearing titled" Hunger in India in Delhi University on 10 January, 2003.

2

Connecting Indian Agriculture : Problems and Prospects

The central government extended National Rural Employment Guarantee Programme in all the districts of the country from April 1, 2008. While presenting Union Budget 2009-10, finance minister said, "It is widely acknowledged that the National Rural Employment Guarantee Act, (NREGA) has been a magnificent success. During 2008-09, NREGA provided employment opportunities for more than 4.47 crore households as against 3.39 crore households covered in 2007-08. We are committed to providing a real wage of Rs. 100 a day as an entitlement under the NREGA. To increase the productivity of assets and resources under NREGA, convergence with other schemes relating to agriculture, forests, water resources, land resources and rural roads is being initiated. In the first stage, a total of 115 pilot districts have been selected for such convergence. Details of these measures and convergence guidelines will be announced by my colleague, the Minister of Rural Development. I propose an allocation of Rs. 39,100 crore for the year 2009-10 for NREGA which marks an increase of 144% over 2008-09 Budget Estimates." Most of the amount spent on works under NREGA will help in agriculture development be it digging of pond, construction of road, etc.

The details of Agricultural Debt Wavier and Debt Relief Scheme 2008 were widely reported in the media with the remit extended to include "other farmers" with more than 5 acres, a one time settlement (OTS) rebate of 25 percent of overdue amount or Rs. 20,000, whichever is higher, on the proviso of their paying the balance 75 per cent in not more than three installments by 30 June, 2009. While announcing the scheme finance minister P. Chidambaram told that the cost of scheme, originally estimated at about Rs. 71,680 crores. He said that both in terms of scope, coverage and the financial cost, this is the most ambitious scheme ever undertaken by any government of India.

The Maharashtra government announced a Rs. 6,208 crore loan waiver package to benefit about 41 lakh farmers in the state not covered by a similar scheme announced by the Centre earlier, including those having pre-1997 debts and those being regular in their repayments. The package gives complete waiver for debts up to Rs. 20,000, waiver for debts over that amount if the borrower repays the excess, and adjustments for those who have repaid their loans regularly. Loans worth Rs. 2,860 crore, for debts up to Rs. 20,000, would be waived completely, to benefit 24.24 lakh farmers in the state. Similarly, for debts over Rs. 20,000 wherein the borrower repays excess amount, the government would extend an assistance of Rs. 3,348 crore to 16.76 lakh farmers by way of waiver. Government would give full waiver for crop failures, amounting to Rs. 20,000 each. Similarly, 1.42 lakh farmers would be given a flat waiver of Rs. 20,000 for loans over that amount, provided they repaid the excess amount, which was estimated to be Rs. 488 crore. Total benefit on this account, thus, would be Rs. 541 crore for 3.55 crore farmers. The government would give full waiver for supplementary loans, amounting to Rs. 134 crore, to 2.29 farmers, for outstanding amounts upto Rs. 20,000. A flat waiver of Rs. 20,000 for loans over that amount would be worth Rs. 184 crore, with the total benefit on this account being Rs. 318 crore. There would be a waiver worth Rs. 36 crore for loans below Rs. 20,000, and a flat waiver of Rs.

168 crore for loans over that amount, provided the borrowers paid the excess of Rs. 728 crore, for loans taken for poultry and fishing. There would be a waiver worth Rs. 341 crore to 3.50 lakh farmers for loans below Rs. 20,000, and a flat waiver of Rs. 304 crore for loans over that amount, provided the borrowers paid the excess of Rs. 446 crore, for term loans. Making identical announcements in the two houses of the legislature at Nagpur, Chief Minister Ashok Chavan said that the loan waiver package would cover 26.01 lakh farmers, who had been regular in their repayment. Such farmers had paid Rs. 1,727 crore by way of repayment of loans, which would be adjusted against their loan repayments for the current year. (UNI, December 30, 2008).

In the budget speech 2009-10 Finance Minister Pranav Mukherjee said, "Agriculture has been the mainstay of our economy with 60 per cent of our population deriving their sustenance from it. In the recent past, the sector has recorded a growth of about 4 per cent per annum with substantial increase in plan allocations and capital formation in the sector. Agriculture credit flow was Rs. 2,87,000 crore in 2008-09. The target for agriculture credit flow for the year 2009-10 is being set at Rs. 3,25,000 crore. To achieve this, I propose to continue the interest subvention scheme for short-term crop loans to farmers upto Rs. 3 lakh per farmer at the interest rate of 7 per cent per annum. I am also happy to announce that, for this year, the Government shall pay an additional subvention of 1 per cent as an incentive to those farmers who repay their short-term crop loans on schedule. Thus, the interest rate for these farmers will come down to 6 per cent per annum. For this, I am making an additional Budget provision of Rs. 411 crore over, Interim BE." He announced :

Debt Relief for Farmers

The one-time bank loan waiver of nearly Rs. 71,000 crore to cover an estimated 40 million farmers was one of the major highlights of the last Budget. Under the Agricultural Debt Waiver and Debt Relief Scheme (2008), farmers having more than two hectares of land were given time upto 30th June, 2009 to pay 75% of their overdues. Due to the late arrival of monsoon, I propose to extend this period by six months upto 31st December, 2009.

It is learnt that in some regions of Maharashtra, a large number of farmers had taken loans from private money lenders and the loan waiver scheme did not cover them. The matter requires special attention. To examine the matter in detail and suggest the future course of action, I propose to set up a Taskforce.

Accelerated Irrigation Benefit Programme

I propose to provide an additional Rs. 1,000 crore over Interim BE for the Accelerated Irrigation Benefit Programme (AIBP), marking an increase of 75 per cent over the allocation in 2008-09(BE). The allocation for the Rashtriya Krishi Vikas Yojna (RKYY) is also being stepped up by 30 per cent over Budget Estimates of 2008-09."

Government has taken following new initiatives to improve the production of agriculture :

National Food Security Mission (NFSM) : To increase the production and productivity of wheat, rice and pulses to ensure food security of the people our country.

Rashtriya Krishi Yikas Yojna (RKYY) : To increase public investment in agriculture and maximize returns to the farmers.

National Agriculture Extension System (NAES) : Strengthened with ATMA in all the districts in the country and 50,000 farm schools along with extensive training, exposure visits and demonstrations for the farmers."

Agriculture and Indian Economy

The performance of the agricultural sector influences the growth of the Indian economy. Agriculture (including allied activities) accounted for 17.8 per cent of the Gross Domestic Product (GDP at constant prices) in 2007-08 as compared to 21.7 per cent in 2003-04. Notwithstanding the fact that the share of this sector in GDP has been declining over the years, its role remains critical as it accounts for about 52 per cent of the employment in the country. Apart from being the provider of food and fodder, its importance also stems from the raw materials that it provides to industry. The prosperity of the rural economy is also closely linked to agriculture and allied activities. Agricultural sector contributed 12.2 per cent of national exports in 2007-08. The rural sector (including agriculture) is being increasingly seen as a potential source of domestic demand, a recognition, that is shaping the marketing strategies of enterpreneurs wishing to widen the demand for goods and services.

Food Production (million tonnes)

1.	Rice	96.69
2.	Wheat Coarse	78.57
3.	Cereals	40.76
4.	Cereals	216.02
5.	Total pulses	14.76
6.	Total food grains	230.78

With an average growth of over 4.9 per cent over three years (2005-6 to 2007-08) the agriculture sector (including allied activities) lent credible support to the overall growth in GDP. However, in 2008-09 the growth originating from agriculture and allied activities declined to 1.6 per cent (as per the revised estimates) while this is lower than the 49 and 40 per cent growth witnessed in 2007-08 and 2006-07 respectively. The performance in 2008-09 needs to be viewed in the light of the high base of the previous years Agricultural growth characterized by sharp fluctuations and remains vulnerable to the vaganes of nature.

2. In terms of composition out of the total share of 178 per cent in GDP in 2007-08 for the agriculture and allied activities sector, agriculture alone accounted for 163 per cent of GDP followed by fishing at 0.8 per cent and forestry and logging at 0.7 per cent of GDP.

Gross Capital Formation in Agriculture and Allied Sector

3. The Gross Capital Formation (GCF) in agriculture as a proportion to the total GDP has shown a decline from 2.9 per cent in 2001-02 to 2.5 per cent in 2007-08. However the GCF in agriculture relative to GDP in this sector has shown an improvement from 11.23 per cent in 1999-2000 to 14.24 per cent in 2007-2008.

4. The share of agriculture and allied sector in total GCF after showing a marginal increase during 1999-2000 to 2001-02 has been continuously declining. It stood at 10.2 per cent in 1999-2000. Increased to 11.7 per cent in 2001-02 and thereafter declined to 7 per cent in 2006-07. The decline was mainly attributed 10 decline in the private sector despite increase in the share of public sector.

Sector in to Share of agriculture & allied at GCF (%) (at 1999-2000 prices)

Year	*Public sector*	*Private sector*	*Total*
1999-2000	6.0	11.9	30.2
2000-01	5.8	11.3	9.7
2001-02	6.7	13.7	13.7
2002-03	6.5	11.5	10.3
2003-04	7.4	9.2	8.8
2004-05	7.8	7.7	7.7
2005-06	7.9	7.1	7.2
2006-07	8.2	6.6	7.0

Source: Agricultural Statistics at a Glance 2008, Directorate of Economics & Statistics.

5. Apart from production the demand and distributional aspects of the agricultural sector especially of food availability and food management, are of importance to the economy. This chapter reviews the production performance of different segments of agriculture and allied activities covering. Inter

alia, horticulture animal husbandry and fisheries as also the developments in the area of food management during the year 2008-09.

Crop Production 2008-09

6. For three consecutive years (2005-06 to 2007-08), foodgrains production recorded an average annual increase of over 10 million tonnes. The total foodgrains production in 2007-08 was estimated of 230.78 million tonnes as against 217.3 million tonnes in 2006-07 and 208.60 million tonnes in 2005-06.

7. As per the third advance estimates. production of foodgrains in 2008-09 is estimated to be 229.85 tonnes, which is a marginal improvement of 1.97 million tonnes over the second advance estimates for 2008-09. This is, however, lower than the target of 233 million tonnes set out for the year as also the final estimates of 230.78 million tonnes for 2007-08.

Cereal Production

8. The overall production of cereals in 2008-09 has shown a decline of 0.2 per cent over 2007-08 and a shortfall of 0.8 per cent over target for the year. While rice production in 2008-09 exceeded both target for the year and the level in 2007-08 wheat production was marginally below the target for the year and production level achieved in 2007-08. (Economic Survey 2008-09)

In 1997, more than three decades after it entered the rural markets, DCM Shriram started setting up the Shriram Krishi Vikas Kendras. The idea was to do some value-addition to its primary business of selling urea, fertilizers and sugar manufacturing. The centers offer services of agriculture experts to local farmers across 100 villages. The company utilized this opportunity to connect its agro products along with other things. The first Hariyali Bazar was established in July 2003. Now DCM Shriram Consolidated (DSCL) had 180 Hariyali Kisan Bazars.

Expenditure Incurred on Agricultur in Five Year Plans

Plan	Total budget	Agriculture and others	Total per cent	Plan	Total budget	Agriculture and others	Total per cent
First	2378	354	14.9%	Sixth	97500	5695	5.8%
Second	4500	501	11.3%	Seventh	180000	10525	5.9%
Third	8577	1089	12.7%	Annual	58369	3405	5.8%
Annual	6625	1107	16.7%	Annual	64751	3851	6.0%
Fourth	15779	2320	14.7%	Eighth	434100	22467	5.2%
Fifth	39425	4865	12.3%	Ninth	8959200	42462	4.9%
Annual	12177	1997	16.4%	Tenth	398890	20668	5.2%

Industry captains are looking good opportunity in retail sector. Now, Mukesh Ambani, Ratan Tata, K.M. Birla, Sunil Mittal and others have joined the retail business. A Me Kinsey 2005 study says India's need for consumer goods itself will touch $400 billion by 2010-making it one of the five largest in the world. Finance Minister P. Chidambaram indicated the importance of food industry that is generating 2,50,000 jobs every years. He said, in his 2005 budget, that this year, the industry has been treated a priority sector for lending, with NABARD creating a separate window with a corpus of Rs. 1,000 for refinancing loans for infrastructure development.

Before starting its hyper-end supermarket venture with Wal-Mart Sunil Mittal started 'Fieldfresh' in 2004 'to link Indian fields to the world : It brought in Ravi Deol, who had earned his spurs at Barista coffee to look after this initiative. A 50 : 50 joint venture with Rothschild of the U.K., it has 5,000 acres of land under cultivation for fruits and vegetables. Aditya Birla Group has planned a big retail plan with a project size of Rs. 4,5000 crore to be scaled up to Rs. 9000 crores.

Reliance entered into the agriculture field in 1999 when it planted 1,00,000 mango trees in Jamnagar, though it was an exercise of green marketing. Reliance roped in Raghu Pillai, who has long experience with RPG group and Pantaloon. Agriculture, being a state subject, has received thousands of crores of rupees over several years from governments on various projects. If we analyze the budget speeches for the past years, focus on marketing and food processing appears regularly.. Reliance Plans to set up high-tech, temperature - controlled warehouses for this across the country where sorting and grading of the fruit and vegetables will take place. It will set up pre-cooling centers in these ware houses, to take the heat out of the fruit or vegetable, to prevent early rotting.

Reliance plans to set up 100 rural business hubs to link millions of farmers. Better quality, pest resistant seeds and advisory services to farmers will be provided through these centers. These centers will play the pivotal role in the rural marketing. Sources said Reliance is setting aside Rs. 50,000 crore to build its farm to fork linkage. Reliance has drawn up plans for presence in 784 towns and 6,000 mandi (whole sale market), towns with 1,600 rural business hubs to service these. It has already rolled out 177 Reliance fresh stores across major towns in states. (Business world, 9 July, 2007)

The inspiration of commercial agriculture started from the time when Pepsi Co. took initiative and transformed agriculture in a part of Punjab where it pioneered the concept of contract farming for bulk procurement of crops like potato, tomato, groundnut, and chili. In partnership with Punjab Agriculture University and Punjab Agro Industries Corporation, it used location-specific R&D to boost yields of tomato and chili by almost three times. India is the second largest producer of fruits and vegetables (15 percent and 11 percent respectively). An impressive network of infrastructure developed by corporates viz. pre-coolers and pack houses to cold stores and refrigerated trucks and cargo, will help in the growth of labour-intensive horticulture. Process of public- private partnership is underway with government interest. Retail interest is happening at the right time when the interest of big business, the farmer and the consumer are coinciding.

Jawahar Lal Nehru at the time of independence said, "Everyone else can wait, but not agriculture." The 4th Report (13th April, 2006) of the National Commission on Farmers notes that, "unfortunately this profound truth is yet to be converted into concrete policies and action on an adequate scale." Agriculture, being source of livelihood of rural population, has been given maximum chunk of financial allocation in budgets. Presenting the interim budget 2004-05, the then finance Minister spared no effort to eulogize: "In India, agriculture is not an economic activity; it is a way of life. Before him the then Finance Minister Yashwant Sinha said his budget was aimed at ensuring freedom of farmer. As per the recent survey report of National Sample Survey Organization 40 per cent of country expressed desire to quit farming.

It is said that allowing direct procurement of farm commodities, setting up special markets for the private companies to mop up the produce, and to set up land share companies, are all directed at the uncontrolled entry of the multi-national corporations in the Indian farm sector. Coupled with the introduction of the genetically modified crops and the unlimited credit support for the agri-business companies, the focus is to strengthen the ability of the companies to take over the food chain. Farmers are being shown the exit gate. In Europe, it has been estimated that one farmer quits agriculture every minute and farming is now increasing in the hands of agri-business giants and corporations. (Sharma 2007)

NSSO survey revealed that despite the gains of green revolution, the average monthly income of a farm household in 2003 stood at a paltry Rs. 2,115. Governments started various programmes for the development of agriculture, but the data shows. that Indian agriculture is stagnating or in fewer crops viz. pulses production is declining.

In a letter, addressed to finance minister, dated 29-6-2004 managing trustee of ZNet Vandana Shiva advocated to check the loss of output estimated annually of more than 1,15,000 crores.

	Loss of crops per year
Oilseed	Rs. 25,000 crore
Potato	Rs. 5,000 crore
Sugarcane	Rs. 1,500 crore
Rice	Rs. 21,000 crore
Wheat	Rs. 27,000 crore
Milk	Rs. 34,000 crore
Tea	Rs. 2,100 crore
Spices and Plantation crops	Rs. 100 crore
Total	Rs. 1,15,800 crores

Source: Srinivasan 2007.

Production of food grains

Year	1950-51	1960-61	1970-71	1980-81	1990-91	2000-01	2001-02	2002-03	2003-04	2004-05	2007-08	2008-09
Food grain production in M.T.	50.8	82.0	108.4	129.6	176.4	196.8	212.9	174.8	213.5	204.6	227.32	230.78

Source: Economic survey 2009, Government of India.

Use of post harvest technology and modern technologies can be helpful in reducing the loss. NDDB's effort to prevent loss of milk in Gujarat is an example. Improved freezing facility, ware housing, transportation, effective marketing channel can certainly control the loss.

According to a survey conducted by Mckinsey in 2007, rural India with a population of 630 million (approximately) would become bigger than total consumer market in countries such as South Korea or Canada in another 20 years and it will grow at least four times from its existing size. The retail sector has a huge potential for growth as a study shows that opportunities in rural retail sector were estimated to be over $34 billion in the year 2007, which is expected to touch $43 billion by the year 2010. It can be seen from the market that companies like Reliance, Subhiksha, etc. expanding in the rural, market. ITC has launched its first rural mall 'Chaupal Sagar,' which offers products ranging from FMCG to electronic appliance to automobiles. Indian Oil is planning to invest $ 189.10 million in the rural areas during the financial year 2009.

Corporate houses operate in niches in rural India. Tata Chemical's promoted Tata Kisan Sansar or Mahindra's Shubh Labh, for instance have retail initiatives. They deal with farmers, advise them on various aspects of scientific agriculture, provide farm credit and even farm equipment.

A recent study by Dun and Bradstreet has estimated wastage of farm produce to the extent of $13 billion in India annually, which affects the farm income and returns on farm investments. Consumer also pays for this wastage. Processing accounts for 2% of total fruits and vegetable production, 35% of milk production. Farmer's distress can be understood as 1050 farmers suicide cases was reported in 2006, which is three times more than year 2004, which saw 324 suicides and 38 in 1999 (Rao 2007). There has been no breather from the spate of farmer's suicides, which has blown in to an epidemic problem. A farmer faces major problem in marketing, where corporates with their improved infrastructure and financial strength can be helpful.

The Legal Restriction

The Agricultural Produce Marketing Committee (APMC) Act prohibits farmers to sell their products in the open market. So far 16 states have amended the rules in accordance with states frame the rules under the amended Act it remains a legislative exercise. Central Government has once again extended the deadline to March 2008 for all 29 states to amend the law. The amendment of the Act has paved the way for contract farming in a number of states although there is a restriction on the lease period. Under the model law on contract farming, a farmer can lease out his land for a minimum of 11 months and a maximum of 30 months. Companies getting into retail complain that 30 months is too short a time to recoup investments. Currently, only 3 states—Punjab, Haryana and Maharashtra allow farmers to lease land. The corporate entrants have been seeking on amendment in the Revenue Act, so that a farmer can lease his land for 10 years. (Jayram 2007)

The India Retail Report 2007, put together by leading Indian and foreign consultancies, estimates that the retail price was worth Rs. 12,00,000 in 2006, with food and groceries accounting for a whopping 63 percent. According to Crisil Research, food and grocery items account for a significant 74 percent of total retail sales, which it places at Rs. 12,80,000 crore in 2006. However, food and grocery accounts only for 18% of the organized retail. Bharti Enterprises launched Fieldfresh Foods in partnership with ELRO Holdings India, an investment company of the Rothschild family. Airtel, the company of Bharti group, revolutionized telecom in 1990s by expanding its reach to millions of customers. Its 300-acre farm leased from the Punjab Agriculture University has been experimenting with exotic vegetables destined for the European Market. Snow peas, cheny tomatoes, bell peppers and sugar snap peas are being tested out at the Ladowal farm close to Ludhiana.

Involvement of corporates in rural marketing is being appreciated by all quarters. The World Bank believes that huge investments by the retail biggies in the supply chain infrastructure could usher in a service revolution that would shorten the distance that fresh produce travels to reach the consumer. In a supply chain analysis of 13 high value commission that covered 1,400 farmers, 200 commission agents and 65 exporters across the country, the bank found that high transport costs and multiple players in the linear supply chain were crippling horticulture.

Tesco in Europe has 7 percent of its $ 40 billion business being managed by 'aggregators' and 'distributors'. Indian retail companies are also working to manage transportation of farm products to a store or work with 'aggregators' of farm produce. 'Aggregator' is the person, whose business is to collect produce from different farms and fill up empty shelves in the store. The profit sharing margins on the particular space leased in the store depends on the retailer. The aggregator can use a mix of warehouses, cold storage facilities and refrigerated trucks depending on the kind of product that is to be put on the shelf. He will also bear loss in the case of perishable items when in transit.

Many corporates started community development initiatives and linked it with business like ITC's e-chaupal. H.S. Bawa, Vice-chairman, Chambal Fertilizers & Chemicals Ltd. (CFCL) said, "We do not look at our growth and profits as our only purpose of being in business. Our core purpose is to help improve the lot of the farming community. Our concern for the people in our area of operations has made us aware that our corporate social responsibility has to be taken up as any other business practice. The concern for our environment has made it possible for us to start planting trees, laying a green belt and creating water bodies simultaneously with the execution of our project." (Bawa 2004).

A recent initiative of Chambal has been its entry in the field of frozen vegetables and fruits. Marketed under the "Ever Fresh" brand, the EF green peas, corn, mixed vegetables, tomato puree and other products are well-received in the quality sensitive middle-east region.

Godrej's FMCG business specially soap marketing has deep penetration in rural markets. Godrej Agrovet has tactfully used its marketing experience in rural areas by opening rural market centres "Adhar". The centre will market centre will advise farmers on scientific agriculture and make available seeds, fertilizers, etc. The company covers 2500 villages and farmers of these villages will be directly linked to its retail business "Nature's Basket", in Mumbai.

Punjab is the first state to set up the terminal market that will act as a major catalyst for farm growth. Impact of green revolution in Punjab changed the face of Indian agriculture in 1970s. Corporates like Bharti Enterprises have chosen Punjab to make farm retailing a successful business.

ITC advertised its 'Ashirwad' atta with a statement that the wheat is procured from its e-chaupal where good quality wheat is purchased from farmers. Rural retail chains are sourcing produce through three routes. One from village markets i.e. haats, second from APMC yards, and third by linking directly with farmers like e-chaupal initiative. Retail chains are in the process of creating a sound supply chain and villages that are better connected to big towns and cities are their first stop for produce. Agri-retail chains such as Reliance Fresh, Field Fresh, Subhiksha, Spinach, Food Bazaar and Nature's Basket have all been sourcing produce from farmers and are either linking to farmers directly or have engaged procurement agencies to do the same for them.

The basic scope of rural marketing initiative will be the mutual benefits of the rural entrepreneurs and industries. The entrepreneurs – primary beneficiaries, SHCs – bridge with the community, participating companies/industries and rural consumers have befitted through a robust commercial relationship. These models of marketing linkages demonstrate a large corporation which can play a major role in reorganizing markets and increasing the efficiency of a rural product generation system. While doing so it will benefit farmers and rural communities as well as shareholders. Moreover, the key role of information technology-provided and maintained by the industry/company for building linkages, and used by local farmers—brings about transparency, increased access to information, and rural transformation. Besides, this strategy of market linkage addresses the challenges faced by rural entrepreneurs due to institution voids, numerous intermediaries and infrastructure bottlenecks. Moreover, the prime scope of this model is the creation of opportunities for the rural entrepreneurs for product differentiation and innovation by offering them choices. Because of this sustainable market linkages, rural producers can participate in the benefits of globalization and will also develop their capacity to maintain global quality standard. Nonetheless, it creates new stakeholders for the industry sector. And subsequently, they become part of the firms' core businesses. The involvement of the private /industry sector at the rural product and market development can also provide opportunities for the development of new services and values to the customers, which will find application in the developed markets. It will be worth mentioning that building a sustainable market linkage through industry's intervention will also empower the rural mass (producers, farmers & entrepreneurs) to cope with socio-economic problems in the rural society and will ensure economic self-reliance.

Farmers in Maharashtra have become part of supply pipeline set up by "Spinach", a Mumbai based retail chain belonging to the Wadhawan group, and are supplying around 10 tonnes of vegetables to it every month. 70 farmers spread across 20 villages near Lonikalbhor have signed as agreement with Spinach to produce vegetables such as cabbage, peppers and cauliflowers for it around the year. Farmers in many villages are shifting away from low-paying staple crops to cash crops that fetch them better prices in the market. Tired of being gripped by middlemen and Corrupt cooperative agencies, farmers are breathing fresh air with agri-retail. According to estimates of SSKI research, the FMCG industry grew by 17% in FY 06, owing to back-end investments and consequently, the sector has sustained this growth through retailing and new product introduction. KPMG claims that the rural market accounts for almost 56% of the total PMGC demand in India. (Business & Economy, June 15-28, 2007)

Food processing industry is on the top of priority sector, government has granted a generous amount of Rs. 10 billion, for agro-processing infrastructure and marketing development. Corporates have penetrated into this industry with an exotic range of premium quality fresh fruits and vegetables to offer the market worldwide. ITC's e-chaupal supply strategy has opened new gate of opportunities for farmers as well as consumers.

Challenges Ahead

The Indian retail market is estimated at $ 300 billion, consumers in rural India spend a whopping $ 165 billion. Therefore, there is hardly any company or retailer who can afford to ignore the rural market. However, according to 2001 census India is home of 720 million consumers across 6,27,000 villages. About 17 percent of these villages account for 50 percent of the rural population as well 60% of rural wealth. Therefore, even if a retailer aims for half of the rural market opportunity, it has to be present in at least 1,00,000 villages (Biyani 2007). Most of these villages are separated by large distances and relatively less density of population. Therefore, the number of customers that a single retail outlet can attract in rural market is significantly low, making existing modern retail formats unviable. Corporates are working on a partnership model to reach rural consumer as well rural producer. Today, a rural retailer has to travel long distances to cities and towns and visit multiple markets to source various products. The challenges in the rural markets are complex but corporates will be able to leverage this market by partnering with small traders, farmers and micro-entrepreneurs.

Though corporates have ventured to tap the rural market, there are many hurdles in the infrastructure space. According to the 2001 census, 62.5% of the smaller villages with population of less than 1000 were not connected by approach roads. According to estimates of the Rural Infrastructure

Report of National Council of Applied Economic Research, it would require a total investment of over Rs. 1,58,313 crore (at 2002-03 prices) for new asset creation in rural India. In the telecom and power sectors, the investment required for full coverage is estimated at Rs. 92,690 crore and Rs. 55,243 crore, respectively. The corresponding expected investment requirements for roads and transport, and water and sanitation sectors are Rs. 5,892 crore and Rs. 4,488 crore. (Sharma, Sarkar & Tiwari 2007)

Rural indebtedness is another problem, which has posed major threat to farming community. Vidarbh region, once known for advanced agriculture, is facing acute problem of farmer's distress. 1050 farmer's suicide cases have been reported in 2006. Government has provision of easier loaning to farmers through Kisan Credit Cards, Private banks like HDFC and ICICI Bank have ventured in to rural markets to offer credit facilities to rural community.

Nobel laureate Amartya Sen, in his well-known theory of entitlements, challenged the then prevailing economic rationale that people died in famines due to scarcity of food. His theory was partly based upon the study of the decisions made by the colonial masters when food was diverted for commercial purposes during the Bengal famine of 1943.

It is hoped the socially responsible investing (SRI) by corporates in rural markets with innovative initiatives like ITC's e-chaupal, Tata Chemical's Tata Kisan Sansar will help in the creation of opportunity in rural markets. Corporates are upbeat about the growing income of rural community but growing inequality is threat to business. Connecting rural markets to corporates will help in the growth of agriculture, farmer and nation.

References

Bawa, H.S. (2004): "Looking back looking ahead," The Hindu, March 31.

Biyani, Kishore (2007): "Challenging but rewarding," The Economic Times, Chandigarh, February 11.

Nayyar, Manjeet Singh(2008): "Rural Markets booming with prospects", Merinews, 4 September.

Rao, GVL Narshima (2007): "Restrictive Laws," Business world, July 9.

Sharma, Devinder (2007) : "Let's budget for farmer suicides," The India Economy Review, Volume 4, pp. 65-66.

Sharma, Shantanu Nandan; Sarkar, John; Tiwari, Dheeraj (2007) : "Back to basics", The Economic Times, Chandigarh, February 11.

Srinivasan R. (2007): "Indian agriculture at the crossroads..." The India Economy Review, Vol. 4, pp. 76-87.

3

The Right to Food

Defining Right to Food

The International Convenant on Economic, Social and Cultural Right (ICESCR) adopted by the United Nations in 1966, to which India is a signatory along with 152 other countries, deals with the issue of the right to food. The international understanding of what constitutes "food security" is elaborated in the Plan of Action of the World Food Summit (1996), which states that : Food security at the individual household, national, regional and global levels is achieved when all people, at all time have physical and economic access to sufficient, safe and nutritious food to meet their dietary needs and food preferences for an active and healthy life". The Council of Food and Agricultural Organisation (FAO) of the United Nations, where India is also a signatary nation, defined the right to food (2004) as "the right of everyone to have physical and economic access at all times to adequte food or means for its procurement".

Lastly, the UN Special Reporter on the Right to Food has articulated the right to food as follows "[The] right to have regular, permanent and free access either directly or by means or financial purchases, to quantitatively and qualitatively adequate and sufficient food corresponding to the cultural traditions of the people to which the consumer belongs, and which ensures the physical and mental individual or collective, fulfilling and dignified life free of fear".

Many other International Covenants and Instruments, to which India is also a signatory, refer to the right to food and elaborate it within their own frameworks. These include the Convention on Elimination of all Forms of Discrimination Against Women (CEDAW, Article 12) and the International Convention on the Rights of the Child (CRC, Articles 27 and 27.3). For instance, Article 12 of CEDAW focuses on the right of women to adequate nutrition during pregnancy and lactation.

Thus, it is not just the legal framework within the country that bind India to obligalions on the right to food but also a range of internationl covenants and related instruments which the Indian State has signed.

Right to Food Act

Social activists and civil society organisations are lobbying to propose Right to Food Bill. Economist Jean Dreeze and others have prepared draft of Right to Food Act. On the other hand, questions are being raised pertaining to various provisions of the Act and its implementation strategy. Writing on the right to food, Professor Bhaskar Datta has critically examined various issues in his article "Stricking against hunger" in The Economic Times dated 17 July, 2009. He wrote, "We first heard of the government's intention to enact such a law during President Patil's speech to Parliament a couple of months ago. The specific promise at that time (and repeated in the finance minister's budget speech) was that the government would provide 25 kg. of foodgrains per month at Rs. 3 per kg. to families below the poverty line (BPL). However, several social activists have expressed a strong preference for a significantly wider definition of the right to adequate nutrition, arguing that access to cheap food grains is just one component of the bundle constituting good nutrition. They believe that an acceptable "right to food" Act must entitle the poor to a balanced basket of nutritious food (and not just grain), clean water, child care and many other essentials.

At an abstract level, there is much to be said for a comprehensive Act which promises the beneficiaries the legal right to a wide range of basic goods and services that are deemed necessary for a minimum acceptable standard of living. However, policies and perhaps more importantly, legislation have to take into account ground realities. In particular, what type of institutional mechanisms can one think of which will immediately – that is, as soon as the Bill is passed – deliver the goods and services to the intended recepients? And is there much point in framing a piece of legislation which has no chance of being implemented properly? That is why a simpler Act which identifies the right to food with the provision of foodgrains alone may be desirable, at least as a first step. As I mention below, even this will pose tremendous challenges in implementation.

The government would like to extend the right to food to the BPL families. But, who are the BPL families and how many BPL families are there in the country? As we know there is a fair amount of controversy about the number of people below the poverty line. Indeed, there is a large variation in the estimates of the incidence of poverty in the country. The 'official' figure, used for instance in the allocation of foodgrains to different states for the public distribution system is roughly 6.5 crore BPL families. But, this is based on somewhat ancient poverty estimates – those pertaining to 1993-94, combined with population estimates for 2000.

While poverty levels must have gone down population has increased, so that the actual number of BPL families may have moved in either direction. Clearly, there is a need to update the number of BPL families, and also to undertake periodic surveys to obtain reasonably accurate estimates of the target group. Another complication is the alarmingly large discrepancy in the numbers of BPL ration cards issued by the state governments totalling 10.68 crore versus the central government's own estimate of 6.5 crore. Of course, as I have mentioned earlier, the latter figure too is outdated!

Even if the right to food is restricted to just foodgrains alone, the delivery mechanism will pose one of the biggest challenge to the government. The public distribution system (PDS) has become something of a sacred cow, and many people will assert that the PDS is the natural—if not the only—option. However, this view completely ignores the shortcomings of the PDS.

Consider, for instance, some characteristics of the PDS. Contrary to popular perception, large sections of poor households do not purchase any foodgrains from the PDS. This could be either because of limited geographical coverage as in the northern states or institutional barriers such as the need to prove residence and buy ration entitlements only once a fortnight. Migrant households do not satisfy the first requirement while the poorest households do not have enough savings to buy in bulk. Apart from inadequate access to the PDS is the huge cost of providing subsidies to the poor through the PDS. Indeed, several, researchers have shown that it costs much more than one rupee to transfer a rupee of subsidy to the target families!

An alternative to the PDS is the system of food stamps. Under this scheme, the government issues coupons to the target families. These coupons can then be re-deemed at — any shop — private or public — for specified quantities of foodgrains at stipulated prices : Obviously, the government will then have to pay private retailers the difference between the stipulated price and the market price.

The PDS and the system of food stamps must both have the same level of leakages due to targeting costs — the identification of BPL families must precede both systems. So, the effectiveness of food stamps obviously depends on how efficient it is delivering foodgrains to the consumers relative to the PDS. By its very nature, food stamps do not have some of the costs associated with the PDS. For instance, there cannot be any chance of illegally diverting grains to the open market. Procurement and storage costs are also substantially higher in the PDS.

On the other hand, private retailers may demand excessive

profit margins in order to enter remote areas. So, the superiority of one system versus another is an empirical issue. This suggests that the sensible option is to allow both systems to co-exist so as to enable researchers to evaluate the costs associated with the two systems.

There is much discussion surrounding the yet to be revealed Right to Food Act. Pragya Singh of Outlook India is not alone in her assessment that the Act "is being crafted as the centrepiece of the UPA's second innings." Singh's article then goes on to look at the debates concerning what the act will ultimately contain. As her article alludes there is some cautious optimism about the development of this Act by those who have worked on the Right to food case and on this issue more generally, but also a very real fear about it. Those fears revolve around, first, whether the legislation will weaken the substance of the right, and second, whether the enforcement mechanisms that go along with any act will be weaker than those currently set-up by the Supreme Court in the guise of the Right to Food Commissioners and regular monitoring of the case by the Court itself.

At first blush the story of this Act looks similar to the development of the Right to Information Act : committed activists rally around a cause, succeed in getting a positive Supreme Court order (or series of orders), and then use the traction and precedent gained from those orders, as well as a great deal of independent organizing efforts, to consolidate (and advance) their gains in legislation. Indeed, one could even tell this story - to some extent - about the development and passage of the National Rural Employment Guarantee Act at the beginning of the UPA's "first inning" (arguably its "centrepiece" at that time). As part of the Right to Food case, the Supreme Court had ordered that the government implement its then existing work-for-food scheme. Many of the same activists involved in the Right to Food Case then pushed to get NREGA drafted and passed, and have worked to implement it. The Supreme Court has since seemed to accept that the passage of NREGS fulfilled its orders concerning the work scheme in the Right to Food case.

This later non-interference by the Court around NREGS highlights an important point. By legislating a "right" the UPA seemingly made the Court more cautious about intervening to implement a right the Court once monitored and (at least on occassion) issued orders to enforce. This doesn't mean they might not issue orders later, but they seem to have adapted a wait-and-see attitude on this relatively new legislation, NREGS is more far-reaching and potentially far more transformative for India's poor than the work-for-food scheme it replaced that was subject of the Supreme Court's initial orders in the Right to Food case. Yet, enforcement of NREGS has been an ongoing problem, in part because the legislation does not provide for either an independent oversight body to enforce it (like a commission) or for a realistic way for those affected to enforce their right in court. As a result, implementation has varied from quite good to quite poor depending on administrators in a locality, state, etc. This sits in contrast to the Right to Information Act which was implemented to both expand and better articulate what the right was, but also to create mechanisms to make it easier to access (i.e. a system of complaint and appeal if requested information is not given and relatively harsh penalties for administrators who unlawfully withhold information).

If a Right to Food Act is passed it is not clear how the Supreme Court will respond. There is a very rare chance that the Court might decide to consider the matter closed if the Act, at least on paper, looks like it is fulfilling its orders in the case. Now in the Right to Food case the Court did expand entitlements in some instances - such as universalizing and mandating the mid-day meal scheme - and these would theoretically be included in any Act. But as far as I can tell the core of the Right to Food case has always been about implementation. Most of the courts orders simply involved telling the government to implement a scheme it already had on the books. I would suggest that when deciding whether to keep the Right to Food case open or not the Court should look most closely at implementation mechanisms in the Act.

Indeed, any right to food act should at its core be about mechanisms of implementation - mechanisms hopefully superior to those that the Court has been able to create on its own.

Biraj Patnaik, the principal adivsor to the Right to Food commissioners appointed by the Court to monitor their orders, has a nice comparative piece in the Mint looking at right to food legislation in different parts of the world. In that article he makes the point that :

"The third key lesson [concerning right to food legislation] is creating a system of not just administrative, but also legal recourse. This is a key feature of the right to food Acts across countries. In Brazil, the public prosecutors' office take up violations of human rights, including socio-economic rights, at the local level. Guatemala, Venezuela, Brazil, Peru, Uganda and South Africa have already put in place or proposed powerful national commissions that act as oversight bodies and also have the power to impose penalties. Although the Supreme Court has appointed its own commissioners to monitor the food and employment schemes of the Indian government, these commissioners do not have the kind of statutory powers to impose penalties that the bodies in other countries do."

Unfortunately, India currently doesn't have a public prosecutor system (i.e. attorney general, advocate generals, etc.) that is independent or resource-rich enough to be relied upon to implement any future Act. Therefore, the independent commission model with the ability to impose stiff penalties could be a potentially good substitute – it is worth noting that if the public prosecutor system could be built up much of the need for always creating yet another commission to implement a law would go away.

Few social activists have opined that Right to Food legislation should include personal judicial remedies, and more generally India should consider legislating a more robust system of constitutional torts. In the U.S. if someone is deprived of a legislated social welfare benefit, this is considered an infringement of his or her right to property in this benefit. If they succeed in litigation, the party is not only given the benefit they were deprived of, but lawyers fees and potentially other damages. This creates a market amongst lawyers to bring these cases. A similar model could be used in any Right to Food legislation to guarantee damages at a sufficiently high level to attract lawyers to enforce the legislation. U.S. legislation also allows public officials to be personally brought to task if they infringe citizens rights (somewhat similar to the Right to Information Act's penalty of Rs. 250 a day on PIOs if they wrongfully withhold information). (Law and other things, July 11, 2009).

Legal Foundation of the Right to Food

The right to food can be seen as an implication of the fundamental "right to life", enshrined in Article 21 of the Indian Constitution. Indeed, the Supreme Court has explicitly stated (several times) that the right to life should be interpreted as a right to "live with human dignity", which includes the right to food and other basic necessities. For instance, in Francis Coralie v. Administrator Union Territory of Delhi and Ors (1981) 1 SCC 708 the Supreme Court observed :

"We think that the right to life includes the right to live with human dignity and all that goes along with it, namely the bare neccesaries of life such as adequate nutrition, clothing and shelter and facilities for reading, writing and expressing one-self in diverse forms, freely moving about the mixing and commingling with fellow human beings. Of course the magnitude and content of the components of this right would depend upon the extent of the economic, developments of this right would depend upon the extent of the economic development of the country but it must in any view of the matter include the right to the basic necessities of life and also the right to carry on such functions and activities as constitute the bare minimum expression of the human self.

Similarly in Shantistar Builders v. Narayan Khmalal Totame (1990) I SCC 520 the Supreme Court stated "The right to life guaranteed in any civilized society. That would take within its sweep the right to food."

The right to food can also be linked with Article 39(a) and 47 of the Constitution, Article 39(a) direct the State to ensure that all citizens have "the right to an adequate means of livelihood". According to Article 47, "the State shall regard the raising of the level of nutrition and the standard of living or its people and the improvement of public health as among its primary duties". These two Articles belong to the "Directive Principles of State Policy", which are not supposed to be enforceable in Court (Article 37). However, it is possible to argue that Articles 39(a) and 47 are enforceable in court as expressions of the fundamental right to life.

It is also worth remembering that while Article 17 states that the Directive principles "shall not be enforceable by any court", it goes on to emphasize that these principles are nevertheless fundamental in the governance of the country and it shall be the duty of the state to apply these principles in making laws" (Article 17).

This argument is presented in Box 1, based on the National Human Rights Commission's interpretation of the right to food. In the same statement, dated 17th January, 2003, the Commission clearly stated that "there is a fundamental right to be free from hunger".

(Proceedings of a hearing held on 17th January, 2003 reprinted in Gonsalvez C. P., R. Kumar and A. K. Srivastava (eds.) (2005). Right to Food second edition (New Delhi Human Rights Law Network, pp. 104-424.)

Box I : Legal Foundation of the right to food

The legal basis of the right to food has been helpfully spelt by the National Human Rights Commission (NHRC) in the proceedings of a hearing held on 17 January, 2003 :

"Article 21 of the Constitution of India guarantees a fundamental right to life and personal liberty. The expression 'Life' has been judicially interpreted to mean a life with human dignity and not mere survival or animal existence.

In the light of this, the State is obliged to provide for all those minimum requirements which must be satisfied in order to enable a person to live with human dignity such as education, health care, just and humane conditions of work, protection against exploitation etc. In the view of the Commission, the Right to Food is inherent to a life with dignity.

And Article 21 should be read with Articles 39(a) and 47 to understand the nature of the obligation of the State in order to ensure the effective realization of this right. Article 39(a) of the Constitution enunciated as one of the Directive Principles, fundamental in the governance of the country, requires the State to direct its policy towards securing that the citizens, men and women equally, have the right to an adequate means of livelihood. Article 47 spells out the duty of the State to raise the level of nutrition and the standard of living of its people as a primary responsibility. The citizen's right to be free from hunger enshrined in Article 21 is to be ensured by the fulfillment of the obligation of the State set out in Articles 39(a) and 47. The reading of Article 21 together with Articles 39(a) and 47 places the issue of food security in the correct perspective, thus making the Right to Food a guaranteed Fundamental Right which is enforceable by virtue of the constitutional remedy provided under Article 32 of the Constitution."

The relevant Articles of the Constitution are as follows:

Article 21 : "No person shall he deprived of his life or personal liberty except according to procedure established by law."

Article 39 (a) : "The State shall... direct its policy towards securing that the citizen, men and women equality, have the right to an adequate means of livelihood.

Article 47 : "The State shall regard the raising of the level of nutrition and the standard of living of its people and the improvement of public health as among its primary duties...."

Article 32 (I) : "The right to move the Supreme Court by appropriate proceedings for the enforcement of the rights conferred by this Part is guaranteed."

Note: Article 32 (I) applies to the rights conferred in Part III of the Constitution, known as "fundamental rights". Article 21 appears in Part III, but not Articles 39(a) and 47. These appear in Part IV, under "Directive Principles or State Policy."

Leaders gathered at the World Food Summit in 1996 committed their countries to cutting hunger in half by the year 2015. A series of international conferences and summits, during the 1990s, identified other major goals and quantified targets with the same time horizon. These were brought together in the Declaration adopted by the UN Millennium Summit in September 2000 and later restated in the form of eight Millennium Development Goals.

Now is the crucial moment for stepping up action if the world is to deliver on the pledges made at the Millennium Summit. The Goals, with their related time-bound targets and indicators, are designed as an agenda for action by countries with support from the international community.

In September 2005 the UN General Assembly will review progress in achieving them. FAO currently is reviewing how its own activities assist countries in this urgent and ambitious effort, and complement the work of UN partners.

The right to food is a human right and is a binding obligation well-established under international law, recognised in the Universal Declaration of Human Rights and the International Covenant on Economic, Social and Cultural Right (1966), as well as a plethora of other instruments. Though the Constitution of India does not contain any explicit indication of a citizen's right to food, the Supreme Court has been able to rule that it had the status of a fundamental right through interpretation. Such a ruling had come about in the context of certain perceived inefficiencies in the right to food programmes that had been initiated by the government of India in response to its international treaty obligations as well as Constitutional Directive Principles.

The Role of the Judiciary in Enforcing the Right to Food

In India, the right to food has been seen as an implication

of the fundamental right to life in Article 21 of the Indian Constitution. The Supreme Court has explicitly stated (several times) that the right to life should be interpreted as a right to live with human dignity, which includes the right to food and other basic necessities. The Supreme Court has affirmed the individual's right to food as a necessary corollary of the fundamental right to life guaranteed under Article 21 and thus, acknowledged the close nexus between the right to life and the right to food. In the right to food case the Supreme Court passed an interim order which focused on eight food-related schemes and the effect of the order was that the government to be held accountable to what it claims to be doing to protect the right to food : implement these food-related schemes.

An international workshop on a 'Code of Conduct on the Right to Food' organised by the German Government in Berlin from 22 to 23 May, 2002 indicated the Indian Government's head-in-the-sand approach to the issue. According to a statement by the Indian Agriculture Ministry: "Our strategies of poverty elevation have paid rich dividends."

It's not just a grammatical error. In the context of food security, the ministry appears to be genuinely unaware of the difference between elevation and alleviation. According to the Food and Agriculture Organisation (FAO), India alone accounts for over 400 million poor and hungry people. For a nation long inured to scarcity and starvation, the nature of this problem is ironic - the problem of plenty. A problem so acute that the Supreme Court has been forced to take notice. Shocked at the increasing number of starvation deaths amidst overflowing foodgrain godowns of the government (public stock exceeding 60 million tonnes), the Supreme Court passed an interim order on November 2001 demanding that the large stocks of foodgrains in the Food Corporation of India (FCI) warehouses be released with immediate effect. The Supreme Court's damning indictment and directive gives the desperately poor a reason to hope. It is however a shameful treatise on both the democratic institutions and the media that the judicially has to step in to ensure what has been overlooked for very long - the fundamental right to food.

Over the past decade, a series of events have brought the question of food security into sharp focus. Vast famine-affected areas juxtaposed against bursting granaries, the World Trade Organisation's attack on agriculture and farmers, the media's spotlight on starvation deaths in Orissa and, finally, the Supreme Court's reaction to the plight of the hungry - all make a case for the recognition of the right to food.

Starvation deaths are not an anomaly in India : the notorious Kalahandi-Bolangir-Koraput region in Orissa is a case in point. This however has not initiated any corrective action. No commission has ever been set up to examine why in a food surplus nation where buffer stocks are three times what is required for food security, thousands still die of hunger and malnutrition. Attorney General Soli Sorabjee has termed the shocking state of starvation amidst plenty a "horrendous state of affairs", condemning it as a criminal neglect of the Constitutional obligations on the part of the government. (www.hrdc.net)

Globalisation and the Right to Food

The Food and Agriculture Organization of the United Nations reported in the State of Food Insecurity in the World 2004 that there were 852 million undernourished people in the world in 2000-2002. This is absurd when, according to FAO, the planet could produce enough food to provide 2,100 kcals per person per day to 12 billion people, that is, almost twice the existing world population. In Africa, a new study by the well-respected International Food Policy Research Institute (IFPRI) has shown that chronic food insecurity in Africa has been increasing since 1970, with the number of malnourished people in sub-Saharan Africa soaring from 88 million to 200 million in 1999-2001. Chronic food insecurity means that as soon as drought strikes, it can quickly turn into catastrophic famine. The IFPRI study shows that hunger could be reduced by investing in development and reducing dependence on rain-fed agriculture. Investments in simple water-harvesting technologies, agricultural extension, education and HIV/AIDS prevention and treatment would dramatically reduce the percentage of malnourished children in Africa.

These findings are used by the Special Rapporteur on the Right to Food to emphasize how famine and food crises are not inevitable. The right to food is a human right that entails government's obligations to guarantee the food security of their populations. In fact, in a world richer than ever before, it is unacceptable that people can be left to die of starvation or condemned to the misery of chronic hunger and malnutrition. He argues that the primary responsibility always rests with national governments. However, all other governments have a responsibility to refrain from taking action that causes food insecurity and to respond to requests for emergency assistance, to the extent that their resources permit. In the context of globalization, when national governments no longer enjoy a full monopoly on power, it is also essential to extend human rights obligations to other powerful actors, such as international organizations and private transnational corporations.

National Governments as Primary Actors : Respect, Protect, Fulfil

By committing themselves to advancing the right to food through ratification of international conventions, governments are bound to respect, protect and fulfil the right to food, which also means that they should be accountable to their populations if they violate those obligations. The obligation to respect the right to food is effectively a negative obligation, as it entails limits on the exercise of State power that might threaten people's existing access to food. Violations of the obligation to respect would occur, for example, if the government arbitrarily evicted or displaced people from their land, especially if the land was their primary means of feeding themselves, if the government took away social security provisions without making sure that vulnerable people had alternative ways to feed themselves, or if the government knowingly introduced toxic substances into the food chain, as the right to food entails access to food that is free from adverse substances. In situations of armed conflict, it would mean that the government troops must not destroy productive resources and must not block, delay or divert relief food supplies to civilian populations.

The obligation to protect means that the Government must pass and enforce laws to prevent powerful people or organizations from violating the right to food. The obligation to protect requires States to regulate non-State actors, including corporations or individuals who may threaten other peoples right to food. The government must also establish bodies to investigate and provide effective remedies, including access to justice, if that right is violated.

The obligation to fulfil means that the government must take positive actions to identify vulnerable groups and to implement policies to ensure their access to adequate food by facilitating their ability to feed themselves. The obligation to fulfil is a positive obligation, as this means that the government must actively seek to identify vulnerable groups and implement policies to improve those people's access to adequate food and their ability to feed themselves. That could mean improving employment prospects by introducing an agrarian reform programme for landless groups or promoting alternative employment opportunities. It could also include, for example, free milk programmes in schools in order to improve child nutrition. The fulfilment of the right to food, like other economic, social and cultural rights, is qualified to the extent that it must be achieved progressively and to the maximum of available resources. Under paragraph 1, Article 2 of the International Covenant on Economic, Social and Cultural Rights : Each State Party... undertakes to take steps ... to the maximum of its available resources ... [with a view to achieving] progressively the full realization of the rights. A poor country is not expected immediately to ensure the same level of economic, social and cultural benefits that a rich country can afford. However, even the poorest country is bound to ensure the highest level its resources will permit.

Extra-territorial Obligations of States

Although globalization is not a new phenomenon, the extent of interdependence between countries is vastly greater than ever before, which means that the policies and programmes of one country can have far-reaching effects on the right to food of people living in other countries. Governments should therefore become more aware of extraterritorial obligations to refrain from violating the right to food in other countries and to respond to emergencies.

Although the primary responsibility to ensure human rights will always rest with the national government, it is not always able to protect its citizens from the impacts of decisions taken in other countries, given the current context of globalization and strong international interdependence. All countries should therefore ensure that their policies do not contribute to human rights violations in other countries.

International trade in agriculture is a case in point. It is widely recognized that subsidies to farmers in developed countries have negative impacts on farmers and the right to food in developing countries if food products are dumped on developing countries. The European Court of Human Rights, for example, ruled in Loizidou v. Turkey, in the context of civil and political rights that the responsibility of Contracting Parties can be involved because of acts of their authorities, whether performed within or outside national boundaries, which produce effects outside their own territory. Unlike civil and political rights, the legal instruments relating to economic, social and cultural rights do not contain any territorial or jurisdictional limitations. On the contrary, there are explicit legal commitments to cooperate for the realization of economic, social and cultural rights of all individuals without limitation. The Special Rapporteur has argued that States must respect, protect and support the fulfilment of the right to food of people living in other territories, to fully comply with their obligations under the right to food. The obligation to respect is a minimum obligation which requires States to ensure that their policies and practices do not lead to violations of the right to food in other countries. The obligation to protect requires States to ensure that their own citizens and companies, as well as other third parties subject to their jurisdiction, including transnational corporations, do not violate the right to food in other countries.

The Responsibilities of International Organizations

Organizations such as the IMF, the World Bank and the WTO are so powerful today that they have enormous influence on the policy and programmes of national governments, particularly in the poorer, weaker countries that are heavily indebted to the international financial system. In relation to the IMF and the World Bank, far-reaching policies of structural adjustment, economic reform and poverty reduction strategies imposed in most developing countries by these agencies have significant impacts on the capacity of a nation State to meet its obligations to ensure the right to food. Far from improving food security for the most vulnerable populations, these programmes have often resulted in a deterioration of food security among the poorest. In Zambia, after a programme of rapid structural adjustment was introduced in the 1990s, an evaluation made by the IMF recognized that the liberalization in agriculture had caused hardship for poor Zambians, with maize consumption falling by 20 per cent between 1990 and 1997 as the poorest could not afford enough to eat. The World Bank is also directly engaged in large-scale investment projects which, while they may promote economic growth, are often at the cost of violating the right to food of poor, vulnerable populations, particularly indigenous people. Many NGOs and civil society organizations have documented violations of the right to food that have occurred in the context of programmes and projects funded by the World Bank, with typical cases including dam construction or mining natural resources in areas occupied by minorities or indigenous people who are forcibly displaced without due process and compensation. WTO rules on agricultural trade, for example, have a significant impact on the policies that governments can choose in terms of maintaining their food security. Unfortunately, the wide disparities in economic power between the negotiating States meant that powerful States have negotiated rules that are neither free nor fair.

There is no question today that international organizations such as the World Bank, IMF and WTO have legal personality under international law. The Special Rapporteur argues that international organizations such as the aforementioned institutions are bound by international law with regard to the human right to food. The General Assembly has supported this view in resolution 60/165 on the right to food.

The Responsibilities of Private Actors

Large private transnational corporations have come to hold power greater than nation States. At the same time, there is no coherent system of accountability. According to UNDP Human Development Report, 2002, global corporations can have enormous impact on human rights - in their employment practices, in their environmental impact, in their support for corrupt regimes or in their advocacy for policy changes. Today, the top 200 corporations control around a quarter of the world's total productive assets. Many TNCs have revenues far exceeding the revenues of the governments of the countries in which they are operating. Concentration has produced huge transnational corporations that monopolize the whole food distribution chain, narrowing choices for farmers and consumers. Under the traditional application of human rights law, it is usually only possible to hold a government to account for violations of human rights; it is still not clear how a corporation could be held to account for such violations. However, new developments are occurring within human rights law. In general, however, there are two ways to make corporations respect human rights - one is indirect, the other, direct. Corporations can be held to account indirectly by governments which have a duty to protect their people and people living in other countries against negative impacts on the right to food of third parties. However, there is a growing perception that corporations can also be held to account for human rights directly, through the development of direct human rights obligations, intergovernmental instruments and voluntary codes of conduct.

The Secretary-Generals Global Compact initiative, by which transnational corporations can commit themselves to support and respect the protection of internationally proclaimed human rights within their sphere of influence and make sure that they are not complicit in human rights abuses is an important initiative.

The underlying causes of malnutrition in many Asian countries include poverty, the low status of women, poor care during pregnancy, high rates of low birth weight, high population densities, unfavourable child caring practices, and poor access to health care. In Sub-Saharan Africa, extreme poverty, inadequate caring practices, low levels of education and poor access to health services are among the major factors conflicts and natural disasters in many countries have further exacerbated the situation The increase in the number of malnourished children in Africa also reflects a rapid rate of population growth in many countries. In Africa, the devastating effects of HIV/AIDS, particularly in the second half of the decade, have reversed some of the gains made in the decade's early years.

Right to Food : An Instance of Human Right

There is no doubt that without food no life is possible and therefore right to food is an aspect of right to life it is necessary to find out its legal status or what kind of statutory recognition is there.

Initial Recognition : Non-Justifiable Right

First time in history right to food was expressly guaranteed as human right in UDHR-1948 under Article 25. It has been provided that everyone has the right to a standard of living adequate for the health and well being of himself and of his family, including food. As it was mere declaration, this right was not enforceable.

Later on this right was adopted in the International Convention on Economic and Social Rights, which provided under Article 11 paragraph 2 the right of everyone to be free from hunger as a fundamental right. Again, as rights guaranteed under this covenant are subject to ratification realized immediately.

In India also the right is not expressly provided under the Constitution, the only relevant provisions are Article 47 of the Constitution which provide that it is the duty of the state to raise the level of nutrition and Article 48 provide for planning of agricultural and animal husbandry but these rights are guaranteed under Part IV of constitution and therefore in pertaining to that it was characterized as a non-justifiable right.

Non-Enumerated Fundamental Right : Outcome of Judicial Activism

First time in Indian history the Supreme Court recognized Right to Food as Right to Life in a significant judgment of the PUCL Vs Union of India [2000(s) SC ALE] Supreme Court held that it is right of every person who is starving because of his or her inability to purchase food grains have right to get food under Article 21. It is the duty of state to provide such persons food grains particularly from stock which is lying with state as unused. And more particularly food grains be provided to all those who are aged, infirm, disabled, destitute women and men, pregnant and lactating women and destitute children and therefore court directed to all states to distribute food grains immediately through PDS shops.

The definition of human rights is provided under Section 2(d) of protection of Human Rights Act 1993, in the light of this definition and after above decision the legal status of Right to Food has been transformed from non-justifiable right to Justifiable right. It can be described as non-enumerated but enforceable fundamental right. Right to food means adequate food, essential for descent standard of life, food free from adulteration.

Right to Food : International Perspectives

'Human Rights' is a universal phenomenon therefore Right to food has to be seen from internalional perspectives, and as it is recognized on International level expressly in many documents/ instruments quite early.

UDHR-1948

The UDHR provides under Article 25 paragraph (1) that everyone has the right to standard of living adequate for the health and well being of himself and of his family, including food, clothing, housing and medical care and necessary social services and the right to security in the event of unemployment, sickness, disability, widowhood old age or other lack of livelihood in circumstances beyond his control. It is expressly provided first time on international level. The right is not absolute, it is an aspect of Right to health, right to livelihood. Persons are entitled only in above-mentioned circumstances.

ICESCR-1966

Article 11 paragraph (2) of the covenant recognized the right of everyone to be free from hunger as a fundamental right.

The paragraph (2) of the same article also provides measure to be adopted individually or collectively by states to achieve above-mentioned object. In particular, to improve methods of production, conservation and distribution of food by making full use of technical and scientific knowledge by disseminating knowledge of the principles of nutrition and by developing or reforming agrarian system in such a way so as to achieve the most efficient development and utilization of natural resources. Further to ensure on equitable distribution of world food supplies in relation to need by taking into account the problems of both food importing and food exporting countries.

UN World Food Conference : 1974

It was convened at Rome from 5th to 6th November, 1974. In that Conference 22 resolutions were adopted and Universal Declaration on the Eradication of Hunger and Malnutrition was also made. In the preamble of the Declaration it was stated that gravity of problem is more in developing countries. The object was enunciated as elimination of hunger and malnutrition. The causes had been mentioned and also their historical circumstances, especially social inequalities, including in many cases alien and colonial domination foreign occupation, racial discrimination, apartheid and neo-colonialism in all its forms which continue to be among the greatest obstacles to the full emancipation and progress of the developing countries and all the people involved.

Three Propositions made

1. Equal right of all persons
2. Adequate resources
3. A common problem in all countries.

Food and Agriculture Organization

One of the objects of FAO of the United Nations is the elimination of hunger and malnutrition and to attain this object FAO has started following actions for ensuring food security :

- International undertaking on world food security of 1974
- The plan of action on world security of 1979
- The agenda for consultations and possible action to deal with acute and large-scale food shortages 1981
- The world food security compact of 1985.

These all are instances of international agreements. These agreements have been entered upon by different states to achieve above purpose laid down.

World Food Programme

It is a joint programme of the United Nations and FAO. Initially it was designed on experimental basis for three years, but later on in 1965 its term was extended and it was made operational continuously for as long as multilateral food aid remained feasible and desirable. The aim of WFP is to provide food aid to support development projects and to meet emergency needs. The Economic Council and the General Assembly review the operation of the programme annually.

Beijing Declaration of the World Food Council

The World Food Council adopted the Beijing Declaration in June 1987. The member states have resolved to join together and in united strength and interest to eliminate the scouroge of hunger forever. The World Food Day is observed on 16th October every year, it was decided by FAO in the year 1979 unanimously.

An action aid discussion paper lamented that Robert L. Bard in his article titled Right to Food published by Iowa Law Review in 1984 said not only does no right to food exists, but it is unlikely that one can be established. That is, both poor and wealthy nations are unlikely to subject themselves to law-based claims of either their own citizens or foreign governments pertaining to access to food. He gave various reasons political and economics related for denial of this right by both poor and well off nations. As there is a tendency on the part of nation-states to insist on a right to retain absolute discretion in determining the level of their contribution to world welfare requirements, he observed that economically developed countries would not be alone in their resistance to the establishment of a right to food. Third World Countries might be happy to impose legal requirements on other nations toward themselves, but they will strongly resist any legal norms that obligate them to their own citizens.

In just three years time, there was turnaround and the right to food was recognized as human right. Goler Teal

Butcher in his article went on to establish the relationship declaration by placing the same on the tripod of the Universal Declaration of Human Rights (UDHR), International Covenant of Civil and Political Rights (ICCPR) and International Covenant of Economic Social and Cultural Rights (ICESCR).[iii] While identifying different dimensions of the hunger problem, Goler Teal Butcher viewed hunger not as a problem of mere geography or of distribution of food but related it to powerlessness - the financial, economic and political powerlessness of individuals and social classes within nations and the international community.

The major breakthrough came in the year 1996 with when world leaders assembled in Rome in November 1996 for the World Food Summit aimed at renewing global commitment to the fight against hunger. The Food and Agriculture Organization of the United Nations (FAO) called the Summit in response to widespread undernutrition and growing concern about the capacity of agriculture to meet future food needs. The results of the Summit are contained in two main documents : Rome Declaration on World Food Security and World Food Summit Plan of Action.[iv]

In the year 1999, this right gained further momentum when it was noticed that hunger exists because of the gross inequities in food production and distribution patterns. For instance, the developing or third world countries account for 75% of the world's population; they produce over 50% of the world's food and yet consume only 40% of agriculture produced. Approximately 75% of all people make their living by cultivating land. Despite this, only a small minority disproportionately controls the vast majority of land through plantations and farms. This small percentage of wealthy individuals enjoy the protection of national and local governments and receive a superfluous percentage of governmental loans, subsidies, investment incentives, and tax privileges. In turn this elite minority becomes wealthier and exercises greater control over the government, which results in legislation that ensures the inequality between the classes and the maintenance of poverty.[v]

Should the denial of such an important right, without which the individual will lack the ability to journey through life and experience the ability to develop a moral sense, love and be loved and participate as a productive member of society [vi].

Meaning of the Right to Food

According to Goler Teal Butcher whereas the practical conception of a right to food arises out of a biological imperative, the theoretical conception of a right to food arises out of a trilogy of factors : one, the evolution of human rights concepts; two, the convergence of moral imperatives and notions of distributional justice; and, three, the reality of collective responsibility regarding both the enormous disparities between the North and South and the situation of the least developed countries and of the almost one billion people living in dire poverty on the edge of existence, utterly without the basic necessities of life.[vii]

The World Food Summit held in Rome in November 1996 took the view that an important aspect of the right to food is food security, the physical and economic access by all, at all times to sufficient, safe, and nutritious food to meet their dietary needs for an active and healthy life.[viii]

Nobel Laureate Economist Prof. Amartya Sen characterized food security as entitlements : production based entitlements, the right to consume the food a person produces; labour-based entitlements, the right to income through sale of labour; trade-based entitlements, the right to get food through the market; and transfer-based entitlements, food donated by others.[ix]

According to Philip Alston, it is not the same as the right not to starve, nor the right not to be hungry. According to Katarina Tomasevski, the right to food is not synonymous with the right to be fed, for that implies an unhealthy dependency upon others.[x]

In his 1987 report, the Special Rapporteur to the Economic and Social Council of the UN said that right to food implies that the physical and institutional environment in which food is procured must be optimally utilized and protected from erosion or distortion. [xi]

Robert E. Robertson, in Right to Food- Canada's Broken Covenant has defined the scope of this right as a condition in which each person can eat food which, be prevailing medical standards, is judged adequate for the full realization of physical and mental health. A persons diet should also consist of food, which satisfies cultural preferences.

Link between Right to Food and Other Rights

Katarina Tomasevski, in a note in the Iowa Law Review in 1984, called for connecting the right to food with other rights. According to this author, to realize the right to food, people need access to resources and therefore right to food cannot be realized unless and until the right to - land, an equal opportunity to grow food for themselves, income-generating activities enabling them to purchase food with salaries earned, work, freedom of movement, freedom of association and trade union rights are granted. Finally, without popular participation in decision-making, strategies and policies negating or violating human rights can be made without people participating or knowing what has been decided on as to their future.[xii] Therefore, the right to information is also a valuable right for the realization of the right to food. In the Indian context, this right assumes tremendous importance for realization of the right to food. Jean Dreze who maps poverty related issues in rural India has evidenced the tremendous disempowerment experienced by ordinary citizens due to lack of information and the inaccessibility of public records. He found that people were given ration cards, but they did not know their entitlement to buy from the ration shops, they were ignorant about the prices they were supposed to pay.[xiii] The right to information, now guaranteed by statute, can aid these disempowered sections by placing responsibility on the state to supply basic information related to all aspects of food distribution to rural population.

International Law and the Right to Food

The international community has broadly recognized the right to food and state's obligations involving the right to food. According to one compilation, there are over 100 international instruments, which are relevant to the establishment and definition of the right to food.[xiv]

Treaty law ICESCR in Article 11 recognizes both a right to adequate food and the right of everyone to be free from hunger.

There have been specific declarations, conferences and resolutions to stress the importance of this right. For instance, Universal Declaration in the Eradication of Hunger and Malnutrition, GA Res. 3180 U.N. GAOR World Food Conference 28th Session convened under General Assembly resolution 3180 (XXVIII) of 17 December, 1973 and endorsed by General Assembly resolution 3348 (XXIX) of 17 December, 1974; World Declaration on Nutrition a product of the International Conference on Nutrition held in December 1992[xvi]; United Nations Millennium Declaration contained in a resolution adopted at the end of the largest-ever gathering of world leaders, known as the Millennium Summit, held at the United Nations between the 6th- 8th September, 2000.[xvii]

Resolutions for example, the UN Commission on Human Rights has issued resolutions, as have the General Assembly of the UN, the Economic and Social Council (ECOSOC) and the FAO regarding the right to food.[xviii]

The international community considers the right to food so integral that international conferences have been held on the right to food, such as the World Food Summit. One commitment of the World Food Summit was to strive to ensure that food, agriculture trade and overall trade policies are conducive to fostering food security for all through a fair and market-oriented world trade system.[xix}

The Committee on Economic, Social and Cultural Rights issued a General Comment that defined the right to adequate food as realized when every man, woman and child, alone or in community with others has physical and economic access at all times to adequate food or means for its procurement.[xx]

The right to food is recognized in international humanitarian law and other commitments which disallow the use of food as a method of warfare. For example, the Protocol Additional to the Geneva Convention of 12 August, 1949 and relating to the Protection of Victims of International Armed Conflicts in Articles 54, 69, 70[xxi]; Geneva Convention for the Amelioration of the Condition of the Wounded and Sick in Armed Forces in the Field, Article 32, etc. obligate states to respect people's right to food. [xxii]

Judicial Protection of Right to Food in India

The Indian judiciary, especially the Supreme Court, has on many occasions reaffirmed that the right to life enshrined in Article 21 means something more than animal instinct and includes the right to live with dignity; it would include all these aspects which make life meaningful, complete and living[xxiii]. Other statutory constitutional institutions like the National Human Rights Commission (NHRC) have also stated : There is a fundamental right to be free from hunger (January 17, 2003).

The Supreme Court in Chameli Singh v. State of U.P., [xxiv]: while dealing with Article 21 of the Constitution has held that the need for a decent and civilised life includes the right to food, water and a decent environment. The Supreme Court further observed :

In any organised society, the right to live as a human being is not ensured by meeting only the animal needs of men. It is secured only when he is assured of all facilities to develop himself and is freed from restrictions which inhibit his growth. All human rights are designed to achieve this subject. Right to live guaranteed in any civilised society implies the right to food, water, decent environment education, medical care and shelter. These are basic human rights known to any civilised society. All civil, political, social and cultural rights enshrined in the Universal

Declaration on Human Rights and convention or under the Constitution of India cannot be exercised without these basic human rights.

In Air India Statutory Corporation, etc. v. United Labour Union and others [xxv] - the Supreme Court held that the enforcement of the provisions to establish canteen in every establishment under Section 16 of Contract Labour (Regulation and Abolition) Act, 1970 is to supply food to the workmen at the subsidized rates as it is a right to food, a basic human right.

In Shantistar Builders v. Narayan Khimalal Totame[xxvi], the Supreme Court held that the basic needs of man have traditionally been accepted to be three - food, clothing and shelter.

In April 2001, a writ petition was filed in the Supreme Court of India by the Peoples Union for Civil Liberties to seek legal enforcement of the right to food. This case, popularly known as the Right to Food Case [xxvii], has since become a rallying point for trade unions, activists, grassroots organizations and NGOs to make the right to food a justiciable right. Here, a primary problem was maladministration : the Court found that about half of the food subsidy was being spent on holding excess stocks.

The Right to Food Case has achieved many milestones. For example, the interim orders have resulted in the Government of India sanctioning 1.88 lakh additional ICDS centres so far. At the macro level the budget of the ICDS has gone up nearly three times from Rs. 1,500 crore in 2003-04 to almost Rs 4,000 crore for 2006-07.

References

[i] Robert L. Bard, The Right to Food, 70 Iowa L. Rev. 1279 (1984-85)

[ii] Ibid.

[iii] Goler Teal Butcher, The Relationship of Law to the Hunger Problem, 30 Howard L.J. 193 (1987) observed that Law is relevant to the problem of hunger and securing food for

hungry people with respect to both the short- and long-term approaches to the problem because it is through law that we structure both the various mechanisms to respond to hunger in a crisis and the means to assist people with pursuit of a development policy aimed at achieving food self-sufficiency. Moreover it is through law that we implement our convictions : on the right of hungry people to food and on the duty of the well-endowed to assist in the alleviation of hunger.

[iv] Available at http://www.org/wfs/index_en.htm

[v] Michael Chossudvsky, The Causes of Global Famine 50th Anniversary of the FAO, available at http://www.harford-hwp.com/archieves/28/039.htm [Jan. 26, 1998].

[vi] Anthony Paul Kearns, The Right to Food exists via Customary International Law, 22 Suffolk Transnational Law Review 223 (1998-99).

[vii] Goler Teal Butcher, Supra note 3.

[viii] World Food Summit : Rome Declaration on World Food Security para 1, available at http://www.fao.org.

[ix] Amartya Sen, Poverty and Famines : An Essay on Entitlement and Deprivation 1-2 (Oxford Univ. Press, 1981).

[x] Philip Alston and Katarina Tomasevski eds., The Right to Food : Guide Through Applicable International Law (Boston: Martinus Nijhoff Publishers, 1984)

[xi] E/CN.4/Sub.2/1987/23 at para 52.

[xii] Katarina Tomasevski, Human Rights : The Right to Food, 70 Iowa Law Review 1321 (1984-85).

[xiii] Jean Dreze, Democracy and Right to Food, Economic and Political Weekly, p. 1723, April 24, 2004.

[xiv] Supra note 11.

[xv] Government representatives from countries of Latin America and the Caribbean and non-governmental organizations (NGOs) from the region met in the Cuban capital for the second Regional Consultation of Non-governmental Organizations, drawing up their own proposals for constitutional guarantees for food security and promoting international solidarity in favour of food sovereignty. The FAO conference's final report.

[xvi] Included official delegations of 159 countries as well as a considerable number of scientists and representatives of non-governmental organizations.

[xvii] All together, representatives from 187 Member States of the United Nations attended this summit.

[xviii] See UN Doc.E/CN.4/RES 2002.25 (2002); UN GAOR, 5th Session, Agenda Item 111 (b), UN Doc A/57/356 (2002); CESCR, 20th Session, Art. 11, UN Doc E/C.12/1999/5 (1999).

[xix] World Food Summit : Rome Declaration on World Food Security, commitment No. 4 available at http://www.fao org/DOCREP/003/W3613E/W3613E00.htm [novo 1996].

[xx] CESCR, 20th Session, Art 11, UN Doc E/C.12/1999/5 (1999).

[xxi] http://www.ohchr.org/ebglishn/law/protocoal1_2.htm;

[xxii] http:/www.umn.edu/humarts/instree/y1 gcacws.htm

[xxiii] Maneka Gandhi V. Union of India AIR 1978 SC 597.

[xxiv] (1996) 2SCC549.

4

Social Capital as Basis of Rights

The concept of 'Social Capital' has added a new dimension to the dialogue on development. In recent times 'Social Capital' has caught the attention of many development practitioners and academicians. While institutions have long been considered as significant in development theory, viewing the density of formal and informal institutions for development as 'social capital' formalizes the link with more conventional labour and capital as inputs into development. Social capital was thought of as a resource that gives people the ability to work together for common purposes (Coleman 1990). The ability of associate depends, in turn, on the degree to which communities are able to subordinate individual interests to those of larger groups and share reciprocal norms and values. Out of such shared values comes trust. Trust facilitates coordinated social action and together they produce an intensive network of civic associations.

Putnam defines social capital as "Features of social organization, such as trust, norms and networks that can improve the efficiency of society by facilitating coordinated actions" (Putnam 1993). The more the stock of social capital a society has, the easier it becomes for its citizens to undertake group activities and sustain collective practices. A rich associational life signified a good social capital in society.

Putnam, therefore, rejects the claim that liberty and community are always inimical. No doubt, this is sometimes true.... The Italian case suggests, however, that because citizens in civic regions enjoy the benefits of community, they are able to be more liberal (Putnam 1993). An engaging trust, then, resides at the heart of social capital. This trust has three basic attributes. It is secular, reciprocal/equal and based on rational interest. For Putnam, trust acted as 'social lubricant' between equals. In a meeting on trust in 1995 he clarified, "Participation in dense networks of horizontal interactions of relative equals produce norms of reciprocity, provides sanctions for defectors, offers some information about others, and creates a 'culturally-defined template for future collaboration" (Levi 1996). This apart trust, in his account reflects neither altruism nor 'irrational' expectation/ obligations, but a productive and calculative interest. I trust you because it is in your interest to do what I trust you to do (Hardin.1993). Social capital is not merely a stock or an asset; it can also be viewed as an overarching condition. As a condition it is seen as something that tends to permeate from one sphere to another and as a consequence norms in society, behaviour of social actors and relationships among them fuse into a predictable pattern. It is in this context that theorists including Putnam posit the positive link between social capital and institutional efficacy (Mahapatra, 2001).

The concept of social capital is best looked at as a characterization of the process that set societies on certain development paths in contrast to the outcomes of those development paths. In common with other kinds of capital, it is the means for achieving well-being which constitutes the end. That is perhaps the reason it is referred to as 'capital' to begin with. In other words, social capital is the networking that helps create linkages which in turn forge rules, conventions and norms governing the development process (Chopra 2002). The role of social capital is defined in the literature as emerging form "the networks and relationships that both encourage trust and reciprocity and shape the quality of a society's social interactions" in providing the inputs into growth. Putnam (1993) examines social capital in terms of the degree of civic involvement as measured by voter turnout, newspaper readership, membership in societies and clubs and confidence in public institutions. He found that northern Italy where these indicators are higher showed higher levels of development that the southern parts. Oslon (1982) on the other hand, hypothesized that associations, in particular horizontal association among trades - people can hurt growth because many of them act as special interest groups lobbying for preferential policies that impose disproportionate costs on society.

The emergence of social entrepreneurs is the consequence of the existence of a vibrant civil society with linkages across agents in different formal sectors. Agents of development play a vital role in reaching out at critical stages of the process leading towards sustainable development. The development catalyst or the social entrepreneur who perceives the problem of backwardness brings them together to formulate a set of values and norms that are acceptable to all to obtain their participation in the proposed process. It is important to secure the ownership of the process and to have a comprehensive coverage of all stakeholders.

The distinctive feature of 'social capital' as an input into development is that it ensures qualitative changes in procedures governing the development process to ensure its embededness and linkage with development at higher levels. State society linkages play an important role in these successes. Examples are to be found in Tendler's description of the social capital created by health campaign in Brazil or Lams evidence from irrigation works in Taiwan. Here "Social capital inheres not just in civil society but in the networks of relationships that span the public-private divide". However, moving from one equilibrium to the next in terms of such networks involves a transaction cost which is approximated by the need for social capital to bridge divides that create bottle necks to sustainability of development processes. (Chopra 2002)

Optimum utilization of locally available resources has

been the strategy for sustainable development. Development strategies in rural area are often rooted in livelihood and intended to strengthen the livelihood base. The case of integrated development of Khaira village in Sidhi district illustrated clearly that reaching out by agents across the government-non-government market divide at each step of the development process to result in the strengthening of social capital constituted an integral part of the experiment. The village is nearly 50 kms. away from district headquarter with 70 percent of tribal population. The low-income levels, unused land almost degraded with lack of irrigation sources attracted the attention of volunteers of Gram Sudhar Samiti (an NGO). The question asked was : Why was this resource left as unutilized and how could better soil and water management lead to improved livelihoods? It was found that non-utilization of the land was a consequence of the interaction of the nature of property rights and minimum scale requirements for a successful intervention on water and soil management. Building up natural capital to initiate a process of development clearly required action in the area of changing property rights or an agreement on temporary pooling to solve the scale problem. Since Khaira is a forest village, most of the land belongs to forest department. Efforts were made to pool unutilized and degraded land to adopt the village under Rajiv Gandhi Watershed Mission and to initiate a process of development.

The users group was formed of stakeholders. The agreement led to a determination of the extent of change in user rights which would be acceptable to owners of land. Stakeholders in the process were identified at the outset and their contribution in terms of land, labour or organization identified. The unique sharing mechanisms evolved by Gram Sudhar Samiti enabled income from the produce to be shared by stakeholders and a part is kept aside for reinvestment the final agreement by the users group members was the outcome of a careful balancing of the economic benefits from participation. The evolution of this mechanism and the keeping apart of a part of the community income for consumption loan constituted parts of networking between different social groups which held the experiment together. It is a live example of the creation of social capital that makes development succeed and was the input of the Gram Sudhar Samiti (GSS). GSS ensured cooperation from government and international agencies. The garnering of complementary inputs from other sectors of the economy constituted the next component of the creation of social capital. Appropriate technologies for successful watershed management was developed by experts with GSS, who after relied on the training by experts and experts from local university. GSS utilized local water harvesting technologies with the help of villagers. Components such as check dams, ponds were used depending on the terrain. GSS under the stewardship of Thakkar Bapa awardee Arun Tyagi, constructed check dams, ponds and various other measures and the water level came up instantly. This helped in the income generation of the self-help group formed by GSS.

The significance of social capital in the process of development can be seen from the many projects that have failed not because of lack of funds or other reasons but because local community did not have a sense of ownership and participation. There are a number of success stories in watershed management - Anna Hazare (Ralegaon Sidhi), Rajendra Singh (Tarun Bharat Sangh), Late Prem Bhai and Dr. Ragini Prem (Banvasi Seva Ashram, Sonebhadra). All these projects and organisations led emphasis on social issues, social mobilization participatory management, transparent project monitoring and evaluation and a strong sense of ownership by the local community.

GSS formed 'users groups' of people affected most. A pond benefited those farmers whose wells are recharged while, on the other hand, the farmers whose land got submerged are adversely affected. There was a third category of resource poor farmers whose need of the water is being met by a new well in the area with augmented ground water. GSS and watershed committees (WC) ensured that benefits are shared equally with a tilt in favour of the poor. Users group members worked jointly with WC in planning, designing and implementation of different programmes.

Equality of social condition was crucial in Alexis de Tocqueville's Democracy in America. It enabled a self-governing democratic community spring up voluntary associations in America of the 1830s. Tocqueville contrasted it to the failure of self-reliance in his native France, which was centralized and bureaucratic. Putnam has been charged for underscoring moral over material resources of social capital and for virtually making civic norms social capital's exclusive marker (Bhattacharya 2001).

Social capital can be broadly described into two types. The geographic social networks are based on the identification of networks based on the concept of a subdivision or neighbourhood whereas non-geographic social capital networks are networks of individuals who share values based upon the basis of hierarchy and nature of association formed i.e. into horizontal and vertical associations, social capital is a set of horizontal associations between people, consisting of social networks and associated norms that have an impact on community productivity and well-being. Social networks can increase productivity by reducing the costs of doing business. Horizontal ties are needed to give community a sense of identity and common purpose, but also stresses that without 'bridging' ties that transcend various social divides (i.e. religion, socio-economic status), horizontal ties can became a basic for the pursuit of narrow interests and can actively preclude access to information and material resources that would otherwise be of great assistance to the community (e.g. access to credit) (Singh 2003). Social capital is most usefully viewed as a system of interpersonal networks. It is an aspect of human capital. If network externalities are more in the nature of public goods, social capital is a component of total factor productivity.

Measuring Social Capital

There generic criteria have been considered for measuring social capital of institutions : productivity, equity, and sustainability. The generic criterion for measuring 'productivity' includes those that enhance productivity or growth of social capital. Group membership is important because the broader the membership base, the more is the coverage of people coming together for a cause. The type of leadership determines the drive of the group.

Keenness and a sense of group responsibility are the advantages of a group in achieving group objectives. With positive group interactions the capacity of the group improves over time and the confidence of group members is boosted with more experience. External linkages, both vertical and horizontal, determines 'connectedness' of the group and provide opportunities for growth. The generic criteria for measuring 'equity' includes criteria such as making sense of group objectives for all its members and active participation of members in decision-making. When group-based activities are broad-based, they help in creating space for participation of the poor and the marginalized women and men. The change is from participation by a few members to participation by many. An important issue in equity is who benefits from group-based activities. For the poor, livelihood impacts of group based activities are crucial for reducing the vulnerabilities they face. It is with the inclusion of poor and marginalized people that local management of natural resources becomes more meaningful. The generic criterion for measuring 'sustainability' includes criteria that promote sustenance and continuity of group efforts, help to recoup from vulnerable situations and maintain assets and capital stocks for future. A group that has a vision for the future can evoke a group strategy. A local knit group is less cohesive than one that is more compact with inner norms, mutual trust and faith. Role clarity helps to lessen conflicts. Ownership feelings for ones group improve the prospects of sustainability. The greater the ability of the group to raise issues and resolve conflicts, the better is the chance for the group staying together. Regular maintenance of assets by the group is also an important indicator of sustainability (Mukherjee 2002).

Several studies have identified useful proxies for social

capital using different types and combinations of qualitative, comparative and quantitative research methodologies.

The question of why some countries are more successful than others in managing to develop their economics and establish a democratic government is still a puzzle, which decades of exercises in cross-country econometric analysis has not been able to solve it. It is apparent that the issue is not the amount of sheer resources pumped into a country, but the existence of certain conditions for resources to be channeled effectively into priority goals. Government's commitment to development and the transparency and efficiency of the bureaucracy are very crucial factors in this respect. The role of civil society, of citizen's awareness of their own rights and responsibilities, and of features of social organization must also be taken into account.

Studies on educational structures and facilities suggest that the source of higher quality of services in Kerla as opposed to Uttar Pradesh lies with the attitude of parents, and their willingness and capability to voice their protest and take appropriate action if needed when teachers are absent, infrastructure is poor and promised funds do not arrive. Mobilization is possible when people share their understanding of the common good and trust one another to achieve this objective. Citizen's voice and reaction might be what makes the difference between malfunctioning and efficient schools in India, providing an appropriate example of the nation that great social capital makes existing physical and human capital more effective. But what are the elements that enable poor people to give voice to their dissent and defend their own right? Qualitative evidence has shown that previous experience of collective action, local presence of NGOs, and rates of literacy are important factors in accounting for local community's capacity to interact with institutions for achieving better outcomes. Women groups have compelled to close liquor shops in their locality. However, these phenomena are hard to capture by means of quantitative indicators, for the lack of comprehensive figures on these movements and activities concerned. It would also be difficult to gauge their presence in terms of states as units of analysis (Serra 2001).

Trust and Production

Trust can be defined as 'a bet on the future contingent actions of others' (Sztompka 1998). Social capital is important for economic development because it facilitates efficient use of information and creation of trust, goodwill and cooperation in society. The result of all this ambiguity is that the machinery of social capital resembles black box. Certain not-so-well defined social variables called social capital enter on one side of the box, and on the other side we find a more efficient governance structure and higher structure. What is going on inside the box is only hinted at and, therefore, to a great extent, left in the dark (Torsuik 2002).

Narain and Prichett (1999) investigate the empirical link between social capital and household income in different villages in Tanzania. They measured social capital as 'quantity and quality of associational life'. Their results indicate that this notion of civil social capital is indeed important for understanding economic development. Based on their empirical findings they conclude : 'a village's social capital has an effect on the incomes of the households in that village, an effect that is empirically large, definitely social and plausibly casual'.

Putnam (1993) mention that social capital can create trust and cooperation among those who live in the village. Trust and cooperation is indeed central to the idea of civil social capital. The hypothesis is that communities with a high density of light and inclusive networks of individual contact will experience an atmosphere of mutual trust; trust which enables individuals to cooperate and work together more efficiently. It is in the environment of behavioural risks and transaction costs that trust becomes an important 'asset'. Trust refers to certain behavioural dispositions that eliminate behavioural risks. Saying that there is mutual trust among traders is the same as saying that everyone is confident that no one will behave opportunistically. Trust can therefore reduce (or eliminate) transaction costs and enhance economic production.

Social capital is one of the important social conditions that can facilitate 'solutions' to the 'logic of collective action'. At its core, social capital theory proposes that variations in the character of social connectedness have a strong impact on our ability to cooperate. Social capital facilitates coordinated action between individuals and is hence a means of making collective action less problematic. Social capital increases communication, since trust, networks and shared norms mean precisely this.

The effort of Gram Sudhar Samiti became a successful initiative positively due to the strong social capital. Watershed development programme increased the per capita income and checked migration of the community. The crop yield of wheat increased from 10 qua to 18 qua and the average yield of Jowar increased from 7 to 12 qua due to irrigation management and application of scientific methods of agriculture. Availability of water ensured increase in milk production and increase in fodder production from 7 to 22 qha and improvement in health and productivity of livestock (Pandey 2007). Livelihood stability is a principal development requirement of people in rural areas. Activities that enable people to raise sustainable crop yields and to improve the availabiity of fodder and drinking water at all times are highly regarded by villagers. Trust and cooperation can increase the effectiveness of all types of collective actions. Collective action depends on reciprocity based trust and strong social capital.

References

Bhattacharya, Dwaipayan (2001), "Civic community and its margins", Economic & Political Weekly, February 24.

Chopra, Kanchan (2002), "Social capital and development process", The Economic & Political Weekly, July 13.

Coleman, S. James (1990), 'Foundations of social theory', Harward

University Press.

Hardin, Russel (1993) "The state level epistemology of trust", Politics & Society, 21, 4 December, pp. 505-529

Putnam, Robert D., Robert Leonardi and Raffella Y. Nanetti (1993), Making Democracy work: Civic Traditions in Modern Italy, Princeton University Press, Princeton.

Levi, Margret (1996), "Social and unsocial capital : A review of Robert Putnam's MDW", Politics & Society, 1 March, pp. 45-55.

Mohapatra, Bishnu N. (2001), "Social connectedness and fragility of social capital', Economic & Political Weekly, February 24.

Mukherjee, Neela (2002), "Measuring social capital", Economics & Political Weekly, July 20.

Narain & Prichett (1999) cited in Prakash, Sanjeev/Selle, Per edited social capital and economic development" Sage publications, New Delhi, pp. 257-279.

Oslon, M. (1982), "The rise and falls of nations', Yale University Press, New Haven.

Pandey, D.P. (2007), "Resource Management through Watershed Development : A Case Study", Northern India Patrika, May 1.

Serra, Renata (2001), "Social capital : Meaningful and measurable at the state level', Economic & Political Weekly, February 24.

Singh, Kultar (2003), "Social capital", Kurukshetra, August, pp. 38-42.

Torrsvik, Gaute (2002), "Social capital and economic development" cited in 'Investigating Social Capital', Sage publications, pp. 257-279.

5

The Programme Partners

1. SIR DORABJI TATA TRUST

The Sir Dorabji Tata Trust was established in 1932 by Sir Dorab Tata, the elder son of group founder Jamsetji Tata, and is one of the oldest philanthropic organisations in India. The Trust's vision of constructive philanthropy has been sensitive to the fast-growing needs of a developing nation, and the projects and programmes it supports bear contemporary relevance.

The grant-making pattern of the Trust involves three broad areas : endowment grants (grants to institutions), grants to non-governmental organisations (NGOs) and grants to individual (medical and educational grants).

Endowment grants

The Trust has promoted, and continued to support, several institutions of learning, research and culture in India. These include the Tata Institute of Social Sciences, Mumbai, the Tata Memorial Centre for Cancer Research and Treatment, Mumbai, the Tata Institute of Fundamental Research, Mumbai, the Tata Agricultural and Rural Training Centre for the Blind, Phansa, and the National Centre for the Performing Arts, Mumbai.

The Trust has also helped in establishing the Sir Dorabji Tata Trust Centre for Research in Tropical Diseases at the Indian Institute of Science, Bangalore, the JRD Tata Ecotechnology Centre, Chennai, and the National Institute of Advanced Studies, Bangalore.

NGO grants

The Trust makes grants to NGOs in five social development sectors :

- *Management of natural resources* : The Trust supports projects related to water and water resources, land degradation and better methods of cultivating and harvesting crops.
- *Livelihoods* : The Trust has backed several projects in this sector, covering unorganised labourers, capacity building of grassroots groups, and business development of a variety of people-based organisations.
- *Education* : The Trust has supported initiatives in the field of education, focusing on children, adolescents and adults (within and outside the formal education system).
- *Health* : The Trust has made contributions in creating and upgrading medical infrastructure and healthcare facilities across India, while focusing on training community health workers. The Trust also supports research studies in alternative systems of medicine such as ayurveda.
- *Social development initiatives* : These cover many areas, including community development, human rights, family welfare, civil society, art and culture, and relief work.

Individual grants

The Trust gives merit and need-based educational and medical grants to individuals.

- *Medical* : Financial help is extended to individuals for

the treatment of diseases and to solve other health problems.

- *Education* : The Trust offers scholarships for higher education and travel grants for studying abroad and for attending conferences, as well as for sports activities.

The Allied Trusts

The Allied Trusts are, primarily, smaller trusts; while some have a specific mandate, the rest are broad-based in their approach to grant-making. The Sir Dorabji Tata Trust administers the Allied Trusts.

JN Tata Endowment: The first of the Tata trusts, it was established by group founder Jamsetji Tata, in 1892 to provide scholarship loans to individuals for the pursuit of higher studies abroad. Over 120 students are selected every year from across India as JN Tata scholars.

Lady Tata Memorial Trust: Established by Sir Dorabji Tata in 1932 in memory of his wife, Lady Meherbai, who died of leukaemia in 1930, the Trust spends four-fifths of its income on international research in leukaemia. The Trust also supports institutional research carried out by recognised Indian institutions, with the emphasis on leukaemia research.

Lady Meherbai Tata Education Trust: Set up in 1932, the Trust grants scholarships to young Indian women graduates of recognised Indian universities to pursue higher studies abroad in the fields of social work and public health.

Additionally, and also coming under the umbrella of the Allied Trusts, are the Tata Social Welfare Trust, the RD Tata Trust, the Tata Education Trust, the JRD Tata Trust, and the JRD Tata and Thelma Tata Trust, all of which focus on women and children. The Jamsetji Tata Trust concentrates on overall developmental issues.

Tata Group's Business

Tata companies operate in seven business sectors: communications and information technology, engineering, materials, services, energy, consumer products and chemicals.

They are, by and large, based in India and take significant international operations. The total revenue of Tata companies, taken together, was $62.5 billion (around Rs. 251.543 crore) in 2007-08, with 61 per cent of this coming from business outside India, and they employ around 350,000 people worldwide. The Tata name has been respected in India for 140 years for its adherence to strong values and business ethics.

Every Tata company or enterprise operates independently. Each of these companies has its own board of directors and shareholders, to whom it is answerable. There are 27 publicly listed Tata enterprises and they have a combined market capitalisation of some $60 billion, and a shareholder base of 3.2 million. The major Tata companies are Tata Steel, Tata Motors, Tata Consultancy Services (TCS), Tata Power, Tata Chemicals, Tata Tea, Indian Hotels and Tata Communications.

Tata Steel became the sixth largest steel maker in the world after it acquired Corus. Tata Motors is among the top five commercial vehicle manufacturers in the world and has recently acquired Jaguar and Land Rover. TCS is a leading global software company, with delivery centres in the US, UK, Hungary, Brazil, Uruguay and China, besides India. Tata Tea is the second largest branded tea company in the world, through its UK-based subsidiary Tetley. Tata Chemicals is the world's second largest manufacturer of soda ash and Tata Communications is one of the world's largest wholesale voice carriers.

In tandem with the increasing international footprint of Tata Companies, the Tata brand is also gaining international recognition. Brand Finance, a UK-based consultancy finn, recently valued the Tata brand at $9.92 billion and ranked it 51st among the world's Top 100 brands. *Businessweek* magazine ranked Tata 13th among the 25 Most Innovative Companies' list and the Reputation Institute, USA, recently rated it 11th on its list of world's most reputable companies.

Founded by Jamsedji Tata in 1868, Tata's early years were inspired by the spirit of nationalism. It pioneered several industries of national importance in India: steel, power, hospitality and airlines. In more recent times. Its pioneering spirit has been showcased by companies such as TCS, India's first software company, and Tata Motors which made India's first indigenously developed car, the Indica, in 1998 and recently unveiled the world's lowest-cost car, the Tata Nano.

Tata companies have always believed in returning wealth to the society they serve. Two-thirds of the equity of Tata Sons, the Tata promoter company, is held by philanthropic trusts that have created national institutions for science and technology, medical research, social studies and the performing arts. The trusts also provide aid and assistance to non-government organisations working in the areas of education, healthcare and livelihoods. Tata companies also extend social welfare activities to communities around their industrial units. The combined development-related expenditure of the trusts and the companies amounts to around 4 per cent of the net profits of all the Tata companies taken together.

Building on a Cherished Legacy—Sir Dorabji Tata

Sir Dorabji Tata was born on 27 August, 1859, the elder son of Jamsetji Tata and Hirabai. Jamsetji, a visionary of his time, was clear about what he wanted to do with the wealth he had amassed—to bring about an industrial revolution in India. He laid the foundation of an integrated steel plant and a hydroelectric power generation company. Unfortunately, Jamsetji passed away without seeing his visions bear fruition. It was left to his two sons, Sir Dorabji Tata and Sir Ratan Tata, to fulfill his dreams. And it was Sir Dorabji, with his drive and enthusiasm—assisted by his cousin RD Tata—who took it up on his shoulders to see the projects through to completion. Jamsetji Tata also gave shape to several pioneering institutions and foundations, the notable among them being the Indian Institute of Science at Bangalore and the J.N. Tata Endowment Fund.

Sir Dorabji initially studied at the Proprietary High School in Mumbai, before he was sent to a private tutor in Kent,

England, at the age of 16. He entered the Conville and Caius College at Cambridge when he was 18 and excelled in sports, especially cricket, rugger and soccer. He was also an avid tennis player, a sprinter and a horseman.

Sir Dorabji returned to Mumbai in 1879, to join St. Xavier's College. lie received his B.A. degree in 1882.

Man with a Mission

Sir Dorabji soon plunged deep into the affairs of the family business. He worked for the realization of Jamsetji's vision of an integrated steel plant. The result was Tata Steel. He explored Central India for iron ore, riding in bullock carts and visiting places where they had no choice but to make tea from soda water.

When Jamsetji passed away, the Tata enterprises comprised three textile mills and the Taj Mahal Hotel, Mumbai. Under Sir Dorabji's stewardship, the business grew to add Tata Steel, three electric power companies and one of India's leading insurance companies. Sir Dorabji had also seen through the establishment of the *Indian Institute of Science, Bangalore.* In 1912, he offered the pioneering institution a donation as large as the one his father had made to establish a *School of Research in Tropical Medicine.* For some reason, the venture did not take off immediately. Notable among his other deeds in the field of education were a sizeable donation to the University of Cambridge for the equipment of a laboratory in the School of Engineering and the constitution of a Chair for Sanskrit studies at the *Bhandarkar Oriental Research Institute, Pune.* During his lifetime he also gave his collection of paintings, statuary and other art objects, generously to the *prince of Wales Museum, Mumbai,* (Chhtrapati Shivaji Maharaj Vastu Sangrahalya) now on display there as the Sir Dorabji Tata Collection.

Sir Dorabji was knighted in 1910.

India into Olympics

Sir Dorabji had an unstinted love for sports. He was

responsible for India participating for the first time in the Olympic Games. It was in 1919, even before the country had an Olympic Committee that he facilitated four athletes and two wrestlers to participate in the Antwerp Games. He also secured for India a place in the 1924 Paris Olympics. He became a member of the International Olyinpic Committee.

Sir Dorabji then embarked on a mission to identify sports talents in the country. He also wanted to propagate the Olympic movement and entrusted the work to the Young Men's Christian Association (YMCA). As President of the Indian Olympic Council, he financed the Indian contingent to the Paris Olympiad of 1924.

A Pillar of Strength - Lady Meherbai Tata

At the age of 38, Sir Dorabji married Meherbai, daughter of H.J. Bhabha. She was beautiful and accomplished, and had a love for English literature and playing the piano. Jamsetji admired his daughter-in-law and in fact he is said to have been responsible for selecting her as Sir Dorabji's companion for life. She shared with Sir Dorabji a love of sports, especially tennis, in which she won many a championship.

Lady Meherbai Tata was a spirited, sensitive woman, deeply concerned about the condition of women. She became one of the founders, first of the Bombay Presidency Women's Council and then of the National Council of Women. She campaigned for higher education for women and against the purdah system and the practice of untouchability.

She introduced India into the International Council of Women when many others felt that India should concentrate on its freedom struggle. In doing so, she brought India into the women's international movement.

She was about 50 when she was struck by leukaemia. Within a year, on 18 June 1931, she died while at Ruthin, North Wales.

In Apri1 1932, Sir Dorabji, as a memorial to his wife, endowed the Lady Tata Memorial Trust with a sum of Rs. 2.5 million for research into leukaemia, and a smaller trust, partly from public donations, called the Lady Meherbai D. Tata Education Trust, for the training of women in hygiene, health and social welfare.

The Later Years

Sir Dorabji was a life-long admirer of the renowned Victorian cricketer, W.G. Grace. He collected several pictures and cartoons of him and displayed them in his homes. He was a diabetic and would eat only boiled vegetables. The diabetes made him crotchety in his old age, but through most of his life, he was good humoured and full of comic stories and anecdotes.

Sir Dorabji and Lady Tata had no children. And like his father before him, Sir Dorabji believed that wealth must be put to constructive use. So, less than a year after his wife died, on 11 March, 1932, he put all his wealth, estimated at Rs. 10 million into a trust for use, "without any distinction of place, nationality or creed", for the advancement of learning and research, the relief of distress, and other charitable purposes. This was the beginning of the Sir Dorabji Tata Trust.

On 11 April, 1932, Sir Dorabji set sail for Europe expecting, among other things, to visit his wife's grave in England. It was on this journey that, on 3 June he died at Bad Kissingen in Germany. A few days later, almost on the anniversary of his wife's death, he was laid beside her at the Brookwood Cemetery.

Also designed from an ancient Persian model, the sarcophagus is of green bronze and stands on a marble plinth. It bears on its two sides the names : Dorab & Mehri.

In her own lifetime Lady Tata gave freely of herself for the causes she believed in. While in the evening of his life, her husband placed all he had in a trust. A trust that would build institutions, uplift the nation and change lives. A trust that would ensure that his father Jamsetji's visions and dreams took concrete shape and made a difference.

The Sir Dorabji Tata Trust—a Historical Perspective

The Sir Dorabji Tata Trust vision of proactive philanthropy has been catalytic to the developmental works carried out in the country, while all its initiatives have had contemporary relevance.

Like his father, Sir Dorabji believed that one must make use of the wealth one had acquired for constructive purposes. So, in less than a year after his wife Meherbai's death, he donated all his wealth to the Trust, insisting that it must be used "without any distinction of place, nationality or creed", for the advancement of learning and research, the relief of distress and other charitable purposes. He died three months later.

The wealth that he turned over to the Trust comprised his substantial share holdings in Tata Sons, Indian Hotels and allied companies, his landed properties and 21 pieces of jewellery left by his wife, including the famous Jubilee Diamond, estimated then to be of the value of Rs. 10 million. Today, these would be worth more than Rs. 500 million.

As the Trust got formed and the trustees deliberated on the policy aspects and finalized them, it decided to adopt a broad framework—that it should undertake such projects, which are too large for individuals to handle and that each of these projects should have a genuine relevance to the welfare of the country.

The Trust is mandated to :

» Maintain and support schools, educational institutions and hospitals
» Provide relief in distress caused by the elements of nature such as famine, pestilence, fire, tempest, flood, earthquake or any other calamity
» Help advancement of learning in all its branches especially research work in medical and industrial problems
» Offer financial aid to the *Indian Institute of Science, Bangalore,* by instituting professorships or lectureships or giving scholarships

- » Award fellowships in any branch of science or assist students to study abroad either by payment of lump sums grants or by payment of periodical sums
- » Give aid to any other charitable institutions or objects endowed by the settler in his lifetime, or by the grandfather, father or both of the settler.

The Trust is best known for promotion and setting up institutions of national importance :

- » Tata Institute of Social Sciences, (1936)
- » Tata Memorial Hosital (1941)
- » Tata Institute of Fundamental Research, (1945)
- » National Centre for the Performing Arts, (1966)
- » National Institute of Advanced Studies (1988)
- » J.R.D. Tata Centre for Ecotechnology (1998)
- » Sir Dorabjit Tata Centre for Research in Tropical Diseases (2000).

Each of these institutions work in frontier areas of learning, research and knowledge dissemination. The ideas that have generated from these institutions and the people who have passed through their portals have enriched the various facets of India's development. Each of these institutions produced a large number of social scientists, cancer specialists, nuclear scientists and distinguished institutional administrators who have all strived to make the country a power to reckon with in science and technology.

In the last decade, the Trust has also given shape to the *National Institute of Advanced Studies* in Bangalore and helped Dr. M.S. Swaminathan Research Foundation to start the *JRD Tata Centre for Ecotechnology* in Chennai.

In addition to these institutions, it has started with the assistance of the Royal Commonwealth Society for the Blind, Asia's first institute for the training of the rural blind, *The Tata Agricultural and Rural Training Centre for the Blind,* and with the cooperation of the United Nations, the International Institute of Demographic Studies.

The Trust also helps various organizations and individuals with its grants. Its grants consist of *Endownment Grants,* grants to *Non-Governmental Organisations* and *Small Grants,* while *Individual Grants* are given to deserving individuals for medical, travel or educational purposes.

What has helped the Trust in achieving its objectives has been the presence of distinguished personalities, most of them industry pioneers, on its board. Among them were JRD Tata, chairman of the Tata Group, Sir Ardeshir Dalal, Dr. John Matthai and Sir Homi Mody.

The involvement of JRD Tata in the affairs of Trust is not just incidental. Being a trustee since the Trust's inception, he held the position of chairman during the last 25 years of his life. His imprint is visible in the setting up the *Tata Memorial Hospital, Tata Institute of Fundamental Research, Tata Institute of Social Sciences, National Institute of Advanced Studies* and *National Centre for the Performing Arts.* His role was especially crucial in the establishment of the Tata Memorial Hospital. Right from its conceptual stages in early 1941, till it became a national centre for cancer research and treatment, JRD Tata was there all along to guide its destinies. In 1957, when the government of India's ministry of health temporarily took over the Tata Memorial Hospital, JRD Tata, along with Dr. Homi Bhabha, the pioneer of India's nuclear energy programme, had the vision to foresee the role of radiation in cancer treatment and prevailed on the government to have the administrative control of the hospital transferred to the department of atomic energy in 1962.

He had also put his own money and efforts to set up, in 1944, the multipurpose JRD Tata Trust. Many years later, he established the JRD and Thelma J. Tata Trust, selling part of his shares and an apartment in Mumbai. The Trust works to improve the lot of India's disadvantaged women.

What is typical of the Trust is that after establishing pioneering institutions, giving them shape and stabilizing them, the Trust handed over their day-to-day running to the Government of India. Thus, *The Tata Memorial Hospital* is now under the government, run by the department of atomic energy. Similarly, the *Tata Institute of Fundamental Research* too has been handed over to Atomic Energy Commission. *Tata Institute of Social Sciences* today is a Deemed University. In the case of TISS and the TIFR, the chairmen of the boards have so far been the representatives of the Tata Trusts. The Trust is represented on the governing council of the *Tata Memorial Hospital*. However, the Trust still takes interest in these institutions and contributes its resources to their running.

As neither Sir Dorabji nor Sir Ratan had any children, their holdings could well have been fragmented and with Tata Sons. The Trusts that Sir Dorabji and Sir Ratan set up gave to Tata Sons a cohesive and a continuing character over decades.

It is easier to manage a social charity with a couple of focused priorities. But, it is not so in the case of a philanthropic organization that changes its focus in terms of the changing needs of the society, responding to them with utmost speed and care. The Sir Dorabji Tata Trust has kept its doors open to the needs of the society, especially of the underprivileged sections, even while functioning within the framework of its set objectives. Its responses, sensitivities and the deep understanding of the Indian society at large, have all helped it to maintain a creditable track record.

Activities of Trust

1. Natural Resource Management and Rural Livelihoods

This thematic area addresses the issues of natural resource management and livelihoods in the rural areas as the rationale is that the bulk of the rural people mostly derive their livelihoods by carrying out their production and collection activities interacting with the natural resource base.

Under this area, the Trusts have identified the following issues as thrust areas :

» Food security at the household, micro- and macro-level. While food security at the macro level results from augmenting food production; food security at the household level can come from both increasing household food production as well as by increasing the household income through expanding and strengthening its other livelihoods options and improving market access to the produce from households. Augmentation of food production in turn occurs through improving productivity of land through watershed development, irrigation, improvement in agronomic practices and introducing new crop combinations and cropping techniques.

» Ecological security, including in particular, efforts at ensuring efficient and equitable use of water. Working towards ecological security includes biodiversity conservation, strengthening technical and social measures for regeneration of fragile ecologies and contributing towards a more prudent and sustainable use of natural resources.

Efforts are afoot also to shift the grant making focus towards the more needy areas in the central, eastern and north-eastern regions. This is the result of a review in 2005 which had noted that until then, much of Trusts' grant making in the theme had occurred in Western and Southern India.

Based upon the new strategy many of the Trusts' efforts are now focused towards two broad thematic areas of Food Security and Ecological Security. Also there has been a focus shift towards livelihood interventions with a market-led approach. Geographically, a lot of new projects have been initiated in the perennially poverty-stricken belts of northern, central, eastern and north-eastern regions. The grant making strategy is also gradually shifting towards a programmatic approach and significant among the programs that the Trusts have mounted, is a national program on promoting System of Rice Intensification (SRI) resulting in bringing in a various players together under a banner, which looks after the issue of food security at the household level.

Similarly, a program on tapping the potential of diversion based irrigation (DBI) was been launched in the latter part of 2008. This initiative too envisages addressing the food security issue with a minimal investment towards creating irrigation infrastructure, agriculture promotion and command area development. Ideas on the line of small ruminants (particularly goat), renewal energy sources (particularly micro hydel), capitalizing on forest-based livelihoods and to strengthen community conservation efforts are on the way of getting shaped in programmatic mode.

SRI Program

During 2006-07, the Trusts conducted a detailed scan of the country on various issues for creating a strategic plan for the next five years. Taking into account, 21 different indicators including agricultural productivity, it generated a district-level human development index covering 596 districts. On the parameters of Income (other parameters being on Health and Education), a district index indicated that many districts in the eastern and central parts of the country were very backward. Since in the rural areas, a major portion of income is generated from farm activities, it was decided to launch a comprehensive program on ensuring food security aiming at small and marginal land holders. Based upon experiments already piloted through NGOs in eastern India and a comprehensive study conducted by a team led by a renown rice breeder in India, the Trusts decided to launch a program on System of Rice Intensification (SRI) targeting the small and marginal farmers.

Progress Made So Far

Thus far, the strategy has been to reach out to a maximum number of small and marginal farmers. For achieving this, a two-track strategy has been implemented of building a cadre of trained people and also of reaching out to a plethora of civil society organizations through nodal agencies. The coverage during the kharif of 2008 has been 30,198 households tilling 6,635 acres of land. This has been achieved in eight states spanning 74 districts. In about half of the districts, SRI has been introduced for the first time. Other salient achievements of the initiative are as below :

» About 80 percent of the farmers covered under this program are small and marginal farmers and they come from rain fed areas without proper irrigation infrastructures. A sample survey of more than 4,000 farmers in the states of Uttarakhand, Orissa, Jharkhand and Assam has suggested that there has been 76 percent incremental yield in rice production under this program over conventional method of rice cultivation.
» The Trust could reach out to a total of 120 agencies for extension of SRI in the field.
» SRI has been adopted in various agro-climatic zones ranging from sea-level fields (Sunderbans) to 2,200 meters above mean sea-level (at Tehri Garhwal).
» In Orissa, the state government has come up with a Government Order for promoting SRI throughout the state with the help of the Trusts' partners. In Uttarakhand the Department of Agriculture is providing financial assistance to the Trusts' partners for SRI promotion.
» The Trusts also supported organizing the Second and Third National Symposium on SRI in India. Additionally, first ever state-level SRI symposiums were organized in Assam, Bihar, Orissa and Jharkhand with active support from the Trusts.
» The Trusts run an e-group on SRI which has 314 members. It is meant for exchanging ideas.

2. Civil Society, Governance and Human Rights

Civil Society, Governance and Human Rights (CSGHR) evolved as a separate portfolio with a pan-India focus as an outcome of the Strategic Planning exercise that was undertaken. At the outset 22 projects slotted under the Social Development Initiatives portfolio until 2006 were brought under the CSGHR portfolio as per the strategic planning exercise.

The thrust areas identified within CSGHR portfolio as outlined in the strategic plan are :

Strengthening Governance

The portfolio will specifically focus on improving the implementation of the 73rd Amendment of the Indian Constitution and Panchayati Raj Extension to Schedule Areas (PESA) to ensure functional democracy.

Protection of Basic Human Rights

Support would be provided towards creating an institutional environment in which basic human rights are protected for the most marginalized communities.

Strengthening Civil Society

Most of the backward areas are not only characterized by poor outreach of basic services, but also a lack of presence of civil society organizations. The portfolio recognizes this need and will support initiatives that will build the capacities of civil society organizations to respond to the complexities of poverty and promote rights of the people.

The portfolio will in a variety of ways seek to professionalize rights-based work through, research, advocacy, documentation and dissemination of relevant materials and also engage with government as well as non-governmental organizations, community-based organizations and the institutional actors such as the police and judiciary.

The program team translated these guidelines and identified various innovative interventions across the country. The projects that are supported in the three main thrust areas focus on :

Strengthening Governance

The focus remained on the grassroots governance in the remote areas of India with emphasis on principles of accountability, transparency and participation of the most marginalized communities in governance.

Several field organizations provide training to the vast number of men and women elected to the Gram Panchayats, in order that they may better understand how to use the legitimate power that they have gained out of an electoral process to ensure better governance at the village level.

Securing Basic Rights

The portfolio of CSGHR also focuses on securing rights of marginalized communities in the most deprived areas of the poorer states of India. The portfolio would respond to appeals that seek to restore and protect the rights of women, Dalits, tribals, homeless, prisoners and basic entitlements of the vulnerable communities. It is found that human rights violations are most rampant among the relatively poorer states. Food insecurity among the poor despite overall economic growth of the country remains a serious problem for the country. In the past few years, a public interest litigation filed by a few organizations have yielded very good orders by the Supreme Court that have strengthened the hands of the rural poor and the civil society organizations working in these areas. These orders have played a significant role in streamlining the Public Distribution System — the major source of grain for the poor. Armed with these orders, the poor and civil society organizations are working towards ensuring the basic right to food.

One of the interesting things about rights is that when its denial becomes apparent only then would you seek justice for the denial. Thus the important thing while working on human rights is to be able to track the violations such as in the case of housing and land rights. For the poor a house is not just a shelter it also doubles on as an important component of their livelihood strategy improper records of land and poor updating of inheritance records on death of the land holder create the conditions for taking away land rights.

Violence against women is a wide spread phenomenon despite legislation protecting women against it. The Trusts' work in this area continues to be ground breaking.

In addition, the Trusts have supported pioneering work in the criminal justice system that looks at securing prisoners' rights and the rights of the undertrails. This unique model - a field action project by TISS - has nurtured several smaller programs across Madhya Pradesh and Maharashtra.

Civil Society Strengthening

In order to sustain social development initiatives, strengthening civil society is one of the main requirements of this sector and hence is a focus area of this portfolio. While there is an increase in the number of formal institutions offering degree courses in social work, the need far outnumbers the supply. There is a need to promote organizations that do both meaningful, good quality work in areas of need as well as to promote activists and professionals who will develop strategies to deal with complex phenomenon such as poverty. Thus this portfolio looks at strengthening small civil society organizations, promoting fellows to work on specific themes to promote basic rights of the poor and marginalized and towards improving governance within civil society. Supporting fellowship programs has emerged as a useful approach to reach out to marginalized communities as well as contribute to the civil society.

While CSGHR has been defined as a separate portfolio and has a pan-India focus, it will be working towards broad basing its work on protection and promotion of basic human rights and strengthening governance within civil society.

2. SAMAJ PRAGATI SAHYOG

Introduction

Over the last two decades, Samaj Pragati Sahayog (SPS) has grown to be one of India's largest grass-roots initiatives for water and livelihood security, working with its partners on a million acres of land across 72 of India's most backward districts, mainly in the central Indian Adivasi belt. SPS took inspiration from the life and work of Baba Amte (its *Pramukh Sahayogi*) who rejected charity and successfully empowered even the most challenged. SPS is headquartered in a drought-prone, tribal area in the Dewas district of Madhya Pradesh, which typifies the most difficult problems of the country. SPS concentrate all its direct interventions in about 220 villages and towns of this area. This work is not so much a model as a living laboratory of learning for others to adapt to their own areas. To facilitate this mutual learning, in 1998, SPS set up the Baba Amte Centre for People's Empowerment in tribal village Neemkheda, where its watershed work began in the early 1990s.

SPS believes that location-specific watershed development combined with low-cost, low-risk agriculture, other nature-based livelihoods and women-led micro-finance, can dramatically raise rural incomes, providing an enduring panacea to India's suicide-ridden drylands. This approach arrests distress migration towards the metros and liberates the rural poor from the clutches of usurious moneylender-traders. Its central mandate is the empowerment of India's most disadvantaged people–women, Adivasis, Dalits and the poor, which it believe contributes to strengthening its fragile democracy at the grass-roots. SPS is working as nodal agency of Right to food programme supported by Sir Dorabji Tata Trust.

Organisational Structure and Principles

SPS is an organisation registered under the Societies Registration Act, 1860. As per the Act, the Executive Committee (EC) is the highest decision-making body and executive powers are vested in the Secretary.

The role of the EC is to provide broad guidance and oversight to SPS work. Day-to-day responsibility rests with the 25-member Core Team of experienced professionals who work full-time at headquarters, leading the team of 225 SPS activists.

SPS is a learning organisation, highly self-critical of its own functioning, in terms of both processes and performance. The regular interface of people across teams, facilitated by the Core Team, acts as a corrective to possible abuse of flexibility. The fluidity of such an organizational structure also demands that decision-making processes are frequently reconstructed—they cannot simply be "read" from an organogram.

The work of SPS shows that farmer-driven, location-specific watershed development combined with bio-diverse agriculture, other nature-based livelihood and micro-finance, can result in sustained higher incomes and empowered communities, providing an enduring panacea to India's suicide-ridden drylands.

Dr. Mihir Shah: The Co-founder

A Ph.D. in Economics from the Jawaharlal Nehru University, New Delhi, Dr. Shah co-authored India's Drylands, a study for the UNDP, which was published and released worldwide by the Oxford University Press in 1998. The study brings out the macro-economic significance of watershed programmes for food security and employment guarantee in India.

Dr. Shah was Adviser to the Commissioner appointed by the Supreme Court of India in the Right to Food case from 2002-2009. As Honorary Adviser to the Technical Committee on Watershed Programmes set up by the Government of India in 2006, he was largely responsible for drafting its landmark report that argues for radical reforms in India's watershed sector. In 2007, he co-founded the National Consortium of Civil Society Organisations that works to support Panchayat Raj Institutions for more effective implementation of NREGA. He was a member of three

Working Groups set up by the Government of India for the 11th Five Year Plan related to rural science and technology and rainfed areas. He was also part of the Hameed Committee set up by the Prime Minister in 2007 to suggest a completely new structure for CAPART.

Dr. Shah graduated in Economics from St. Stephen's College, Delhi (where he won the KC Nag Economics Prize) and did his post-graduation from the Delhi School of Economics (where he was Merit Scholar). In the 1970s, before going on to complete a much-acclaimed doctoral dissertation at the Centre for Development Studies, Kerala. After teaching for some years at the Centre, he resigned to explore fresh terrain beyond the ivory towers of conventional academia. During this time, he travelled extensively in rural, tribal India in pursuit of a fresh understanding, necessary for the formulation of an alternative Indian vision of development. These travels culminated in 1990 in the formation of Samaj Pragati Sahayog.

Dr. Shah has combined 20 years of living and working at the grass roots with academic research and policy advocacy, deeply informed by his endeavours in the field. He has received national and international recognition for his work, including the Social Entrepreneur of the Year Award from the American India Foundation and the Doreen Mashler Award of ICRISAT.

Dr. Shah is working as Member- Planning Commission, Government of India. He writes regularly for the Economic and Political Weekly and The Hindu.

ACTIVITIES OF SPS

Watershed Development

SPS has taken up 45,000 acres for direct implementation of watershed programmes spread over 34 villages, spending Rs. 60 million. This has generated nearly a million person-days of employment. The total storage capacity of the water harvesting structures created by SPS is over 1 million cubic metres. This has had the primary impact of ensuring drinking water security to all households in these villages. Rabi irrigation has shown a rise of 300% and the overall irrigation ratio has more than doubled. A significant impact of the work has been drought-proofing of the kharif crop. As in any typical dryland region, rainfall in our area is low, highly erratic and characterized by long dry spells between rainy days. Water harvesting structures help farmers tide over this crisis by providing crucial "life-saving" protective irrigation. We see the watershed programme as crucial public investment to incentivise private investments by even the poorest farmers on their own lands.

The value of agricultural output has gone up mainly due to expansion in irrigated area and higher per hectare yields. The yield of kharif (mostly rainfed) crops has shown a rise in the range of 10-20% and that of rabi (mostly irrigated) crops has shown a rise of 50-60%. Overall, the value of production of kharif and rabi crops together has gone up in the range of 80-160%. The Benefit-Cost Ratio ranges from 1.49 to 1.96 and Internal Rate of Return on investments from 30% to 49%. An 80% reduction in external migration has been observed during the years of ongoing watershed implementation.

With significant expansion in irrigated area and crop productivity, high labour absorption in agriculture is visible even after the watershed programme closes. It is this "sedimented employment" which reduces external migration from the area in the long run. Hundreds of tribal farmers who have grown a single rainfed crop all their lives are now cultivating 2-3 crops. Many have returned home after years to reclaim land they had virtually given up for good.

Micro-Finance

SPS believe that the full potential of watershed work can only be realised if it is supplemented by a micro-finance programme. SPS is convinced that no micro-finance programme can be successful until it is tied up with livelihood programmes such as agriculture, dairying, marketing etc.

Thus, micro-finance and livelihood programmes are complementary to each other and their simultaneous implementation is the key to poverty alleviation. Incomes rose through livelihood initiatives need to be saved. Of these women are the best custodians. These savings must be reinvested in livelihood options that in turn raise incomes, setting up a virtuous cycle.

The micro-finance programme is based on the Self Help Group-Bank Linkage (SBL) model. Over the last four years, SPS has formed about 900 women's Self-Help Groups (SHGs) with around 14,000 members. Most members of these SHGs belong to marginalised sections, such as the poor, Adivasis, Dalits, landless and displaced people. SHGs offer their members a range of financial products including interest on savings, recurring deposits, fixed deposits, loans against fixed deposits, loans for genuine needs and emergencies (the veracity of each of which is judged by the members themselves), loans for cattle and well construction, cattle insurance, life insurance etc. So far, SPS SHGs have saved a total of Rs. 20 million and provided loans worth Rs.100 million to their members. Individual loans range from Rs. 3,000 to Rs. 30,000.

But the central goal of its SBL model goes beyond finance. It is the empowerment of these disadvantaged women who learn to run their own series of nested institutions - SHGs, Cluster Development Associations (of 15-20 SHGs) and Federations (of around 200 SHGs).

The persistence of endemic poverty and hunger six decades after independence points to the glaring lack of good governance in rural areas. It is vision of SPS that Federations of these women's SHGs will emerge as a key building block for effective empowerment of the poor in the tribal drylands of India, giving these regions the necessary voice in the development process. The members of these Federations will also be able to provide effective and capable leadership to Panchayat Raj Institutions, which SPS see as the centerpiece of governance in rural India. The unique strength of SHG programme is financial and procedural discipline and transparency. It is mandatory for each group to go through an external audit every year, conducted by reputed chartered accountants. Thus, running SHGs is a great learning experience and allows these women a space to become powerful articulators of their perceptions and interests. They carry forward this strength into the panchayat arena.

In this extremely important task of nation building through people's empowerment, public sector banks have a critical role to play. India has the largest banking network in the world. SHG Federations and banks in remote rural areas are complementary entities, whose existence depends on each other. Today, when the very existence of some of these public sector banks is under threat, Federations of SHGs can be a massive support to them. The credit extended by banks to SHGs is their lifeline. The repayment rate of SHGs is unprecedented. Therefore, if public sector banks become partners of Federations on a large scale, the financial situation of banks can also improve.

Kumbaya

Kumbaya, garment fabrication centre of SPS, has empowered women by creating a new skill and employment opportunity in the area. SPS trained over 500 women from 45 villages in ready-to-wear garments and patchwork products. In the absence of a traditional marketable craft, by designing products that compete with mainstream fabrication units, Kumbaya guarantees work and a market to women producers for 300 days a year. Most of these tribal women had never stitched a garment before and had no options other than manual labour. Kumbaya makes a range of Indian and western casual wear, duvets, patchwork cushion covers, table and bed linen, curtains, wall hangings and different types of bags and rucksacks.

The accomplishment of Kumbaya has been that the product by itself instantly leaves a brand imprint leading to an ever-growing demand from customers, retailers and exporters in Delhi, Bangalore, Pondicherry, Bombay and

Indore. The compelling pressure from hundreds of women in the area demanding fair livelihood opportunities and the ever-increasing demand for its products has enabled Kumbaya to open three training and production centres in the area. Kumbaya is also hope for many differently abled people, particularly women, whose inability to contribute manual labour in an agricultural area leads to their abandonment. The Kumbaya centres are supervised by a team of skilled and trained local people, who manage training, production, and accounts.

Agriculture

Based on the building blocks of watershed and micro-finance, SPS is developing a series of sustainable livelihoods for the poor.

Dry land Agriculture

SPS has worked out a package of agricultural practices finely tuned to the resource endowments of the watershed, which is accessible to the poor (low-cost) and sustainable (low-risk). It has experimented with 36 improved varieties based on indigenous seeds of 9 crops – sorghum, maize, pigeon pea, cotton, soyabean, gram, pearl millet, groundnut and wheat—which give good yields even with low external inputs. These varieties have been developed from the local germplasm by scientists working on-location across India's dry lands and are, therefore, well adapted to this challenging environment. Of these, SPS has short listed 15 varieties of sorghum, maize, pigeon pea, cotton, soyabean, gram and wheat. Under its agricultural extension programme, SPS encourage a few carefully selected farmers to set up seed production plots of some of these varieties. SPS buys back seeds from these farmers and then distributes them to farmers in the area. With an increasing number of these farmers, the SPS team is encouraging the adoption of No Pesticide Management (NPM) agriculture.

Along with seven other partner NGOs, in 2008, SPS

initiated an All-India Consortium on NPM Agriculture. The NPM idea came up as a response to the difficulties faced in Organic Certification, which is both expensive and inaccessible to small farmers. The idea of the NPM movement is to encourage farmers to grow crops without any chemical pesticides, create an identity for their produce and link these small producers to markets. The need to use small doses of chemical fertilizers arises because of the poor soil health in these areas. Unless soil health is built up over time, a move to full organic agriculture will be impossible. Hence, NPM agriculture stresses building up soil fertility through appropriate management practices (such as composting and recycling of agricultural residues, use of farm yard manure, green manuring crops and bio-pesticides) with a gradual phasing out of chemical fertilizers.

Livestock Support

Over the last two years, SPS has started a livestock support programme for small and marginal farmers. While people have large stocks of cattle in our area, milk yields have been poor due to lack of health, water, fodder, affordable credit and a market. Its watershed programme had already ensured water and fodder. SPS has now introduced quality preventive and curative veterinary care. Its painstaking efforts have ensured that the Indore Milk Union includes its area in their milk collection route. In addition, SHGs have extended credit to their members (at low rates of interest with long repayment periods) to purchase quality indigenous breeds. These animals are insured through a tie-up with the Oriental Insurance Company.

Having first minimized risk, the programme now emphasises building up systems to ensure transparency and provide incentives to the farmer to increase production. On the procurement side, activities focus on building up a fair and efficient milk collection and payment system. On the production side, various programmes like pregnant cow care, fodder production, regular deworming and vaccination, support in selection of good animals and improved breeding services have tried to raise productivity of farm animals. In these efforts, it has been its endeavour to strike a balance between getting better yields from the present stock as well as induction of indigenous and crossbred animals. A dedicated cadre of paravets and milk cooperative society secretaries provides feet to the programme by making available these services in far-flung villages.

Right to Food

SPS is working hard to generate awareness among the people about schemes such as the mid-day meal scheme, the ICDS and the Public Distribution System and build pressure on the government to reform the way they run and increase the resources allotted to them. Its work has provided extensive relief to people living in malnutrition hotspots of Madhya Pradesh and ensured greater transparency and accountability in the functioning of the administration.

SPS is working as Nodal Agency with Sir Dorabji Tata Trust on Right to Food programme in which Gram Sudhar Samiti is associated as programme partner.

3. GRAM SUDHAR SAMITI

Gram Sudhar Samiti (GSS) is a registered voluntary organisation under the Societies Rgistration Act in 1987. GSS started its action oriented programme in the year 1993 in Sidhi district. The brief account of report of the activities undertaken by GSS is as follows:

Work on watershed development with assistance from CAPART

With its proven expertise in watershed development programme, GSS is selected as project implementing agency (PIA) with CAPART. GSS formed watershed committee. Mass awareness programmes were organized including a rally with school children to create awareness on water harvesting and soil conservation. Wall writing, slogan writing and street plays sensitized community to understand the importance of water conservation. GSS organized a Jal Sammelan in which prominent personalities and experts in watershed development and water harvesting participated. The participants expressed their opinion on the sustainable water harvesting techniques. GSS organized a health camp in Dhunna Nallah watershed area on July 25, 2005 with the assistance of Block Health & Medical Officer Dr. R.K. Thakur and doctors of PHC Majhauli. Total 247 patients reported in the camp with diseases like Malaria, Asthma, Skin ailments, Anaemia and other diseases. 40 children and 5 pregnant women were vaccinated in the camp. The BMO with its team also distributed Bleaching Powder and chlorine tablets to ensure hygiene and sanitation.

Another health camp was also organized under watershed committee in village Kochila on July 30. Medical team under the guidance of Dr. M.K. Gupta of Semaria PHC managed the camp with volunteers of Gram Sudhar Samiti, Sidhi. Total 181 patients participated in the camp and were examined by expert and distributed free medicines by GSS.

Under the CAPART project, work on environment building for group formation was started with the meeting of informal groups and watershed committee members. The participant women were motivated to form self-help-groups (SHGs) to improve their economic condition. GSS organized training programme for the members of watershed committee on various aspects of the project and their role in the project. A training programme was also organized on micro-finance through which SHG members were imparted knowledge on different aspects viz. account upkeep, bank linkages, deposit and withdrawal.

GSS constructed 104 soil check dams benefiting 89 beneficiaries, 8 boulder bunds benefiting 15 beneficiaries, 338 contour trenches benefiting 20 beneficiaries. To develop orchards, GSS planted 1495 saplings benefiting 35 farmers of the area. GSS repaired and maintained a well benefiting 15 families. Members of SHGs were imparted training in bee keeping and agarbatti making. Total 67 beneficiaries are working to improve their socio-economic condition through their micro-enterprises.

Work on Panchayat Institutions with the Hunger Project:

GSS started its work with the Hunger Project to improve the quality of existing structure of panchayats and promotion of gram swaraj theme of M.P. Government. GSS organized 3 days residential workshop from July 1 to 3 to sensitise panchayat members on different aspects. 20 villages and 10 women sarpanch participated in the training programme.

GSS instituted Bal Panchayat and 'Mahila Mandals in the 17 villages to enlist their cooperation in organizing various activities of the project. Meetings of Bal Panchayat and Mahila Mandal were organized at the village level in which members resolved that social networking need to be strengthened at the village level to develop understanding on social harmony. The committees resolved to work on participatory development to fulfill the objectives of Gram Swaraj. GSS formed a network of women sarpanch of Rampur Baghelan block of Satna district. This network will work as an apex organization (federation). The federation will improve the level of confidence of fellow women sarpanch to take decision and implement programmes with social equality and distributive justice GSS organized a one day workshop on 'Panch Parmeshwar' in which ex-MLA Prabhakar Singh elaborated on various provisions of 73rd amendment in the constitution and said that gram sabha as legal entity has to play significant role in realizing gram swaraj. GSS organized a leadership training programme for the women sarpanch of project area to develop leadership attributes. In the village meeting of gram panchayat Konia Kothar, Sarpanch Meera Devi along with the members of Mahila Mandals resolved to collect Rs. 10 per month from each student and appointed additional teacher with the permission of Parent-Teacher Association, this has improved the performance of students. Women Sarpanch of project villages were taken out to exposure visit in Mendha Lekha village of Garh Chirauli block of Maharashtra in November. Members of the exposure visit team realized the fruits of participatory development in this village and learnt from the sarpanch of Mendha Lekha about the strategic intervention. After coming from the visit, women Sarpanch are exercising same strategies to replicate the success story of Mendha Lekha.

Work on Elimination and Rehabilitation of Child Labour

As a responsible citizen, GSS always treated child labour a curse on society. With its demonstrated expertise in the field of social development, GSS is selected as partner NGO under Indus Child Labour Project. GSS is running a bridge school in Satna in which 50 child labourers are studying. Each child is paid a scholarship of Rs. 100 and regular health check-up is being done by doctors. Efforts were made to mainstream these children in the formal schools being run by government and non-government agencies. Regular motivation and behavioural correction remedies helped these children to develop their personality through education and skill development training. 50 school children have been streamlined and have taken admissions in formal schools.

GSS organized counseling programmes for the parents of these children, with regular contact and monitoring by the volunteers of GSS, parents have asked their children to continue their education.

Watershed Development

GSS started watershed development programme in 1996-97 as project implementing agency (PIA) under Rajiv Gandhi Watershed Mission. The programme was conceived on the basis of Hanumant Rao Committee with the objective to increase in employment opportunities and agriculture production. Since then, GSS has been implementing various activities under watershed development programme. GSS adopted area development strategy with water and soil as main subjects. GSS worked continuously to recharge water level, checking depletion of water level.

GSS adopted various techniques developed by villagers based on local needs, knowledge and cost effectiveness, invited scientists and engineers, experts like Magsasay awardee Rajendra Singh to construct good quality structures. Watershed development and its ancillary activities like afforestation, soil and water conservation, pasture development, etc. are being carried out by GSS since last 7 years. The watershed development programme is conceived to achieve objectives of natural resource management through people's participation to improve ecological well-being and thereby enhance its productivity and life supporting systems for the betterment of community. A watershed area is a geo-hydrological unit or piece of land that drains at a common point. Optimum utilisation of locally available resources has been the strategy for sustainable development. The optimum use of land scientifically tantamount to an optimum use of. the available land, water and other natural endowments. GSS's watershed development programme consists of the survey and mapping of the village level natural resources, not as an external scientific input but participative with the local community. It is conceived through the strategy developed by Robert Chambers in his book 'Putting the Last first', which says, "The links of modern scientific knowledge with wealth, power and prestige condition outsiders to despise and ignore rural people's own knowledge". GSS always ensured people's participation since the programme benefit was to tickle down to them. Knowledge of local community in the construction of stop dam, digging of ponds, etc. was thought of as necessary input. For this, GSS organised 8 Participatory Rural Appraisals (PRAs) in the planning and management of watershed development programmes towards participatory management.

GSS used innovative scientific tools like geological information systems (GIS) and remote sensing to study the map showing extent land use, terrain features, availability of water and other natural resources. It developed a permanent data bank in the villages based on reliable and relevant micro-level terrain characteristics. The watershed committees (WC), formed at village level, resolved that the use pattern be based on locally available input and items of work should lead to sustainable land use.

Watershed activities completed by GSS under DPAP-II in 2006-07:

(i)	Digging of Ponds	:	8Nos.
(ii)	Soil bund	:	7Nos.
(iii)	CPT	:	4000 run meters
(iv)	Farm pond	:	92Nos.
(v)	Check dam	:	35Nos.
(vi)	Plantation	:	54900Plants
(vii)	CPW	:	1100 run meters.

The result of the watershed development programme under Rajiv Gandhi watershed Mission is motivational to farmers and others. With the increased activities of water harvesting and conservation, the water level recharged 3.50 ft. in Komar Nallah, 1.50 ft. in Banas Nallah Part-1 and 1.00 ft in Banas Nallah Part-II. Water harvesting in the constructed structures was 70.65 ha mt. in Komar Nallah, 40.35 ha mt. in Banas Nallah Part-I and 35.70 ha mt. in Banas Nallah Part-II. With the availability of water and application of scientific methods of agriculture, the agriculture production increased to 20% in project villages. The ongoing construction and other activities like plantation made available the employment of 131150 man-days in Komar Nallah, 65400 man days in Banas Nallah Part-I and 75800 man-days in Banas Nallah Part-II. GSS formed 165 users groups in Komar Nallah, 117 in Banas Nallah Part-I and 115 in Banas Nallah Part-II. GSS formed 15 SHGs in Komar Nallah area, 8 SHGs in Banas Nallah Part-I and 6 SHGs in Banas Nallah which helped in the 50% increase in annual income of group members 5 groups undertook diesel pump for irrigation purpose, a group is working with flour mill, 2 groups have general stores.

The impact of watershed programme is evident through the live example of Khaira village where 150 acres of land is being irrigated through permanent natural water, outlet which is the result of water harvesting in two stop dams. The recharged water level is flowing throughout the year and is helpful for the local community in earning their livelihood.

Sl. No.	*Committee name*	*Received Amount (in Rs. Lakh)*	*No.of benefi-ciaries*	*Expenditure (in Rs. lakh)*	*Treated land (in ha.)*
1	Bahri	7.60	190	8.05	130
2	Shehauliya	2.43	210	9.85	162
3	Fulwari	-	165	7.76	126
4	Dhutpura	12.80	198	9.58	159
5	Jethula North	6.07	190	8.56	142
6	Jethula South	5.67	212	9.85	164
7	Duara	8.789	188	7.98	133
8	Khaira	-	-	-	-
9	Dubri Khurda	-	-	-	-
10	Dubri Kala	-	-	-	-
11	Umariya	-	-	-	-
12	Kanchanpur	3.89	155	3.89	64
Total		**47.249**	**1508**	**68.52**	**1080**

Work on 'Right to Food' with support from Sir Dorabji Tata Trust

As part of corporate social responsibility, Tata group has established many trusts and societies to discharge its social responsibility practices. Sir Dorabji Tata Trust supported GSS in the implementation of Right to Food programme. GSS conducted base line survey of 100 villages of Sidhi, Majhauli and Kusmi blocks of Sidhi district. 50 Adhikar Paramarsh Kendra (Rights counseling centers) are established in the villages through which a villager can get information about government schemes, Right to Information Act, and any other information. The centre makes available stationary and other necessary inputs to villagers. Mahila Adhikar Sangathan (women rights organization) and Dalit-Adivasi Sangathan (for men) are established in all the villages to discuss various problems of the village, GSS organized cycle rally in 17 villages of Sidhi block to spread awareness about government schemes, volunteers of GSS, people's elected representatives and opinion leaders participated in rally. Mass awareness campaign is being organized through wall writing, street plays, etc. GSS organized leadership development training to develop leadership attributes among its volunteers, group organizers. Posters and pamphlets showing information on Rights to Information Act, NREGA and Rights to Food were distributed in villages through which villagers got information about various schemes.

Based on the non-compliances of various applications of complaints of villagers, GSS organized a sit-in programme in front of the office of the SDM, Majhauli under the banner of Dalit Adivasi Adhikar Manch. Memorandum consisting list of complaints and applications were sent to chief minister with a copy to district collector. Total 32 complainants got relief and delivery mechanism of Anganwadi centres smoothened and work under NREGA was made transparent. To make groups empowered, GSS organized training programmes for the capacity building of group coordinators. GSS worked on advocacy on 254 applications related with Antyodaya card, social security pension, NREGA, Anganwadi centres and inclusion of name in BPL, correction in the delivery mechanism of PDS, etc.

Work on Handicapped Welfare with Hope Foundation

GSS worked with Hope Foundation and handed over 3 computers alongwith furniture to Vivekanand Viklang Ashram Sidhi through which 56 hearing impaired and 15 intellectually challenged children are learning computers.

GSS obtained software from Care & Cure to train intellectually challenged.

Work on Integrated Rural Development with Action Aid

Considering the outcome of the programme, Action Aid continued its support to GSS as partner NGO, GSS organized various rights based programmes with a tilt in favour of poor with the help of Mahila Adhikar Manch, GSS is able to create pressure on concerned officials to include names of 69 persons in the BPL and 6 families got assistance under the national assistance programme. Manch locked PDS shops in Chaufal and Rauser with villagers to correct the malpractices in the system. Mahila Adhikar Manch worked to protect the interests of women fellows. Illegal liquor units were closed by the activists of Manch and GSS volunteers in Ghusmunia, Khamh, Chakdor and Chaufal. Members of Manch organized sit-in programme against the liquor shop and with this result the liquor shop was replaced from Chakdor Panchayat. Subhaua Saket, President of Mahila Adhikar Manch organized agitation and 32 names are included in the list of employment guarantee through Tehsildar.

GSS organized training programmes for the adolescent girls in Sarethi, Khamh, Barhai and Mata to aware them on different changes and suitable technologies to meet with these changes. A legal awareness training programme was organized in regional training centre, Ghordand on 24-25 August in which Shubhra Pachauri worked as resource person. 40 participants from project area were given necessary information related to court procedures, different provisions of the government, protection from exploitation, and self-defence. Legal awareness camp was organized in Sarethi on October 29 under the chairmanship of district magistrate in which 300 men and 250 women participated and presented their application for relief from lower judiciary, 63 matters were accepted and 3 cases were solved in 'Lok Adalat'. GSS organized 'Bal Sanjeevani Abhiyan' in 11 panchayats which included health check-up of pregnant and lactating women and awareness rally from Sapni Duari to Ghordand. GSS organized two days training programme on gender sensitization on 20-21 June in which 56 participants learnt on social stigma with girl child and social inequality with girls and women and how to sensitise community to be gender sensitive. Membes of Mahila Adhikar Manch visited Akhil Bhartiya Samaj Seva Sansthan Manikpur under exposure visit with the objective to learn on organization and management of rights based activities. Two days legal training programme was organized for the members of Dalit Adivasi Mahapanchayat. GSS organized workshop on land rights in Sarethi in which MLA of Gopad Banas K.K. Singh and Deputy Collector Kalika Prasad Tripathi, Tehsildar and members of Mahapanchayat participated in the workshop and expressed their views. GSS organized training programe for the Kala Jatha and street play team of the Panchayat, these teams demonstrated in different Nyaya Panchayats from 16.06.06 to 30.11.06.

Work on National Rural Employment Guarantee Programme (NREGA)

GSS is actively involved in the implementation of NREGA in the Sidhi district. The mandate of government to provide 100 days employment to needy families is being fulfilled through constructive works and infrastructure development in the rural areas.

A Learning Centre : Gram Sudhar Samiti has been regarded as learning centre by many educational institutions and NGOs. Students of MSW and MA(Rural Development) of Nehru Gram Bharati University, Kotwa, Allahabad visited various projects of Samiti to learn and practice on different issues under field stay programme. Volunteers of different NGOs visited various ongoing activities of GSS under exposure visit to learn on strategic management.

Work on Forest Rights : Considering its geological coverage in the far remote and forest villages, GSS started its activities linked with the forest rights of Adivasis in Sidhi district with the assistance of Winrock International. Volunteers of GSS actively participated in the workshops organized on different issues related with the forest rights.

Education Programme

Action Aid supported GSS in Madhya Pradesh Shiksha Abhiyan in which 485 children were enrolled in schools. Dropped out 50 girls and 37 boys were admitted in bridge course. GSS volunteers motivated parents and arranged to get disability certificate for 29 children. 6 boys and 4 girls were freed from child labour, now they are enrolled in schools. GSS organized training of members of education and health committee of villages in which 42 male and 7 female participated. Parent Teacher Association training programme was organized in which 194 male and 26 female ways and means to improve the education standard. GSS organized orientation programme for the head masters and teachers of the project area, emergency assistance materials were issued in 48 schools. An Anganwadi Kendra was constructed and handed over to Bal Adhikar Suraksha Samiti in Barhai with the assistance of M.P. government.

6

Strategic Intervention by Gram Sudhar Samiti on Right to Food

Sidhi District is a reflection of proud history of the state of Madhya Pradesh. It makes the North-eastern boundary of the state. Sidhi district is a repository of natural, historical and cultural history. This district is known for luxuriant natural resources with the river Sone draining the district.

On one side the spectrum of its floristic socio-cultural diversity and ethnic history of tribal, the district has a panoramic view of the Kaimur, Kehejua and Ranimunda hills blazing with flowers of flame of forest and intoxicated by the sweet smell of mahua flowers.

Blocks

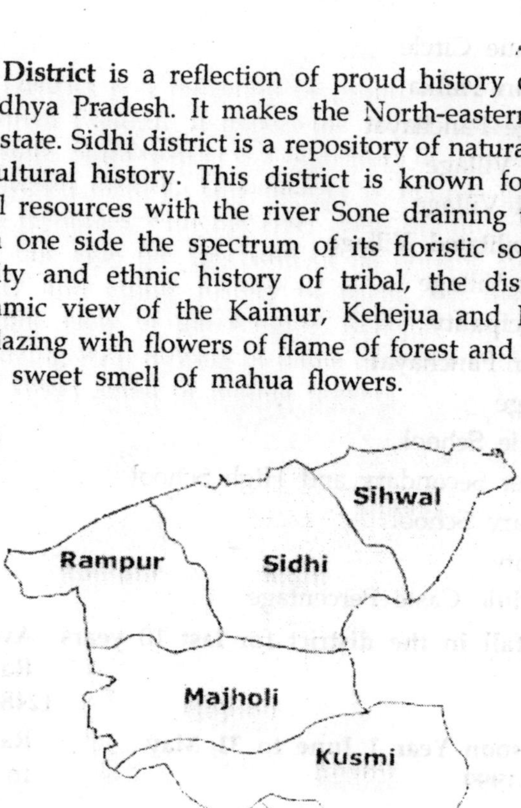

General information of district Sidhi (as per the district Hand Book

1.	Population	910983 (2001)
	a. Tribal Population	351660 (2001)
2.	Geographical Area	10536 Sq.Km.
3.	Sex Ratio	923
4.	Sub-Division	03
5.	Legislative Parliament Area	01
6.	Legislative Assembly Area	04
7.	Block/ Janpad Panchayat	05
8.	Tribal Block	01
9.	Tehsil	06
10.	Revenue Circle	12
11.	Patwari Halka	186
12.	Village Panchayat	402
13.	Totāl Village	1024
14.	Forest Village	1
15.	Rehabilitated Village	992
16.	Viran Village	32
17.	Municipality	01
19.	Nagar Panchayat	02
20.	College	7
21.	Middle School	257
22.	Higher Secondary and High School	100
23.	Primary School	1350
24.	Density	130
25.	Schedule Caste Percentage	11.9
26.	**Rainfall in the district for last 10 years**	**Average Rainfall 1248.3mm**
	Monsoon Year 1 June to 31 May	**Rainfall in m.m.**
	1998-1999	**0922.3**

1998 - 1999	0922.3
1999 - 2000	1182.4
2000 - 2001	1093.2
2001 - 2002	1246.8
2002 - 2003	0842.7
2003 - 2004	1397.7
2004 - 2005	0864.8
2005 - 2006	0982.2
2006 - 2007	1014.7
2007 - 2008	0661.2

Location

On the Northern boundary of the district lies Mirjapur district of Uttar Pradesh : Sarguja in south; Rewa on the west and touches Sonebhadra district of Uttar Pradesh.

Geographic Background

Sidhi district is located on the North-eastern Boundary of the state between 22", 47" 5" and 24.42" 10" North Latitude and 81:18"40 and 82"48"30 East longitude

Sidhi District is one of the four district of Rewa Division in Madhya Pradesh. Sidhi is also known as penultimate North-eastern frontier of the state. Sidhi district is situated approximately 632 km. from the state capital Bhopal and 80 km. from Divisional Head Office. The district stretched between 155 km. from East to West and 95 km. from North to South. The total geographic area covers 4,854 sq. km.

Population

Sidhi District has a total population of 910983 sharing almost 3.03%of the total population of erstwhile state of Madhya Pradesh (2001).

Total Schedule Castes population is 11.9% while 29.9% are tribal.

Male literacy rate is 67.4% and female literacy is as 36.0% as per 2001 figures.

Tehsil wise Population of the District Sidhi (2001)

S. No.	*Name of Tehsil*	*Total Area in Sq. kn.*	*Total Population*
1.	Gopad Banas	845.11	232028
2.	Churhat	309.63	102090
3.	Rampur Naikin	645.67	166478
4.	Majhauli	724.23	128893
5.	Kusmi	1448.37	65108
6.	Sihawal	744.74	216386
	Total	4717.75	910983

Indicators of the District Sidhi

1.	% of the girls married below 18 years	68.80 (2000)
2.	Birth order 3 and above	59.20
3.	% of current users of family planning	29.50
4.	Complete antenatal Care	2.50
5.	Safe Delivery	10.40
6.	Complete Immunization	40.80
7.	Female Literacy	13.61
8.	Coverage of safe drinking water	79.23
9.	% of village not connected by Pakka road	21.53
10.	Infant Mortality Rate (q2p)	136
	i. Infant Mortality Rate Male q2 (m)	133
	ii. Infant Mortality Rate Female q2 (f)	138*
11.	Gender Difference in Infant Mortality Rate	5(1991)
	q2 (f) - q2 (m)	16.50
12.	Sex Ratio	16.50
13.	Nutrition Grade of Children below 6 years (Grade I, II, III and IV)	34.62 (1998-99)
	Composite Index	27.61

Health Profile

Death Rate	11.2
Infant Mortality Rate	110
MMR	1110
Fertility Rate	4.3
Growth Rate	3.86
Birth Rate	38.2
Unmet Need for Contraception	25.1
Woman Receiving ANC Care	17.0
Woman Receiving full ANC Care	2.5
Female with RTI/STI Symptoms	35.8
Male with RTI/STI Symptoms	16.9
Female Literacy	56(2000)

No. of Blocks	Distt. Hospitals	CHCs	PHCs	SHCs
05	01	06	23	145

National Rural Employment Guarantee Act in Sidhi

NREGA Statistics
District : SIDHI

Emp. provided to households:	1.9824 Lakh
Person days [in Lakh]:	
Total:	104.48
SCs:	22.98 [21.99%]
STs:	39.7 [38%]
Women:	39.77 [38.06%]
Others:	41.8 [40.01%]
Total fund: Rs.	147.58 Crore.
Expenditure:	158.85 Crore.
Total works:	9573
Works completed:	1365
Works in progress:	8208

NREGA Statistics
State : MADHYA PRADESH

Employment provided to households:	23.68012 Lakhs
Person days [in Lakh]:	
Total:	932.48
SCs:	167.71 [17.99%]
STs:	421.07 [45.16%]
Women:	379.39 [40.69%]
Others:	343.7 [36.86%]
Total fund:	2361.97 Crore.
Expenditure:	1269.54 Crore.
Total works taken up:	367303
Works completed:	57427
Works in progress:	309876

Strategic Intervention by Gram Sudhar Samiti (GSS) on Right to Food

Gram Sudhar Samiti has been involved in undertaking rights based internventions to ensure effective delivery of government programmes. Considering the severity of problems linked with efficient delivery mechanism, GSS worked out on plan to work on right to food considering the need and objective of programme Sir Dorabji Tata Trust offered assistance to implement the programme. The programme was planned to solve problems related with malfunctioning of delivery system. GSS selected 70 villages under Right to Food programme for the effective access among villages. After working for six months, it increased its access in all the villages. GSS organised participatory rural appraisal (PRA) in all the selected villages to find out problem and its solution through the community members.

Vilages Selected under Right to Food Programme in the First Six Months

S. No.	*Village*	*Panchayat*	*Block*
1.	Chamradol	Chamradol	Majhauli
2.	Bodari	Bodari	Majhauli
3.	Semariha	Semariha	Majhauli
4.	Karmai	Karmai	Majhauli
5.	Naurhia	Nauriha	Majhauli
6.	Khamchaura	Khamchaura	Majhauli
7.	Deem	Khamchaura	Majhauli
8.	Pond	Pond	Majhauli
9.	Garaur	Pond	Majhauli
10.	Jamua 1	Jamua 1	Majhauli
11.	Kolgarh	Jamua 1	Majhauli
12.	Paniha	Paniha	Majhauli
13.	Gijwar	Gijwar	Majhauli
14.	Pathraula	Pathraula	Majhauli
15.	Gangiai	Murheria	Majhauli
16.	Gajri	Gajri	Majhauli
17.	Barseni	Naro	Majhauli
18.	Naro	Naro	Majhauli
19.	Dariya	Dariya	Majhauli
20.	Lohjhar	Dariya	Majhauli
21.	Nachin Mahua	Dariya	Majhauli
22.	Kochila	Kochila	Sidhi
23.	Andharigadai	Kochila	Sidhi
24.	Sendura	Sendura	Sidhi
25.	Uraisa	Uraisa	Sidhi

S. No.	Village	Panchayat	Block
26.	Khamh	Khamh	Sidhi
27.	Barhai	Barhai	Sidhi
28.	Ghusmunia	Barhai	Sidhi
29.	Barmani	Barmani	Sidhi
30.	Rausar	Barmani	Sidhi
31.	Bhagohar	Bhagohar	Sidhi
32.	Sukhi	Bhagohar	Sidhi
33.	Badera	Bhagohar	Sidhi
34.	Murkuda	Bhagohar	Sidhi
35.	Thengarahi	Bhagohar	Sidhi
36.	Bareraha	Dol	Sidhi
37.	Dol	Dol	Sidhi
38.	Piprahi	Piprahi	Kusumi
39.	Baheradol	Piprahi	Kusumi
40.	Majra	Bastua	Kusumi
41.	Bastua	Bastua	Kusumi
42.	Ramgarh	Bastua	Kusumi
43.	Pondi	Pondi	Kusumi
44.	Kota	Kota	Kusumi
45.	Khairi	Khairi	Kusumi
46.	Haiki	Khairi	Kusumi
47.	Pankhora	Khairi	Kusumi
48.	Gijohar	Khairi	Kusumi
49.	Dadri	Dadri	Kusumi
50.	Harraha	Dadri	Kusumi
51.	Nagpokhar	Dadri	Kusumi
52.	Naganna	Dadri	Kusumi
53.	Hardi	Hardi	Kusumi

S. No.	Village	Panchayat	Block
54.	Lurghuti 1	Lurghuti 1	Kusumi
55.	Lurghuti 2	Lurghuti 2	Kusumi
56.	Saidol	Lurghuti 2	Kusumi
57.	Kudaur	Kudaur	Kusumi
58.	Amgaon	Amgaon	Kusumi
59.	Biraura	Amgaon	Kusumi
60.	Mavanagar	Amgaon	Kusumi
61.	Duhukaria	Amgaon	Kusumi
62.	Kamachchh	KamachchhKusumi	
63.	Karauti	KamachchhKusumi	
64.	Medra	Medra	Kusumi
65.	Dhupkhad	Dhupkhad	Kusumi
66.	Tharhipathar	Tharhipathar	Kusumi
67.	Duari	Duari	Kusumi
68.	Gajar	Gajar	Kusumi
69.	Tiliya	Gajar	Kusumi
70.	Tirchuli	Gajar	Kusumi
71.	Ledgarh	Gajar	Kusumi

Village Selected after Six Months

S. No.	Village	Panchayat	Block
1.	Barkadol	Podi	Majhauli
2.	Sendhwa	Sendhwa	Majhauli
3.	Kotro	Sendhwa	Majhauli
4.	Parsili	Parsili	Majhauli
5.	Chunguna	Parsili	Majhauli

S. No.	Village	Panchayat	Block
6.	Ghonghi	Naurhia	Majhauli
7.	Pondaratal	Khamchaura	Majhauli
8.	Dhanauli	Dhanauli	Majhauli
9.	Silwar	Silwar	Majhauli
10.	Sulkhan	Silwar	Majhauli
11.	Dudhmania	Silwar	Majhauli
12.	Dhaniganwa	Patharaula	Majhauli
13.	Sahijanaha	Sahijanaha	Majhauli
14.	Charwa	Dewai	Majhauli
15.	Rupaidol	Tilwari	Majhauli
16.	Kundintola	Dariya	Majhauli
17.	Kudaria	Piprahi	Kusumi
18.	Korwahi	Piprahi	Kusumi
19.	Matkhania	Bastua	Kusumi
20.	Sarsaidol	Kundaur	Kusumi
21.	Dharamduari	Karhipathar	Kusumi
22.	Sajadol	Tarhipathar	Kusumi
23.	Tala	Gajar	Kusumi
24.	Medhaki	Bastua	Kusumi
25.	Chhirhat	Doal	Kusumi
26.	Barmani	Barmani	Kusumi
27.	Tilwari	Tilwari	Kusumi
28.	Dhanigawa	Pathraula	Kusumi
29.	Amjhar	Gajri	Kusumi

Block-wise Information of 100 Village Adopted Under Right to Food Programme

Sl. No.	*Block*	*No. of villages*	*No. of families*	*Total population*	*Male*	*Female*	*S.T.*	*S.C.*	*Others*	*BPL*	*Antyodaya Cardholder*
1	2	3	4	5	6	7	8	9	10	11	12
1.	Sidhi	17	3655	15775	7991	7784	11820	846	3109	2333	697
2.	Majhauli	39	12017	48146	24689	23457	20745	3775	23626	6225	2113
3.	Kusumi	44	5075	23664	11955	11709	15991	1270	6403	2729	759
	Total	100	20747	87585	44635	42950	48556	5891	33138	11287	3569

Primary Information about Selected Villages of Kusumi Block

Sl. No.	Name of the village	Name of village panchayat	No. of families	Population							BPL Families	
				Female	Male	S.T.	S.C.	OBC	General	Total	BPL	Antyodaya
1.	Haiki	Khairi	185	185	194	231	0	96	52	379	77	10
2.	Khairi	Khairi	226	326	382	132	258	303	15	708	77	20
3.	Karauti	Kamachh	235	371	340	537	22	117	35	711	85	9
4.	Tilaya	Gajar	45	88	96	151	0	27	6	184	25	3
5.	Navanagar	Amgaon	101	162	186	343	2	3	0	348	38	10
6.	Vidaura	Amgaon	80	136	138	237	15	0	22	274	34	15
7.	Podi	Podi	423	827	845	1049	113	446	64	1672	90	27
8.	Amgaon	Amgaon	103	306	282	376	7	169	36	588	21	20
9.	Kamachh	Kamachh	189	272	338	477	27	33	73	610	67	17
10.	Kota	Kota	337	619	608	345	58	795	29	1227	75	28
11.	Duhakuria	Amgaon	94	179	172	318	5	28	0	351	38	10
12.	Kundaur	Kundaur	312	751	736	1155	74	210	48	1487	25	147
13.	Saidol	Lurghuti 2	28	49	51	100	0	0	0	100	9	6
14.	Taal	Gajar	102	225	221	375	0	71	0	446	74	21
15.	Piparaha	Dadri	52	161	184	305	0	40	0	345	43	10

(Contd.)

Sl. No.	Name of the village	Name of village panchayat	No. of families	Population							BPL Families	
				Female	Male	S.T.	S.C.	OBC	General	Total	BPL	Antyodaya
16.	Hardi	Hardi	95	428	433	698	110	41	12	861	138	33
17.	Naganna	Dadri	34	47	63	110	0	0	0	110	2	2
18.	Dadri	Dadri	78	244	278	384	24	101	13	522	42	-
19.	Nagpokhar	Dadri	65	269	269	460	14	66	0	540	44	20
20.	Lurghuti 1	Lurghuti	187	395	382	404	78	150	145	777	114	-
21.	Lurghuti 2	Lurghuti	185	359	379	607	0	77	54	738	111	14
22.	Narraha	Dadri	36	63	66	115	0	14	0	129	10	6
23.	Medhaki	Bastua	76	114	138	4	0	236	12	252	58	-
24.	Matkhania	Bastua	51	66	72	81	0	18	39	138	22	1
25.	Bastua	Bastua	224	400	429	562	18	205	44	829	107	-
26.	Ramgarh	Bastua	150	335	338	267	43	346	17	673	102	3
27.	Madra	Madra				1252	116	253	5	1626	53	38
28.	Ladgarh	Ladgarh				121	0	10	3	134	32	
29.	Tirchuli	Tirchuli				67	0	5	4	76	2	
30.	Tala	Tala				126	0	6	0	132	5	22
31.	Gajar	Gajar				372	71	120	37	600	12	

(Contd.)

Sl. No.	Name of the village	Name of village Panchayat	No. of families	Population							BPL Families	
				Female	Male	S.T.	S.C.	OBC	General	Total	BPL	Antyodaya
32.	Naurhia	Naurhia				433		24		457	1	16
33.	Duari	Duari				846	5	124		975	112	36
34.	Tharipathar	Tharipathar				926	43	55		1024	9	15
35.	Dharam-dauri	Dharamdauri				80		105		185	17	8
36.	Sajadol	Sajadol				286	3	45		334	19	
37.	Dhupkhad	Dhupkhad				1378	42	39	5	1464	169	40
39.	Karwahi	Karwahi	36	94	82	155				155	19	
40.	Magra	Magra	29	42	47	3		86		89	14	
41.	Baheradol	Baheradol	114	320	287	166	50	200	191	607	38	40
42.	Kuduria	Kuduria	58	111	134			224	21	245	11	
43.	Pankhora	Khairi	45	81	88	169				169		
44.	Gigohar	Khairi	50	73	76	121		28		149	50	36

Majhauli Block

Sl. No.	Name of village	No. of families	Total population	Male	Female	S.T.	S.C.	Others	BPL families	Antyodaya
1	2	3	4	5	6	7	8	9	10	11
1.	Rupaidol	132	527	281	246	235	0	292	84	20
2.	Tilwari	327	1310	661	649	576	113	621	130	18
3.	Chorba	223	810	396	414	560	41	209	74	1
4.	Sahijanaha	495	1962	987	975	346	240	1376	312	48
5.	Kogarh	122	487	251	236	162	0	325	36	10
6.	Poniha	243	973	495	478	140	55	778	92	14
7.	Gangai	279	1090	575	515	235	181	674	212	34
8.	Jamua 1	508	2032	1049	983	345	64	1623	73	14
9.	Dhangaona	129	518	263	255	53	0	465	68	11
10.	Patharawh	384	1535	753	782	123	0	1412	312	45
11.	Budhmania	49	198	106	92	181	0	17	43	11
12.	Sulkhan	58	224	118	106	126	33	65	38	5
13.	Silvar	675	2500	1334	1166	661	76	1763	524	104

(Contd.)

Sl. No.	Name of village	No. of families	Total population	Male	Female	S.T.	S.C.	Others	BPL families	Antyodaya
1	2	3	4	5	6	7	8	9	10	11
14.	Gijwar	1045	4154	2120	2034	1885	297	1972	654	68
15.	Naro	324	1215	608	607	242	52	921	113	34
16.	Barsehi	366	1382	720	662	777	247	358	98	6
17.	Daria	255	961	483	478	621	8	332	220	20
18.	Lohjhar	171	636	318	318	380	126	130	94	14
19.	Nachani Mahua	129	471	250	221	421	38	12	115	10
	Total	5914	22985	11768	11217	8068	1571	13345	3202	487

1. Amjhar	162	376	432	808	219	243	462	37	41	78	276	77	45
2. Ganjari	448	1558	1633	3191	876	915	1791	123	119	242	1158	458	136
3. Sendhwa	307	597	630	1227	423	445	868	25	27	52	307	26	70
4. Kotri	118	233	238	471	118	132	250	37	30	67	154	25	6
5. Dhanuwli	488	948	1004	1952	58	66	124	71	97	168	1660	277	54
6. Khamchaori	287	408	452	860	156	174	330	43	58	101	429	159	111
7. Deem	83	164	168	332	110	104	214	25	29	54	64	62	80
8. Pond	702	1365	1441	2806	368	373	741	151	187	338	1727	500	132
9. Semrha	178	330	378	708	203	226	429	27	28	55	224	42	40
10. Bodari	346	651	729	1380	339	355	694	72	98	170	516	102	70
11. Chamradol	357	866	919	1785	544	549	1093	85	99	184	508	25	281
12. Parsili	275	552	548	1100	329	330	659	41	52	93	348	268	97
13. Chunguna	182	459	453	912	318	298	616	28	33	61	235	82	29
14. Naurhia	568	1439	1399	2838	742	709	1451	165	150	311	1076	339	108
15. Karmai	651	1250	1354	2604	888	959	1847	89	89	178	579	307	154
16. Ghonghi	62	106	135	241	36	52	88	8	21	29	124	51	16

17.	Shankarpur	37	70	76	146	0	0	0	13	6	19	127	25	13
18.	Madra Taal	41	74	86	160	61	74	135	-	-	-	25	17	38
19.	Dadaur	203	388	422	810	171	178	349	2	2	4	457	116	21
20.	Barkadol	208	406	424	830	266	277	543	-	-	-	287	65	125
	Total	5703	12240	12921	25161	6225	6459	12684	1042	1166	2204	10281	3023	1626

Sidhi Block

Sl. No.	*Name of village*	*No. of families*	*Total population*	*Male*	*Female*	*S.T.*	*S.C.*	*Others*	*BPL families*	*Antyodaya*
1	2	3	4	5	6	7	8	9	10	11
1.	Dol Kothar	833	423	410	512	12	309	160	25	235
2.	Baheraha	1301	628	673	859	268	174	174	26	256
3.	Chhirhar	299	146	153	296	-	3	150	35	135
4.	Gochila	2185	1103	1082	1942	81	162	369	47	396
5.	Anddarigarh	535	251	284	461	27	47	133	100	133

Sl. No.	Name of village	No. of families	Total population	Male	Female	S.T.	S.C.	Others	BPL families	Antyodaya
1	2	3	4	5	6	7	8	9	10	11
6.	Sendura	1205	595	610	894	65	246	162	60	257
7.	Bhajohar	616	298	318	287	58	271	74	17	112
8.	Sukhi	636	302	334	577	-	59	125	22	119
9.	Badera	643	295	348	502	108	33	90	18	127
10.	Murkuda	448	228	220	408	-	40	68	15	97
11.	Thegarhi	661	324	337	386	63	212	87	15	129
12.	Barmani	1042	549	493	880	36	126	206	80	372
13.	Rausar	408	204	204	403	-	5	77	26	88
14.	Barhoi	1007	481	526	852	11	144	146	25	247
15.	Ghosmunia	667	349	318	621	-	46	101	18	162
16.	Khamh	1884	924	960	893	72	919	36	130	410
17.	Udaisa	1405	684	721	1047	45	313	175	38	380
	Total	15775	7784	7991	11820	846	3109	2333	697	3655

Allocation of Responsibilities

Programme functionaries have been assigned responsibilites according to the objectives and operational areas.

Programme Director : Programme director is working as leader of the programme and is responsible for the efficient and effective management of all the activities of the programme. He is responsible for the organisation of training programmes, workshop, public hearing and capacity building exercises. His responsibilities include preparation of monthly plan, budget and monitoring of the programme.

Programme Coordinator: The programme coordinator works in all 100 villages of Sidhi, Majhauli and Kusumi Tehsils of Sidhi district with the cooperation of supervisor and gramdoot. His responsibility includes coordination among community workers, gramdoot and supervisor, increase in the level of understanding among team members, inspiration of team members to achieve programme objectives. He works on the creation of pressure for the solution of problems linked with functioning of government departments with the strong relationship with media, people's elected representatives and follow-up with government departments. Programme area is divided between two sectors comprising of Sidhi and Majhauli in one sector of Kusumi in another sector. Programme coordinator devotes comensurate time in both the sectors and work on the documentation, media relation, reporting, submission of bills and vouchers in accounts department. He works with programme director in the programme planning, meeting of volunteers, strengthening of team work, advocacy of cases, and preparation of monthly progress and financial reports.

Supervisor : There are two supervisors to looks after 44 villages of Kusumi while another looks 56 villages of Sidhi and Majhauli blocks. These supervisors spent 25-26 days in the field. Their responsibility includes meeting with gramdoot, follow up with the help of community workers participation in programmes being organised in the respective sectors.

Supervisor participate in the quarterly meeting organised at Panchayat level in which gramdoot of different villages participate to enlist the progress of activities, preparation of case studies reporting and documentation.

Community Workers : Work area of community workers is distributed on the basis of geographic and social conditions. Area, which falls under deep forest with no transport and road connectivity, has 11 villages under a worker while a community worker looks after 19-20 villages under Sidhi and Majhauli blocks. A community worker works as link between Gramdoot and programme coordinator.

Gramdoot (Village level functionaries) : Gramdoot work as assistant to community workers in the organisation of different activities. Responsibility of a gramdoot includes investigation of problems, search of evidence, promotion of voluntary efforts among youths, advocacy of cases of denial of entitlements and community organisation.

Challenges during programme implementation :

1. Access and rapport building in the village which are away from road and transport connectivity is difficult. There is always danger in the forest villages due to wild animals.
2. Due to social factors, it is difficult to penetrate into home and form women groups.
3. Due to lower level of literacy, volunteers found it difficult to increase the awareness on right issues.
4. Considering wide gap between poor and rich in project area, there has been reports of diversion of benefits from poor to rich. Holding grip on rich villagers is difficult and risk taking exercise.
5. Those who are misappropriating the benefits always create environment against volunteers and have at many occassions tried to disrupt the programme activities. Despite all these odds volunteers are involved in undertaking various activities.
6. Due to poor accessibility and lack of irregular contact, volunteers found difficulty in raising the level of confidence.

7. GSS has developed leadership attributes among villagers and they are improving their image in the community, which, at few occassions, is perceived in negativity by the people's elected representatives.
8. Village hamlets are far away from each other, due to which presence in meetings or programme activities was very less. Sometimes volunteers have to cancel or postpone the meeting.
9. Poor literacy among scheduled tribes forced GSS volunteers to adopt various strategies to communicate on right to food.
10. The process of social change is very slow and S.T. community react very slow on any change, be it in their favour.

Progress Under Right to Food Programme

Right to food programme is being implemented in Sidhi, Majhauli and Kusumi block of Sidhi district. Due to continuous effort being done by the volunteers of GSS, social change is taking place and the community is raising voice for their entitlement. Following is the achievement of GSS under right to food programme :

1. Application filed for inclusion of name in the BPL: 856.
2. Award of social security pension to 374.
3. Issue of ration card: 758.
4. Application filed for job card under NREGA: 964.
5. Job card issued to villagers: 837.
6. Application filed for the issuance of card under Pt. Deen Dayal Upadhyay Scheme: 671.
7. Card issued to: 563.
8. Opening of closed schools: 13
9. Application for the improvement in mid-day meal (MDM): 84.
10. Mid-day meal improved in the schools: 79.
11. Application filed for the functioning of parent-teacher association: 43.

12. Application filed to issue BPL card under public distribution system: 278.
13. Complaint filed for opening of PDS shop: 27.
14. Complaint filed for the allotment of ration as per norms: 35.
15. Application filed for the timely release of pension under National Family Assistance Scheme.
16. Application filed for inclusion of name under pension: 57.
17. Efforts made for the arrangement of building for Anganwadi centre: 16.
18. Efforts made for the maintenance of Anganwadi Centre: 11.
19. Application filed for the regular functioning of Anganwadi Centre: 17.
20. Application filed for the timely release of nutritious material under ICDS: 14.

7

Management of Right to Food Programme

Programme Management at Gram Sudhar Samiti

Selection of Villages : GSS adopted following criteria for the selection of villages under the programme :

(i) Villages which were far long from block and district headquarter.
(ii) Villages with maximum number of S.T. families.
(iii) Villages where public delivery system was weak.
(iv) Villages with poor infrastructure and transport connectivity.
(v) Villages where youths expressed desired to work as volunteers.

GSS volunteers selected total 100 villages consisting of 44 from Kusumi, 39 from Majhauli and 17 from Sidhi. Volunteers visited villages, met with villagers and chalked out strategies to implement programme. During the meeting, applications were invited to work as Gram Doot (village volunteers) and supervisor. GSS received total 56 applications from youths to work on strategy. A selection committee comprising of experts, people's elected representatives and functionaries of GSS selected village volunteers.

Meeting with Programme Functionaries

After selection of volunteers, GSS organised a sensitisation meeting, volunteers were informed on various aspects of programme and strategies to work in favour of deprived section of society. Volunteers were informed on the programme strategy and various welfare schemes which are being handled by Panchayats like ICDS, Mid-Day Meal, NREGA, etc. Volunteers were informed about the orders passed by Supreme Court.

Survey Work : A questionnaire was developed by the staff and volunteers were informed about the methodology to conduct survey and to complete the questionnaire. 7 villages were selected on pilot basis to assess whether survey work was compled in 100 villages with the help of gramdoot, supervisor and other project staff of Gram Sudhar Samiti (GSS). A master plan was prepared on the basis of information collected through the survey work. GSS volunteers worked to chalk out the strategic intervention under Right to Food Programme. The information collected through the survey helped in assessing the level of effectiveness of delivery mechanism.

Establishment of Right Counselling Centres : GSS established 50 Rights Counselling Centres on the basis of consultation through community. The objectives of these centres are as follows :

- *(i)* To inform community about different programmes.
- *(ii)* To make available different forms of schemes of benefits to rural community.
- *(iii)* To work with villagers on filing an application under Right to Information Act.
- *(iv)* To ensure free availability of stationary etc. to villagers for easy filing of cases.
- *(v)* To work on advocacy of cases in favour of S.T. community.

There are 20 counselling centres in Majhauli, 20 in Sidhi and 22 in Kusumi block. These centres facilitated villagers to file cases and submit application forms for effective delivery of government programmes in their village.

Group Information : GSS formed groups of poor, deprived and victims of exploitation eligible to get benefits of different programmes. It constituted 16 women groups in the name of 'Mahila Adhikar Manch' and 90 male groups in the name of 'Dalit-Adivasi Mahapanchayat'. These groups are playing pivotal role in ensuring effective delivery of government programmes at village level. These groups are investigating individual cases of exploitation and harassment and reporting it to GSS volunteers. These cases are being advocated in favour of the deprived community. GSS volunteers work with groups in the problem solving from village level to district level.

Programme Strategy: GSS adopted following strategy for successful implementation of the programme :

(i) *Cycle Rally* : Gram Doot, supervisors and members of counselling centres and groups organised a cycle rally from village Uraisa in Ledripar Panchayat to Naro Panchayat covering 17 panchayats. Participants in the rally worked on awareness generation through street plays. A workshop was also organised in which people's elected representatives, group members and GSS volunteers expressed their views and formulated a work plan to implement the right to food programme. The rally helped in the enhancement of knowledge level of community members to ask for their entitlements.

Training Programme on Capacity Building of Volunteers : A 3 days training programme was organised at Regional Training Centre, Ghordand by GSS under Right to Food programme. Gramdoot, supervisor and other staff members of GSS participated in training programme. Experts from academic and development field delivered lectures on different aspects of rights based activities. Training was imparted on the development of leadership among community members, group formation and organisation, reporting and documentation, strategic intervention for social change and other relevant issues.

A group discussion was organised in which trainees were asked to present their views on given topic with reference to Right to Food. Participants prepared their cases and discussed with others to compile suggestions from co-participants. The training programme was organised from 6 to 9 July, 2007.

The taining programme helped in the successful formation of groups and effective advocacy of different cases. Group meetings are being organised continuously and volunteers are reporting and documenting all the cases effectively.

Training Programme for group members under progress.

Wall Writing

GSS found wall writing as sound medium of rural communication. Volunteers worked on mass level for slogan

writing on different schemes like mid-day meal, NREGA slogans on Right to Information Act, orders of hon'ble Superme Court are written on walls nearby road. This exercise helps in the creation of environment for the awareness generation on Right to Food. The slogan facilitated in the efficient group formation.

Mass Demonstration

GSS organised mass demonstration programme on 10 August, 2007 at Majhauli Tehsil in which villagers from all the select villages participated and submitted a 10 point charter of demands to collector, Sidhi with a copy to chief minister Madhya Pradesh and honourable high court Madhya Pradesh. Members of Mahila Adhikar Manch and Dalit Adivasi Mahapanchayat worked effectively in the organisation of demonstration. The demonstration helped in the making of synergy of efforts to work more radically for the entitlement of poor community.

In search of solution through mass demonstration.

Poster and Pumplet Distribution

GSS printed three posters : one on Right to Food, second on orders of Supreme Court and the third on Right to Information Act. Posters were distributed among villagers for spread of information. Information on right of entitlements, benefits under NREGA, etc. This helped in the capacity building of common man and they are raising their demands.

Street Play

GSS organised street plays in different villages to spread strong message to rural communities about different schemes, irregularities and struggle towards their rights. GSS developed a street play alongwith Swabhiman Kala Natya Samiti, Sidhi which organised street plays in all villages. In fact, the community which was not capable of reading the slogan or poster liked it and promised to fight for their rights.

A street play under progress.

Mass gathering to learn through street play.

Detail of Street Plays Organised

Sidhi Block

Sl. No.	*Name of village*	*Name of Block*	*Date*	*No. of Villagers*
1.	Barhai	Sidhi	27.04.07	150
2.	Barmani	Sidhi	27.04.07	90
3.	Ghumunia	Sidhi	27.04.07	110
4.	Uraisa	Sidhi	27.04.07	122
5.	Ledripar	Sidhi	27.04.07	88
6.	Sendura	Sidhi	27.04.07	60
7.	Kochila	Sidhi	27.04.07	55
8.	Andhigorai	Sidhi	30.04.07	80
9.	Dol	Sidhi	30.04.07	122
10.	Dolkothar	Sidhi	30.04.07	60
11.	Baheraha	Sidhi	01.05.07	90
12.	Jhirhat	Sidhi	01.05.07	75

Majhauli Block

Sl. No.	Name of village	Name of Block	Date	No. of Villagers
1.	Naro	Majhauli	02.05.07	112
2.	Poniha	Majhauli	02.05.07	103
3.	Kolgarh	Majhauli	02.05.07	90
4.	Jamua 1	Majhauli	03.05.07	140
5.	Murharia	Majhauli	03.05.07	72
6.	Tilwari	Majhauli	03.05.07	95
7.	Pond	Majhauli	04.05.07	110
8.	Daraur	Majhauli	04.05.07	80
9.	Semariha	Majhauli	04.05.07	120
10.	Badari	Majhauli	05.05.07	108
11.	Chamradol	Majhauli	05.09.07	90
12.	Dodi	Majhauli	25.09.07	85
13.	Karmai	Majhauli	26.09.07	90
14.	Sedhwa	Majhauli	27.09.07	95
15.	Parsili	Majhauli	28.09.07	102
16.	Norhia	Majhauli	29.09.07	90
17.	Khamchaura	Majhauli	30.09.07	88
18.	Gijwar	Majhauli	01.10.07	118
19.	Pathraula	Majhauli	02.10.07	103
20.	Dariya	Majhauli	03.10.07	120
	Total			4210

Kusumi Block

Sl. No.	Name of village	Name of Block	Date	No. of Villagers
1.	Bastua	Kusumi	20.09.07	88
2.	Karwahi	Kusumi	20.09.07	65
3.	Piprahi	Kusumi	21.09.07	95
4.	Ramgarh	Kusumi	22.09.07	80
5.	Podi	Kusumi	23.09.07	90

Sl. No.	*Name of village*	*Name of Block*	*Date*	*No. of Villagers*
6.	Khairi	Kusumi	23.09.07	95
7.	Nagpokhar	Kusumi	24.09.07	80
8.	Hardi	Kusumi	24.09.07	65
9.	Kudaria	Kusumi	25.09.07	92
10.	Dadri	Kusumi	25.09.07	105
11.	Lurghuti	Kusumi	26.09.07	175
12.	Kundaur	Kusumi	26.09.07	110
13.	Amgaon	Kusumi	27.09.07	90
14.	NavanagarKusumi		27.09.07	85
15.	Duhukuria	Kusumi	28.09.07	105
16.	Karaunti	Kusumi	28.09.07	60
17.	Medra	Kusumi	29.09.07	125
18.	Duari	Kusumi	29.09.07.	103
19.	Dhari Pathar	Kusumi	30.09.07	70
20.	Gajar	Kusumi	30.09.07	65
21.	Ledgarh	Kusumi	01.10.07	82
22.	Tala	Kusumi	01.10.07	60
	Total			1985

Training on Group Empowerment

GSS organised a training programme on strengthening group activities and building confidence among them. Group members were informed on different strategies to fight for the right of entitlements under different government programmes at panchayat level. Training was conducted under the leardership of Vedanti Prasad Mishra and Awadh Raj Singh.

Training programme commenced with an organisational song and expectations of the participants. After assessing needs of participants, trainers informed trainees about strategies to formulate groups, creating an environment of group pressure, strategies of conflict resolution and financial management through saving.

A Training Programme for group Coordinators.

On-going training programmes

Detail of Training Programmes Organised by GSS

Sidhi Block

Sl. No.	*Date*	*Panchayat*	*Block*	*No. of participants*	*Other participants*
1.	22.09.07	Dol	Sidhi	35	6
2.	23.09.07	Kochila	Sidhi	28	7
3.	24.09.07	Sendura	Sidhi	15	5
4.	25.09.07	Uraisa	Sidhi	20	4
5.	26.09.07	Bhagohar	Sidhi	25	12
6.	27.09.07	Barmani	Sidhi	35	9
7.	28.09.07	Barhai	Sidhi	40	13
		Total		198	58

Kusumi Block

Sl. No.	*Date*	*Panchayat*	*Block*	*No. of participants*	*Other participants*
1.	24.09.07	Lurghuti	Kusumi	45	25
2.	25.09.07	Kundaur	Kusumi	25	17
3.	26.09.07	Amgaon	Kusumi	32	15
4.	27.09.07	Mendara	Kusumi	38	9
5.	28.9.07	Bastua	Kusumi	42	12
6.	29.09.07	Ledgarh	Kusumi	25	10
7.	30.09.07	Khairi	Kusumi	35	18
8.	01.10.07	Piprahi	Kusumi	35	12
9.	02.10.07	Podi	Kusumi	30	16
10.	03.10.07	Dadri	Kusumi	35	15
11.	04.10.07	Hardi	Kusumi	25	14
12.	05.10.07	Kamachh	Kusumi	25	11
13.	06.10.07	Thadipathar	Kusumi	28	15
14.	07.10.07	Doari	Kusumi	22	16
15.	08.10.07	Gajar	Kusumi	26	14
			Total	464	219

Majhauli

Sl. No.	*Date*	*Panchayat*	*Block*	*No. of participants*	*Other participants*
1.	26.09.07	Naro	Majhauli	45	25
2.	27.09.07	Paniha	Majhauli	35	23
3.	28.09.07	Jamua 1	Majhauli	25	32
4.	29.09.07	Gijwar	Majhauli	13	28
5.	30.09.07	Silwar	Majhauli	28	19
			Total	146	127

Training on NREGA and Right to Information Act

GSS organised two days training programme on 10-11 October, 2007 in which 29 participants from Right to Food programme participated at Regional Training Centre, Ghordand. Trainer Arvind Shukla, Senior Advocate informed on different provisions of these acts and process to file an application under Right to Information Act. He lamented on the provision of appeal and imposition of fine under the act.

Trainer Kedar Rajak informed participants on different provisions under NREGA. He told participants on the site selection, wage rate, monitoring and evaluation of work so that trainees could learn from planning to implementation.

Publication of Booklet Titled,"Our Rights"

GSS published above booklet to inform villagers on different provisions of government programmes. The booklet was distributed among villagers of all panchayats. The booklet comprised of relevant rules and regulations of different programmes. Now, equipped with knowledge on different provisions of programme, villagers are asking for their rights.

Publication of Booklet on Rights of Dalits and Scheduled Tribes

GSS published 2000 copies of this booklet to inform members of dalit and scheduled tribe about their rights and entitlements.

Workshop on Media Advocacy

Media plays significant role in the effective and transparent functioning of government delivery system. GSS organised one day media advocacy programme in Sidhi in which 28 correspondents and representatives of regional and national level print and electronic media participated and worked on a strategy to fight for the cause of rural poor towards right to food.

Media advocacy programme being organised.

District Level Public Hearing

GSS organised a public hearing at district headquarter Sidhi to address public grievances directly through the administration. 430 villagers from select villages participated and submitted their grievances to the present government authorities and people's elected representatives.

Large number of participants in public hearing.

On the Spot Redressal of Grievances

GSS organised on the spot redressal exercise of grievance of villagers pertaining to denial of their entitlement, apathetic and autocratic behaviour of government officials, syphoning of benefits, etc. Senior government officials and people's elected representatives instructed concerned departments and village level functionaries to correct the anamoly and work in favour of poor community.

Towards quick redressal of grievances.

Organisation of Baiga Mahapanchayat

Baiga tribe forms majority in the project villages. GSS promoted Dalit Adivasi Mahapanchayat which organised Baiga Mahapanchayat to enlist their problems and work a strategy to solve problems through public cooperation. It may be mentioned that Girdhari Lal Baiga has been treasurer of GSS in the past and based on his contribution he has been awarded with Godfrey Philips Bravery Award in social field. The programme was organised in Krishi Vigyan Kendra, Sidhi.

Girdhari Lal Baiga speaking in Baiga Mahapanchayat

Organisation of Group Coordinators Meet

GSS organised group coordinators meet to formulate implmentation strategy and discuss on the problems and

Meeting of group coordinators under progress.

solution of hurdles being faced by GSS volunteers at the village level.

Organisation of Panchayat Level Public Hearing

GSS organised panchayat level public hearing in all the

On going public hearing at panchayat level.

panchayats of three blocks to enlist the problems being faced by villagers in getting their entitlements. Matters were reported to the concerned departments and authorities and most of the cases were solved through this exercise.

Annexures

Annexures 1 : Honourable Supreme Court Orders on Right to Food Case

The Supreme Court Orders

So far, over fifty "interim orders" have been issued by the Supreme Court in the "right to food case" (PUCL vs. Union of India and others, Writ Petition [Civil] 196 of 2001). Many of these orders are of no consequence, e.g. adjournments or listings of dates for further hearings. The substantive orders are given below. This is the full text, without any change in wording. However, we did correct types and spelling mistakes, to improve readability.[1]

1. Text of the Order of 23rd July, 2001

Counsel for the petitioner is permitted to file a fresh application for interim relief. A copy of the same is given to the counsel for the Union of India as well as to the counsel for the States and for the Food Corporation of India. Learned Attorney General states that this should not be regarded as an adversarial litigation and it is a matter of concern for all. In our opinion, what is of utmost importance is to see that food is provided to the aged, infirm, disabled, destitute women, destitute men who are in danger of starvation, pregnant and lactating women and destitute children, especially in cases where they or members of their family do not have sufficient funds to provide food for them. In case of famine, there may be shortage of food, but here the situation is that amongst plenty there is scarcity. Plenty of food is available, but distribution of the same amongst the very poor and the destitute is scarce and non-existent leading to mal-nourishment, starvation and other related problems. Reply affidavits be filed within two weeks by the States and the Union of India as well as the Food Corporation of India.

In the meantime, we are sure that the responsible Governments will act for the benefit of their people. By way of an interim order, we direct the States to see that all the PDS shops, if closed, are re-opened and start functioning within one week from today and regular supplies made. Leave is granted to the petitioner to impaled other States also as parties to this petition. On such an application being filed today, notice to issue to them. List the matter for further consideration on 20th August, 2001.

2. Text of the Order of 20th August, 2001

The anxiety of the Court is to see that the poor and the destitute and the weaker sections of the society do not suffer from hunger and starvation. The prevention of the same is one of the prime responsibilities of the Government - whether Central or State. How this is to be ensured would be a matter of policy which is best left to the Government. All that the Court has to be satisfied and which it may have to ensure is that the foodgrains which are overflowing in the storage receptacles, especially the FCI godowns, and which are in abundance, should not be wasted by dumping into the sea or eaten by rats. Mere schemes without any implementation are of no use. What is important is that the food must reach the hungry.

3. Text of the Order of 3rd September, 2001

Issue notice to the Union of India as well as, in the first instance, to the States of Andhra Pradesh, Chhattisgarh, Gujarat, Himachal Pradesh, Karnataka, Maharashtra, Madhya

Pradesh, Orissa, Rajasthan and Kerala. Notice to serve through the standing counsel. Liberty is given to the petitioner to file a supplementary affidavit giving fresh suggestions after taking into consideration the affidavit of these states as well as the Union of India and the statutory order dated 31st August, 2001. Affidavit be filed within a week. Response to the application as well as to the additional affidavit be filed within a week thereafter. To come up on 17th September, 2001. Learned Attorney General brings to our notice that 16 States and Union Territories have not as yet identified the below poverty line families under the Antyodaya Anna Yojana. We direct these 16 States and Union Territories, namely, Arunachal Pradesh, Assam, Bihar, Delhi, Goa, Manipur, Nagaland, Orissa, Sikkim, Tamil Nadu, Tripura, Uttarakhand, West Bengal, Chandigarh, Lakshadweep and Pondicherry to comply with the Central Government's directions within two weeks from today and report compliance.

4. Text of the Order of 17th September, 2001

With reference to this Court's direction dated 3rd September, 2001 requiring 16 States & Union Territories who, according to the learned Attorney General, had not identified the below poverty line families under the Antyodaya Anna Yojana, to identify, we are not satisfied that any such exercise in the right earnestness has been undertaken. Some of the States mention that the exercise is underway. Considering the seriousness of the matter, one further opportunity is granted to these 16 States and Union Territories to comply with the Central Government's directions within three weeks and to inform the Central Government about the number of below poverty line families under the Antyodaya Anna Yojana which they have identified. Copies of the communication said by the said 16 States/Union Territories should also be forwarded to the Attorney General who will inform the Court on the next date of hearing whether compliance has been made or not.

In I.A. No. 8/2001 at pages 66-68, certain schemes of the

Central Government are mentioned which are required to be implemented by the State Governments. These schemes are : Employment Assurance Scheme which may have been replaced by a Sampurna Gramin Yojana, Mid-Day Meals Scheme, Integrated Child Development Service, National Benefit Maternity Scheme for BPL pregnant women, and National Old Age Pension Scheme for destitute persons of over 65 years, Annapurna Scheme, Antyodaya Anna Yojana, National Family Benefit Scheme and Public Distribution Scheme for BPL & APL families. The Chief Secretaries of all the States & the Union Territories are hereby directed to report to the Cabinet Secretary, with copy to the learned Attorney General, within three weeks from today with regard to the implementation of all or any of these Schemes with or without any modification and if all or any of the Schemes have not been implemented then the reasons for the same.

The Central Government shall collate all the facts and thereafter take necessary action in order to ensure the implementation of the said Schemes. A status report with regard thereto may be filed in Court within five weeks. Before giving the status report, the Central Government will also ascertain with regard to the actual implementation of the various Schemes. In the meantime, we direct all the State Governments to forthwith lift the entire allotment of food grains from the Central Government under the various Schemes and disburse the same in accordance with the schemes.

The Food for Work Programme in the scarcity areas should also be implemented by the various States to the extent possible. To come up on 5th November, 2001.

5. Text of the Order of 28th November, 2001

After hearing learned counsel for the parties, we issue, as an interim measure, the following directions :

1. *Targeted Public Distribution System (TPDS)*
   (i) It is the case of the Union of India that there has been full compliance with regard to the allotment

of food grain in relation to the TPDS. However, if any of the States gives a specific instance of non-compliance, the Union of India will do the needful within the framework of the Scheme.

(ii) The States are directed to complete the identification of BPL families, issuing of cards and commencement of distribution of 25 kgs. grain per family per month latest by 1st January, 2002.

(iii) The Delhi Govt. will ensure that TPDS application forms are freely available and are given and received free of charge and there is an effective mechanism in place to ensure speedy and effective redressal of grievances.

2. *Antyodaya Anna Yojana*

(i) It is the case of the Union of India that there has been full compliance with regard to the allotment of food grain in relation to Antyodaya Anna Yojana. However, if any of the States gives a specific instance of non-compliance, the Union of India will do the needful within the framework of the Scheme.

(ii) We direct the States and the Union Territories to complete identification of beneficiaries, issuing of cards and distribution of grain under this Scheme latest by 1st January, 2002.

(iii) It appears that some Antyodaya beneficiaries may be unable to lift grain because of penury. In such cases, the Centre, the States and the Union Territories are requested to consider giving the quota free after satisfying itself in this behalf.

3. *Mid-Day Meals Scheme (MDMS)*

(i) It is the case of the Union of India that there has been full compliance with regard to the Mid-Day Meal Scheme (MDMS). However, if any of the States gives a specific instance of non-compliance, the Union of India will do the needful within the framework of the Scheme.

(ii) We direct the State Governments/ Union Territories to implement the Mid-Day Meals Scheme by providing every child in every Government and Government assisted Primary Schools with a prepared Mid-Day meal with a minimum content of 300 calories and 8-12 grams of protein each day of school for a minimum of 200 days. Those Governments providing dry rations instead of cooked meals must within three months start providing cooked meals in all govt. and govt. aided primary schools in all half the Districts of the State (in order of poverty) and must within a further period of three months extend the provision of cooked meals to the remaining parts of the State.

(iii) We direct the Union of India and the FCI to ensure provision of fair average quality grain for the Scheme on time. The States/ Union Territories and the FCI are directed to do joint inspection of food grains. If the food grain is found, on joint inspection, not to be of fair average quality, it will be replaced by the FCI prior to lifting.

4. *National Old Age Pension Scheme (NOAPS)*

(i) It is the case of the Union of India that there has been full compliance with regard to the National Old Age Pension Scheme. However, if any of the States gives a specific instance of non-compliance, the Union of India will do the needful within the framework of the Scheme.

(ii) The States are directed to identify the beneficiaries and to start making payments latest by 1st January, 2002.

(iii) We direct the State Govts. / Union Territories to make payments promptly by the 7th of each month.

5. *Annapurna Scheme*

The States/ Union Territories are directed to identify the beneficiaries and distribute the grain latest by 1st January, 2002.

6. *Integrated Child Development Service (ICDS)*
   (i) We direct the State Govts. / Union Territories to implement the Integrated Child Development Scheme (ICDS) in full and to ensure that every ICDS disbursing centre in the country shall provide as under :
      (a) Each child up to 6 years of age to get 300 calories and 8-10 gms. of protein;
      (b) Each adolescent girl to get 500 calories and 20-25 grams of protein;
      (c) Each pregnant woman and each nursing mother to get 500 calories & 20-25 grams of protein;
      (d) Each malnourished child to get 600 calories and 16-20 grams of protein;
      (e) Have a disbursement centre in every settlement.
   (ii) It is the case of the Union of India that there has been full compliance of its obligations, if any, under the Scheme. However, if any of the States gives a specific instance of non-compliance, the Union of India will do the needful within the framework of the Service.

7. *National Maternity Benefit Scheme (NMBS)*
   (i) We direct the State Govts. / Union Territories to implement the National Maternity Benefit Scheme (NMBS) by paying all BPL pregnant women Rs. 500/- through the Sarpanch 8-12 weeks prior to delivery for each of the first two births.
   (ii) It is the case of the Union of India that there has been full compliance of its obligations under the Scheme. However, if any of the States gives a specific instance of non-compliance, the Union of India will do the needful within the framework of the Scheme.

8. *National Family Benefit Scheme (NFBS)*
   (i) We direct the State Govts. / Union Territories to implement the National Family Benefit Scheme and pay a BPL family Rs. 10,000/- within four weeks

through a local Sarpanch, whenever the primary bread winner of the family dies.

9. We direct that a copy of this order be translated in regional languages and in English by the respective States/ Union Territories and prominently displayed in all Gram Panchayats, government school Buildings and Fair Price Shops.

10. In order to ensure transparency in selection of beneficiaries and their access to these Schemes, the Gram Panchayats will also display a list of all beneficiaries under the various Schemes. Copies of the Schemes and the list of beneficiaries shall be made available by the Gram Panchayats to members of public for inspection.

11. We direct Doordarshan and AIR to adequately publicise various Schemes and this order. We direct the Chief Secretaries of each of the States and Union Territories to ensure compliance of this order. They will report compliance by filing affidavits in this Court within 8 weeks from today with copies to the Attorney General and counsel for the petitioner.

We grant liberty to the Union of India to file affidavit pursuant to the order of this Court dated 21st November, 2001. List the matter for further orders on 11th February, 2002. In the meanwhile, liberty is granted to the parties to apply for further directions, if any.

6. Text of the Order 8th May, 2002

After hearing learned counsel for the parties we issue the following directions :

(a) The Gram Panchayats shall frame employment generation proposals in accordance with the Sampurna Gramin Rozgar Yojana (SGRY) guidelines for creation of useful community assets that have the potential for generating sustained and gainful employment such as water and soil conservation, a forestation and agro-horticulture, salvipasture, minor irrigation and link roads, These proposals shall be approved and sanctioned by the Gram Panchayats and the work started expeditiously.

(b) The respondents shall focus the SGRY programme towards agricultural wage earners, non agricultural unskilled wage earners, marginal farmers and, in particular, SC and ST persons whose wage income constitutes a reasonable proportion of their household income and to give priority to them in employment, and within this sector shall give priority to women.

(c) The respondents shall make the wage payment on a weekly basis.

(d) The respondents shall prohibit the use of contractors in the SGRY programme.

(e) The Central Government shall make financial releases under the different employment generation schemes to each State on schedule, provided that the State Governments fulfil the conditions as prescribed by the SGRY. The State Governments are directed to fulfil these conditions and implement the SGRY expeditiously. The State Government will furnish utilisation certificate and it is only on the furnishing of the same that further amounts shall be released. The funds provided shall only be utilised in respect of SGRY programme.

(f) The Gram Sabhas are entitled to conduct a social audit into all food/employment schemes and to report all instances to misuse of funds to the respective implementing authorities, who shall on receipt of such complaints, investigate and taken appropriate action in accordance with law.

(g) On a complaint being made to the Chief Executive Officer of the Zila Panchayat (CEO)/Collector regarding non-compliance of the orders of this Court the concerned CEO/ Collector shall record the salient features of the complaint.

(h) Register maintained for this purpose, acknowledge receipt of the complaint and forthwith secure compliance with this Court's order.

(i) The CEO/Collector of all the Districts in the States and territories shall scrutinize the action taken by all the implementing agencies within their jurisdiction to ensure compliance with this court's orders and report to the Chief Secretary.

(j) The responsibility for implementation of the order of this Court shall be that of the CEO/Collector. The Chief Secretary will ensure compliance with the order of this Court.

(k) Dr. N.C. Saxena, former planning secretary, government of India, and Mr.S.R. Shankaran, former secretary, rural development, Government of India, shall function as Commissioner's of this Court for the purpose of looking into any grievance that my persist after the above-mentioned grievance resolution procedure has been exhausted.

(l) On the Commissioner's recommending a course of action to ensure compliance with this Court's order, the State Government/UT administrations, shall forthwith act upon such recommendation and report compliance.

(m) The Commissioner's shall be at liberty to take the assistance of individuals and reliable organizations in the State and Union Territories. All officials are directed to fully cooperate with such persons/organizations, to bring about effective monitoring and implementation of the order of this Court.

(n) The Gram Sabhas are empowered to monitor the implementation of the various schemes and have access to relevant information relating to, inter alia, selection[2] of beneficiaries and the disbursement of benefits. The Gram Sabhas can raise their grievance (s) in the manner set out above and the redressal of the grievance (s) shall be done accordingly.

(o) It has been started by the Petitioner that the identification of BPL families is not being done properly and that the criteria for the identification of the BPL families are neither clear nor uniform. The Central and the State Governments are directed to frame clear guidelines for proper identification of BPL families.

(p) The respondents shall ensure that the ration shops remain open throughout the month, during fixed hours, the details of which will be displayed on the notice board.

To come up for further directions after 12 weeks.

7. Text of the Order 29th October, 2002

On 8th May, 2002, detailed directions were given by this Court with regard to the implementation of various schemes which had been floated for giving relief to the poor, impoverished and the hungry. In the said order Dr. N.C. Saxena and Mr. S.R. Sankaran were appointed as Commissioner's of the Court, inter alia, for the purpose of looking into any grievance that may persist after the grievance resolution procedure set out in the said order has been exhausted.

Pursuant to the said order Dr. N.C. Saxena has filed the first report dated 12th October, 2002. In the said report, there is a reference with regard to the food requirement in the State of Rajasthan. We had not go into this aspect but what requires to be considered is the directions which are sought for by the Commissioner's in the said report.

We have heard the learned Attorney General, Mr. Colin Gonsalvez and Dr. A.M. Singhvi and in furtherance and in addition to our aforesaid order of 8th May, 2002; we issue the following directions :

The Chief Secretaries/Administrators of the States/ Union Territories are directed to respond promptly to the correspondences addressed to them by the Commissioner's and provide full information as required.

In case of persistent default in compliance with the orders

of this Court concerned Chief Secretaries/Administrators of the States/Union Territories shall be held responsible.

The Chief Secretaries/Administrators are given one last chance to translate and permanently display the order dated 28th November, 2001 and 8th May, 2002 of this Court, on all the Gram Panchayats, school buildings and fair price shops and give wide publicity on the All India Radio and Doordarshan. This should be complied with within eight weeks from today.

It is clarified that the scope of the work of the Commissioner's appointed by this Court is to include the monitoring of the implementation of this Court's orders as well as the monitoring and reporting to this Court of the implementation by the respondents of the various welfare measures and schemes.

The respective State Governments shall appoint Government officials as assistants to the Commissioner's within eight weeks from today. The appointment shall be made by the chief secretaries/administrators of the States/ Union Territories in consultation with Dr. N.C. Saxena. The assistants so appointed will render such assistance to the Commissioner's as the Commissioner's may require and help them in discharging the responsibility which has been cast upon them.

In order to ensure that there is effective implementation of the Governmental Schemes, the States as well as the Central Government shall appoint one Nodal Officer each. The assistants appointed to help the Commissioner's, as well as the Commissioner's would remain in constant touch with the said Nodal Officers for the purpose of ensuring the due implementation of the Schemes.

The Nodal Officers so appointed shall provide to the Commissioner's full access to relevant records and provide relevant information.

Whenever the States/Union Territories have a meeting in relation to food scarcity it will be appropriate that the Commissioner's and in their absence the assistants are notified to participate in the same.

It is the duty of each States/Union Territories to prevent deaths due to starvation or malnutrition. If the Commissioner reports and it is established to the satisfaction of the Court that starvation death has taken place, the Court may be justified in presuming that its orders have not been implemented and the chief secretaries/administrators of the States/ Union Territories may be held responsible for the same.

We reaffirm our earlier order dated 8th May, 2002 and direct the parties to comply with the same, and in particular the Central Government shall formulated the scheme to extend the benefits of the Antyodaya Anna Yojana to the destitute section of the population.

Adequate funds shall be made available to the Commissioner's by the Union of India to enable them to perform the functions. To await the next report of the Commissioner's, and to come up for further orders after four months before a bench of which Hon'ble Mr. Justice Y.K. Sabharwal is a member.

8. Text of the Order 2nd May, 2003

In this petition that was filed little more than two years back various issues have been framed many of which may have a direct and important relevance to the very existence of poor people; their right to life and the right of food of those who can ill-afford to provide to their families two meals day. There misfortune becomes further grave during the times of famines and drought. The petitioner has sought directions for enforcement of famine code. The petitioner seeks immediate release of surplus food-grains lying in the stocks of Union of India for drought affected areas. Directions are also sought requiring the Government to frame fresh schemes of Public Distribution for Scientific and Reasonable Distribution of food-grains. In order that any meaningful and immediate relief is given by the Central Government and the State Government without any delay various applications have been filed by the petitioner. Considering the importance of the matter particularly in relation to those who are Below

Poverty Line (BPL) an order was made by this Hon'ble Court on 3rd March, 2003 requiring the respondents to file replies to the applications and place on record the requisite materials, while adjourning the case to the 8th April, 2003. In respect of the directions that the Central Government shall formulate the scheme to extend the benefits of the Antyodaya Anna Yojana (AAY) to destitute section of the population, learned Attorney General stated on the last date of hearing which was on 3rd March, 2003 that for the budget for the year 2003-2004 a provision has been made for it. Despite the order of this Court the document has not been placed on record. The approach of Government is more distressing since this matter which was to come up on 8th April, 2002, has come up today after nearly four weeks of the scheduled date but neither the documents have been filed nor other aspects required to be dealt with in the last order have been adverted to. In I.A.25 one of the grievance that has been made is that names of various persons have been removed from BPL arbitrarily. In I.A.26 it has been highlighted that the allocation made for supply of grain in lieu of the labour of BPL family has been recommended to be reduced from 10 kgs. per day per household to 5 kgs. and for 10 days in every month till June, 2003. In terms of the last order the specific instructions were required to be obtained on the relevant schemes mentioned in I.A.26 including in the matter of reduction of supply of the grain and the number of days. In I.A.26 directions sought against Union of India are to release 20 million tones food-grains, at the very minimum, free of cost every year for the Food for Work Programmes besides other reliefs. Response from Government was sought within three weeks.

Declining request for filing of replies we have heard learned counsel since it is necessary to consider issuing certain directions without any further delay with a view to provide some ad hoc interim relief to a class which deserves a sympathetic approach. We have heard Mr. Colin Gonsalvez, learned counsel for the petitioner, Mr. Mukul Rohtagi, learned Additional Solicitor General for Union of India, besides Mr. B. B. Singh, for State of Bihar, Mr. Ashok Srivastava, for State of U.P. and Ms. Indra Sawhney, for Food Corporation of India.

This Court in various orders passed in the last two years has expressed its deep concern and it has been observed, in one of the orders, that what is of utmost importance is to see that food is provided to the aged, infirm, disabled, destitute women, destitute men who are in danger of starvation, pregnant and lactating women and destitute children, especially in cases where they or members of their family do not have sufficient funds to provide food for them. In case of famine, there may be shortage of food, but here the situation is that amongst plenty there is scarcity. Plenty of food is available, but distribution of the same amongst the very poor and the destitute is scarce and non-existing leading to mal-nutrition, starvation and other related problems. The anxiety of the Court is to see that poor and the destitute and the weaker sections of the society do not suffer from hunger and starvation. The prevention of the same is one of the prime responsibilities of the Government-whether Central or the State. Mere schemes without any implementation are of no use. What is important is that the food must reach the hungry.

Article 21 of the Constitution of India protects for every citizen a right to live with human dignity. Would the very existence of life of those families which are below poverty line not come under danger for want of appropriate schemes and implementation thereof, to provide requisite aid to such families? Reference can also be made to Article 47 which inter alia provides that the State shall regard the raising of the level of nutrition and the standard of living of its people and the improvement of public health as among its primary duties.

In the light of the aforesaid, we are of the view that for the time being for the months of May, June and July, 2003, it is necessary to issue certain directions so that some temporary relief is available to those, who deserve is the most.

Our attention has been drawn to the famine code

(Annexure Petitioners/ Appellants herein-VIII). That famine code, we are informed, is the one formulated by State of Rajasthan and similar codes have been formulated by other States. A perusal of this famine code shows that first three chapters deal with the steps to be taken as preventive measure before the famine and drought and Chapter IV onward deal with declaration of distress and commencement of relief setting out in detail the relief's and the officers responsible thereof. One of the reliefs claimed in the petition is for enforcement of the famine code. Learned Additional Solicitor General submitted that the famine codes were formulated long time back and many of the aspects have been dealt with under various schemes that have been formulated later like Sampurna Gramin Rozgar Yojana (SGRY). This should not present any difficulty in implementing the Famine Code for the time being. Under the circumstances, we direct the implementation of the famine code for the period May, June and July, 2003 as and when and where situation may call for it, subject to the condition that if in subsequent schemes the relief to be provided and preventive measures to be undertaken, during famine and drought, are better than the one stipulated by the famine code, the same may be implemented instead of famine code.

The next aspect pertains to Food for Work. We have been taken through Employment Assurance Scheme of the Government of India. Though the same stands merged into SGRY, but it has been submitted by learned counsel for the petitioner that the reliefs under SGRY, instead of improvement, have since been reduced. SGRY provides for an outlay of only Rs. 5000 crores and 5 million tonnes of free grain. It was pointed out that as far as the guarantee of employment is concerned, in the employment assurance scheme, it was 100 days, whereas according to SGRY, it is 15 days and rather 10 days according to States and at the most 20 days which is according to Union of India. Our attention has also been drawn to the report of the high level committee on long-term Gramin Policy-July, 2002. A detailed reference to report has been made in I.A.25. That committee was constituted by Department of Food and Public Distribution, Ministry of Consumer Affairs and Food and Public Distribution, Union of India. In the summary and recommendation the report inter alia states that an importantly social and security measure in the context is provision for employment on public works. While a food component can and could be part of such employment generation in the short run or in periods of local food shortages in long run, employment generation should be distinct from the food delivery system. This should not, however, undermine the importance of employment and income generation in eliminating hunger and malnutrition. The report further states that no long run policy can be effective unless present imbalances, specifically, the large excess holding of public stocks, the report has outlined a two year plan of action which includes immediate steps to lower procurement inflows on the one hand, and to raise outflows, on the other hand, by several means including a large Food for Work programme, a revitalized universal PDS and other grain-based welfare schemes. It has also recommended a major food-based employment programme for the short run. In ultimate, the recommendation of the said committee is that the present SGRY scheme should be expanded and at least doubled. It says that this implies doubling grain allocation from 5 to 10 million tonnes, and also an increase in the cash allocation to States by at least 5000 crores.

The prayer of the petitioner, in fact, is for allocation of 20 million tonnes though, according to it, the requirement is of 40 million tonnes. The high level committee was appointed by the Government of India. It gave its report in July, 2002. Ten months have passed. We do not know what consideration the report has received if at all it has been considered by the Government. We may also note that the report has further mentioned that currently, about half of the food subsidy is being spent on holding stocks in excess of the buffer stock levels necessary for food security. As these stocks are reduced to normal levels, very large fiscal resources of around Rs. 10,000 crores annual will become available.

While directing the Government of India to place on record by 8th August, 2003, the consideration bestowed on the report of the committee and the decision, if any, we direct that on pro rata basis, the recommendation that present SGRY scheme should be expanded at least doubled be implemented, both in regard to allocation of food-grain as also cash, for the months of May, June and July. The State Government shall lift those allocations and ensure that the same reach those for whom it is meant. In case, however, after considering the response of Union of India, we hold that the allocations do not deserve to be doubled as recommended, the question of adjustment being made for the future supplies on the basis of the allocations in terms of SGRY can be considered.

Further, it is necessary to issue immediate directions to evolve a system whereby eligible BPL families, which may not be on BPL list, are so included as also regarding the ration shops and other outlets remaining open and giving deliveries of food-grains to those, who are on the list and hold the requisite cards. For the present, we are not going into the question whether only 41% of the poorest households are on BPL list. We may note that in May last year and order was passed that the respondents shall ensure that the ration shops remain open throughout the month during fixed hours and the details of which shall be displayed in the notice board.

To facilitate the supply of the grain, we issue the following directions :

(1) Licensees, who
- (a) do not keep their shops open throughout the month during the stipulated period,
- (b) fail to provide grain to BPL families strictly at BPL rates and no higher,
- (c) keep the cards of BPL households with them,
- (d) make false entries in the BPL cards,
- (e) engage in black-marketing or siphoning away of grains to the open market and hand over such ration

shops to such other person/organizations, shall make themselves liable for cancellation of their licenses. The concerned authorities/functionaries would not show any laxity on the subject.

(2) Permit the BPL household to buy the ration in instalments.

(3) Wide publicity shall be given so as to make BPL families aware of their entitlement of food-grains.

What was observed in the order dated 23rd July, 2001 in regard to the making available of food to aged, infirm, disabled etc. has already been noticed hereinabove. According to the figures supplied by the petitioner, approximately 1.5 crore persons are eligible to get Antyodaya Anna Yozana (AAY) card. We direct the Government of India to place on AAY category the following groups of persons :

(1) Aged, infirm, disabled, destitute men and women, pregnant and locating women, destitute women;
(2) Widows and other single women with no regular support;
(3) Old persons (aged 60 or above) with no regular support and no assured means of subsistence;
(4) Households with a disabled adult and assured means of subsistence;
(5) Households where due to old age, lack of physical or mental fitness, social customs, need to care for a disabled, or other reasons, no adult member is available to engage in gainful employment outside the house;
(6) Primitive Tribes.

What we have stated above in regard to BPL cardholders for effective supply of grains to them, would equally apply for those, who are on AAY list.

Regarding Mid-Day Meals, on 28th November, 2001, this Court directed the State Government/Union Territories to implement the Mid-Day Meals Scheme (MDMS) by providing every child in every Government and Government assisted primary schools with a prepared Mid-Day Meals with a minimum content of 300 calories and 8-12 grams of protein each day of school for a minimum of 200 days. It was further directed that those Governments which provide dry rations instead of cooked meals, within three months start providing cooked meals in all govt. and govt. aided primary schools in all half the Districts of the State (in order of poverty) and must within a further period of three months extend the provision of cooked meals to the remaining parts of the State. Some States in implementation of the said direction are supplying cooked Mid-Day meal to the students. We are, however, told that despite the fact that 1½ years has passed, some of the States have not even made a beginning. Particular reference has been made to States of Bihar, Jharkhand and Uttar Pradesh. It is not in dispute that in these three States even beginning has not been made whereas some of the other States are fully implementing directions for supply of cooked Mid-Day Meals. Counsel for Uttar Pradesh and Jharkhand could not give any satisfactory reason for non-implementation. No reply or affidavit was filed by the said State. In so far as the State of Bihar is concerned, Mr. B.B. Singh has drawn our attention to the affidavit filed by Secretary and relief Commissioner, relief and rehabilitation department, Government of Bihar, inter alia stating that the State Government proposes to implement this scheme in few blocks on a pilot basis through panchayat, pending settlement of the issue regarding funding of conversion cost and to establish the capacity of the Panchayat Raj Institution to supply hygienic cooked meals to all eligible students on a regular basis, without compromising teaching activities. The affidavit could not be more vague than what it is. When they propose to start, in how many districts they propose to start, what scheme has been formulated and every other conceivable detail is missing from the affidavit. We are told that there are 38 districts in the State of Bihar. For the present, we direct the said State to implement the cooked Mid-Day Meals Scheme in terms of the directions of this Court in at least 10 Districts, which may be most poor according to the State's perception.

We also direct the State of Uttar Pradesh, Jharkhand and other States to make a meaningful beginning of the cooked Mid-Day Meals Scheme in at least 25% of the District, which may be most poor.

By order dated 8th May, 2002 Dr. N.C. Saxena, former planning secretary, Government of India and Mr. S.R. Shankaran, former secretary, rural department, Government of India were appointed to function as Commissioner's of this Court for the purpose of looking into any grievance that may persist after the grievance resolution procedure has been exhausted. In subsequent orders, directions have been issued to the Government to fully cooperate with the learned Commissioner's. Mr. Shankaran has said to have written a letter to the Government expressing personal difficulty in functioning as Commissioner on account of ill-health. Mr. Gonsalvez states that he has recovered and now is in a position to so function. We would, therefore, request Mr. Shankaran to start functioning as Commissioner with Dr. Saxena in terms of the orders already passed.

The copies of the order shall be sent to the Chief Secretaries of all States/Union Territories. The State Governments/Union Territories are directed to file affidavits showing the compliance and extent thereof. The affidavits may be filed on or before 8th August, 2003. Union of India may also file its affidavit(s) by the same date. For further consideration the matter shall be placed on 19th August, 2003.

9. Text of the Order 5th May, 2003

The matter has been mentioned by Mr. Colin Gonsalvez, learned counsel for the petitioner. He has also produced copy of the letter dated 3rd May, 2003 written to the learned Attorney General for India in addition to the orders passed on 2nd May, 2003. None is present for the Union of India. Having heard learned counsel for the petitioner, we direct that till the date of hearing the Government of India will not insist the State Governments to remove any person from the existing Below Poverty Line (BPL) list.

10. Text of the Order 19th August, 2003

Fourth report dated 14th August , 2003 has been filed by the Commissioner's, Dr. N.C. Saxena and Mr. S.R. Sankaran. Copy of the report may be supplied to such of learned counsel who may approach the registry. In respect of the report of the high powered committee, the same may be supplied by the petitioner to the States through their counsel on payment basis.

In the report dated 14th August, 2003, various issues have been dealt with such as Mid-Day Meals, ICDS, Targeted Public Distribution System, Antyodaya Anna Yojana, and other social security schemes, employment programmes, urban destitution, corruption and transparency and various directions have been sought from this Court. We are of the view that many aspects dealt in the report can be sorted out between the Central and /or State Governments and the petitioners, particularly, having regard to the fact that it is a non-adversary litigation and the aspects dealt with pertain to that class of citizens which cannot afford even two times meal. Mr. Gonsalvez states that he had discussed the matter with Mr. Soli J. Sorabjee, learned Attorney General and he was also of the view that many aspects can be thrashed out across the table during mutual discussions. It is also so stated by learned counsel for the Union of India. If necessary, at appropriate stage, States can also be involved in the aspect of resolution of some of the matters. Let this be done within four weeks. The matters which remain unresolved, parties can seek directions from the Court.

11. Text of the Order 2nd December, 2003

A report dated 28th November, 2003 has been filed by the committee. Such of the parties who have not been supplied with the said report may obtain it from the registry, response to the report may be filed within six weeks.

Mr. Gonsalvez, learned counsel, submits that though some aspects have been sorted out, some still remain on which directions may be issued by the Court. Let a compilation be filed stating the matters which have been sorted out and which remain to be resolved, within a period of six weeks.

12. Text of the Order of 16th January, 2004

IA No.31

We have perused the Report annexed to I.A. No 31 of 2003. The Report seems to be as a result of visit of Sukumar Gaine, Convenor, Right to Food and Work West Bengal Network and Anuradha Talwar, Advisor to the Commissioner's appointed by this Court, to Tea-Plantations in Jalpaiguri District between 12th December, 2003-14th December, 2003. The Report reveals alarming state of affairs. The State of West Bengal shall respond to the Report and, in the meanwhile, take such action as it may consider appropriate having regard to the various aspects and incidents of malnutrition and other problems highlighted in the Report. The response be filed within 10 days.

In the meanwhile, the Commissioner's are also requested to give their suggestions on the aspects highlighted in the Report, particularly on directions 1-7 sought for in the Report.

13. Text of the Order of 20th April, 2004

Upon hearing counsel the Court made the following order :

Mid-Day Meals Scheme

We have heard Mr. Colin Gonsalvez, learned senior counsel appearing for the petitioner, Mr. Raju Ramachandran, learned Additional Solicitor General appearing for Union of India, Mr. M.L.Verma, learned senior counsel appearing for intervener-Health India, and learned counsel representing various States. We have also perused the special report of the Committee dated 28th November, 2003 and report dated 28th January, 2004 and other relevant material on record. In one of the orders earlier passed, this Court had observed about the impact of this public interest litigation on the very existence of large section of poor people, their right to life and right to food to those who can ill-afford to provide to their families two meals a day and their misfortune becoming further grave during famine and drought.

On 28th November, 2001, this Court directed the State Governments/Union Territories to implement Mid-Day Meals scheme by providing every child in every government and government aided primary school with a prepared Mid-Day Meals with a minimum content of 300 calories and 8-12 grams of protein each day of school for a minimum of 200 days. The said order further directed that those governments which provide dry rations instead of cooked meals, within three months, should start providing cooked meals in all government and government aided primary schools in half of the districts of the State (in order of poverty) and must, within further period of three months, extend the provision of cooked meals to the remaining parts of the State.

By an order dated 29th October, 2002, it was made clear that in case of persistent default in compliance of the orders of this Court, the concerned Chief Secretaries/ Administrators of the States/Union Territories shall be held responsible. It was brought to the notice of the Court that despite orders having been passed, some of the States had not even made a beginning. In the order dated 2nd May, 2003, this Court observed the manner in which the directions were being flouted in some of the States. In that order, specific reference was made to the States of Bihar, Jharkhand and Uttar Pradesh. The type of the affidavit that was filed has also been commented upon since it was not stated in the affidavit as to when the State of Bihar proposed to start the supply of Mid-Day Meals, in how many districts they proposed to start it and what scheme had been formulated. The order noticed that every conceivable detail had been missing. Ultimately, the State of Bihar was directed to make a beginning by supplying cooked Mid-Day Meals and implement the said scheme in at least ten districts which might be most poor according to the State's perception. Similarly, the States of Uttar Pradesh, Jharkhand and other States were also directed to make a meaningful beginning of the scheme in at least

25% of the districts which might be most poor.

After the orders were made on 2nd May, 2003, various reports have been filed in regard to the implementation of the directions for supply of the cooked Mid-Day Meals in schools in terms of directions contained in the order dated 28th November, 2001.

We have perused the affidavits and heard learned counsel representing the States of Bihar, Uttar Pradesh, Maharashtra, Delhi, West Bengal, Himachal Pradesh, Uttarakhand, Jharkhand, Madhya Pradesh and Haryana. There are other States and Union Territories as well in respect whereof the aforesaid Reports of the Commissioner's have commented upon. Some of the States/Union Territories have not made even a beginning despite lapse of so many years; some have only made a partial beginning; some have made a token beginning and only few of the States have fully implemented the order in respect of cooked Mid-Day Meals that was passed on 28th November, 2001.

Some of the States which claim that they have made a beginning and are partially implementing the scheme have also not given the full and complete details so that this Court could know the extent of the implementation. Most of the affidavits only set out the number of schools and the students where the scheme was being implemented. What was required to be done was to simply state as to how many schools in a particular State/Union Territory would be covered under the directions for supply of cooked Mid-Day Meals, how many students in the said school would be eligible for the benefit and then give the number of the schools and the students who are being supplied cooked meals. The affidavits provide only a part of information without specifying the number of eligible schools and students.

Be that as it may, Table-1 to the second Report of the Commissioner's sets out broadly the States which have implemented it fully or partially or have not responded to the queries of the Commissioner's. We may, however, note that after the said Report, there has been some improvement by a token beginning having been made by some of the

States. The report of the Commissioner's, on the basis of their earlier experience, states that nutritious Mid-Day Meals at schools can be a highly effective way of protecting children from hunger and can also boost school attendance among girls. It also notices some of the areas where such meals are supplied even during the school vacations, especially in drought affected areas. None can question the desirability of extension of this facility even during vacations in drought affected areas where children are deprived of even one day meal.

It is a matter of anguish that despite lapse of nearly three and half years, the order dated 28th November, 2001 has not been fully implemented by all the States and Union Territories. As already stated earlier, many of the States have given only half-baked information and figures. Further, we wish to make it clear that the fact that some of the States were permitted to at least make a start in some of the districts in terms of the order dated 2nd May, 2003 does not mean that this Court has modified or varied the earlier order dated 28th November, 2001. It is a constitutional duty of every State and Union Territory to implement in letter and spirit the directions contained in the order dated 28th November, 2001. We may also note that the suggestions given by Health India would be considered at an appropriate stage.

The petitioner has also made a reference to the announcement made by the Prime Minister extending the Mid-Day Meals scheme upto 10th Standard during his address to the Nation on 15th August, 2003. The suggestion is that extension should be made operational at the earliest. In reply, it has been contended that once the Mid-Day Meals scheme at primary level is consolidated, the question of extension of the scheme upto 10th Standard can be taken up in a phased manner. In this connection, it has been pointed out that the views of various States have been asked in regard to the cost and logistic requirements for the extension of the scheme upto 10th standard.

Further, the petitioner, referring to the recommendations of the Abhijit Sen Committee appointed by Government of

India regarding sharing of conversion cost of implementing the cooked Mid-Day Meals scheme, suggests that the Government should implement that scheme. The Government is stated to be presently discussing the modalities with the concerned ministries and planning commission to provide assistance for meeting with a part of conversion costs towards effective implementation of the said scheme.

Having regard to the aforesaid, in respect of cooked Mid-Day Meals scheme, we issue the following directions :

1. All such States and Union Territories who have not fully complied with the order dated 28th November, 2001 shall comply with the said directions fully in respect of the entire State/Union Territory, preferably, on the re-opening of the primary schools after a long vacation of 2004 and, in any case, not later than 1st September, 2004.
2. All Chief Secretaries/Administrators are directed to file compliance report in regard to directions No.1 on or before 15th September, 2004.
3. The conversion costs for a cooked meals, under no circumstances, shall be recovered from the children or their parents.
4. In appointment of cooks and helpers, preference shall be given to Dalits, Scheduled Castes and Scheduled Tribes.
5. The Central Government shall make provisions for construction of kitchen sheds and shall also allocate funds to meet with the conversion costs of food-grains into cooked Mid-Day Meals. It shall also periodically monitor the low take off of the food-grains.
6. In respect of the State of Uttarakhand, it has been represented that the scheme is being implemented in all the schools. It would be open to the Commissioner's to inspect and bring it to the notice of the Court, if it is otherwise.
7. In drought affected areas, Mid-Day Meals shall be supplied even during summer vacations.

8. An affidavit shall be filed by the Government of India, within three months, stating as to when it is possible to extend the scheme upto 10th standard in compliance with the announcement made by the prime minister. The affidavit shall also state the time frame within which the Government proposes to implement the recommendations of Abhijit Sen committee in respect whereof the modalities have been discussed with the concerned Ministries and Planning Commission.
9. Attempts shall be made for better infrastructure, improved facilities (safe drinking water etc.), closer monitoring (regular inspection etc.) and other quality safeguards as also the improvement of the contents of the meal so as to provide nutritious meal to the children of the primary schools.

The issue as to the implementation of this scheme will be considered in the month of September, 2004.

SGR Y-Employment Guarantee

In respect of this Scheme, the following directions are issued :

1. The directions for doubling the food-grains as also cash in terms of the order dated 2nd May, 2003 shall be applicable this year also.
2. The State Governments/Union Territories are directed to pay minimum wages to the workers under the scheme and shall stop use of labour displacement machines.
3. Access to all public documents including muster rolls shall be allowed to such persons who seek such access and the cost of supplying documents shall not be more than the costs of providing copies of the documents.
4. The allocation of funds and food-grains shall be timely made by the Central Government to the State Governments.
5. The State Governments are directed to utilise the entire

allocation, as aforesaid, so that the allotted funds and food-grains neither lapse nor result in reduction in subsequent years.

6. In case, some of the State Governments, as a result of financial constraints, wish to pay 100% wages in shape of food-grains and not partly food-grains and partly cash, it would be open to them to approach the Central Government. On examination of each case, the Central Government may permit payment of 100% wages in the shape of food-grains.

Antyodaya Anna Yojana

In regard to this scheme, the following directions are issued:

1. The Government of India shall issue, within two months, guidelines so that the existing condition of possession of a BPL card for inclusion in AAY category is dispensed with.
2. The State Governments should be directed by the Central Government to accelerate the issue of Antyodaya cards especially to primitive tribes. The guidelines issued to State Governments shall be implemented in letter and spirit. List the Writ Petition on 27th April, 2004 for consideration of other Schemes.

14. Text of the Order of 27th April, 2004

Upon hearing counsel the Court made the following order :

National Social Assistance Programme (NSAP)

We have further heard for some time Mr. Gonsalvez, learned senior counsel and Mr. Raju Ramachandran, and learned Additional Solicitor General. The various schemes for the poorer sections of the citizens of this country have been the subject matter of the orders passed by this Court from time to time. It seems that some States have discontinued some of the schemes. As an interim measure, till the matter is fully heard in detail, we direct that no scheme covered by the orders made by this Court including the National Old Age Pension Scheme, National Family Benefit Scheme, in particular Annapurna, and National Maternity Benefit Scheme shall be discontinued or restricted in any way without the prior approval of this Court. In other words, it means that till further orders, the schemes would continue to operate and benefit all those who are covered by the schemes. We hope that the Government of India and the State Governments would simplify the procedure so that high proportion of eligible persons remain to be covered by the schemes.

A copy of this order shall be sent to the Chief Secretaries of every State Government/Union Territory. The Union of India, through the concerned ministry, shall also issue directives to the State Governments/Union Territories to comply with this order.

Integrated Child Development Scheme (ICDS)

In respect of Integrated Child Development Scheme, directions were issued on 28th November, 2001. It seems that most of those who are covered by the said order are not getting benefit under the said scheme. We have heard the submissions of Mr. Gonsalvez and perused the report submitted by the Commissioner's and the directions sought. From the facts and figures that have been furnished to us, it seems evident that there are a large number of malnourished children between the age group of 0 to 6 years. These figures are based on the survey conducted under the National Family Benefit Health Scheme. The position is quite alarming. These young children are the future of the nation. Further, it appears that except Kerala and Tamil Nadu where the benefit under the scheme is said to be reaching to about 50 per cent of the children, in the rest of the country the average seems to be below 25 per cent. The position in the States of Bihar, Uttar Pradesh, Jharkhand and Uttarakhand seems to be quite alarming. According to the survey for the period 2002-2003 the access to supplementary nutrition for the children in Bihar reaches about 12.6 per cent of those who are otherwise covered by the scheme. Mr. Raju Ramachandran, learned ASG prays for a short adjournment to discuss the matter with the concerned officials and make submissions on the directions that may be issued to ensure the compliance of the Order dated 28th November, 2001.

As prayed, the case is adjourned to 29th April, 2004. BPL (Below Poverty Line Scheme).

The case may be put up for hearing on a non-miscellaneous day after re-opening of the Court after summer vacation.

15. Text of the Order of 29th April, 2004

Upon hearing counsel the Court made the following order :

With the assistance of learned counsel, we have perused various documents including report No.1 of 2000 prepared by CAG and a working paper on Health, Nutrition and Family Welfare Programme review of progress during the Ninth Plan period by planning commission, Government of India (February, 2001). It is evident that Integrated Child Development Scheme (ICDS) is perhaps the largest of all the food supplementation programmes in the world, was initiated in the year 1975 with the following objectives as per the aforesaid document prepared by the planning commission.

(i) To improve the health and nutrition status of children 0-6 years by providing supplementary food and by coordinating with state health departments to ensure delivery of required health inputs;

(ii) To provide conditions necessary for pre-school children's psychological and social development through early stimulation and education;

(iii) To provide pregnant and lactating women with food supplements;

(iv) To enhance the mother's ability to provide proper child care through health and nutrition education;

(v) To achieve effective coordination of policy and implementation among the various departments to promote child development.

From the facts and figures given in the documents it appears that despite the fact that for the development of children, in particular, mal-nourished and under nourished children, the scheme is elaborate and intends to cover all the children under the age group of 0-6 years but it appears that a lot more deserves to be done in field to ensure that nutritious food reaches to those who are under nourished or mal-nourished or others covered under the scheme.

The food is supplied to children through Anganwadis Centers (AWCS). In all, there are 6 lakh centers. The norms of Government of India provide for one center for the population of 1000 (700 in case of Tribal area). According to the petitioner, going by the said norms there should be 14 lakh ACWS. It appears that according to the calculation of Government of India the AWCS would be 12 lakhs. We direct the Government of India to file within 3 months an affidavit stating the period within which it proposes to increase the number of AWCS so as to cover the 14 lakh habitations. We notice that the norm for supply of nutritious food worth rupee one for every child was fixed in the year 1991. The Government of India should consider the revision of the norm of rupee one and incorporate their suggestion in the affidavit.

In respect of sanctioned AWCS, we direct that the same shall be made fully operational by 30th June, 2004. We further direct that the sanctioned AWCS shall supply nutritious food/ supplement to the children, adolescent girls and to pregnant and lactating women under the scheme for 300 days in a year.

We direct the Chief Secretaries to file reports showing that for the period from 1st April, 2003 till 31st March, 2004 from the sanctioned AWCS how many children, adolescent girls and pregnant and lactating women were supplied nutritious food/supplement and for how many days during the said period. The report shall be filed by 31st July, 2004. List the matter in the month of August, 2004.

The question regarding Below Poverty Line Scheme will also be taken up on that day instead of July, 2004. Not to be treated as part heard.

16. Text of the Order of 17th August, 2004

Four weeks' time is granted by way of last chance to the States of Andhra Pradesh, Assam, Bihar, Gujarat, Himachal Pradesh, Jharkhand, Mizoram, Orissa, Sikkim and Union Territories of Daman & Diu and Lakshadweep to file report of the respective Chief Secretaries on affidavit, failing which the Chief Secretary of the defaulting State shall be required to remain present in-person in Court on the next date of hearing.

So far as the States of Chhattisgarh, Meghalaya and Nagaland are concerned, though counsel have entered appearance on their behalf, but neither report/affidavit of the Chief Secretaries have been filed nor the States are represented through any counsel. Report of the Chief Secretaries on affidavit must be filed within the aforesaid time, otherwise the Chief Secretary of the defaulting State shall remain present in-person in Court on the next date of hearing.

I.A. No. 37 :

Issue notice to the petitioner.

Place this petition on 16th September, 2004.

17. Text of the Order of 16th September, 2004

Mr. Colin Gonsalvez, learned senior counsel appearing for the petitioner has handed to us the fifth report of the Commissioner's of August 2004. According to the learned counsel, in some of the States there is hardly any implementation of the Mid-Day Meals Scheme and other schemes as extensively stated in the report. It is further submitted that urgent directions are required to be made on the basis of the recommendations made in the report so that schemes can be meaningfully implemented and the benefits of the Scheme reaches the downtrodden for whom the schemes have been made from time to time by the Central Government. Copy of the report shall be supplied to such counsel appearing for the State Governments who may approach Ms. Aparna Bhat, learned counsel within three days. It would for be open to the Central Government and / or the State Governments to respond to the recommendations made and the findings of the report on or before 1st October 2004. We direct the following State Governments to positively respond to the report: Uttar Pradesh, Bihar, Jharkhand, Chhattisgarh, Madhya Pradesh, Delhi, West Bengal, Assam, Manipur and Rajasthan.

We also expect the Union of India to respond within the stipulated time. List the matter for consideration of the Report and hearing on 7th October, 2004. Till further orders, the Union of India shall not transfer the Mid-Day Meals Scheme to the State Governments. The order shall not be construed to mean that we have restrained the Central Government from transferring funds or grains to the State Governments or restrained the implementation of the Schemes by the State Governments.

Further Mr. Gonsalvez has brought to our notice a Note which, according to the petitioner has been prepared by its Rajasthan branch and sets out the details of hunger related deaths and a situation of nutritional emergency amidst primitive tribes in Baran district of Rajasthan. According to the said Note, in the month of August 2004 twenty-six deaths took place in Baran district of Rajasthan as a result of malnutrition and hunger. As per the note, mostly children have died on that account. Reference is also made in the Note to a special package for tribals announced by the State Government on 15th September, 2004, which prominently appeared in major newspapers like Hindustan Times, Dainik Bhaskar, Rajasthan Patrika etc. The said announcement includes:-"100 days 'employment assuarance scheme' for one person from every Sahariya household in Shahbad and Kishanganj block of Baran district, for which the Government has allocated 21.30 crores and 4000 quintals of grain to Baran. Also 100 days 'employment assuarance scheme' for one person of every household of the Kathori tribals of Kotra and Jhadol blocks of Udaipur. According to the announcement this scheme is already being implemented.

15,000 families of Sahariyas will be taken under Antyodaya Anna Yojana and be provided according to the scheme 35 kgs. of grain at the rate of Rs. 2 per kilogram every month. For which an amount of Rs. 2 crore and 90 lakhs has been budgeted by the State Government. 1200 Sahariya families will be given economic support for housing facilities.

We have requested learned counsel appearing for the State of Rajsathan to seek instructions and file an affidavit of a responsible officer responding to what has been stated in the aforesaid Note filed by the People's Union for Civil Liberties dealing specifically as to the State Government's version of the cause of death of so many children within a span of few days in one particular district of the State. If the special package as claimed has been announced in the newspapers for the Tribals, it ought to be implemented without further delay. The affidavit shall also be filed by 1st October, 2004, so that matter can be taken up on 7th October 2004.

18. Text of the Order of 7th October, 2004

We have gone through the 5th August, 2004 Report of the Commissioner's Shri Dr. N.C. Saxena and N.R. Sankaran. First of all, we wish to place on record our compliments and appreciation for the enormous work done by the learned Commissioner's and presenting the report under consideration.

The report is in three parts. First part is divided into 14 sections covering different schemes. Under Section 1, Integrated Child Development Services (ICDS) has been considered. Part II sets out summary of findings and Part III sets out recommendations. We would first consider the aspect of ICDS. In order to fully appreciate the problem, it would be useful to notice the background briefly.

ICDS, as noticed in the Order dated 29.4.2004 is perhaps the largest of all the food and supplementation programmes in the world that was initiated in the year 1975 with the following objections as per the document prepared by Planning Commission :

1. To improve the health and nutrition status of children 0-6 years by providing supplementary food and by coordinating with state health departments to ensure delivery of required health inputs;
2. To provide conditions necessary for pre-school children's psychological and social development through early stimulation and education;
3. To provide pregnant and lactating women with food supplements;
4. To enhance the mother's ability to provide proper child care through health and nutrition education;
5. To achieve effective coordination of policy and implementation among the various departments to promote child development.

The scheme intends to cover all the children under age group of 0-6 years. The food is supplied to the children through Anganwadis Centres (for short, 'AWCS'). The norms of Government of India provide for one Centre for a population of one thousand (700 in case of Tribal area). It is not in serious dispute, as contended by Mr. Mohan Parasaran, learned Additional Solicitor General that according to norms, there should be approximately 14 lakhs ACWS. Admittedly, nearly 6 lakh centres have been sanctioned. Many of the sanctioned centres are also not operational as is evident from the report under consideration. The problem seems to be more acute in States like Bihar, Uttar Pradesh and Jharkhand.

It deserves to be noticed that the directions in respect of ICDS were issued as far back in 28.11.2001. The order dated 27.4.2004 notices that most of those covered by the order dated 28.11.2001 are not getting the benefit under

ICDS. That observation was made on the basis of figures which were provided under National Family Benefit Health Scheme on conducting survey. The result was that a large number of children between the age group of 0-6 years were malnourished. That order also noticed that the position was alarming in the aforesaid three States as well as the State of Uttarakhand. By order dated 29.4.2004, the Government of India was directed to file within three months an affidavit stating the period within which it proposed to sanction the remaining number of AWCS. The Government of India was also directed to consider the revision of norms of supply of nutritious food worth rupee one to every child in the centres as norm of rupee one was fixed way back in the year 1991 and incorporate its suggestion in the affidavit.

It is most unfortunate that instead of three months, nearly six months have expired, the Government of India has still not filed the affidavit and instead an oral application has been made by learned Additional Solicitor General for grant of further time to file an affidavit in terms of the Order dated 29.4.2004. We are shocked at the attitude of the Central Government which is in respect of giving nutritious food to all children though in practice it concerns those unfortunate section of the society who can ill-afford to provide nutritious food to the children of the aforesaid age group. In absence of the affidavit, we could have straightway issued directions for the sanction of the remaining AWCS and for increase of norm of rupee one to rupees two but having regard to the totality of the circumstances, we grant one final opportunity to the Central Government to file affidavit within a period of two weeks where after we would consider these two aspects, namely, (i) sanction of 14 lakh AWCS; (ii) increase of norm of rupee one to rupees two.

We make it clear that if the affidavit is not filed, this Court will be left with no option but to issue directions for implementation of the two aspects.

Now, we would deal with the aspect of sanctioned AWCS and their working. In the Order dated 29.4.2004, it was directed that the sanctioned AWCS shall be made fully operational by 30th June, 2004. Further direction issued was that the sanctioned AWCS shall supply nutritious food/ supplement to the children, adolescent girls and to pregnant and lactating women under the scheme for 300 days in a year. The report presents a glooming picture both in regard to the operation of the sanctioned AWCS in some of the States like Uttar Pradesh, Bihar and Jharkhand and the position in those which are operational. Instances have been given in the Report where for months the supplies were not made to the children. For example, in the State of Jharkhand, the sanctioned AWCS were not working from May to December, 2003. No satisfactory reply is forthcoming from that State. Further, there are material discrepancies in two affidavits filed by the said State one in September and the one handed over in the Court today. In the September affidavit, it was deposed on oath that 16689 AWCS were operational. In the affidavit filed today, the figure of operational AWCS is stated to be 7429. According to the report, on an average, 42 paisa as against the norm of rupee one was being allocated per beneficiary per day by the State of Jharkhand. The position in Bihar and Uttar Pradesh is also no better. Out of 394 sanctioned ICDS projects, only 249 were operational in the State of Bihar. As per the affidavit dated 30th September, 2004, all the projects were being made operational from 4th October, 2004. Whether that has happened or not, Mr. B.B. Singh, learned counsel appearing for the State is unable to state for want of instructions. Be that as it made, if all have not been made operational since 4th October, 2004 has already passed and gone we direct that the same shall be made operational in period not later than one week from today.

In the State of Uttar Pradesh, though percentage of non-functional/non-operational AWCS is more as per the Report but according to the State, admittedly 24 per cent are not operational. In the affidavit, it has been claimed that the remaining will be operational by 30th November, 2004. We direct the State Government to make operational all sanctioned AWCS by 30th November, 2004. After that, we would not entertain any application for extension of time.

The report also mentions that some of AWCS are operating from private houses including those of grain dealers which it is suggested is not a healthy way of working as it is likely to increase the chances of pilferage of the grain etc. We are happy to note that as stated in the affidavit of State of Uttar Pradesh, it has made efforts to shift AWCS to primary schools. It is a good example for other States to follow. The Report also mentions about the attempt to centralise the procurements in some of the States which has many fallouts. It has been explained in one of the affidavit that the procurements is at district level and not at the State level. Further, the problem of using contractors for procurement has also been mentioned in the report suggesting that it should be done by agencies and officers at the Government level. These are only by way of illustrations as to facts and figures given in Section 1 of the report relating to Integrated Child Development Services.

Having heard Mr. Colin Gonsalvez, learned senior counsel appearing for the petitioner and learned additional Solicitor General appearing for the Central Government and learned counsel appearing for the State Governments in particular, the States of Bihar, Jharkhand and Uttar Pradesh, for present, we issue following directions :

1. The aspect of sanctioning 14 lakhs AWCS and increase of norm of rupee one to rupees 2 per child per day would be considered by this Court after two weeks.
2. The efforts shall be made that all SC/ST hamlets/ habitations in the country have Anganwadis Centres as early as possible.
3. The contractors shall not be used for supply of nutrition in Anganwadis and preferably ICDS funds shall be spent by making use of village communities, self-help groups and Mahila Mandals for buying of grains and preparation of meals.
4. All State Governments/Union Territories shall put on their website full data for the ICDS schemes including where AWCS are operational, the number of beneficiaries

category-wise, the funds allocated and used and other related matters.

5. All State Governments/Union Territories shall use the Pradhanmantri Gramodaya Yojana fund (PMGY) in addition to the state allocation and not as a substitute for state funding.
6. As far as possible, the children under PMGY shall be provided with good food at the centre itself.
7. All the State Governments/Union Territories shall allocate funds for ICDS on the basis of norm of one rupee per child per day, 100 beneficiaries per AWC and 300 days feeding in a year, i.e., on the same basis on which the centre make the allocation.
8. BPL shall not be used as eligibility criteria for ICDS.
9. All sanctioned projects shall be operationalize and provided food as per these norms and wherever utensils have not been provided, the same shall be provided (Instance of Jharkhand State has been noticed in the report where utensils have not been provided). The vacancies for the operational ICDS shall be filled forthwith. (Instance of Uttar Pradesh where vacancies have not been filled up is quite alarming though in the affidavit it has been stated that a drive has been initiated to fill up the vacancies).
10. All the State Governments/Union Territories shall utilise the entire State and Central allocation under ICDS/PMGY and under no circumstances, the same shall be diverted and preferably also not returned to the Centre and, if returned, a detailed explanation for non-utilisation shall be filed in this Court.
11. All States/Union Territories shall make earnest effort to cover the slums under ICDS.
12. The Central Government and the States/Union Territories shall ensure that all amounts allocated are sanctioned in time so that there is no disruption whatsoever in the feeding of children.

Our attention has been drawn to what is stated at page

20 in box 2 regarding failure of authorities to take appropriate action despite Commissioner's intervention in the case of Madhya Pradesh pertaining to the area mentioned therein and the non-payment to the work force. We direct the State Government to either make payment of wages to the labourers or file an affidavit giving detailed explanation within two weeks.

List the matter after two weeks.

19. Text of the Order of 17th November, 2004

Sampurna Gramin Rozgar Yojana

The Order dated 7th October, 2004 notices as to what is stated at page 20 in box 2 regarding failure of authorities to take case of Madhya Pradesh in respect of payment of wages to the labourers. The State of Madhya Pradesh was directed to file an affidavit giving explanation. Our attention has been drawn to letter dated 22nd September, 2004 written by the Commissioner's appointed by his Court to the Chief Secretary of the state requesting for arranging payments of Rs. 88,996/ - (Rupees eighty eight thousand, nine hundred and ninety six only) for the work done at Limbi. The said letter makes a grievance of about non-payments of wages and also refers to joint enquiry report. We have also perused that report. It appears from the material on record that a resolution was passed by Gram Sabha on 14th April, 2003 for construction of the dam in question in Limbi village. Further, it appears that the work of construction commenced on 22nd May, 2004 and it was completed on 2nd June, 2004. The inauguration was done by Naib Tehsildhar. It further appears from the material on record that even post evaluation estimate shows that the work was of over eighty thousand rupees. In the report dated 10th September, 2004, the following summary recommendations have been made.

The Collector Badwani must ensure that the process of social audit is taken seriously by all Gram Panchayats in the district. All records must be made available at meeting of the Gram Sabha, which, must be regularly held. Copies of records must be made available to any citizen on demand. Strict action must be initiated on any dereliction of duty in this respect.

The Collector Badwani must be fully co-operated with any individual/ organization seeking to enforce transparency and accountability in governance.

A payment of a total of Rs. 88,995.78/- be immediately made to labourers who worked at the earthen dam site in Dadwani Pahlia (near Iohania s/o Hira's field) in village Limbi, block Pati, Tehsil Badwani, and district Badwani as per the record of work done.

The payments must be made in a transparent manner at village Limbi in full public view in the presence of an officer of rank not less than Tehsildhar.

The Collector should report to the Commissioner's of the Supreme Court on India that the payment has been made not later than 20th September, 2004. Non-compliance with this would necessitate bringing the issue to the notice of the Hon'ble Supreme Court.

We have also perused the reply dated 8th October, 2004 sent by the Collector to the Commissioner's letter dated 22nd September, 2004. That reply has been annexed with the affidavit of the State Government which commences from pages 4003 of volume 1(I). The factum of the construction of the Dam is not in dispute. The cost of the work is also not in dispute have, however, been raised, such as lapse of the resolution passed by the Gram Panchayat, Authority of the Naib Tehsildhar and the like.

To decide the larger question and to issue appropriate directions on the aforesaid summary recommendation, we have asked learned Additional Solicitor General whether the Central Government has taken any decision and issued orders for the effective implementation of various schemes. Here we are concerned with Sampurna Gramin Rozgar Yojana (SGRY). The schemes are to be properly implemented, amounts properly released and spent. We have also asked in other States, in particular, Andhra Pradesh so that keeping entire backgrounds into consideration, appropriate directions can be issued. Mr. Parasaran, learned ASG prays for time to obtain instructions and place on record the appropriate material in the form of an affidavit. Let that be done within three weeks.

Pending consideration of the aforesaid larger question, we see no reason as to why the payments of Rs. 88, 996/- to the labourers should be further delayed, particularly when the construction of the Dam and its appropriate cost is not in dispute. In this view, without prejudice to the rights and contentions of the parties and without it being treated as a precedent, we direct State of Madhya Pradesh to release to Jagrat Adivasi Dalit Sanghtana the aforesaid amount, for the Sanghtana in turn to pay the same to the concerned labourers on obtaining receipts from them. The receipts so obtained shall be given by the Sanghtana to the appropriate officers of the State Government. The State Government is granted two weeks time to make payments to the Sanghatan and within two weeks thereafter Sanghtana will provide the receipts to the State Government.

Mid-Day Meals Scheme

In the order dated 28th November, 2001 , directions were issued for supply of prepared Mid-Day Meals in implementation of Mid-Day Meals scheme by directing that cooked meal in all Government and Government aided primary schools within three months thereafter. That order should have been implemented by May, 2002. In the order dated 20th April, 2004, noticing that despite lapse of nearly 3-1/2 years, the order dated 28th November, 2001 was not being fully implemented in all States and Union Territories and, expressing anguish, further directions for supply of cooked Mid-Day Meals were issued directing for supply of cooked Mid-Day Meals were issued directing that those States which have not implemented the order of 28th November, 2001 shall implement it immediately and, in any case, not later than 1st September, 2004. The report filed by the Commissioner's show that in many of the States of Manipur, Nagaland, U.P and Assam, as per the 5th report of the Commissioner's filed in August, 2004. There has been some progress thereafter inasmuch as there was partial implementation in the States of U.P and Assam. In the State of Himachal Pradesh, till August, 2004, the coverage was only 3.1%, in Assam, there is partial implementation of 18% whereas in Jharkhand, it is 15% and in Bihar 24%. One of the difficulties put forth in providing cooked meal is the cost involved therein. Now, the Government of India, in terms of its letter dated 6th October, 2004 sent to Chief Secretaries of all States and Union Territories of Andaman & Nicobar, Pondicherry and Delhi, Advisor to Administrator of UT of Chandigarh and Administrators of UT Daman and Diu, Dadra Nagra Haveli and Lakshadweep, has informed all concerned that the Central Government had taken a decision to augment central assistance under Mid-Day Meals Scheme by providing at the rate of Rs. 1/- per child per school day to meet cooking cost as from 1st September, 2004. The letter also refers to further assistance such as increasing transport subsidy. In this view, at present, without going into the past non-implementation , we see no reason why Mid-Day Meals Scheme, read with the directions issued in the order dated 28th November 2001, for supply of cooking meal, shall not be implemented forthwith in letter and spirit.

The letter dated 6th October, 2004 further postulated that actual release of Central assistance to States for meeting cooking cost would take place soon after the central Government's first supplementary budget is passed by the parliament in the winter session and necessary appropriation Act comes into force. It further states that once this happens, the assistance to meet cooking cost will be provided retrospectively with effect from 1st September, 2004.

The aforesaid letter further stipulates that detailed guidelines if the revised Mid-Day Meals Programme will be issued in the next few weeks which will, inter alia, also lay soon the procedure for claiming central assistance to meet cooking cost. It further requests the State Government and Union Territories that in the light of the firm commitment conveyed under the letter, the government shall immediately take all necessary steps, using available resources to universalize the cooked meal programme in all school and EGS & AIE centers for children studying in classes I- V.

In view of the aforesaid, we direct that very child eligible for cooked meal under the Mid-Day Meals Scheme in all States and Union Territories, shall be provided with the said meal immediately and, in any case, not later than the month of January, 2005. Affidavits shall be filed by the Chief Secretaries by 16th December, 2004 placing on record necessary steps taken to implement this order. Further affidavits shall be filed by 2nd week of January, 2005 detailing the full implementation of direction of supply of cooked meal to all eligible children.

The responsibility to monitor the implementation of the scheme essentially lies with the Central Government which is providing assistance. The letter dated 6th October, 2004 gives some indication that revised guidelines are being prepared for the purpose of management, monitoring and evaluation of the programme. We direct the Central Government to file, within four weeks, an affidavit stating how it is meant. We make it clear that it would not be open to the State Government/ Union Territories to delay the implementation of the scheme so that the benefit under the scheme reaches those for whom it is meant. We make it clear that it would not be open to the State Government/ Union Territories to delay the implementation of the Scheme beyond January, 2005 on the ground that the necessary assistance has not been released by the Central Government. The scheme should be implemented forthwith and cooking costs can be claimed from the Central Government in terms of letter dated 6th October, 2004 which, in fact, requires those governments to use available resources and recover it late from the Central Government.

Antyodaya Anna Yojana

This scheme is meant for the poorest of the poor. A person entitled to the benefit under this scheme is issued a red card. The holder of red card entitles him to obtain grain and rice from the dealer of Public Distribution System (PDS) at a highly subsidized rate which at present is rupees two per kilogram for wheat and rupees three per kilogram for rice.

First of all it is of utmost important that those who have already been issued red card shall straightaway be supplied the rice and grain as per their entitlement. It is also important that those falling under this category should be immediately identified. The special attention is required to be given to Primitive Travel Groups, which we are told, are in large in Maharashtra, West Bengal, Jharkhand and Madhya Pradesh, which are still to be identified in large numbers, card issued and grains supplies. We direct all the State Governments to complete the process of identification of persons falling under this scheme and issue then the red card by the end of the year so that immediately thereafter supply of food grains to them may commence.

For supply of the food grains to red card holders, we are told, that no commission is being paid to the dealer. Mr. Parasaran, learned ASG states that guidelines are being framed in that regard. The Central Government shall file an affidavit within eight weeks placing on record those guidelines. The object is that the red card holders should not be made to pay, directly or indirectly, any amount other then what they are liable to pay for the supply taken.

To be taken up on 18th November, 2004.

20. Text of the Order of 18th November, 2004*

We direct that the amounts paid by the Central Government to the State Governments as Additional Central Assistance under NOAPS shall not be diverted for any other scheme. However, we wish to make it clear that the beneficiaries under the said scheme would continue to be paid the benefits being paid by the State Government. Further, the State Government would continue to pay them, the other additional benefits which the State Government which the

* This is an extract of the order pertaining to the 'directions' given by the Court.

State may be giving them. No benefit would be withdrawn as a result of this order till further orders, by any of the State Governments/ UT's.

21. Text of the Order 9th May, 2005

By IA 37, permission is sought to modify the National Maternity Benefit Scheme (NMBS) and to introduce a new scheme namely Janani Suraksha Yojana (JSY). Whereas in IA 54, the prayer is that the scheme should not be modified by reducing, abridging or qualifying in any way the social assistance entitlements created under the original scheme of NMBS for expecting BPL mothers, including cash entitlement of Rs. 500/ - provided therein. We have requested learned Additional Solicitor General to place on record further material in the form of affidavit to effectively implement the new Scheme sought to be introduced. The further material shall include the approximate distance of Public Health Centre from the residential complexes and the facility of transportation etc. The Commissioner shall also examine the matter in depth and file a report. The response to the application may be filed within eight weeks. Meanwhile, the existing National Maternity Benefit Scheme will continue.

On oral application of Mr. Gonsalvez, for the present, we permit Mr. Harsh Mander to continue to assist the Commissioner - Dr. Saxena.

In 5th Report of August, 2004 of the Commissioner's it has been reported that on ground level, Public Distribution System is not working well, many poor people living BPL have not been issued the BPL ration cards. Orders of this Court are not being implemented and to support details have been given at page 3411 along with recommendations up to page 3421. The recommendation is that the Chief Secretaries shall put in place a mechanism to ensure suitable action against the officials who hesitate in taking action against the guilty; the State Government shall set up committees to frame detailed procedure and time frames for dealing with various types of grievances and complaints received from the public; an independent Public Service Commission be constituted to listen to the grievances and provide redressal in a time bound manner and the said body should be vested with necessary powers and finances to carry out its functions and to ensure implementation of Court's orders. Some of the States mentioned are Rajasthan, M.P., Orissa, Delhi, Bihar, West Bengal, Chhattisgarh and Assam. The State Governments have not responded to the report. A grievance has also been made by Mr. Gonsalvez that despite letters from the Commissioner pointing out the violations of the Court's Orders appropriate actions are not taken. Learned counsel suggests that the licenses of the violators shall be cancelled and work of Public Distribution System be assigned to Panchayat or other bodies. Before we consider these aspects, we deem it appropriate to give a last opportunity to the State Governments to respond to the report, particularly those States whose names have been mentioned in the report, to file their response within eight weeks.

IA No. 45.

Issue notice only to Delhi State. Mr.Ashok Bhan, learned counsel, accepts notice. Reply may be filed within eight weeks.

IA No. 48.

Response to this application may be filed within eight weeks.

IA No. 50.

The prayer of the nature made in the application cannot be entertained. If the applicant is aggrieved for non-issue of BPL Card, she may have recourse to appropriate remedy. IA is dismissed.

Rest of the matters are adjourned.

22. Text of the Order 14th February, 2006

Counsel for the parties state that a settlement has been arrived at between the petitioner and Ministry of Rural

Development and the Ministry of Consumer Affairs, Food and Public Distribution, Government of India. The terms of which are as follows :

1. Food grain allocations by the Central Government to beneficiaries under TPDS will be continued to be made at the present to States on the basis of Planning commission estimates of 1993-94 poverty rations, which is at 36% applied to the population projections of the Registrar General of India as on 1.3.2000 or on the basis of families identified and issued ration cards by the State Government whichever is less.
2. The survey methodology for the next BPL census will be designed by the Ministry of Rural Development in consultation with the Supreme Court Commissioner's in the right to food matter Case No. 196/2001 along with other sections of the society latest by the beginning of the 11th Five Year Plan.
3. Provisions will be made to allow new names to be added and ineligible names deleted from the BPL

List 2002 on a continuous basis during the period that the list will be applicable.

In view of the afore-stated settlement arrived at between the parties, counsel for the petitioner states that additional affidavit, as directed by this Court on 15.12.2005 is not required to be filed. Counsel for the parties further state that I.A. Nos. 25, 26, 31, 32, 48 and 53 may be disposed of in terms of the settlement arrived at between the parties. Ordered accordingly.

The stay order dated 5th May, 2003 is vacated. Adjourned by four weeks.

23. Text of the Order 1st May, 2006

Heard learned counsel for the petitioner.

It appears that the High Court declined to interfere only on the ground that the matter is sub-judicial before this Court.

We notice that this court in D.K. Basu vs. State of West Bengal 1997 (1) SCC 416 passed the following order : "Failure to comply with the requirements herein above mentioned shall apart from rendering the official concerned liable for departmental action also rendered him liable to be punished for contempt of court and the proceedings for contempt of court may be instituted in any High Court of the country having territorial jurisdiction over the matter".

Instead of contempt proceedings, it would be appropriate if the High Court shall take up the matter as a writ petition so that the matter can be appropriately dealt with.

With the aforesaid observations, the special leave petition is disposed of.

24. Text of the Order 12th July, 2006

After having heard learned counsel for the parties, we find that there is practically no monitoring over the sums allotted for the Public Distribution System (in short PDS) by the Central Government, and its utilisation. The amount involved, we are told, is in the neighbourhood of rupees thirty thousand Crores annually.

Certain suggestions have been given by Mr. Colin Gonsalvez, learned senior counsel, as to the modalities to be adopted in such cases. At the present stage, we feel it would be necessary to constitute a Central Vigilance Committee, headed by a retired Judge of this Court to be assisted by Dr. N.C. Saxena, the Commissioner earlier appointed by this Court. We request Mr. Justice D.P. Wadhwa to head the Committee.

The Committee shall look into the maladies which are affecting the proper functioning of the system, and also suggest remedial measures. For this purpose, the Committee shall, amongst other things, focus on :

(a) The mode of appointment of the dealers,
(b) The ideal commission or the rates payable to the dealers, and

(c) Modalities as to how the Committees already in place, can function better.
(d) Modes as to how there can be transparency in allotment of the food stock to be sold at the shops.

While dealing with the question of the mode of appointment, the committee shall also suggest as to a transparent mode in the selection of the dealers. The committee shall also indicate as to how more effective action can be taken on the report of the Vigilance committees already appointed. It goes without saying that the same shall be in addition to the legal remedies available to any citizen in setting law into motion. We request the committee to give its report within a period of four months so that further instructions/directions can be given.

The committee would invite suggestions from general public, organizations and would consider the suggestions, if any received, in the proper perspective.

We are giving this unusual direction in view of the almost accepted fact that large scale corruption is involved and there is hardly any remedial step taken to put an end to this. The ultimate victim is the poor citizen who is deprived of his legitimate entitlement of food grains. The Public Distribution System is intended to ensure that a citizen gets the food grains at a reasonable price keeping in view his economic standards. The expenses including honorarium to the Chairman and the Member Convener and other financial involvements of the committee shall be borne by the Food Ministry of the Central Government. The honorarium shall be same as the pay and allowances of a sitting Judge of this Court and a Joint Secretary of the Union of India. The necessary infrastructure shall be provided by the concerned ministry within three weeks from today. This direction is initially given for the Government of Delhi to be followed on All India basis. List the matter after the report is filed.
I.A. Nos. 34, 35, 40 and 49

List on 27th July, 2006.

I.A. Nos. 58 and 59

Mr. Ravindra K. Adsure, learned counsel accepts notice on behalf of the State of Maharashtra. Response, if any, shall be filed before the next date of hearing, i.e.,27th July, 2006.

I.A. Nos. 60 and 61

Learned counsel for the State of Maharashtra waives notice. However, it is stated that an affidavit indicating the factual position shall be placed on record before the next date., i.e. 27th July, 2006.

S.L.P.(C) No. 17906 of 2003

Delay condoned.

We find that the grievance made in this petition can be considered by the authorities in the light of orders to be passed in the connected matters, if occasion so arises. This special leave petition is, accordingly, disposed of.

25. Text of the Judgement 13th December, 2006*

Keeping in view the submissions made and considering the materials placed on record we direct as follows :

(1) Government of India shall sanction and operationalize a minimum of 14 lakh AWCs in a phased and even manner starting forthwith and ending December 2008. In doing so, the Central Government shall identify SC and ST hamlets/ habitations for AWCs on a priority basis.

(2) Government of India shall ensure that population norms for opening of AWCs must not be revised upward under any circumstances. While maintaining the upper limit of one AWC per 1000 population, the minimum limit for opening of a new AWC is a population of 300 may be kept in view. Further, rural communities and slum dwellers should be entitled to an "Anganwadis

* This is an extract of the order pertaining to the 'directions' given by the Court

on demand" (not later than three months) from the date of demand in cases where a settlement has at least 40 children under six but no Anganwadis.

(3) The universalisation of the ICDS involves extending all ICDS services (Supplementary nutrition, growth monitoring, nutrition and health education, immunization, referral and pre-school education) to every child under the age of 6, all pregnant women and lactating mothers and all adolescent girls.

(4) All the State Governments and Union Territories shall fully implement the ICDS scheme by, inter alia,

(i) Allocating and spending at least Rs. 2 per child per day for supplementary nutrition out of which the Central Government shall contribute Rs. 1 per child per day. (ii) Allocating and spending at least Rs. 2.70 for every severely malnourished child per day for supplementary nutrition out of which the Central Government shall contribute Rs. 1.35 per child per day. (iii) Allocating and spending at least Rs. 2.30 for every pregnant woman, nursing mother/ adolescent girl per day for supplementary nutrition out of which the Central Government shall contribute Rs.1.15.

(5) The Chief Secretaries of the State of Bihar, Jharkhand, Madhya Pradesh, Manipur, Punjab, West Bengal, Assam, Haryana and Uttar Pradesh shall appear personally to explain why the orders of this Court requiring the full implementation of the ICDS scheme were not obeyed.

(6) Chief Secretaries of all State Governments/UTs are directed to submit affidavits with details of all habitations with a majority of SC/ST households, the availability of AWCs in these habitations, and the plan of action for ensuring that all these habitations have functioning AWCs within two years.

(7) Chief Secretaries of all State Governments/UTs are directed to submit affidavits giving details of the steps that have been taken with regard to the order of this Court of 7th October, 2004 directing that "contractors

shall not be used for supply of nutrition in Anganwadis and preferably ICDS funds shall be spent by making use of village communities, self-help groups and Mahila Mandals for buying of grains and preparation of meals". Chief Secretaries of all State Governments/UTs must indicate a time-frame within which the decentralization of the supply of SNP through local community shall be done.

(8) It is a matter of concern that 15 States and Union Territories have not submitted any affidavit in compliance with the order dated 7.10.2004. They are the States of Orissa, Uttar Pradesh, Sikkim, Arunachal Pradesh, Nagaland, Goa, Punjab, Manipur, Tamil Nadu, Andhra Pradesh, Mizoram, Haryana, Bihar and the National Capital of Delhi and the Union Territory of Lakshadweep. Within four weeks reply shall be filed through the concerned Chief Secretary as to why action for contempt shall not be initiated for the lapse.

The matters shall be listed after three months. Upto date statistic report shall be filed by the different States, Union Territories and the Central Government.

26. Text of the Order 1st February, 2007

A detailed memorandum has been filed by Mr. Colin Gonsalvez and certain directions have been prayed for. Essentially the National Maternity Benefit Scheme (in short the 'NMBS') and Janani Suraksha Yojana (JSY) are the schemes with which the present I. As. i.e. I.A. No. 37/2004 and I.A. No. 54/2005 are concerned. With reference to the report of the Commission appointed by this Court and certain statistical data, it has been highlighted that there is practically no step taken for implementation of the schemes in question.

Additionally, it is submitted that because of lack of monitoring the schemes have not taken up in the way they were intended to be put in place. Let the Union of India, which is providing the funds for the implementation of the schemes; file its response to the suggestions given by Mr. Colin Gonsalvez. It has also been highlighted that there has been total non-implementation of the schemes in certain States including Delhi where it is stated the number of persons getting benefits i.e. targeted beneficiaries is nil.

Let the States of Uttar Pradesh, Uttarakhand, Bihar, Delhi, Jharkhand, Madhya Pradesh, Chhattisgarh, Assam, Rajasthan, Orissa and Jammu and Kashmir file their response as to why there has been such dismal inaction in implementation of the schemes. While filing the response, the Union of India shall indicate as to how the Union of India proposes to monitor the implementation of the schemes by the State Government and in what way there can be more coordinated effort for implementing the schemes. In the response to be filed, the Union of India shall also indicate as to whether it would be in the interest of the beneficiaries if the funds are directly placed at the disposal of the Gram Panchayats so that without unnecessary delay beneficiaries can get immediate benefit of the schemes. The intention of the schemes appears to be providing nutritional assistance to the expecting mothers. It is apparent from the report of the Commissioner that in the rural areas the non performance is more acute. It is brought to our notice that there have been some modifications in the JSY scheme which do not appear to have been made known to the beneficiaries.

It would be appropriate if the Union of India and the State Governments take steps to make the beneficiaries aware of the benefits of the schemes and the entitlements flowing there from. Let the response be filed within three weeks by the Union of India and by the State Governments within four weeks. The State Governments shall also indicate their suggestions as to what effective steps can be taken for better implementation of the schemes and how there can be more coordinated effort between the Union of India and the State Governments.

Mr. Colin Gonsalvez learned senior counsel is also requested to compile the responses, if any filed, and give his suggestions as regards the modes to be adopted for better results.

Call this matter in the third week of March 2007.

The budget estimates required for the Commissioner by this Court is placed on record. A copy has also been handed over to the learned counsel for the Union of India; let him take the instructions so that necessary orders can be passed on the next date of hearing.

27. Text of the Order 9th July, 2007

1. Grievance of the writ petitioner in these I.As. Is that a number of Anganwadis centres which are required to be sanctioned by December 2008 is 14 lakhs. But the number of centres sanctioned as on March, 2007 is 10.53 lakhs. Therefore, about 3.47 lakhs centres need to be sanctioned. As per the data available, the numbers of Anganwadis centres which are operational as on 30.9.2006 is 7.81 lakhs. Therefore, even the sanctioned centres have not become operational and their number is 2.72 lakhs. The details of some of the States where sanctioned Anganwadis centres have not been operationalized to a large extent are as follows :

From the affidavit of the Union of India it appears that the position is as follows :

State	*No. of sanctioned Anganwadis**	*No. of sanctioned Anganwadis centres Not operationalised**	
		As per UOI	*As per State Govt. Affidavits*
Bihar	80528	22761	19602
Jharkhand	32097	10638	7680
Madhya Pradesh	69238	19432	16165
Punjab	20169	5439	5439
Haryana	17192	1225	1225
West Bengal	92152	37088	37092

Uttar Pradesh	150727	33987	22087
Manipur	7639	3138	3138
Assam	37082	11635	11666

* This includes the ICDS centres sanctioned in December 2006 under Phase II expansion. None of these centres have obviously been operationalised.

2. By 31.3.2005-7, 64,709, by 30.9.2006-9, 46,000 (approx.) and by December 2006- 1.02 lakhs centres have been sanctioned with a total of about 10, 48,000.
3. By order dated 13.12.2006 it was inter-alia directed as follows :

"(1) Government of India shall sanction and operationalize a minimum of 14 lakh AWCs in a phased and even manner starting forthwith and ending December 2008. In doing so, the Central Government shall identify SC and ST hamlets/ habitations for AWCs on a priority basis.

(2) Government of India shall ensure that population norms for opening of AWCs must not be revised upward under any circumstances. While maintaining the upper limit of one AWC per 1000 population, the minimum limit for opening of a new AWC is a population of 300 may be kept in view. Further, rural communities and slum dwellers should be entitled to an Anganwadis on demand "(not later than three months) from the date of demand in cases where a settlement has at least 40 children under six but no Anganwadis."

4. It is a matter of concern that even the sanctioned centres (the number of which is much less than the targeted one) have not been made operational.
5. Learned counsel appearing for different States has indicated various reasons for the same. Prima facie we are not satisfied with the reasons indicated. The need for having functional Anganwadis centres has never been questioned and cannot be questioned.

6. The importance of Anganwadis centres has been highlighted by this Court in several orders. By order dated 7.10.2004 it was noted as follows :

"Now we would deal with the aspect of sanctioned AWCs and their working. In the Order dated 29.4.2004 it was directed that the sanctioned AWCs shall be made fully operational by 30th June, 2004. Further direction issued was that the sanctioned AWCs shall supply nutritious food/ supplement to the children, adolescent girls and to pregnant and lactating women under the scheme for 300 days in a year. The Report presents a glooming picture both in regard to the operation of the sanctioned AWCs in some of the States like Uttar Pradesh, Bihar and Jharkhand and the position in those which are operational. Instances have been given in the Report where for months the supplies were not made to the children. For example, in the State of Jharkhand, the sanctioned AWCs were not working from May to December, 2003. No satisfactory reply is forthcoming from that State. Further, there are material discrepancies in two affidavits filed by the said State one in September and the one handed over in the Court today. In the September affidavit, it was deposed on oath that 16689 AWCs were operational. In the affidavit filed today, the figure of operational AWCs is stated to be 7429. According to the Report, on an average, 42 paisa as against the norm of rupee one was being allocated per beneficiary per day by the State of Jharkhand. The position in Bihar and Uttar Pradesh is also no better. Out of 394 sanctioned ICDS projects, only 249 were operational in the State of Bihar. As per the affidavit dated 30th September, 2004, all the projects were being made operational from 4th October, 2004.

Whether that has happened or not, Mr. B.B. Singh learned counsel appearing for the State is unable to state for want of instructions. Be that as it may, if all have not been made operational since 4th October, 2004 has already passed and gone we direct that the same shall be made operational in period not later than one week from today.

In the State of Uttar Pradesh, though percentage of non-functional/non-operational AWCs is more as per the Report but according to the State, admittedly 24 per cent are not operational. In the affidavit, it has been claimed that the remaining will be operational by 30th November, 2004. We direct the State Government to make operational all sanctioned AWCs by 30th November, 2004. After that, we would not entertain any application for extension of time.

The report also mentions that some of AWCs are operating from private houses including those of grain dealers which it is suggested is not a healthy way of working as it is likely to increase the chances of pilferage of the grain etc. We are happy to note that as stated in the affidavit of State of Uttar Pradesh, it has made efforts to shift AWCs to primary schools. It is a good example for other States to follow. The report also mentions about the attempt to centralise the procurements in some of the States which has many fallouts. It has been explained in one of the affidavits that the procurements are at district level and not at the State level. Further, the problem of using contractors for procurement has also been mentioned in the report suggesting that it should be done by agencies and officers at the Government level. These are only by way of illustrations as to facts and figures given in Section 1 of the report relating to Integrated Child Development Services.

7. Learned counsel for the State of U.P. has pointed out that because of elections there was some delay.

8. In the circumstances, we direct as follows :

   The backlog has to be cleared immediately and the centres which have been sanctioned upto September 2006 shall be made operational and functional by 15th July, 2007 in the case of all States except the State of U.P. where the last date is fixed to be 31st July, 2007. Those centres which have been sanctioned upto January 2007 shall be made functional by 30.9.2007.

9. It is made clear that if there is any non-observance of the time period fixed would be seriously viewed. Affidavits shall be filed by 20th July, 10th August and

10th October, 2007 by the States in respect of the date lines fixed indicating the action taken.

10. List this matter on 20th July, 2007.

28. Text of the 25thJuly, 2007

Upon hearing the counsel the Court made the following Order :

Inspite of several orders of this Court, the pace at which operationalization of the sanctioned Anganwadis Centres is taking place is a sad reflection on the sincerity and seriousness of various State Governments to carry out the policy decisions relating to functioning of the Anganwadis centres. It is shocking to note that even in respect of Anganwadis Centres sanctioned in 2005-2006, in several States, the percentage of functional centres is very low. Glaring examples are the States of Bihar, Rajasthan, Himachal Pradesh, Keral and Orissa. Though in some of the other States, 100% operationalization has not been done, keeping in view the deadlines of phases as fixed by this court, but they are in most cases more than 90%. It needs no reiteration that by various previous orders, emphasis was laid on the need for making the sanctioned Anganwadis Centres functional. Taking note of the lapse so far as named States are concerned, notice of contempt is issued to the Chief Secretaries of the States of Bihar, Himachal Pradesh, Keral, Rajasthan and Orissa to appear in person in this Court on 30th August, 2007. They shall file affidavits indicating the reason for non-compliance with this Court's orders. In the affidavits, they shall also indicate the names of the other officers who are responsible for not complying with the Court's orders. The affidavit shall be filed latest by 24th August, 2007.

29. Text of the Order 30th August, 2007

Upon hearing the counsel the Court made the following Order :

Heard learned amicus curiae and learned counsel for different States. From the details filed, it appears that more or less the stipulated operationalization has been done, so far as the Anganwadis Centres which were sanctioned upto September 2006. For the subsequent period it is expected that the zeal shown after the notice of contempt was issued shall be continued to see that there is no further lapse.

The matter shall be listed after six weeks. The personal presence of the Chief Secretaries who are present in Court is dispensed with for the present. So far as the State of Orissa is concerned, though there is substantial progress, because the chief secretary has not appeared today, he shall appear on the next date of hearing to consider whether his appearance can be dispensed with.

Further affidavits, if any, are permitted to be filed. A copy of Mr. Justice D.P. Wadhwa's report be supplied to the learned amicus curiae and learned counsel appearing for the Union of India.

30. Text of the Order 20th November, 2007

As regards Suo Moto Contempt Petition (C) No. 128 of 2007 in W. P. (C) No. 196/2001 IN R E : Chief Secry. State of Bihar & 4 Ors. The I. As. are disposed of in terms of the signed judgment.

31. Text of the Order 20th November, 2007

1. By this order two IAs. No. 37 of 2004 and No. 54 of 2005 stand disposed of IA No. 37 of 2004 is an application by the Union of India for permission to modify the National Maternity Benefit Scheme (in short 'NMBS') and to introduce a new scheme called the Janani Suraksha Yojana (in short 'JSY'). IA No. 54 of 2005 is an application by the petitioner questioning legality of the discontinuation of the benefit under the NMBS due to introduction of JSY. By order dated 27.04.2004 this Court directed as follows :

"No Scheme...in particular...National Maternity Benefit Scheme shall be discontinued or restricted in any way without prior approval of the Court."

2. Again by order dated 09.05.2005 this Court directed as follows:

"By IA 37, permission is sought to modify The National Maternity Benefit Scheme (NMBS) and to introduce a new scheme namely Janani Suraksha Yojana (JSY). Whereas in IA 54, the prayer is that the Scheme should not be modified by reducing, abridging or qualifying in any way the social assistance entitlements created under the original scheme of NMBS for expecting BPL mothers, including cash entitlements of Rs. 500/- provided therein. We have requested learned Additional Solicitor General to place on record further material in the form of affidavit to effectively implement the new Scheme sought to be introduced. The further material shall include the approximate distance of Public Health Centre from the residential complexes and the facility of transportation etc. The Commissioner shall also examine the matter in depth and file a report. The response to the application may be filed within eight weeks. Meanwhile, the existing National Maternity Benefit Scheme will continue."

3. The government set a numerical ceiling of 57.5 lakh beneficiaries as the annual target for NMBS. However, the number of beneficiaries under JSY in 2006-07 was only 26.2 lakh i.e. 45.5% and in the year 2005-06 this was as low as 5.7 lakh i.e. 10%. While there has been an improvement in the last one year, the coverage under this scheme is still very below the target number of women to be covered by the NMBS.

4. According to the Union of India the JSY was introduced to put a premium on the willingness of poor women to go in the institutional delivery instead of home delivery. But it was recognized that in States with lower institutional delivery rates, one of the reasons for low performance have been lesser availabilities of facilities in the Health Centres, which act as disincentive for the poor illiterate women to seek the services.

5. Pursuant to the order of this Court dated 09.05.2005 the Commissioner had prepared a report.
6. After discussions with the Commissioner appointed by this Court, senior officials, the Central Government took a decision to modify the JSY Scheme to continue the benefits of NMBS and also to improve upon such benefits for non-institutional delivery, where the women chooses to deliver her baby at home. In this connection, a letter dated 13.07.2006 was written to the Commissioner by the Secretary Health and Family Welfare under the amended JSY. The Low Performing States and High Performing States were defined as follows :

   "4.1 The scheme focuses on the poor pregnant woman with special dispensation for states having low institutional delivery rates namely the States of Uttar Pradesh, Uttarakhand, Bihar, Jharkhand, Madhya Pradesh, Chhattisgarh, Assam, Rajasthan, Orissa and Jammu and Kashmir. While these states have been named as Low Performing States (LPS), the remaining states have been named as High Performing States (HPS)."
7. The table below gives details of the number of beneficiaries under JSY (all these would have received the Rs. 500/- under NMBS irrespective of place of delivery) vis-à-vis the annual targets set by the Government of India for NMBS.
8. The scheme as the details above go to show has virtually not taken off in many states. Delhi has given the benefit under the NMBS to only 20 women in 2006-07, while in Chandigarh the number of beneficiaries is 0. In Sikkim Meghalaya, Himachal Pradesh, Uttar Pradesh, Haryana and Dadar and Nagar Haveli have less than even 10% of the eligible beneficiaries have been covered under the NMBS. Except for the states of Andhra Pradesh, Jammu & Kashmir, Rajasthan, Madhya Pradesh, Assam, Orissa and Mizoram where more than 75% of the eligible beneficiaries seem to have been reached out to, the performance of this scheme has been very poor in all the other states.

Percentage of Eligible Beneficiaries Covered Under NMBS

State	*No. of Women eligible for NMBS*	*No. of Beneficiaries in 2006-2007*	*Percentage of Eligible Benefici-aries covered*
Andhra Pradesh	296033	457000	154.4
Rajasthan	28123	387648	138.4
J&K	50494	57798	114.5
Assam	122894	183231	100.2
Orissa	264249	227204	86.0
Madhya Pradesh	472840	401184	84.8
Mizorum	4429	3330	75.2
Chhattisgarh	148876	74778	50.2
Uttarakhand	37117	18614	50.1
West Bengal	425520	199000	46.8
Tamil Nadu	301676	136091	45.1
Karanạtaka	28939	81152	28.0
A & N Islands	2295	600	26.1
Kerala	107602	27683	25.0
Bihar	732891	171353	23.4
Pondicherry	6446	1315	20.4
Gujarat	212845	42373*	20.0
Punjab	41297	8276	20.0
Maharashtra	529777	97390	18.4
Tripura	20601	3203	15.5
Manipur	11112	1684	15.2
Goa	3188	483	15.1
Lakshadweep	333	42	12.6
Sikkim	4598	446	9.7
Meghalaya	22768	2031	8.9
Himachal Pradesh	29222	2508	8.6
Uttar Pradesh	1073341	71456	6.7
Haryana	92856	3294	3.5
D & N Haveli3850		76	2.0
Chandigarh	2108	0	0.0
Delhi	42447	20	0.0
Arunachal Pradesh	1039	NR	NR
Damman and Diu	632	NR	NR
Jharkhand	208592	NR	NR
Nagaland	12763	NR	NR
Total India	**5925554**	**2618889**	**44.2**

Indicated Below are Percentage of Home Delivery Figures

State%	*Home delivery reported of JSY beneficiaries (2006-2007)*	*% Home delivery in out the state (NFHS 3)*
Assam	4.4	77
Madhya Pradesh	0.9	70
Haryana	0.0	61
Rajasthan	13.5	68
Manipur	0.0	51
Delhi	0.0	39
Meghalaya	41.4	70
Orissa	33.3	61
Chhattisgarh	59.2	84
Sikkim	44.8	51
Tamil Nadu	5.7	10
Bihar	75.9	78
Karanataka	37.6	33
Kerala	5.2	0
Mizorum	44.1	35
Tripura	60.5	51
Uttar Pradesh	90.2	78
Uttarakhand	96.9	64
Punjab	82.9	47
Maharashtra	86.0	34
Goa	67.9	7

9. In the States of Madhya Pradesh, Haryana, Manipur and Delhi there are almost no JSY beneficiaries who had a home delivery. This indicates that in these States the scheme's focus continues to be only on institutional deliveries and not all deliveries. Even in the States of Assam, Rajasthan, Meghalaya, Orissa and Chhattisgarh the JSY has been disproportionately given to only those who have had institutional deliveries.
10. At this juncture, the financial performance needs to be noted.

11. The Janani Suraksha Yojana is a centrally-sponsored scheme with the centre providing 100% of the funds. Some states e.g. Andhra Pradesh make their own contribution thereby increasing the amount of cash assistance for in-stitutional deliveries. Tamil Nadu has introduced a separate scheme for providing mothers with Rs. 1000/- per month for six months i.e. three months prior to the delivery and three months after. Given below are the details of allocation and utilization of the funds provided by the Central Government.
12. Out of the funds provided for JSY for 2006-07, about 71.2% of the funds allocated have been utilized in the year 2006-07.

Utilization of Funds Allocated by JSY
(Rs. in Lakhs)

State	*Fund realeased in 2006-2007*	*Expenditure reported by state*	*% Utilization*
Andaman Nicobar Island	10.00	1.99	19.9
Andhra Pradesh	4073.20	4550.00	111.7
Arunachal Pradesh	26.2	0.31	1.2
Assam	1300.00	1331.32	102.4
Bihar	610.00	190.00	31.1
Chandigarh	5.23	0.00	0.0
Chhattisgarh	513.00	516.55	100.7
D & N Haveli	9.17	0.73	8.0
Daman & Diu	5.23	0.00	0.0
Delhi	65.49	0.20	0.3
Goa	7.86	0.38	43.0
Gujarat	851.85	185.56	21.8
Haryana	350.00	39.11	11.2
Himachal Pradesh	100.00	20.66	20.7
J & K	138.33	123.84	89.5

State	*Fund realeased in 2006-2007*	*Expenditure reported by state*	*% Utilization*
Jharkhand	392.89	64.67	16.5
Karnataka	916.00	594.02	
Kerala	511.94	284.45	55.6
Lakshdweep	4.83	0.31	7.1
Madhya Pradesh	4261.00	2482.00	58.2
Maharashtra	785.79	209.07	26.6
Manipur	78.57	13.45	17.1
Meghalaya	39.29	42.75	108.8
Mizorum	78.57	37.27	47.4
Nagaland	65.49	0.00	0.0
Orissa	1600.00	1571.31	98.2
Pondicherry	19.64	6.10	31.1
Punjab	145.37	56.84	39.1
Rajasthan	4085.00	3056.35	74.8
Tami Nadu	13.1	7.46	56.9
Sikkim	1827.00	1441.00	78.9
Tripura	117.86	43.70	37.1
Uttar Pradesh	1375.00	436.80	31.8
Uttarakhand	79.56	56.06	70.5
West Bengal	1678.99	1233.67	733.5
Total	**26141.00**	**18600.93**	**71.2**

13. Looking at the State-wise break-up it is seen that states like Delhi, Nagaland and Arunachal Pradesh, and union territories of Chandigarh and Daman & Diu have not at all utilized the funds allocated to them for the purpose of JSY. Among other states, Manipur, Jharkhand and Haryana utilized less than 20% of the funds released to them. Only 10 states spent more than 70% of the funds allocated to them under JSY.

14. At the time of hearing of the applications, learned counsel for the petitioner and the Union of India

highlighted various aspects. Considering the submissions and the material data placed on record we direct as follows :

(a) The Union of India and all the State Governments and the Union Territories shall
  (i) continue with the NMBS and
  (ii) ensure that all BPL pregnant women get cash assistance 8-12 weeks prior to the delivery.

(b) The amount shall be Rs. 500/- per birth irrespective of number of children and the age of the women.

(c) The Union of India, State Governments and the Union Territories shall file affidavits within 8 weeks from today indicating the total number of births in the State, number of eligible BPL women who have received the benefits, number of BPL women who had home/ non-institutional deliveries and have received the benefit, number of BPL women who had institutional deliveries and have received the benefit.

(d) The total number of resources allocated and utilized for the period 2000-2006.

(e) All concerned governments are directed to regularly advertise the revised scheme so that the intended beneficiaries can become aware of the scheme.

(f) The Central Government shall ensure that the money earmarked for the scheme is not utilized for any other purpose. The mere insistence on utilization certificate may not yield the expected result.

(g) It shall be the duty of all concerned to ensure that the benefits of the scheme reach the intended beneficiaries. In case it is noticed that there in any diversion of the funds allocated for the scheme, such stringent action as is called for shall be taken against the erring officials responsible for diversion of the funds.

15. At this juncture it would be necessary to take note of certain connected issues which have relevance. It seems from the scheme that irrespective of number of children, the beneficiaries are given the benefit. This in a way

goes against the concept of family planning which is intended to curb the population growth. Further the age of the mother is a relevant factor because women below a particular age are prohibited from legally getting married. The Union of India shall consider this aspect while considering the desirability of the continuation of the scheme in the present form. After considering the aforesaid aspects and if need be, necessary amendments may be made.

16. The IAs is accordingly disposed of.

32. Text of the Order 10th January, 2008

We have perused the report submitted by the Commission headed by Justice D.P. Wadhwa. The report is very comprehensive and gives a detailed analysis of various aspects which needed to be addressed. There is unanimity at the Bar that the report deserves acceptance. Therefore, we direct acceptance of the report. In terms of the earlier order, let a similar exercise be undertaken for the entire country, because the factors highlighted by the Commission are not restricted to Delhi alone, and appear to be prevalent throughout the country. The Commission is requested to submit its report within a period of six months. The earlier modalities relating to salary etc. shall be continued. The various suggestions given and shortfalls noticed by the Commission shall be addressed after the subsequent report is received.

The order dated 28.11.2001 is modified to the extent that the allotment shall be 35 kg. in view of the increase, subsequent to the order.

Annexure-2
Reports of Commissioners

Introduction and Summary of Recommendations

In the dark shadows of this land, the silent tragedy plays out, of millions of women and men, boys and girls, who sleep hungry. The experience of chronic hunger in distant villages as much as on city streets is one of intense avoidable suffering; of self-denial; of learning to live with far less than the body needs; of minds and bodies stymied in their growth; of the agony of helplessly watching one's loved one's—most heartbreakingly children—in hopeless torment; of unpaid, arduous devalued work; of shame, humiliation and bondage of the defeat and the triumph of the human spirit.

Such high levels of hunger and malnutrition are a paradox, because they stubbornly survive surging economic growth and agricultural production which outpaces the growth of population (although it has worryingly stagnated in recent years). The riddle deepens because the State in India runs some of the largest and most ambitious food schemes in the world. The persistence of widespread hunger is the cumulative outcome of public policies that produce and reproduce impoverishment; of failures to invest in agriculture especially in Central and Eastern India and for rain-fed and small farmers; of unacknowledged and unaddressed destitution; of embedded gender, caste, tribe, disability and stigma which construct all social barriers to accessing food; but in the last analysis it is the result of a profound collapse of governance.

The State in India implements massive food, livelihood and social security programmes - some of the largest in the world - which theoretically support vulnerable people from even before their birth to their survivors after death. Expectant mothers are fed in ICDS centres, along with infants, children up to the age of six and adolescent girls. The child in school gets school meals. As adults, women receive maternity support, bread earners are guaranteed 100 days of wage employment in public works; and if identified to be poor, they can buy subsidised cereals from a massive network of half a million ration shops. The aged - and in many states widows and disabled people - are given pensions. And if an earning adult dies prematurely, the survivor is entitled to insurance.

These programmes are plagued by corruption, leakages, errors in selection, delays, poor allocations and little accountability. They also tend to discriminate against and exclude those who most need them, by social barriers of gender, age, caste, ethnicity, faith and disability; and State hostility to urban poor migrants, street and slum residents, and unorganised workers.

The most evolved definition of food security so far at the time of writing that we could locate in the literature appears in the State of Food Insecurity 2001: 'Food security [is] a situation that exists when all people, at all times, have physical, *social* and economic access to sufficient, safe and nutritious food that meets their dietary needs and food preferences for an active and healthy life'. (emphasis added). The inclusion in the definition of 'social' access is highly significant, because it acknowledges that people may be barred from access to food even if it is locally available and they have the economic means. These social barriers to food security may include gender, caste, race, disability or stigmatised ailments.

The brutal expulsion of those who most need it, from support and succour, from care and rights - often by their own families, by local communities, but most importantly by the State - is one of the most profound public crimes of our times. It is important therefore to identify those classes, social categories and local communities, who are destitute and socially expelled, which is the task this report sets itself. These are people who lack the resources, financial and material, the employment, assets, access to credit, and social and family support and networks, to secure the means for dignified survival. In the first instance, this would entail sufficient and assured food for themselves and in many cases for their dependents. These are men and women, girls and boys who are powerless and disenfranchised, socially isolated and devalued, sometimes stigmatised and even illegalised, and often with special needs born out of disability, illness, social standing and age.

Even in the more intimate context of a village, many of these socially excluded groups are invisible, barely known and acknowledged. In most contemporary cultural contexts, social categories that consistently tend to be very dispossessed and vulnerable in their access to food include disabled people, both as bread winners and dependents, single women and the households that they head, aged people especially those who are left behind when their families migrate or who are not cared for by their grown children, people with stigmatised and debilitating ailments such as TB, HIV AIDS and leprosy, working and out of school children and bonded workers. In addition, in diverse cultural and socio-economic contexts, others may be added, such as some specially disadvantaged dalit groups like Musahars or Madigas in another, weavers, artisans and particularly disadvantaged minority groups in yet another, all designated 'primitive tribal groups', survivors of conflict and internal displacement, and many other diverse forgotten people. Many of them are of contested citizenship.

In the bridge between rural and urban destitute are the distress migrants, at the bottom of the heap both where they move for work, and from where they come. In urban contexts are street children, with or without responsible adult caregivers, urban homeless people, slum dwellers and a wide range of unorganised workers, both seasonal migrants and settlers, such as rickshaw pullers, porters, loaders, construction workers and small vendors, and people dependent on begging.

Overcoming corruption, theft, leakages, inefficiencies, and constraints of costs, are imperative, but still not sufficient, in a highly unequal society like ours, to overcome the barriers that powerless and expelled dispossessed people face to access food and livelihoods with dignity. They may not be able to find work and food only because they are women, and worse single women, because they are aged or disabled, because they suffer from caste discrimination of millennia, because of the discrimination fostered against ethnic and religious minorities and indigenous people, because of the stigma of dreaded diseases like leprosy or HIV AIDS, and for a host of other social barriers.

Government programmes are also woefully inadequate to address destitution; in fact they tend to be blind to or in denial of the fact that large numbers of people lack even the elementary means and power to survive with dignity. Our evidence is that apart from major leakages and corruption, the coverage of government food schemes is so meagre that they leave huge gaping holes in the social security net, through which large numbers of most destitute women and men, girls and boys slip into starvation and hunger. It is stressed again that this is a duty of the State not to the dead, but to the precariously living. It requires public vigilance about individuals, communities and several categories living with starvation and absolute hunger. It requires the State to act, not after there is an emergency like a drought or flood, not even *after* people die of starvation, but pro-actively before people slip into destitution, and fail to access in an assured and reliable manner, with dignity, the nutritious and culturally appropriate food they require to lead healthy lives.

In a sense, this set of duties are of pro-active measures by the State to prevent hunger and starvation and to promote well being and the right to food of all people : to anticipate and forestall starvation, by recognising and arresting destitution well in time, before it pushes hapless people into starvation. After a starvation death, the State's response is reactive, whereas what is imperative is that it is actively protective and deterrent, to end an enormous amount of avoidable and extreme human suffering.

As Commissioners of the Supreme Court in the writ petition (Civil) No. 196 of 2001 (People's Union for Civil Liberties Vs the Union of India & Others) dated 23/07/2001, we have submitted seven reports to the Court so far, which attempted to assess in depth the performance of various governments, central and state, in securing the right to food of its citizens. We attempted to do this mainly by tracking the compliance by governments of various instructions and directives of the Supreme Court regarding food schemes, and the actual performance of these schemes in terms of allocations, utilisations, coverage and field level performance issues like leakages and quality.

However, our field studies confirm distressingly that large numbers of the most vulnerable women and men, boys and girls in the country, are uncovered or inadequately covered by any government food schemes. An estimated eighty to two hundred million still sleep hungry every night. It is about these excluded and hungry people that the Supreme Court in its order in the writ petition (Civil) No. 196 of 2001 dated 23/07/2001, expressed deep worry :

> '...it is a matter of concern for all. In our opinion, what is of utmost importance is to see that food is provided to the aged, infirm, disabled, destitute women, destitute men who are in danger of starvation, pregnant and lactating women and destitute children, especially in cases where they or members of their family do not have sufficient funds to provide food for them. In case of famine, there may be shortage of food, but here the situation is that amongst plenty there is scarcity. Plenty of food is available, but distribution of the same amongst the very poor and the destitute is scarce and non-existent leading to mal-nourishment, starvation and other related problems'.

The Commissioners decided therefore to dedicate an entire report to these people who are condemned to live at the edge of hunger, to highlight the most urgent unfinished agenda of the right to food in India. We have titled our Eighth Report to the Supreme Court 'A Special Report on the Most Vulnerable Social Groups and their Access to Food'. In it, we have focussed on single women, the aged, the disabled and their dependents; 'primitive' tribal groups and most discriminated against dalit groups; bonded workers; urban homeless men, women, boys and girls, and residents or urban slum shanties. The chapters in this report elaborate their special social and economic vulnerabilities; estimates of their numbers and locations; the nature of and reasons for their intense nutritional denials; and the barriers to their access to food, livelihood and social security schemes of the government.

Each chapter ends with a set of detailed recommendations for public policy, and for consideration of the Supreme Court of India, to help surmount or dismantle these barriers, and ensure better access of these most vulnerable people who routinely subsist at the edge of starvation, to adequate and assured food with dignity. There is considerable diversity between the groups; therefore the recommendations are also specific. However, for convenience, some of the **most important recommendations** are summarised below :

Identification

1. One feature which is common to public policy relating to each of these dispossessed groups is the fact that for almost all, there is very little authentic official data, about their numbers and lists. This is not a chance or random default. It is the outcome of what we describe as **'invisibilisation**' of these powerless people by the state.

   We therefore recommend an effort at least once every two years do not just estimate these groups, but to conduct a full listing. This should be undertaken in each district of the country, led by the state government and district collectors, but with active participation of local bodies such as gram sabhas and municipalities, professionals, experts, civil society groups and representatives of these populations. These lists updated every two years, and form the basis for them to receive the entitlements detailed in this report.
2. It is remarkable that although persons deemed by the state to be 'below poverty line' in rural areas have been

surveyed and listed, no such survey has been undertaken for urban areas since Independence, although around a third of the country's poor live in cities. Targeted schemes like the TPDS are then accessible to them only when they apply to the concerned officials, who make their estimates of whether the applicant is 'poor' in each specific case. But directly asking people's incomes is not a reliable and verifiable criterion. And asking people only to certify income without any objective criteria is bound to be misused, leading to corruption, and the poorest will be left out.

It is proposed to identify and list the most poor and vulnerable segments of urban populations by identifying them along objective and verifiable criteria of vulnerability and denial of rights. These are: a) place of residence and access to public services: (shelterless, unauthorized slum dwellers, authorized slum dwellers and residents of resettlement colonies); b) social vulnerability: children without protection and child headed households, single women and single women headed households, disabled people and family with PWD, old people without care givers, people in destitution; c) vulnerable occupational categories: such as rag pickers, casual daily wage workers, rickshaw pullers, porters, construction workers, street vendors, domestic helpers etc; and d) affirmative action categories: Scheduled Castes/ Scheduled Tribes, Muslims.

The details of the proposed process of identification (which incidentally has been approved recently by the Delhi government on the recommendations of the Commissioners, and endorsement by the Planning Commission) are given in the pages of this report, but all state governments should be directed to survey the urban poor on these objectives and verifiable criteria.

3. Single adult women who live with or without dependents, as well as old people, who live with relatives by blood or marriage under the same roof, should be treated for purpose of all food schemes as separate

families. Specifically this means that single adult women and old people will be eligible for separate ration cards, even if they live under the same roof and share the same kitchen. This will assure them greater dignity and autonomy. The samewould of course apply to bonded workers who may stay with their employers.

Subsidised food grains under AAY

1. It has been recommended that almost all the groups identified in this report as most vulnerable are assured highly subsidised food grain under AAY (35 kilograms a month at the rate of two rupees a kilogram for wheat and three rupees a kilogram for rice). The only group that would be eligible for BPL rather than AAY grain are urban slum residents, who may not be the poorest of the poor.

   The Supreme Court already in its interim order of 2nd May, 2003, deliberated on the Antodaya Anna Yojana (AAY) and directed the Government of India directed to place on AAY category the following groups of persons:

   1) Aged, infirm, disabled, destitute men and women, pregnant and lactating women, destitute women;
   2) widows and other single women with no regular support;
   3) old persons (aged 60 or above) with no regular support and no assured means of subsistence;
   4) households with a disabled adult and no assured means of subsistence;
   5) households where due to old age, lack of physical or mental fitness, social customs, need to care for a disabled, or other reasons, no adult member is available to engage in gainful employment outside the house;
   6) primitive tribes."

   The only additional groups to this order that the Commissioners recommend for inclusion for universal coverage under AAY, are (a) urban homeless people; b) persons undergoing treatment for stigmatised ailments of TB and HIV AIDS; c) most discriminated dalit groups (identified by criteria and processes listed in this report) and d) Released bonded labourers.

However, we have found that interim order of 2nd May, 2003 of the Supreme Court is one of those least implemented by most state governments. We believe that there are 3 main reasons for this wide failure : a) the political powerlessness of these groups and the absence of authentic data about the groups; b) state governments have not interpreted the orders to be one of ensuring, in a phased manner, universal coverage of these groups with AAY cards, although in the absence of such universalisation, the most vulnerable will slip through this social security net; and c) the quotas for AAY in most states were already exhausted before the said 2003 order.

In order to remedy these problems, it needs to be reiterated by explicit Court directions that all members/ households of the following social groups must be covered by AAY cards within a maximum of 2 years, without being bound by BPL identification or state BPL quotes : (a) Primitive Tribal Groups; (b) identified 'most discriminated against' dalit groups, starting with the Musahars, the Madigas, and all households engaged in socially despised 'unclean occupations' such as manual scavenging, disposal of dead bodies and sewer workers; (c) single women headed households (except income tax payers); (d) households with disabled heads of families or dependents (except income tax payers); (e) released bonded workers; (f) urban homeless people and households; (g) aged people (except income tax payers); and (h) people undergoing treatment in government hospitals for TB and HIV/ AIDS, and the households to which they belong. As stated earlier, every district collector in collaboration with civil society groups and local bodies should ensure the comprehensive survey of each of these groups every two years.

A special additional AAY quota should be approved for each state government by the central government, by an amount which is not less than 50 per cent of the present AAY quota, and this should be used exclusively for the universal coverage of each of these groups. In case the surveys reveal that eligible members of these most identified social groups are left out even with this additional quota and after state governments weed out ineligible members from existing AAY cards, they will make special demands on the central government for additional AAY quotas specifically to ensure full coverage of these groups as a preventive measure against their slipping into destitution and starvation.

2. Migrant workers who move with their families should be permitted to use their ration cards anywhere in the country, in situations in which they migrate with their families. This should be an automatic process, not requiring additional paper work, because any further bureaucratic interface would result in dangers of corruption and harassment.
3. State governments should be advised to enable and encourage tribal (especially PTG) panchayats; and dalit SHGs to run their own ration shops, with adequate grants from the departments.

Social Security Pensions and Stipends

1. Every aged person must have access as a legal right to a pension that is sufficient for a dignified, active and healthy life. All designated BPL aged people above the age of 65 years have recently been made entitled to a pension of 200 rupees from the central government; with the state governments encouraged to at least match this amount. This is welcome. But it needs to be expanded to ensure that all workers who are not part of the organised sector of the economy must be covered by pension benefits. The government should ensure within one year pensions for all aged people above the age of 65 years who in rural areas are landless, artisans, and

small or marginal farmers, and all SC and ST aged persons; and in urban areas all aged persons who are residents of slums or homeless, and all unorganised workers.

2. Many state governments have indeed exceeded 400 rupees pension, which is also welcome. The matching contributions by the state governments should be made mandatory; and they should be directed to cover all aged people mentioned in the earlier paragraph with pensions within one year.
3. This pension must be secured as a universal entitlement to each of these men and women (in the way that mid-day meals have become for all school going children in government and aided schools). This means that central and state governments cannot plead financial constraints or fix any quotas on the numbers of such persons who are to be covered.
4. A centrally sponsored scheme should be introduced to ensure pensions of the same amount to all BPL single women and disabled adults.
5. Central Government employees and pensioners get an increment twice a year that is pegged to the Consumer Price Index (CPI). Likewise, the pension amount should also be linked to inflation in the economy and appraised every half a year, using Rs. 400 in the year 2007 as the baseline.
6. Pensions must be paid by the seventh of every month, regardless of the availability of specific budgetary allocations.
7. Arrangements must be put into place in one year for either payment into bank accounts, or doorstep delivery of pensions to all rural and urban aged, disabled people or single women. Any commission payable to the Postal Department or banks for making these payments should be waived or borne by the Ministry concerned.

Special food credit under NREGA

Many families will have the modest resources required

for monthly purchase of the highly subsidised food grains under AAY. But in case they do not, those who rural residents should be permitted to draw their ration on credit, against their future labour in NREGA works. Since NREGA is a demand led legal guarantee, there is little risk of failures to recover the required amounts. This should apply particularly to released bonded workers; but also to single women, old and disabled people.

Special Feeding Arrangements

1. A ll old people from the neighbourhood should be permitted to share in the school mid-day meal of hot cooked meal in schools or ICDS centres without any conditions, as practiced in the state of Tamil Nadu. This serves as a last defence against starvation of the aged destitute, without requiring any additional administrative costs. This may become possible without significant additional resources, by merging present allocations under the Annapurna Scheme (which was meant to provide 10 kg. to old people not covered by pensions, but which has now become superfluous because the scheme has been universalised) with food allotments with the mid-day meal.
2. Establish community kitchens across cities and urban settlements to provide inexpensive, subsidised nutritious cooked meals near urban homeless and migrant labour settlements, with committed source of external funds (preferably government funded or in partnership with civil society: both citizens and private sector), which are managed by community groups of homeless people, preferably women, and will provide employment as cooks to homeless people themselves (at least 50 such kitchens per city with population less than one million; and 100 with populations more than one million, and 500 in those more than ten million).
3. Hot cooked meals should be provided to all children who attend all alternative educational settings, such as remedial schools, bridge classes, extension schools, and evening schools.

ICDS

1. Children of migrant workers should be admitted and permitted to avail of all facilities and services in ICDS, regardless of their place of origin, with no paper work required by their parents/guardians.
2. State governments should be directed to ensure full coverage of urban slums latest in 2 years.
3. In urban areas, ICDS should develop prefabricated structures, to enable it to function in unauthorised slum settlements, or construction and brick kiln sites.
4. In rural areas, care should be taken to locate ICDS centres on priority within one year in all settlements of PTGs and most discriminated dalit settlements, without any ceiling of minimum children; and all other hamlets with more than 50 per cent SC/ ST/minority population within a maximum of 2 years. In all these centres, ICDS staff should be local from the discriminated communities, and two hot meals served instead of one to children of 3 to 6 years; and double weaning foods given to children below 3 years.
5. Data should be disaggregated at the ICDS level for enrolment and actual coverage, to reflect the numbers and proportion of disabled children; and children from vulnerable local SC /ST /minority communities; and poor coverage should be penalised.
6. ICDS centres should extend their nutrition and health services which at present cater to expectant and lactating mothers, also to all categories of single women, recognising them to be intensely nutritionally vulnerable.

NREGA

1. Ensure that single women, aged and disabled people in practice enjoy at least equal legal claim to employment in NREGA works as households 'led' by able-bodied men, and that their work guarantee should be extended to 150 days.
2. NREGA guidelines and handbooks in each state should

carefully identify specific tasks in public works which can be undertaken by disabled adults and aged people; and they should be encouraged to undertake such tasks when people of these categories apply for work.

3. The NREGA Standard Schedule of Works should be modified to include and give priority to these categories to be hired to fill temporary vacancies (when the staff are unavailable due to maternity leave, vacations, election duty, vacant posts etc.) across other social welfare programmes of the government on a time-rate basis for example as cooks or helpers or additional teachers in schools, as anganwadi helpers, additional helpers in ICDS centres, caregivers for disabled children etc. Likewise the NREGA Schedule of Work should identify physically less demanding work which should be prioritised for these categories like standing guard at the sites, the work of 'mates' who supervise and measure the work, taking care of children, serving water, filling stones and soil in baskets, and planting and irrigating saplings etc.
4. Special proactive campaigns should be undertaken by panchayats and district authorities, with support from civil society groups, to create awareness and mobilise and assist to enrol persons from each rural vulnerable categories mentioned in this report, to get job cards and demand as a legal right guaranteed days of wage work per family.
5. Provide separate NREGA job cards for all 'single' women, regardless of whether they live alone, with dependents, or in their natal or husband's home. Likewise for aged, infirm and disabled people who may or may not live with 'able-bodied' caregivers.

Residential Care for food security of most vulnerable children

1. For children of rural seasonal migrants, the village school should be converted into a community based temporary residential school, to enable the child to

access food and education, without having to migrate every year with their guardians. The aged of the village, who are often left behind in destitute conditions, may take care of the children in return for sharing the food in the community based hostels. This model has been adopted by Orissa Government for Bolangir district, and is widely recognised internationally as a best practice, applauded among others by Dr. Amartya Sen.

2. For children who still migrate, it should be the duty of the education department of the host state to provide education in local language at work sites, and permit the child to access midday meals at the nearest government school. This is again a best practice adopted by the governments of Andhra Pradesh for migrant families from Orissa.
3. For children who live and work on the streets, the only way to secure their right to food (and with this their rights to education, health and protection), is to provide them alternatives to move decisively away from the streets and any kind of work. This is possible only through guarantees of comprehensive long-term care in open voluntary residential homes. Every city would need a large network of such schools. This could be done by converging the Sarva Shiksha Abhiyan (a programme to bring every child to schools) and the Women and Child Department's night shelter programmes, as well as Labour Department programmes for child workers, to pool resources to create hostels for urban street and working children, and greatly enhancing allocations. This best practice has been adopted by the governments of Andhra Pradesh and Delhi. The aim should be in the first phase of 3 years to start at least 100 such centres in all metropolises; and 50 in all other urban areas of population more than 5 lakhs.

A prodigious amount of work that has been put in for more than a year by our young colleagues in the office of the Commissioners to the Supreme Court, without whose industrious research, this report would not have been possible. They are led by our very capable Principal Advisor Biraj Patnaik, and also include a committed team of Dipa Sinha, Tanveer Ahmad Dar and Oommen C. Kurian, who contributed significantly to the work of the Commissioners.

We would also like to acknowledge the support received from our research staff Swati Narayan, V. Manikandan and Arpan Tulsyan. We have also been assisted by our friends in the right to food campaign, like Kavita Srivastava, Jean Dreze, Colin Gonsalves, Aruna Roy and Nikhil Dey, committed official colleagues like Rakesh Mehta, K. Raju, Alok Shukla, Vijay Dev, Debashree Mukherjee, Rashmi Singh and Rajeev Jaiswal; and also our Advisors like Veena Shatrugna, Kodandaram, Arundhati Dhuru, Rama Melkote, Anuradha Talwar, Vandana Prasad, Ginny Srivastava, Joseanthony Jose, Sunil Kaul, Samir Garg, Pradeep Bhargava, Rajkishore Mishra, Tarun Bharatiya, Mihir Shah and Chingmak Chang, among others. We are also deeply indebted to the network of other State Advisers who voluntarily undertake the responsibility of monitoring the food and employment schemes in the States.

This is a report about some of the most excluded, destitute, socially devalued, invisible people for whom hunger and food denials are a way of life. It is constructed around the conviction about the intrinsic equal human worth of every human being, regardless of whether and what they produce and contribute; of their difference; their departures from social norms; their physiological and social diversity from the majority; their disenfranchisement and powerlessness.

Gandhi offered us a 'talisman' to use in moments of doubt and confusion. He asked us to recall the face of the poorest, most defenceless, most powerless man we have encountered. (Today he would have recognised that she would probably have been a woman!). Ask ourselves whether what we are attempting has meaning for this person : does it touch her life with dignity and worth? Does it augment her power and self-reliance? If it does, it must surely be the right thing to do. It is this talisman that this report strives to hold up to public policy, but ultimately also to ourselves.

NC Saxena
Commissioner

Harsh Mander
Special Commissioner

Single Women

Introduction

Women produce between 60 and 80 per cent of the food in most developing countries, and are culturally food providers in most homes. Yet social and cultural practices determine in India that within households, women not only eat least and last, but in situations of absolute household food insecurity, they may not eat at all. 'Single' women face additional discrimination and social barriers to food and livelihood, even if not within their homes if they live independently, but as they battle alone the world beyond.

Single women are of many kinds, and they face discrimination in similar and different ways. They may have never married; they may have left their spouses or have been abandoned by them; they may have been widowed young or old; they may live with natal families, or with the family of their spouse, or with children, with unmarried partners or alone; they may be rich or poor; and may have been born and married into varied caste or faith groups with their diversity of rules and norms. But what binds them all together is the absence of male 'protection', 'security' and eventually *control*. This erodes their social status in our largely patriarchal society.

Social Exclusion

Irrespective of whether she is from a wealthy or

impoverished household, widowhood has a deep social stigma attached to it in most communities. But it is most severe among upper caste Hindus. Women are seen as protecting the 'honour' of the family. There is a perceived threat to this notion when she is widowed (especially when she is young), as it makes it difficult to control her sexuality, fertility and control of property, unless she is completely isolated. Paradoxically, a widowed woman (as also other single women without male 'protection') is also seen as sexually 'available'. Women widowed in the Orissa cyclone of 1999, and the Gujarat earthquake of 2001, confided about horrific sexual exploitation even by close family members within days of the calamity. Likewise, widows of the communal carnage in Gujarat in 2002 experienced stigma and exploitation within their families and communities.[1]

Whatever their age, there persist formidable social barriers to the remarriage of Hindu widows. A woman once widowed is not treated with respect and a lot of restrictions are imposed upon her. At times she is still expected to shave her head, wear extremely simple and coarse white clothes and not wearing symbols of marriage ('*sindoor*' or vermilion in the parting of the hair), eating separately a frugal vegetarian diet, not participating in auspicious occasions. The rituals of widowhood signify symbolic rejection/deprivation of the widow's sexuality.

The widow has no perceived value to the family after the death of her husband. She is considered to be a burden who will need to be given a share in property and her presence at festivals and family occasions is viewed as inauspicious. Young widows are even considered to be responsible for the death of the husband. Sati as a practice evolved based on the belief that a women doesn't deserve to live without her husband.

Even more ostracised are women who are alone despite living spouses. Many married women are trapped in dehumanising personal situations in the family. A large number persist in tolerating battering, humiliation and physical and mental cruelty, unable or unwilling to strike out on their own. This inertia in degradation may be for a variety of reasons, such as social and cultural beliefs that enjoin that it is the duty of a woman to continue to live with her husband even if she suffers cruelty, and that a woman's social acceptance and security in the community necessarily derives from her married status. Even if a woman is able to herself overcome such beliefs, her parents are frequently unwilling to accept back a married daughter who leaves her husband and, therefore, a woman is trapped also because she has nowhere to go if she breaks ties with her husband's home. She may lack education and professional qualifications, and therefore lack the confidence that she would be able to survive economically alone. And finally she may be paralysed by concern for the welfare of her children.

The peculiar culturally imposed tragedy of widows, particularly in Hindu society, is not only one of condemnation to live cold, deprived and unfulfilled lives in either their parents' or husband's homes, vulnerable always to sexual exploitation. It is also one of destitution and abandonment, in religious towns such as Vrindavan and Varanasi, or on the streets. The North Indian religious cities of Varanasi and Vrindavan contain hubs of widows. From the early nineteenth century onwards widows, especially from Bengal, were sent on a pilgrimage to these 'holy' places. Often they were taken on a pilgrimage by family members and abandoned there. Widows from different parts of the country continue to migrate to these cities in search of a life of security and some peace[2], but in these towns a vast multitude of widows live forgotten in conditions of appalling neglect and deprivation. The number of widows living in Vrindavan, especially those from West Bengal, has been increasing over the years. A Vrindavan Nagar Palika survey in 2004 enumerated 3,105 widows and the figure is estimated to be anywhere between 5,000 and 6,000 now[3].

Magnitude

6.9 per cent of women in India are widows, while 0.5 per cent are divorced or separated.[4] Further, another 1.4 per cent of all women above the age of 30 are unmarried (0.5 per cent of all women) and can also be considered to belong to the category of 'single women'.[5] In total, at least 7.5 per cent of Indian women are single - i.e. 40 million women (more than the entire population of Canada).

In India's largely patriarchal society, 10.4 per cent of households are headed by women.[6] A third of these are managed by married women largely in unique matriarchal communities[7] or due to the local prevalence of mass-migration of men in search of livelihoods. The remaining two-thirds are headed by single-women - largely widows but also women who have left or been left by their husbands- who either live alone or take care of all their dependents. Female headed households are growing rapidly across the world. This is the cumulative outcome of stresses and breakdown of family, such as by violence, alcoholism, divorce, separation, widowhood, and male or female migrations. These may be lone family units with single females, households in which women earners receive significant remittances from absent males, or homes in which single women are the principal earners, and they support young or aged dependants.

Almost 58 per cent of widows (20 million women) are more than 60 years of age. Incidence of widowhood among the total female population rises sharply with age. In other words, two-thirds of women who cross their seventieth year outlive their husbands. Also, 45 per cent of women who complete their sixtieth birthday are widows. They face the double burden of age and a lonely future without the companionship of their lifelong partner. This undoubtedly has important implications both for policies relating to single women as well as those for the elderly.

Lack of Support

Although widows are traditionally supposed to be taken care of by the husband's extended family; this does happen very often. Widows typically find themselves under pressure in their homes by marriage to part with their share of property, and are unsafe physically. The crumbling of joint families, with their assurances both of security and patriarchy, have led women to either the threshold of their natal homes, if their parents and brothers are willing and able to take them and their dependents in, or to tenuous and arduous independent living. This section analyses the economic plight of single women and their daily struggles for food and livelihood. To earn more money when in distress, women often engage in self-employment, sell or mortgage their assets in distress, beg, send their children to work, or are even involved in undignified appeasement of those who can help them.

Almost 80 per cent of widows either take care of themselves or are dependent on their son/s (if they have one).[8] Very few who live alone receive any 'maintenance' or qfood on a regular basis from other households. They have to fend for themselves. The 'Living with Hunger' study in three states indicates that 47 per cent of single women earn to support themselves, 27 per cent primarily depend on government programmes, 20 per cent get support from other family members, 3 per cent live on the money from sale of assets/land and another 3 per cent depend on charity/ begging. More than half the women studied not only supported themselves but also had dependents to look after.[9]

In instances where widows, depend on their family, it is usually in the home of one or more of her sons. But here, she is even more likely to be neglected unless she is able to contribute to the household in terms of childcare, housework, land, other assets, wages or a pension. Many widows often also need to repay the debts incurred by their late husbands or to pay for his medical treatment before he died or death ceremonies[10].

Property Rights

Widows in India have a legal right to their husband's property. While these legal entitlements exist for women's rights to property, the inheritance rights of the majority of Indian rural widows are governed by actual practice (which is influenced by traditional or customary law). Practice can differ from village to village, caste to caste, but even in the same region and among the same caste.

But actual legal ownership is a rarity. Just the process of establishing one's rights over the land and getting the property/land registered can be quite daunting for a widow with no family support. Even where use-rights have been established, control often doesn't lie with her.

Access to Livelihood and Employment

Even though the need for gainful employment is great among single women, finding such work is fraught with difficulties. Social exclusion includes economic deprivation due to the taboos regarding what a woman can and cannot do. One of the most direct impacts is restricted mobility. It makes widows, in particular, invisible and they are unable to access work outside the home.

Worse still, is the vulnerability and stigma associated with being a widow. This amounts to highly unequal access and unfair treatment in the 'job market'. Young single women, who live on their own, though able-bodied are systematically secluded from outside work because of the burden of household work; need to fetch water from distance sources (many kilometres away) and to cook food, without any familial support. The other reason in-laws do not allow them to work outside, is that it could lead to the financial independence of women which is resented by traditional communities.

But due to the acute need and desperation of single women to support themselves and their dependents, they are compelled to find work outside the home. Female headed households participate as much as 74 per cent in the labour market as compared to 54 per cent of married women in male-headed households.[11] The National Family Health Survey also reveals similar results amongst able-bodied women largely in the age group of 15-49 years. Despite the innumerable barriers they faced, more single women are forced to work outside the house in the absence of any family, community or state support.

But since most widows in India are above 60 years of age, the vast majority of them are unable to undertake hard physical work.[12]

Even if they were able to find work, however, single women invariably face barriers in relation to the type of work they can take up. That apart, they also face gender discrimination in the payment of wages. The average agricultural daily wage for women in 2006 is estimated at only Rs. 48.6 for women, against Rs. 69.7 for men.[13]

1. Access to credit

Single women also face severe restrictions in trying to access credit. Even if she has the same earning capacity as a man or a married woman, she finds it more difficult to get a loan. At best they receive charity or loans in-kind. Shopkeepers charge them more and give them less than their due because they are too weak to protest. They are therefore forced to work at very low wages and for long hours. This ordeal is even harder for elderly women. Single women report that even formal banks turn them away, as do self help groups.

2. Poverty

Economists acknowledge a phenomenon of what is described as the "feminisation of poverty", i.e., poverty among women is rising faster than poverty among men. It has many related faces : women have a higher incidence of poverty then men; women's poverty is more severe that than of men; and that there is a trend to greater poverty among women, particularly associated with rising rates of female headship of household.

Based on data from Karnataka, Jean Dreze analyses that households with a widow have low per capita expenditure levels. Those with both widows and their young children have higher-than-average levels of poverty[14]. Similarly, at an all India level, households headed by widows have lower consumption levels and higher levels of poverty compared with other households[15].

Food Deprivation

Due to the undue disadvantages in the access to livelihood and assets, single women are more food insecure when compared to others who probably belong to the same economic category. They have to struggle harder in order to access food. Even in cases of single women living with families, of which they are the not the primary earning members, they do have an equal access to food as a result of their low status in the household.

To cope with their hunger pangs they employ a range of strategies. The common ones include - rationing of food, substitution by inferior foods, cooking only once a day, sharing from the same vessel, sacrificing their share of food for the children.

There is an identifiable difference in the proportion of single women in comparison to married women who consume less than 90 per cent of the required calorie norm. The calorie consumption of an average married woman each day is 2086 calories, of widows is 2005 calories and for divorced/separated women 1989 calories (NSS, 61st round).

Access to Food Schemes

There are various schemes that exist in the country that can potentially contribute to the food security of single women. But most often they prove to be beyond their reach. Single women face many barriers to access them. The greatest impediments are their invisibility, powerlessness and even lack of knowledge about these schemes.

The choice of beneficiaries of each of these schemes is often arbitrary and dependent on the hands of local elites. A review of these schemes shows that although they have laudable objectives, there are serious problems in implementation : access, regularity and corruption.

1. Swadhar Scheme

There are no major schemes of the Government of India for widows or single women, in general. The only scheme that is available is Swadhar Scheme, run by the Ministry of Women and Child Development, which is a shelter based scheme "to cater the requirements of various types of women in distress in diverse situations including destitute widows. The package of services made available under the Scheme include provision for food, clothing, shelter, health care counselling and legal support, social and economic rehabilitation through education, awareness generation, skill upgradation and behavioural training"[16]. Currently, there are 208 shelter homes running under this scheme in the entire country. In a positive step, the budget for this scheme has been increased to Rs. 15 crores from Rs. 8.7 crores last year, but it is patently microscopic in relation to the need and scale of the problem in the country.

The scheme since its inception, has reached out to very few beneficiaries. In one year since it started in 2001 was the number of beneficiaries more than about 3000. This renders the scheme tokenistic. Further, the expenditure of the budgets allocated under this scheme also has been low. The Planning Commission mid-term appraisal notes, "The Tenth Plan outlay for Swadhar is Rs. 100 crore. The progress under the scheme is not satisfactory. Only 35 projects have been sanctioned so far and utilisation of funds has also not been up to mark. Though the outlays were Rs. 14.46 crore and 14.02 crore in 2002-03 and 2003-04 respectively, only Rs. 3.90 crore was utilised in 2002-03 and Rs. 1.05 crore in 2003-04. Such under-utilisation of funds defeats the objectives and concerns with which the scheme had been launched."

State governments have various schemes for the benefit of widows. Most state governments have widow pensions of some sort or the other. Further, some state government's offer monetary support for re-marriage of widows, for the marriage expenses of daughters of widows, scholarships in government schools for the children of widows and so on.

2. Pension Schemes

Widows constitute the single largest proportion of 'single' women. 58 per cent of them are above the age of 60 years and excessively vulnerable not only because of old-age and their inability to work but also because of regressive social customs which makes them suffer from daily indignities. Their social security needs are therefore acute.

Although several states have schemes for widow's pensions, the amount of pension allotted is abysmally low and the actual coverage even worse. For instance, calculation based on an estimation of the number of eligible beneficiaries and the actual number of beneficiaries in Maharashtra and Delhi shows that the coverage is only 19.5% and 24.4% respectively[17]. A study in Rajasthan found almost 50% of BPL widows to be widow non-pensioners[18].

Moreover, the eligibility criteria of age restrictions and absence of sons (irrespective of whether they take care of their mothers) are often quite restrictive making it very difficult for women to access the scheme.

The process of application can also be quite cumbersome with many bureaucratic hurdles, making it very difficult for single women to access these schemes. Often beneficiaries have to miss their entire day's work (and hence wages) to travel to the panchayat and block offices to get what they are rightfully entitled to.

However when pensions do reach they offer an invaluable sense of dignity for elderly widows; providing a sense of freedom and autonomy to fulfil their small wishes without depending on others. There is therefore a need to have a uniform central scheme offering pensions to poor widows, with no additional restrictions such as having adult sons and so on.

Given that many widows are also old, effective implementation of this scheme and the universal coverage of all who are eligible would also ensure that some economic support is available, however minimal, for their survival with dignity. However often if an elderly person does receive an old age pension they are often denied widows' pension or vice-versa.

Studies do show that for those women who do get pensions, it represents a significant source of independent support for widows who live as dependents. But they do not enable a widow who heads a household to support her dependents[19]. The quantum of pension therefore needs to be revised to at least Rs. 500 for all social security schemes. This would make it about 50 per cent of the current deemed poverty line, assuming that a widow supports on an average 3 dependents[20].

3. National Family Benefit Scheme

Single' women could potentially substantially benefit from this scheme which provides one-time cash assistance of Rs. 10,000 when the primary breadwinner of a family dies. It can provide immediate relief to women who have lost their husbands and are suddenly left on their own to support their children.

But it suffers from abysmal implementation. In the year 2006-2007, it reached only 30 per cent of the eligible beneficiaries.[21] In the previous year, states such as Haryana, Karnataka and Delhi reported NO beneficiaries under the NFBS[22], which should be viewed as a grave abdication of official responsibility to a segment of people who are most in need. The procedure to benefit from the NFBS is lengthy and bureaucratic. The bereaved family needs to present several supporting documents such as death certificate etc. which are often practically very difficult to obtain.

4. Public Distribution System / Antodaya Anna Yojana

The Public Distribution System which is a household based scheme has the obvious problem of not addressing intra-household inequities. The ration card is usually in the name of the man and in case of separation the wife is not given another card.

The Antodaya Anna Yojana scheme as part of the PDS is supposed to reach out to the poorest of the poor. The Supreme Court order dated 2nd May, 2003 specifically, stated that 'widows and other single women with no regular support' should be included in the scheme. However, the selection of families is often quite arbitrary. None of the states even collect data on how many AAY cards have been issued to the various vulnerable groups, including single women. This remains significantly one instruction of the Supreme Court that has been ignored by most state governments.

5. National Rural Employment Guarantee Scheme

The NREGS which provides employment on demand, for 100 days a year, is also a household based scheme. One job card is issued per household, typically in the name of the male member. Even when the work is done by others, the wage is paid to this man. Therefore single women, who are part of larger households and not provided an 'independent job card' often do not have access to their own wages.

Another common reason why single women fail to get work is that it is often handed out to pairs of male and female workers. Instead of creating slots for single women workers, the programme has effectively eliminated them.

Women are also paid far less than men[23]. The culprit is the Standard Schedule of Rates (SSR) which makes invisible the work of women. While the extent of digging and soil conditions forms the basis of payment for men's work; the carrying of load, its weight, the underfoot conditions and its distance do not figure in wage calculation. So if two men dig and four women carry the soil, the two men collectively want as wages half the payment while the four women are left to divide the other half between them. This leads to wage differential especially as there is a clear cut sexual division in such works. Further, men work with tools while women do not but no efforts are made to compensate their contribution, much less consider the drudgery of the tasks done by them.

Recommendations : Single Women

It is grudgingly and belatedly acknowledged today that most government policies and laws are 'blind' to the lower power - economic, social, political and administrative - of women. Therefore they fall very short of redressing gender inequalities. This is even truer of women who are single, by choice or circumstance. They grapple with patriarchal social norms, which create tall and diverse barriers to their access to food, livelihoods and food schemes. These have been illustrated in this chapter, and government food and livelihood programmes need to be resolutely refashioned to reach and partner single women as they battle the world alone.

Identification

1. Conduct a periodic **census** of single women every two years through panchayats, urban local bodies and women's group to ensure universal coverage of all social security, food and livelihood schemes.
2. Recognise single women and their dependants if any as separate family units for all purposes such as job cards and ration cards, regardless of whether or not they live with their natal or husband's family and share a common kitchen. Even single women alone or with joint families should be accepted as separate family units, and this should be explicit in all government instructions. If single women have no permanent address (on the streets or in professions like casual sex work) this should not be a bar to eligibility to all the programmes listed below.

Cash Entitlements

3. Create a centrally sponsored scheme (with central government contributions of 50 : 50) and implement for all single women (including widows, separated, divorced, deserted, unmarried women) who are below the poverty line (BPL), scheduled caste (SC) or scheduled tribe (ST) and from minority communities, similar to the old-age pension, a **universal pension scheme.** All eligible single women should be covered with no limits or quotas imposed.
4. **Increase the amount** of pension to a minimum of Rs.

400 for all social security schemes, and revise these every year based on the Consumer Price Index (CPI).

5. Ensure that single women pensions **do not have any restrictions** on their own age, or the age and sex of their children.
6. Ensure that separated and abandoned women are accepted as 'single' for the purposes of all government social security support and food schemes, even if they are not formally divorced, based on a written undertaking by the woman confirming her separation.
7. Ensure that a person entitled to two or more **pensions receives all** of them e.g. widow and old-age pension.
8. Universalise coverage of the National Family Benefit Scheme and **reduce the red tape** for its eligibility, ensuring mandatory payment within 3 months of the death of the bread-winner.

Food Entitlements

9. Provide **separate ration cards** for all single women, whether or not they live with their natal or husband's family.
10. Ensure that all these single women have access to the **Antyodaya Anna Yojana.** This would require the central government to make specific additional allocations of AAY cards to cover all single women households, as per the order the Supreme Court to universalise AAY for this group.[24]
11. Extend **ICDS food provisions**, currently available for nursing and expectant mothers, to all single women, in recognition of their special vulnerabilities.
12. For all single women who are head of households with dependent children or living alone provide high protein **dry take home rations (THR)** once a week from the ICDS anganwadi centres.
13. In addition to these dry rations, single women should be entitled to enrol and eat hot cooked meals at ICDS centres of they so choose.

Provide Special and Differentiated Treatment

14. Children of single women should be entitled to assured **admission in SC/ST hostels** run by state governments, where their education and food security would be better secured.
15. In cities and towns, government should start **residential hostels** with priority to children of single women, especially those who are homeless. All children of urban homeless single women should be taken into hostels and governments should confirm this within a maximum period of 2 years, and adequate financial provisioning should be made for this.
16. Process all social security application at the **panchayat level** where a **list** of all single women should be maintained and updated every month.
17. Provide **funds for training** and making single women aware of their rights and entitlements with the aim of creating a federated association of single women.
18. Allocations for **shelter homes** for women survivors of domestic violence should be expanded manifold to ensure at least one in every district of the country, and women's organisations, especially those of single women, encouraged to run these. These homes should provide for women in distress a safe place to go with children in safety; psycho-social and family counselling services; legal advice and assistance; vocational guidance and training; crèches for children; financial assistance; assistance in employment/self-employment in secure vocations; assistance to find homes for eventual self-reliant rehabilitation; and long stay homes for older destitute widows.
19. Likewise the allocations on the excellently conceived **Swadhar** scheme, which provided for food, clothing, shelter, health care counselling and legal support, social and economic rehabilitation for women in most difficult circumstances should be greatly expanded to cover as a priority programme every district in the country.

Employment Guarantee

20. Provide **separate NREGA job cards** for all 'single' women, regardless of whether they live alone, with dependents, or in their natal or husband's home.
21. Ensure that single women in practice enjoy **at least equal legal claim to employment** in NREGA works as households 'led' by men, and that their work guarantee should be extended to 150 days.
22. Modify the NREGA Standard Schedule of Works (**SSW**) to identify and calculate **women's share of work** and compensate them equitably and justly.
23. The NREGA Standard Schedule of Works can be modified to include and give priority to single women to be hired to fill temporary vacancies (when the staff are unavailable due to maternity leave, vacations, election duty, vacant posts etc.) across other social welfare programmes of the government on a time-rate basis for example as cooks or helpers in schools, as anganwadi helpers, additional helper-teachers in schools and ICDS centres, caregivers for disabled children etc.
24. Single women should be paid **daily wages,** rather than weekly or fortnightly.

Impoverished and Old

From a social security and policy point of view, the largest concern of the elderly in India is poverty. Thirty percent of the elderly in India are estimated to live below the poverty line. Another one-third is not even acknowledged to be poor; even though live marginally above the poverty line. National policy on older persons estimates that about seventy per cent of the population above 60 are economically 'fragile', of whom half are BPL and the other half APL, belonging to the low income group. However, it is often observed that the assessment of only one-third of the elderly being BPL, is an understatement.[25] With their bodily capacities already under the stress of years, most are unable to engage in active employment. Their impoverishment is even more crippling.

Double Burden of Widows

The chances of being taken care of are greater when one's spouse is still alive. One-third of the elderly population is however widowed, and faces a precarious existence.[26] There is also a marked gender disparity in the case of widowhood. Though the incidence of widowhood among elderly women is declining, it remains an important social phenomenon affecting more than half of the women who are more than 60 years. The reason for the acute gender disparity in widowhood is largely three-fold. The life expectancy of women is greater compared to men. Secondly, in Indian society, men largely marry women who are younger. Again, due to societal customs widowed men are more likely to remarry than women.[27]

Ageing Population

The population aged 60 and above is expected to increase from 77 million (7.5 percent) to 301 million (17 percent) in the fifty years since 2001 with a marked increase in the elderly aged more than 70 years. The structure of the population would be undergoing some dramatic changes in the next fifty years or so[28]. Unlike many parts of the world, in India sex ratios show that for most aged cohorts across time, men out-number women. This situation is interesting because female life expectancy in India at 60 and 70 is higher than male life expectancy. Some reasons for this higher number of males in old ages are given to be "under-reporting of females, especially widows, age exaggeration, low female life expectancy at birth, and excess female mortality among infants, children and adults".[29]

Multiple Vulnerabilities

Poverty has many dimensions of deprivation and denial - social, political, economic, psychological - therefore estimates of income and expenditure have limited utility in capturing the depth and range of the deprivation of the impoverished. Where large proportions of the population are subject to high morbidity and mortality, poor access to even minimal healthcare, lack of clean water and sanitation, inadequate housing, lack of education, social exclusion, etc. along with hunger and malnutrition, income poverty measures tend to underestimate the degree of poverty.

This is particularly the case for groups like the aged whose needs and risks are different than the general population. Their material deprivation is exacerbated by their powerlessness and marginalisation, and ultimately their social dispensability. They end up being more vulnerable to risks than the general population, even when they might be technically 'above the poverty line' constructed by planners and economists.[30] There is therefore an acute need to define poverty in a way that takes into account the needs of the aged as different from young men and women. The dependency ratio in India has been sharply on the rise. On an average every 1000 persons in the working age in the rural areas had to provide support, physically or otherwise, to 141 aged persons, to maintain their daily life, as opposed to 94 aged persons in 1981. In the urban areas, the number of dependent elderly persons rose to 107 from just 71 in 1981.[31]

Field studies have illuminated the anatomy of such dependency of the aged. A study by Kumudini Dandekar of the aged in rural Maharashtra (EPW, June 5, 1993) found that unlike the small section of the elderly who can fall back on their provident fund, pension, savings, insurance or property, 33 per cent in the rural and 37 per cent in the urban areas are totally economically dependent. Of these, 9 per cent depended on their spouse, 50 per cent on their children, and 6 per cent on their grand children and the remainder on others. Their dependence is aggravated because most elderly people have no financial assets. For the country as a whole, for 1,00,000 old men and women, only 581 and 482 respectively had some financial assets.

Nearly 80 per cent of the dependent elderly expressed a need for old age pension. The fact that they are so dependent does not mean that there are social and cultural guarantees that the family members on whom they are dependent will necessarily provide for them. The state has an obligation to the fully dependent elderly to ensure for them economic support in old age; as many are below the poverty line and suffer multiple disabilities, therefore they should be assisted with poverty alleviation and social security programmes.

But it cannot be assumed that those who are not 'dependent' need no state support. On the contrary, more than 15 per cent of all the elderly live alone or only with their spouses. The study by Kumudini Dandekar of the aged in rural Maharashtra (EPW, June 5, 1993) also found 18 per cent old people in villages lived alone, comprising of 4 per cent men and 14 per cent women. Often, economic 'independence' is forced upon them. Such pseudo-independence, therefore, cannot be taken as a proxy for well-being and there are chances that some amount of poverty gets invisibilised amongst those elderly persons who are technically perceived to be 'not dependent'. The enormity of the degree of dependence is undeniable. 65 percent of the aged depend on others for their day-to-day existence[32]. Women are particularly vulnerable. 85 percent of women are economically dependent on others, largely because of cultural constructions of gender relations and opportunities and preparation for self-reliance.

The mere process of ageing - the continuous decline of functional ability of the body and to a point the mind, over time – often creates and exacerbates intra and inter-household inequalities. Visual impairment, hearing problems, difficulty in walking and speech are the most common forms of disability among elderly[33]. Senility and neurosis are also common. Without familial or institutional support, these added disadvantages seriously affect their ability to survive and fend for themselves[34]. 45 per cent of the elderly suffered from chronic health problems in both rural and urban areas. The percentage of physical immobility due to chronic illness and old age was found to be consistently higher for women than men in all states of the country.

Poor health, unfavourable socio-economic conditions,

widening inter-generational gaps and non-working status contribute towards added vulnerability to the aged.[35] Even meagre financial assistance would substantially alleviate their burden. Their relatively lower bargaining power makes them vulnerable to a higher risk of poverty, especially at the time of contingencies.[36]

Amongst the elderly; poor people, widows and disabled people are invariably the most disadvantaged. Widows, in particular, face direct and indirect forms of cultural stigma linked with their gender accentuated by their marital status. In comparison to aged widowers, women suffer from lack of ownership of property and financial assets. Even in cases where they may legally inherit such property, they often fail to gain actual control over the property and are harassed by male members of their deceased husband's family. This deprivation, in turn, adversely affects their access to food, housing and health.

Social security in many developing countries like India largely focuses on the workforce in the formal sector. Other provisions that have an old age focus largely 'exist on paper' with their effectiveness 'hardly ever analysed'. Research on old age itself largely has a bias towards the middle class and basic issues like old people's access to food and livelihood are largely left unexplored.

It has been observed that the elderly from indigent groups, when their dependence is accompanied by ill-health, no savings and no assets, complicated further by cultural biases such as against widows and economic pressures faced by poor families such as for distress migration, are viewed as a burden by their families, and are often denied their basic needs in life, including food. They are routinely subjected to neglect, indignity and ill-treatment.

It is estimated that at least 50 per cent of the population of the elderly in this country, especially among the indigent, are in need of some form of supportive services. An analysis of their problems reveals the following major areas of need, namely :

- economic deprivation and insecurity
- restricted mobility due to ill-health
- physical insecurity
- reduction in dignity, self-esteem
- loneliness due to rejection
- lack of meaningful occupation, leisure activities, and
- lack of protective supportive shelter.

Government Programmes for the Aged

Historically, the focus of social security measures in India has been promotive rather than the protective; justified by the unacceptably high incidence of poverty, the scarcity of resources, and the tacit assumption of the lower claim of those who are perceived to be no longer 'productive'. At the same time, it is well recognised that to achieve higher levels of human development societies need a judicious mix of both forms of social security.

Even though the elderly were identified as a priority group for social protection from the initial years of India's independence, policy initiatives like old age pensions were pioneered by various state governments and not the Centre. It was only in 1995 that an all India pension scheme was introduced, with very small financial provisioning for small numbers of aged people. In effect, to date, pension is not perceived as a right of unorganised workers.

From 2002-03, NOAPS as well as Annapurna have been transferred to the States; money being given in the form of Additional Central Assistance. Every year, the Ministry of Finance, Government of India, releases funds to the states in equal monthly instalments till December, and the payment for the remaining three months is conditional to "reporting of satisfactory progress of implementation of the Schemes and utilization of funds". The ACA thus provided could be utilized by the States/UTs "by taking up one or two or all of the three (schemes[37]) or in any other combination in accordance with their own priorities and needs". The guidelines categorically state that failure to submit physical and financial progress reports will result in the non-release of funds for the last quarter of the financial year.

This was done, according to the government, to provide States with the required flexibility in choice and implementation. However, in practice, this shift has affected performance of the scheme. Even after the pension amount got enhanced from Rs. 75 to Rs. 200, many state governments did not pay pensions for more than six months, due to inordinate delays. Old people are politically powerless, and the stepping back of the central government after their belated entry as late as 1995 to first introduce a national programme of (highly modest) pensions for aged people, has tended to erode even the small gains that aged people had secured. The central government even stopped reviewing the performance of state governments in extending pensions to old people, and it required an order of the Supreme Court to direct them to restart monitoring the programme.

The central government contributes collectively to a combination of three schemes and the states determine the proportion to be spent on each of the three schemes. The total allocation by the Central Government compared with the actual expenditure reported for all the states indicates that the money utilized was close to optimum with less than 5 percent of the funds left unused in 2003-4.

But since then, the expenditure reported has declined steeply. Unused balances were as high as 29 percent in 2004–2005 and 22 percent in 2005–2006. Last year, however, showed lowest levels of utilization with almost half the funds allocated left unused. This surprisingly, despite the fact that the old age pension was increased from Rs. 75 to Rs. 200.

2007 was perhaps the most significant year for public policy for the aged. The Prime Minister announced in his politically significant address to the nation from the Red Fort in Delhi on Independence Day that old age pensions would at last be universalised for the poor. Accordingly, NOAPS was replaced by the Indira Gandhi National Old Age Pension Scheme[38], which would provide a monthly pension to *all* people over 65 years and who are identified by government to be living below the poverty line. The quantum of pension would also be enhanced. The central government would provide Rs. 200 to each beneficiary and the State were expected to contribute an equal amount.

But the actual disbursement varies significantly across state governments. Till the close of the financial year 2007, the coverage of the pension scheme was also been far from satisfactory. However, with the introduction of IGNOAPS, there seems to have been a dramatic improvement, as shown in the following table. However, it must also be borne in mind here that, coverage on paper often does not translate into benefits reaching the needy.

Gap between IGNOAPS beneficiaries (2007-08) and the number of eligible persons (2004-05 poverty estimates) (in Lakhs)

Bihar	1.120670
Goa	0.065790
Gujarat	3.946050
Haryana	0.390940
Kerala	2.510440
Maharashtra	11.092840
Orissa	3.727600
Punjab	0.826890
Tamil Nadu	3.405660
Uttar Pradesh	2.240870
Uttaranchal	1.255160
A & N Island	0.022360
Pondicherry	0.105460

Calculations by Ministry of Rural Development, Government of India.

1. Antyodaya Anna Yojana Scheme

Directions from the Supreme Court of India (order dated of May 2, 2003) specifically instruct that all aged, disabled persons and single women should be given Antyodaya cards which entitle them to 35 kilograms of rice or wheat every month at the rate of 2 rupees per kg. for wheat and 3 rupees per kg. for rice, which is well below the soaring market rates. However, in reality, some have BPL cards at best, on which the government subsidy is less.[39]

Distance to government institutions often acts as an access barrier. In some Orissa villages, old people and even those with disability have to trudge more than 7 kilometres to collect their pensions and their rations. However hard and painful it is for them to walk, they have to do so two or three times a month to check whether grains have arrived.

When the rations do arrive, they have to trudge back carrying the heavy load over long distances. Each day spent visiting the ration shop or the office to collect pensions means the loss of earnings or foraging for food. Often at the beginning of each month, the delayed grain arrives earlier than the pension, which causes the elderly much anguish as they do not have the money to buy the grain.

To compound these issues, there are illegal restrictions on the amount of grain that they get from the cards. Most of the elderly reported that they get 4, 8 or 16 kilograms on grain against their BPL cards as against an entitlement of 35 kilograms every month. Many are convinced that they are duped or short-changed by the ration shop dealers, but feel powerless to resist.[40]

2. Able to Work

NREGA which in principle gives every person who is willing to work, the statutory right to 100 days of guaranteed wage labour at minimum wages per family, is legally open to all destitute persons including the elderly. But in practice, it is found that to most it remains barred. Old people report that they are discouraged to apply for work, with commonplace remarks such as : *'you are too old and will fall sick because of the heavy work involved'*.

Most of the NREGA work involves digging of soil which is often too hard and unyielding. Also workers are paid based not on the time worked but the actual work accomplished, which further leaves them with small earnings. Instead of identifying less physically demanding work like standing guard at the sites, taking care of children, filling stones and soil in baskets, and planting and irrigating saplings, they are given the most back-breaking work, and are therefore themselves eventually compelled to opt out.[41]

Recommendations : Old Age Security

The nation must at last redeem its duty to its senior citizens, who have contributed to it in many ways : built it up through difficult times, raised its young, and enriched its diverse wealth of wisdom, songs and material well being. People in the formal sector have pensions to fall back on, but for the vast majority of men and women who toil in the unorganised sector, there is no retirement : they still have no pension without work, and no food withoutwork. Sickness is an inevitable companion of age, but each time it falls, it is a calamity. We need to ensure that as people grey, they can live with dignity and self-reliance, with adequate food and health care, with protection, rest and recreation. This is a public policy imperative that can brook no further delay.

Cash Transfers

1. Every aged person must have access as a legal right to a pension that is sufficient for a dignified, active and healthy life. This means that all workers who are not part of the organised sector of the economy must be covered by pension benefits. The government should ensure within one year pensions for all aged people above the age of 65 years who in rural areas are landless, artisans, and small or marginal farmers, and all SC and ST aged persons; and in urban areas are residents of slums or homeless, and all unorganised workers.
2. This must be secured as a universal entitlement to each of these men and women (in the way that mid-day meals have become for all school going children in government and aided schools). This means that central

and state governments cannot plead financial constraints or fix any quotas on the numbers of such persons who are to be covered.

3. The gram panchayat, youth and women's groups, and literacy activists, and college NSS groups may be involved in a campaign to cover all eligible elderly people with old age pensions in a campaign mode. Transparency in selection and disbursement should be ensured by involving the Gram Sabhas, pensioners' organisations, and citizens' committees.
4. The quantum of pension should be adequate. In line with the Working Group on Social Protection Policy's recommendation, the rate of minimum pension should be fixed at Rs. 400 per person and the State Governments may be required mandatorily to contribute their share of the pension. This can best be done by treating the Scheme a Centrally Sponsored Scheme under which the expenditure is shared by the Central and State Governments in the ratio of 50 : 50.
5. Central Government employees and pensioners get an increment twice a year that is pegged to the Consumer Price Index (CPI). Likewise, the pension amount should also be linked to inflation in the economy and appraised every half a year, using Rs. 400 in the year 2007 as the baseline.
6. The pension should be paid through banks or post offices either via money order or in cash or deposited in the nearest bank accounts. Any commission payable to the Postal Department for making these payments should be waived or borne by the Ministry concerned.
7. Based on the Supreme Court Order dated 28th November, 2001 pensions should be paid to the beneficiaries by the 7th day of each month. Even if the budgeted funds from the central or state government are unavailable or delayed, the state government should make use of alternative arrangements to arrange these funds and prevent delays in disbursement. In the way that salaries and pensions of public servants are not

delayed despite delays in financial allocations and disbursements, the pensions of aged people should also be seen as having a 'first call' on state finances, because they are essential for the survival of a highly vulnerable group.

8. The minimum age criteria for pension eligibility should be reduced to 60 years instead of 65 years, as has already been implemented across many states.
9. Whereas non-pensioners are in most desperate conditions, pensioners, especially those from lower rungs of government and corporate hierarchies, tend to suffer from delays of sanction and disbursements, and other forms of harassment. At present, there are about 25 lakh pensioners of central government and there is an addition of one lakh every year. There is almost an equal number of pensioners drawing pension from state governments. The government pensions include family pensions. More than one lakh persons draw pension from banks, insurance companies and public sector undertakings. In mid 1980s a Supreme Court decision added nearly 10 lakh more pensioners. In 1985, the central government took a policy decision that minimum pension it will pay will be Rs. 375/-p.m. Pensioners frequently suffer harassment, humiliation and long delays in disbursement of pensions. For this, a single-window payment with simple procedures for pension disbursement involving also pensioners' groups and local bodies to control corruption in the disbursement needs to be ensured.
10. District officers must held responsible to personally monitor the timely processing of pension claims of all government servants due to retire in the next three years. Paper work should commence at least two years before the date of retirement, and special pension camps for disposal of pending cases may be organised from time to time. The target should be to hand over pension papers to the retiring functionary on the date of superannuation.
11. National Family Benefit Scheme amount must be

increased to Rs. 25,000 and must cover deaths of any 18 - 64 years old member of the family in a BPL household. The ratio of 36 percent applied to the current population estimates for 2006–2007 must be used to calculate the percentage of persons eligible. The amount of insurance must be pegged to the Consumer Price Index (CPI) and upwardly revised accordingly at least once every two years.

12. Payment under NFBS must be disbursed to the family within 3 months of the death, failing which interest at the rate of 5 per cent per month should be payable.
13. Families of persons who died allegedly of starvation, farmer suicides, natural and human-made disasters should get first priority in NFBS releases.
14. Measures have to be taken to check an reduce under-utilisation of funds in various programmes serving the elderly.
15. Ensure that a person entitled to two or more pensions receives all of them e.g. widow and old-age pension.

Social Safety

16. In view of the universalisation of IGNOAPS, if all the eligible persons over time are covered under the NOAPS, the eligibility for the Annapurna Scheme would become defunct. However, given the multiple benefits of the scheme of direct food transfers, it is instead suggested to modify the programme to a. Continue to serve as an additional assistance to the most vulnerable groups amongst the elderly, who have multiple vulnerabilities (such as single women, disabilities or debilitating ailments) and b. Merge its food allotments with the mid-day meal, and all old people from the neighbourhood should be permitted to share in the school mid-day meal of hot cooked meal in ICDS centres without any conditions, as practiced in the state of Tamil Nadu. This serves as a last defence against starvation of the aged destitute, without requiring any additional administrative costs. The presence of aged

disabled people are not even aware that they can demand work under NREGA. Their exclusion starts from the very first step, and often are not provided with separate job cards nor is their name included in the job cards owned by their family. Out the 19 disabled people interviewed in Sitapur block of Chhattisgarh in December 2006, 15 had no job cards.[90] In Deogarh panchayat, the sarpanch has refused to issue job cards to all disabled applicants with the disdainful explanation, *"You cannot take care of your own bodies how will you work?"*[91] In Bardihi Panchayat though 6 disabled people had their names on the job cards, but they are not called for work[92].

The problem also lies in the attitude of the community, local panchayat and government officials, who presume that people with disability are unable to do work. The exception is Badwani block in Madhya Pradesh, where due to a concerted community-based movement and pressure more than 200 people with disabilities have participated in NREGA work.

Almost 20 per cent of disabled persons usually find their place in among the poorest. It is therefore ironical that poverty alleviation programs including the dynamic NREGA exclude this vulnerable section of society in violation of the PWD Act 1995.

6. Other Poverty Alleviation Programmes

Most poverty alleviation schemes like the Swarnjayanti Gram Swarozgar Yojana (SGSY), Indira Awaas Yojana (IAY), Swarna Jayanti Shahari Rozgar Yojana (SJSRY) have stipulated in their guidelines or budgets that a 3 per cent reservation of coverage or finances is mandatory for disabled people. However these targets are invariably not met. In 2006-7 (up to Jan. 2007)[93], disabled people constituted only 1.07 per cent of Swarozgaris and were allotted only 0.94 per cent of IAY houses. While the performance of SJSRY was better in aggregate terms, it is still below the 3 per cent norm and in the case of states like Arunachal Pradesh, Meghalaya and Goa according to official data is a stark 0 per cent.[94]

The minimal participation of disabled persons in government schemes is a result of a range of issues including lack of awareness about these poverty-alleviation schemes and their specific entitlement based on reservation. It would also be faulty to assume that disabled people through mere information alone would be in a position to come forth and claim the benefits. Societal prejudice and the physical inaccessibility of government offices serve as important barriers. To ensure inclusion, regular awareness campaigns combined with rigorous door-to-door identification of poor disabled persons is a first and necessary step.

Recommendations for People with Disability

1. Work is the right of every adult individual, not only because it is the source of economic self-reliance but also because it leads to dignity and self-esteem. The state must accept and operationalise **the right to work** of persons with disabilities. Special employment agencies should be created for disabled people. In guiding, training and placement of the disabled for livelihoods, the key is to recognise and build upon the unique strengths of disabled persons; one may be led even to tasks which the disabled can do better than non-disabled. The hearing impaired for instance, can do all jobs except those in which speech and hearing are essential, and would be in fact at an advantage in situations of high noise level such as the aeroplane industry, and have been found to be more accurate in computer data entry work. The mentally slow may be better equipped for assembly-line simple repetitive tasks, as well as tasks requiring physical stamina. In China, under what is described as a 'special warmth' schemes, a number of 'welfare factories' have been established in which the majority of workers are disabled. Able-bodied workers undergo sensitisation workshops to develop appropriate attitudes to the disabled. Such factories are functioning at a profit, and have greatly built the morale of the disabled workers.

2. Likewise, the state must be serious about implementing its constitutional and statutory duty to **educate every disabled child**. Education may be defined as guided learning to help a child gain skills and understanding for meeting life's needs. The school is an important institution for education, but even countries which have successfully implemented programmes for universalising elementary education have often excluded the disabled. It is important for policy makers and teachers to understand that many disabled children have quick minds, and can do as well or better than other children, but only if they have certain basic facilities and support. What is more, schooling may be even more important, say, for physically disabled children than for able-bodies children in villages, because they may not be able to perform hard physical farm labour, but have a good chance for employment or community leadership through schooling.

   The preference should be for the integrated and not segregated special schools, in which model all motor disabled and other mild or moderately disabled children attend regular schools. This is not only cost-effective because it utilises the existing school infrastructure, but it also enables disabled children to aspire for and achieve higher goals and helps disabled and able-bodies children to understand and work and play comfortably with one another. Even for severe disabilities, there may be a special class in a normal school, with shared eating and recreation spaces.
3. Special bus/transport services should be provided for disabled students to go to school/college. For issuing disability and income certificates, and identity cards for availing concessions, district officials may **recognise certificates** issued by notified and specific NGOs especially disability rights organisations, instead of insisting on government doctor's certification.
4. Wherever a disabled children enrols herself into a school, ramps or other required aids should be put in place

within a period of one month and the specific class/ group should be made to sit at the ground floor to ensure that the child is **not excluded** from mid-day meals and supplementary nutrition programme (SNP).

5. In all the anganwadis or school where a disabled child has been enrolled, the anganwadi worker or one teacher from the school should be **trained within 3 months** specifically on the disability needs and rights.
6. All anganwadis and schools must consistently show at least **5 per cent attendance** of disabled children, else the CDPO and District Education Officer must be held personally responsible.
7. Any education provided in an alternative setting should be of equal quality, recognition and value as the general school system. Children with disability face both direct and indirect discrimination and exclusion. They are out of school and pre-school ICDS centres mainly due to the inaccessibility of schools, attitude of teachers and workers and lack of proper support for their equal participation in education. There is a strong case, to make arrangements to provide all disabled children (both moderately and severely disabled) who are registered with the nearest schools (but do not attend regularly for any reason[95]) with **mid-day meals and supplementary nutrition** in the school and ICDS centre during feeding time if the child comes from the nearest school or anganwadi, or at home in the way of weekly dry rations, irrespective of whether they receive home-based education.
8. The government should actively promote **organisations and self-help groups of the disabled** and their families, and work mainly with them. These should not be dominated by middle class, male and urban persons with disabilities but include rural village level groups of disabled people and their families, with equal representation to girls and women. This helps them to realise that they are not alone, promotes mutual support and assistance, and provides important resources for

many community based activities. It ensures that government programmes are designed and implemented with the real needs of persons with disabilities. The slogan of disabled people worldwide must be respected, *'Nothing about us without us'*.

9. There should be a **mass education and mobilisation** programme with *jathas*, banners, posters, wall-writing, discussions in schools and colleges, use of mass media and so on the abilities and rights of persons with disabilities. The success of the campaign would be measured firstly by the extent to which the community begins to introspect about its prejudices regarding the disabled and overcomes these prejudices, recognising both the potential and the right of the disabled to a life of dignity and self-reliance; and secondly to how much more inclusive schools, public buildings and work places become for persons who live with disability.
10. All the states governments should conduct detailed **surveys** to understand the prevalence of disability in total and also separately in different socio-economic groups. It would be useful to commence with a **detailed house-to-house survey of disability**, through youth volunteers including many disabled youth. The surveyors should be sensitised and trained in advance not only with regard to identifying and classifying disability, but also appropriate attitudes towards the disabled, otherwise they would also invisibilise the disabled like census workers. Alternatively, as was successfully tried out in Pakistan, the survey may be conducted through school children.
11. State governments should also undertake a special campaign for the **identification** of disabled persons as beneficiaries for the range of existing government schemes without any ceiling on the number of beneficiaries. All the disabled persons who qualify to be eligible should be able to avail the benefits without any ceiling on number of beneficiaries.
12. All disabled persons should be given **'entitlement cards'**

with all benefits - both specific and general - clearly mentioned based on the gender, age and eligibility. The procedure for application for these benefits should also be mentioned, in two languages including the local language.

13. In all **poverty**-alleviation and feeding programmes including the ICDS, MDM, NREGA, AAY, etc. state governments should gather information separately on the **coverage** of disabled persons vis-à-vis the total number of the PWD eligible for the scheme.
14. Provide **free healthcare** in government hospitals for all disabled persons without any ceiling on the extent of severity of disability or obligation to produce a disability certificate or BPL card.
15. Most disabled persons require some kinds of **aids and appliances** for a fuller life, for mobility and communication. For mass and locally appropriate production, the best approach would be to develop local design of these aids and appliances using local materials and skills and to train local artisans for cottage-based or cooperative workshop manufacture. Organising training of disabled persons as artisans for this purpose would be an excellent idea, and distributing these through disabled peoples' organisations.
16. The quota of Antyodaya Anna Yojana (AAY) should be increased to provide universal coverage among all disabled-headed families or families in which there are disabled children or in which disabled adults are dependent, who are BPL or SC or ST.
17. There should be **clear directions** to issue NREGA job cards and to provide on priority work when demanded by people with disabilities. The Schedule of Works should also be modified to provide a listing of all the physically **light tasks** like carrying drinking water for labourers, looking after children in the crèche who are accompanying nursing mothers, maintaining muster rolls and attendance register etc. which can be allocated for disabled persons.

18. In most families in which disabled children or adults need home based care, one adult member normally misses work in order to provide care for the disabled person. Therefore, all families with a disabled member should be allocated a minimum of **150 days** of work under NREGA.
19. All disabled children under eighteen who cannot take care at themselves should be allowed to join the **worksite crèche** for children under six. Women preferably from the families with disabled children should be deputed to look after the children in the proportion of one woman for every five disabled children and they should be provided the full applicable NREGA minimum wage.
20. Create a **centrally sponsored scheme** for disability pension scheme of a minimum of Rs. 400 covering all BPL, SC and ST disabled persons with a centre-state contribution of in the ratio of 50 : 50.
21. Ensure that a person **entitled** to two or more **pensions receives all** of them e.g. old-age and disability pension, because such a person suffers from multiple disabilities.
22. Enforce uniform **guidelines** for the **construction** of buildings, roads and other infrastructure to make them equally accessible to the persons with disability.
23. All the **pre-service training** programmes should include a component on sensitization to the needs and rights of the disabled.

Annexure 1
Coverage of Disabled Persons under State Disability Pension Schemes

S. No.	*States/UTs*	*No. of BPL disabled Persons**	*Coverage under Disability Pension Schemes by the States***	*Percentage Coverage*
1.	Andhra Pradesh	**350527**	200000	57
2	Bihar	**1037431**	150000	14

S. No.	States/UTs	No. of BPL disabled Persons*	Coverage under Disability Pension Schemes by the States**	Percentage Coverage
3	Chhattisgarh	**178536**	63865	36
4	Goa	**2350**	4257	181
5	Gujarat	**253107**	174642	69
6	Haryana	**113988**	116444	102
7	Himachal Pradesh	**63721**	26922	42
8	Jharkhand	**246428**	7980	3
9	Karnataka	**311917**	453331	145
10	Kerala	**218900**	176596	81
11	Madhya Pradesh	**598906**	183620	31
12	Maharashtra	**578548**	313911	54
13	Orissa	**495960**	203000	41
14	Punjab	**49966**	91338	183
15	Tamilnadu	**575367**	81137	14
16	Uttar Pradesh	**1410701**	400000	28
17	Uttarakhand	**79563**	26216	33
18	West Bengal	**658702**	8264	1
19	Tripura	**24083**	839	3
20	Chandigarh	**1764**	1590	90
21	NCT Delhi	**34652**	200	1
22	TOTAL	7285117	2684152	37

* Calulation based on Census Data 2001 and taking into consideration the BPL percentage what MoFCS is using and assuming that Disability is equally prevalent among all the sections of Society.

** Estimates from Ministry.

Urban Homeless

Homeless people on city streets are invisible to public policy, though they are visible daily to policy makers as they drive the same city streets. Homeless women, men and children share the cities virtually as non-citizens. Many die unmourned in the bitter winter cold, the merciless summer heat or in the deluge of the monsoons. They are forced to live and sleep each night under the open sky. Life for them is an unremitting struggle against hunger, loneliness, sickness.

The bitter winter often proves to be a messenger of death.[96] In 2002, the police found 3040 corpses of homeless people defeated by Delhi's harsh winters. 400 of these were victims of a single cold wave. The onus lies entirely with the government to build a comprehensive policy to support the city's most marginalised residents, but the governance amnesia across the nation has been acute.

India is estimated to have the largest population of street children in the world. Often, they escape from abusive homes and get caught in yet another world of exploitation, hunger, physical violence and sexual abuse. Poor education and the bitter reality of their lives kill any hope of a better future.

'Houseless people', of all age-groups, are defined by the census as those who do not live in 'census houses' i.e. a structure with roof. Enumerators are instructed to observe possible locations where the houseless populations are likely to congregate : roadside, pavements, drainage pipes, under staircases, or in the open, temple-mandaps, platforms, welfare institutions.

Based on this restricted vision, in 2001, the census enumerated 1.94 million homeless people, of whom almost three-fifth live in villages and remaining 0.78 million live a precarious existence in India's cities and towns. However, these numbers are likely to be gross underestimates, because people without a home tend to be a highly invisible especially to officialdom. In Chennai city, a civil society survey in 2003 was able to list twice the official estimate of homeless people (i.e. 40,500 persons from 11,000 households) and also revealed that 83 percent of them are *dalit*.

The largest majority of homeless people sleep on pavements and sidewalks, under ledges of shops and homes, in market corridors, at bus-stands and railways stations, outside places of worship often in daily danger to their lives from rash and drunken drivers. In some cities, single women seem to prefer shrines, children bus stands and railway stations and families pavements.

Street Children

Some estimates indicate that the number of street children alone is 18 million with twice as many boys as girls.[102] Street children belong to two kinds: children *on* the streets and children *of* the streets. This distinction is very crucial for planning relevant intervention strategies. Children of the street are more vulnerable than children on the streets, because they have no adult protection. They either have no parents or have escaped on the streets abusive, violent, alcoholic or irresponsible parents. They can be mainstreamed for formal education in schools; but they have no home to go back to, only the streets. They therefore need comprehensive long term residential care for the entire duration of their childhood and youth, but in ways that are voluntary and non-custodial.

As distinct from children of the street, children on the street do retain live contact with their families in the city, who may live on the streets or in slums. However, because of extreme poverty, substance abuse or irresponsible parentage, the children are left largely to their own devices especially through the day. At an early age, they often learn to beg, at places of worship or traffic lights, or they forage in rubbish heaps not only for food but also for various materials that can be sold for recycling. As they grow older, girls are often drawn into casual street-based sex work, whereas boys may diversify from rag picking to working in garages and catering establishments.

Undefined

It is remarkable that so little is known about the lived experiences of those without a home : why do they live on the streets, how do they survive; how do they manage to sleep, where do they bathe; what do they eat; what work they do, do they access public services?

As an itinerant population, they are almost intractably

difficult to identify, reach and research for many reasons. First, the homeless population is extremely heterogeneous, in terms of age group, gender, livelihoods, place of origin and reasons for living on the streets.

Often the relationship between homeless families and the state is one of extreme mutual acrimony and distrust, an unending undeclared cold war. State authorities are distrustful of homeless people as parasitical, lazy, unhygienic, illegal and largely criminal. Homeless people return the compliment by regarding the government as implacably uncaring, hostile, corrupt and neglectful.

Criminalised

Homelessness itself is perceived to be a crime. Homeless families are vary of both the government and the middle class, particularly because both perceive homeless people of any age and gender to be vaguely dangerous and intractably on the wrong side of the law. Homeless people are taken as illegal elements who need to be weaned out of the city. Due to the above reason police brutality and harassment is more common for homeless people.

Worse still, vagrants, mentally ill itinerants, 'illegal' squatters, pavement dwellers, are all considered 'guilty' of violating penal statutes or those whose entire enforcement is at the mercy of the police and the junior magistracy.

Across India, large numbers of homeless people are routinely rounded up by the police. This is done usually to fulfil targets of 'preventive detention' as proactive measures to maintain civic peace under Sections 109 and 151 of the Criminal Procedure Code, 1973. Homeless people then languish for long periods in the jail, because they are too poor, asset less and without legal aid or literacy, to secure bail.

Even apart from their acute need for shelter, their daily efforts of survival are hindered at every step by their absolute 'illegality' of existence. At the heart of the problem are existing laws and policies of regulating urban land, which systematically exclude the poor from building or acquiring legal shelter. As a result, even all self-help efforts of the poor to live are condemned by law to the twilight zones of illegality.

Invisiblised

The processes of illegalisation and criminalisation work together. Any state would prefer to take steps towards invisiblising the powerless. Imprisonment is one of the common tools. Another is de facto denial of citizenship.

In an age of targeting as opposed to universal access, the fate of the poor increasingly hinges on possession of 'legal' documents. These have become indispensable not only for protecting citizenship and assets but also as instruments for the needy to rightfully avail of the services of a welfare society as enshrined in the constitution of the land.

In the case of homeless people, the very concept of citizenship is denied by the State itself in India. Two basic documents that are widely perceived as de facto proof of citizenship - ration card and voter's card - are not available to the overwhelming majority. The reason often cited by the authorities is their unavailability of a permanent address.

Informal Jobs

The majority of homeless people survive through casual, unprotected, uncertain and hard labour, through a range of occupations like daily wage work, construction labour, pulling rickshaws, carrying and pushing loads, domestic work, street vending and of course soliciting alms. A small number admit to living by professional blood donation and casual street based sex work (both male and female), although the actual numbers in these professions that are in conflict with law and routinely stigmatised, is likely to be larger.

India has an estimated six million beggars.[104] The Delhi School of Social Work reports that over 71 percent of Delhi's, estimated 60,000 beggars, are driven to solicit alms by poverty.[105] But India's anti-beggary laws are derived from obsolete European vagrancy laws, which hold the helpless poor criminally responsible for their situation. The Anti-

Beggary laws in particular are used as weapon against homeless people. Some state laws actually assume that all who are houseless are no more than beggars. The Bombay Prevention of Begging Act, 1959 and its later avatar Delhi Prevention of Begging Act, 1960 define begging as soliciting or receiving alms in a public place and includes any one having no visible means of subsistence and, wandering about or remaining in any public place in such condition or manner, as makes it likely that the person doing so exists by soliciting or receiving alms. This amounts to criminalising destitution and homelessness and even stigmatised ailments like leprosy. This broad definition allows the police to arrest anyone who looks poor and unfairly targets those who are houseless and live in public places such as pavements or parks.[106]

Last year, more than half the people surveyed by the Centre for Equity Studies[107] reported that work is not available on a regular basis. In Delhi, Chennai and Patna more than three-fifths held the same opinion. Only in Madurai, where the dominant occupation is begging, did 90 percent of homeless people report regular earnings.

Even these meagre urban livelihoods of the poor are subject to a great deal of harassment by the municipal and police authorities. Despite the Supreme Court's ruling, that their informal occupations merit protection based on their fundamental right to livelihood under the Constitution, street vendors conduct their business amidst ominous insecurity. Whenever eviction drives are conducted their wares are confiscated or even destroyed. Section 34 of the Police Act empowers the police to remove any obstructions on the streets. Even licensed street vendors can be evicted under this law.

Often the street vendors organize themselves into unions or local associations who negotiate with the local authorities for occupying public space. This invariably means offering bribes to the authorities for warding off eviction drives or forewarning them of impending drives. In some cases local musclemen, more often than not with the backing of local political leaders, collect protection fees through threats.[108]

Delhi itself has about two lakh rickshaw pullers and more than three lakh street vendors, mostly run by first-generation rural migrants. But the city government has put a limit of 50,000 on licences to pull rickshaws. Therefore, every day about 1.5 lakh rickshaws operate illegally in the city. A vast majority of street vendors have no license either. They all operate outside the legal economy and are routinely harassed by the police and municipal authorities. The licence-permit raj remains as entrenched as ever for the poor to earn their livelihood. The formal economy is closed to them and so is formal housing. They are compelled to get their *roti* (livelihood) and *makaan* (living space) from the informal sector, in their case from the road itself.[109]

Debt Bondage

As homeless people find their income streams become increasingly insecure in the informal sector and state interventions fails to bring them in the ambit of policy spaces, homeless people are increasingly pushed into unmanageable hunger, debt, sometimes forced to take loans from private moneylenders who charge exorbitantly high rates of interest. While this might ease immediate consumption needs, mainly food expenses, it creates a mountain of future problems.

In fact, there is a great amount of distrust that the moneylenders have for people without homes. If they do manage to procure loans, the interest rates vary between 10-30 percent per month, which is again very high compared to the common bank interest rates. However, they are left with little other options to access credit.

Lack of Access to Public Services

The urban homeless people often have little and troubled access to even the most elementary public services much of which people who are privileged to live on homes take for granted. Worse still, everything that they can use has to be paid for - every visit to the toilet, every bath - must be paid for, in cash, immediately. The wider range of services, including healthcare, education and law and order, on the grounds of cost and discriminatory practices, remain a distant dream.

The Centre for Equity Studies survey revealed that 45 percent of homeless respondents pay for to relieve themselves in public toilets. Drinking water, often not potable and erratic in supply, is however available free at roadside taps. In Chennai, however, women complained that they have to wait at public taps for long, until other more authorized citizens including even slum dwellers, fill their needs before homeless people get their turn.

Even the night shelters sometimes charge a fee. In Delhi, the Municipal Corporation runs 12 night shelters with a total capacity of 2,500. But the occupancy rate is minimal as each person has to pay Rs. 6 for 12 hours, but the basic facilities like toilets, blankets, mats, clothing and sense of safety are rarely available .or are in terrible disrepair.[110]

Homeless life can therefore be paradoxically costly! Especially in urban areas, the costs of living are higher than rural areas as all essential items including food, rent, energy, transport, water from private vendors, and sanitation from pay-as-you-use facilities have to be purchased. Poor people's capacity to meet these needs is purely dependent on having a secure to live preferably close to their work, their capacity to sell their labour for money, and their ability to draw on and use social support systems[111] - all of which are prohibitively difficult for homeless people.

Hunger on the City Streets

The availability of food to urban homeless people is mixed. The quantities may (but are not always) sufficient. The quality however uniformly tends to be monotonous, elementary, often of poor nutritional value and (in the nature of their existence) unhygienic. It is indeed the search of food which has led many to the streets.

Sufficiency of the food seems far more important to the homeless than the nutritional content. Except those with families in the streets, they rarely get home cooked food. Many buy cooked food, sometimes from humble eateries on the pavements themselves. Homeless people are forced to depend extensively on external sources for their food – through purchase, foraging, or receiving food in charity.[112]

Many who live by soliciting alms, eat only what they get as charity and save all the cash they are given as alms to send back to their village. At times, they have to be content with only one meal, but usually they are able to manage two half meals a day. Leprosy patients in Madurai, Patna were found to depend upon stale leftovers that they are given as they beg in the day. But at night, they try to set up a make shift stove between two bricks, and boil some hot rice. [113]

Street children buy their food from food stalls. On bad days the younger ones even forage for food in rubbish heaps. The rag pickers start their day with a single cup of tea as they can spend only a little money and only after they complete their work by late afternoon do they buy their first meal of the day from the stalls. When they have enough money, they eat from relatively good places as violence of the streets makes it difficult to save money. Later they forage in the bins for bits of biscuits and samosas, and sometimes beg at temples.

Unhealthy Diets

Recurring bouts of irregularity in food consumption also deprives them of nutrition and poor health. Repeated infections result in low food absorption, further worsened by their substance abuse, including excessive drinking of tea in cold winters. Yet they spend the greatest part of their earnings in the daily struggle to feed themselves and their dependents.

In Chennai, homeless women set out their stoves only close to midnight after the streets are emptied of pedestrians, and they wake their sleeping children to groggily eat their only 'home'-cooked meal for the day. But during the rainy season, it is an almost impossible luxury as their fires burn under the pouring rain. Many resort to other modes of foraging their food.[114]

Nearly half of the respondents of the CES study reported that they have taken ill during that last one month due to which they could not continue their work and had to forgo their earnings. Nearly one fourth of those who experienced illness were unable to access any medication. 56 percent who were advised to be hospitalized, were unable to afford to enter one. Shockingly, hazardous drug usage is found more among the street children than adult homeless persons. In Bangalore city[115], seven of every ten street children were found to be drug users. These habits add to their poor health.

In Patna, none of the homeless respondents store any food due to its perishable nature. Besides, fuel is something that is beyond their means. Often they cook on fires burning between bricks with dry twigs or cakes of cow dung collected with great difficulty. [116]

Myth of Public Help for the Urban Homeless[117]

Across cities, invariably 60 percent of more of the homeless people reported never receiving any form of assistance either from non-government organizations or the government. This assistance mainly consisted of provision of food or shelter during rains and a few relief measures during the tsunami in Chennai.

Some charitable organizations are focused on not serving any able bodied homeless person with free food but only the elderly, disabled and mentally disturbed. However, there is a singular lack of a long term vision for rehabilitation.

There is also a general but illusory idea that the free food provision in religious places serves the homeless people. In Madurai Meenakshi Temple preference is accorded to devotees and homeless people are served only left overs, if available. In major Gurudwaras of Delhi like Sis Ganj in Chandni Chowk, our researchers have observed that it is often college students, who eat the free food while homeless people often are not allowed to enter the premises, which is a grave distortion of the religious teachings on which the practice is based.[118]

Schemed Out

Food and livelihood schemes of government often fail to reach poor men and women, boys and girls who live in urban slums and shanties, because they most frequently face a hostile administration who believes they should not live in the city, and wishes only to break their makeshift homes and drive them out. But those who are most comprehensively excluded are those who are forced to make the pavements and railway platforms their home - because they need to save every rupee to keep alive family in their villages, or because they are brutalised and abandoned by those who should have cared most are also those who are most comprehensively barred from every government initiative.

1. Integrated Child Development Scheme (ICDS) and Mid-day Meals

In any Indian city, one would invariably come across homeless children playing on the streets and dirty by-lanes, who never go to schools or anganwadis. This stark exclusion of homeless children in the two major food schemes of India is very visible across cities. Either the schools or anganwadis do not exist at a convenient location, or what is much more the case, the homeless are routinely turned away, for want of a permanent address and also because of stigma.

Chennai seems to be the interesting exception. Homeless children have been found sometimes to be allowed to join government schools, on the basis of their living in the same pavement for generations. But mothers reveal that most of the children go to school but on an irregular basis.[119]

As for those street children who live away from their families, there arises no question of admission without familial or external support. In Delhi, even children of rag-pickers, construction workers and migrant labourers were found to be left out from the ICDS.[120] Irregularities and the inconsistencies with the anganwadis that are function in urban areas is a different issue altogether.

2. *Public Distribution System (PDS)*

Not having any proof of identification and address proof means not being able to claim BPL or Antyodaya cards and the other food schemes, which in practice depend on this. The other menace that homeless people face is the perpetual threat of being forcibly displaced or dislocated from their place of stay.

Only one-fifth of the respondents of the CES study possess ration cards and the rest either have never been issued one, or have it in their village address which cannot be used once they migrate. Others have lost them in their transition from the native houses to the homeless life. Some lose it of they lived in slums earlier and these were demolished without notice.

Of course, mere possession of a ration card does not assure them any food security. There are often discriminated against them in the PDS outlets. Even if majority of adults without a home are aware of ration card and voters ID, due to their powerlessness they would be able to rarely access it.

Due to the recent civil society efforts, some state governments have considered the need of homeless people for having a ration card.[121] In Chennai in early 2007 many homeless persons had been issued with a ration card recently but had yet to start availing the benefits. Other were denied the cards as they claimed

> "We are also denied ration cards as the officials fear that we may claim for houses and televisions[122] by showing the BPL cards".

3. *Other Welfare Programs*

Other social assistance programmes such as old age pensions, NFBS (death insurance) and NMBS (maternity benefit) are simply out of the reach of urban poor, either due to their contested citizenship because of no permanent address, or due to the lack of political will and administrative rigour in delivering the benefits to the homeless.

Rashmi Singh[123], Joint Director, Social Welfare Department, in a recent consultation in Delhi[124], emphasised the need for the convergence in the social sector programmes to reach the urban poor, as there was lack of clarity in the official mandate which was unable to fix the responsibility of service delivery with any particular department.

Recommendations

The homeless have a seamless continuum with those who are precariously housed under a plastic sheet, often on pavements or construction sites, and those who live in illegalised and insecure slum shanties. Therefore recommendations have been listed together for all these segments of the city's poorest, and the end of the subsequent chapter on slum dwellers.

URBAN SLUM DWELLERS

The term 'slum' is used in a loose sense to designate such settlements of the urban poor, that are overcrowded, dilapidated, faultily laid out and generally lacking in essential civic services. NSSO defined 'slum'[125] as 'a compact area with a collection of poorly built tenements, mostly of temporary nature, crowded together usually with inadequate sanitary and drinking water facilities in unhygienic conditions'. UN HABITAT[126] has officially defined as, "a heavily populated urban area characterised by substandard housing and squalor……and lacking in tenure security…usually inhabited by the very poor or socially disadvantaged. Most slums lack clean water, electricity, sanitation and other basic services".

In 2001 census enumerators estimated that 42 million people live in slums, in 640 cities and towns spread across the country. They constituted 4 per cent of the total population and a seventh of the total urban population and almost a quarter of the population in the 640 cities and towns which officially report the existence of slums. However, even this is likely to be a gross under-estimate, due to definitional problems, and problems of dealing with the transience of marginal populations, forced on to the wrong side of the law. Many slums are not recognised by the state, as it can then refuse to provide it any amenities. Independent studies have established that any thing between a quarter or one-third of the population in most cities and towns lives in slums or are precariously housed or houseless, and that at least half the population in slums are below the official poverty line.

India is home to two-thirds of all slum dwellers in South Asia[127]. The distorted world map indicates that 17 per cent of the world's slum dwellers reside in India (represented by the orange bulge). These 170 million urban dwellers with legally insecure housing and poor conditions are spread across 640 cities and towns in India and constitute 32 per cent of the urban population.[128] Today, there are about 52,000 slums in India, but only half are 'legal' or slums which are authorised and recognized by governments.

Most urban poor people are believed to be migrants from villages i.e. as temporary visitors to cities. Therefore, governments and city dwellers themselves regard them as a corrupting influence, disregarding their contribution to the city economy and its development. Rural and urban poverty are inextricably inter-linked and urban poverty is not merely a spill-over of rural poverty. They must therefore be seen together and addressed simultaneously as two aspects of a single problem and at the same time as autonomous problems that need to be addressed in distinct ways. [129]

A Profile

Interestingly, the male population in slums is far more predominant on an average. The sex ratio is skewed in favour of men. For every 1000 men there are only 876 women, which is lower the proportion in the general urban population. The only exception is in states with matriarchal communities like Meghalaya, Pondicherry and Kerala.

But the sex ratio in slums is lower than non-slum urban population in 9 states and union territories, while in the remaining 17 states/union territories the sex ratio of slum population is higher than the non-slum urban areas of the respective states. Contrary to the expectation that migration to slum areas would be of males initially and is followed by their families which would give a lower sex ratio in slum areas, the higher sex ratio in slums for many states is suggestive of the migration to slums more often of the complete families.

More than 6 million children i.e. 16 per cent of the total child population live in slums. In other words, every sixth urban child in the country who is less than six years is a slum dweller.

In another contrast, while 81 per cent for male slum dwellers are literate, only 64 per cent of women have been imparted the same skills. The 16 percentage point differential in literacy levels is large and the male-female gap among slum dwellers is highest in Rajasthan at 26 per cent. Across cities and towns, the literacy level among the slum dwellers is lower than the general population.[130]

Surrounding Insecurities

Livelihoods of slum residents are typically unorganized, insecure and the wages irregular, *uncertain and nominal. Many a times, their occupations are even illegalised.*[131] For children in slums who are forced to work, conditions are particularly precarious.

Despite all their toil, the sense of social security is minimal. Slum dwellers constantly live with the fear of losing their homes (where they have often invested their life savings) and their possessions due to demolitions. Many settlements have been demolished repeatedly. Though many of these people have proper legal documentation (ration cards, voter ID cards) to prove their domicile, there is often no justice. Often the residents are not even provided advance notice, which is mandatory, to at least recover their valuables. After all, demolitions are perfect opportunities for money to pass hands between the police, criminal gangs and corporations and for grabbing of prime urban real estate.

Slums are the direct outcome of the failure of state policy and law to intervene effectively to ensure legal access of the urban poor to land and financial resources, which would be necessary to enable them to construct for themselves legal and adequate shelter.

Despite stated commitment in official documents to ensuring access of housing to the poor, we shall see that actual investments in this regard have been niggardly and misdirected. Law as well as administrative and judicial prejudices aggravate this. In effect, these have not only consistently blocked the access of the urban poor to shelter, but have actually rendered illegal and criminalised the spirited, sometimes valiant, endeavours of the poor to survive, not with the help of but despite the state.[132]

Exclusion Path

Often the urban poor, residing in slums, are worse off than their rural counterparts. They face issues of legitimacy, insecure tenure rights, are cut off from their community and are thrown into anonymity and formality of urban life. They have to pay for every civic amenity like, toilets and water.

Urban slums are characterised by unhygienic and unsanitary conditions, high levels of environmental pollution. The poor repeatedly confront the police and civic authorities, face exploitation because of their low literacy and are highly dependent on the government to provide legal housing, livelihoods, health care etc.

India's slum population has doubled since the eighties[133] as rising urbanisation has not been coupled with rise in infrastructure facilities. But governments have sought to reduce the visibility of mushrooming slums by pushing them to periphery and refusing to notify or legalise them. Further, slum dwellers face constant neglect from the administration and are forced to live in terrible squalor. Given the commercial value of every square inch of urban space, every attempt is made to push slums to periphery, deny them any access to sanitation facilities, credit, legality and often even citizenship.

One-fifth of the slum dwellers belong to either the scheduled caste i.e. *dalits* (17 per cent) or scheduled tribe (2 per cent). The *dalit* population is far higher in the slums than in non-slum areas (11 per cent). In fact, of the total *dalits* in urban areas, 22 per cent live in the slums. Similarly, 17 per cent of scheduled tribes find themselves in the same situation compared to only 14 per cent of the general population.

Food Insecurity and Issues of Malnutrition

In the city, the poor are necessarily immersed in a cash economy and informal employment. Their incomes are often erratic and meagre. The purchase of basic food is therefore often threatened by employment and income crises.

Slum dwellers not only suffer from lack of nutrition but since they are able to buy only in small quantities, they also spend more. In urban areas, the higher prevalence of stunting implies that malnourishment is not as much a function of lack of access to food; but is primarily because of lack of access to infrastructural and institutional factors like health care, clean drinking water, mother's nutrition.

Absorption or assimilation of food by the slum people constitutes the major barrier as it makes them food insecure. They largely live in unsanitary conditions, amidst high levels of pollution, with limited access to clean drinking water and sanitation facilities. Within a city, per capita availability of water varies ten times between rich and poor areas. [134] Lack of public heath facilities is also pitiable in most slum areas.

More than half of the children under six years were found to be malnourished in the slums in Rohtak town in Haryana.[135] But the situation is even worse across the country. 70 per cent of slum children are malnourished compared to the national average of 46 per cent. Due to low calorie intake, children suffer the most as they need a proportionately higher intake for their growth and development.

Long-term food security is dependent on livelihood security. However, most slum dwellers continue to work in the informal sector, with harsh work conditions and payment much below minimum wages.[136]

State and the Schemes

1. Public Distribution System : Low Coverage, Lower Consumption

At the turn of this century, the average cereal consumption of the poorest decile in cities was 9.55 kg/month[137] and less than 1 kg. of this was obtained through the PDS. More recently, the 'National Sample Survey Organisation (NSSO) 61st round report[138] indicates startling facts :

- Since the launch of Targeted PDS in the late nineties[139], BPL card holders in urban India have risen only by 10.5 per cent
- Among the poorest decile, only 29 per cent hold BPL cards (as against 41 per cent in rural areas)
- PDS rice is consumed by only 5 per cent of urban households in West Bengal, 2 per cent in Assam and 0.7 per cent in Bihar, even though rice is the major cereal food
- Only 9.5 per cent of the urban poor have benefited from any government food assistance scheme.

People's tribunals in Mumbai and Delhi found that unlike for rural areas, there are no systematic BPL surveys. People apply for BPL ration cards, and food department officials estimates people's income, processes testified to be corrupt and arbitrary. Almost every state has faltered on conducting regular urban BPL surveys, while it has been done regularly for rural areas. Regular surveys are necessary to eliminate the bogus cards[140], renewal of old cards and sanction of new cards to overcome exclusion errors and also ensure that the food grains meant for the poor actually reach them.

A pilot study from Cuttack[141], Orissa, estimates that as many as 78 per cent households in the surveyed slums of the city have no ration cards. From amongst those who do have cards, only about 15 per cent have Antyodaya cards (although 40 per cent of all BPL persons are deemed eligible officially for Antyodaya cards). Not only the quality of food grains was rated as bad, the quantity was insufficient and most families had to buy rice also from the local market. The shops usually open only for 2-3 days or even if it opens regularly, they are allowed to collect their ration during certain days of a month. From amongst families without ration cards, about 42 per cent of them have not even applied for cards. The most commonly encountered reason is lack of awareness of procedures and documents to be submitted. Next is because the process is cumbersome and results uncertain. From amongst those who have applied, most cite the elected councillors' and government officials' negligence for rejection. About 31 per cent are not sure why their application has been rejected, whereas, 12 per cent were refused ration cards for lack of documents.

For migrants, accessing the PDS has become increasingly difficult. Those who move from other states generally do not have ration cards. This restricts their ability to economize by purchasing food at lower cost from PDS. A study in Bhuj town[142] revealed that only 22 per cent of migrants were able to purchase food from the PDS largely due to difficulties in the application process, eligibility requirements and distance.

2. ***Anganwadis (ICDS)***

Every sixth urban child in India who is less than six years is a slum dweller. Nevertheless, although government claims that a little more than one-third of the urban poor are covered by the existing 360 ICDS projects,[143] the coverage of the poor in slums and on the streets is probably even far less. Only 10 per cent of the anganwadis are located in urban areas. The National Advisory Council in 2004 recommended that 2970 additional ICDS centres need to be operationalised in urban India to ensure universal coverage. All of these need to cater to the poor in slums.

As many as 40 per cent of slums are routinely excluded from ICDS coverage as they are construction is 'illegal' or 'unauthorised'. Further, BPL lists used to identify ICDS beneficiaries may exclude the 'hidden' construction site workers, pavement dwellers and other homeless populations. This is despite the Supreme Court order[144] to ensure the coverage of all children below six years, all pregnant and lactating mothers and adolescent girls in all urban slums with all nutritional and health services of the ICDS in a phased manner latest by December 2008.

Of the existing ICDS centre in urban areas, only 40 per cent have adequate separate cooking space. Cooking utensils were also available in only 49 per cent of anganwadis[145].

In Madanpur Khadar slum pocket of Delhi city, Mobilie Crèches[146] ascribes high frequency of diarrohea and other illness among children to lack of child care facilities and supplementary feeding. Dehydration due to diarrohea and acute respiratory tract infections are the largest reason for mortality and malnutrition for children under six. Only 53 anganwadis of the 67 allotted are functional in Madanpur Khadar. In Dakshinpuri, "the anganwadi is merely a distribution centre for some food like biscuits, bread. Even this has not been available for many months. Anganwadi workers have not received either rent or salary for about a year". The anganwadis in slum areas are clearly crying for attention.

As another disturbing example, in Cuttack city[147] though most of the Anganwadis open everyday, the supply of food grains to anganwadis is irregular and it takes a fortnight to replenish the stock. As a natural consequence no supplementary nutrition (either cooked meal or raw material) could be provided and the attendance of children falls very low in these no-food days.

3. *Mid-Day Meal : Contractor's Quality*

In many urban areas, mid-day meals are contracted out

to either NGOs (many with religious identities) or contractors who use centralized kitchens to prepare in bulk and supply to several schools. There have been a few media reports that this food is served stale and the quantities are inadequate or excessively wasteful. On the other hand, in urban areas due to lack of space, it has also been argued that, it makes sense to have centralized kitchens.

The Comptroller and Auditor General's (CAG) 2006 report, however, has indicated that a large proportion of the children in the urban areas of Arunachal Pradesh (87 per cent), Chandigarh (95 per cent), Mizoram (84 per cent) and Punjab (88 per cent) do not receive mid-day meals. There is also the possibility of false reporting by schools and diversion of funds allotted.

Low financial allocations are a major problem as suppliers get only Rs. 2 per child. There are also delays in reimbursement for upto 3 months. Foodgrains provided by the government are also erratic, insufficient and of very poor quality. Nutrition Federation of India[148] found that the minimum goal of 300 calories and 8-12 gms. of protein was rarely met.

Further, the dominance of the suppliers is so entrenched that in none of the 60 households visited across Delhi was any parent involved in cooking or distributing the meal (as part of a SHG or an NGO). Neither did were they involved in monitoring the mid-day meal (by tasting it at the school) or in giving the authorities feedback on the content, quality or quantity of the food. Dalits, scheduled castes (SCs) and scheduled tribes (STs) are also not given preference in appointment as cooks and helpers. But fortunately there have been no reports of segregated distribution of food as in some rural areas.

4. *Swarna Jayanti Shahari Rozgar Yojana (SJSRY)*[149]

This centrally sponsored scheme was launched afresh in 1997 in lieu of the erstwhile urban poverty alleviation programmes. Its two main components are Urban Self-

Employment Programme (USEP), and Urban Wage Employment Programme (UWEP).

However, it is questionable to which extent these wage schemes are of real help to the urban slum dwellers (and even less the homeless). As for the self-employment component, many small entrepreneurs face genuine problems, such as lack of markets and infrastructure which is not addressed by SJSRY. It is based on the simplistic assumption subsidized credit alone will help in creating new entrepreneurs and augmenting incomes. However the high cost of appraising, monitoring and enforcing small loan agreements deters the banks from extending credit and therefore the overall coverage of the scheme is still limited. It is also inconceivable that traditional banks, with their emphasis on collateral and creditworthiness, would provide loans to homeless people irrespective of their entitlement under the scheme.

Recommendations for Urban Slum dwellers and Urban Homeless

Urban governance in India and most parts of the world is not geared to identify and deliver social services to the urban poor, especially to the most vulnerable segments of society, in slums and on the streets. We therefore need to rise to the challenge.

1. *Identifying the Most Vulnerable Urban Poor*

The first challenge is to find a mode of identifying the urban poor and vulnerable people using the existing administrative machinery, with least dangers of corruption. This is possible if discretion is reduced, and the criteria are clear and verifiable.

Directly asking people's incomes is not a reliable and verifiable criterion. And asking people only to certify income without any objective criteria is bound to be misused, and the poorest will be left out.

The way forward : It is possible to identify the most

vulnerable segments of urban populations by identifying them along objective and verifiable criteria of vulnerability and denial of rights. These are :

Place of residence and access to public services : (Shelter-less, unauthorized slum dwellers, authorized slum dwellers (both owners of the shanties who actually live in these and those who live on rent to owners or slum lords) and residents of resettlement colonies {only direct allottees of houses in resettlement colonies and not second or third purchasers})

Social Vulnerability : Children without protection and child headed households, single women and single women headed households, disabled people and family with PWD, old people without care givers, people in destitution.

Occupational Categories : Rag pickers, casual daily wage workers, rickshaw pullers, porters, construction workers, street vendors, domestic help etc.

Affirmative Action Categories : Scheduled Castes/ Scheduled Tribes, Muslims.

Income Factor

It is important to note that these criteria do not address household income directly, because it is very difficult to assess and verify. But these are in the nature of reliable proxy indicators of income.

Household income is indirectly addressed by the occupational categories, because these characteristically have low and uncertain incomes. Also that this does not necessarily claim to be a *measure* of urban poverty, but of providing an instrument to identify the most vulnerable segments of urban populations, so that government can better target these programmes to those who are genuinely most in need.

Higher income in itself does not mean better food, shelter, health and a better life. In the absence of public services, with high social vulnerability and in unprotected and unorganised occupations, the same income can amount to very little of nutrition, health and well-being.

Operationalising this identification process

Residence in authorized and unauthorised slums, and resettlement colonies {only direct alottees of houses in resettlement colonies and not second or third purchasers} would prima facie make you eligible for BPL or AAY, subject to further criteria as below :

For these residents, they will be considered BPL if they are also in the unorganized sector: such as rag pickers, casual daily wage workers, rickshaw pullers, porters, construction workers, street vendors, domestic help etc.

For these residents, they will be considered AAY if they belong to these socially vulnerable categories : Children without protection and child headed households, single women and single women headed households, disabled people and family with PWD, old people without care givers, destitute people.

All homeless people will be eligible for BPL with no other qualifying criteria. Homeless people will be included for AAY, if they are also in the unorganized sector : such as rag pickers, casual daily wage workers, rickshaw pullers, porters, construction workers, street vendors, domestic help etc.; and if they belong to these socially vulnerable categories: Children without protection and child headed households, single women and single women headed households, disabled people and family with PWD, old people without care givers, destitute people.

Conduct detailed surveys of urban slums with community participation, both authorised and unauthorised, and homeless populations to identify and officially legitimise their existence through provision of voter ID and ration cards and to make them aware of their rights and entitlements. The residential address can be the nearest building to where they reside, stating that they live on the pavement near it, or care of the nearest PDS shop.

2. *Rationalisation of Schemes for the Most Vulnerable Segments*

i) The Groups to be Served : The existing range of food and livelihood schemes and programmes for the various departments need to be reviewed and only those retained which are most suited to the problems and needs of the most vulnerable segments of urban populations.

We should not take the schemes as given, and then try to adapt them into needs that they may not fulfil. Most schemes are inappropriate as they are designed with the rural poor in mind.

Let us first identify which groups we wish to serve. It must be those identified as most vulnerable :

- Shelterless, especially street children and single women
- Slum residents and residents of resettlement colonies { only direct alottees of houses in resettlement colonies and not second or third purchasers}
- Children without protection and child headed households, single women and single women headed households, disabled people and family with PWD, old people without care givers, destitute
- Unorganised workers especially in unclean, unsafe and hazardous occupations.

Based on their need identifications, appropriate schemes can be identified and converged. To take one illustration, the Sarva Shiksha Abhiyan (a programme to bring every child to schools) and the Women and Child Department's night shelter programmes for hostels for street kids could be converged to meet the needs of these children for comprehensive long-term care in open voluntary residential homes.

For those marginalized groups whose needs are unmet, there can be additional programmes.

ii) Adopt a single-window approach to make all applicable social security schemes available for urban homeless people from a centralised location e.g. the municipal office, or the office of the district collector.

iii) Distribute Food and Pensions :

(a) Identify the urban poor based on the process indicated above.

(b) Provide AAY and BPL ration cards and pensions to

all households who qualify by this identification process.

(c) Ensure that there is sufficient expansion of food and financial quotas to ensure universal coverage of all segments of the urban poor and vulnerable.

(d) Ensure that ration shops are open on all designated days throughout the month in urban slums

(e) Migrants should be allowed to use their ration cards across the country.

iv) Cooked Food :

(a) Establish community kitchens across cities and urban settlements to provide inexpensive, subsidised nutritious cooked meals, which are managed by community groups of homeless people, preferably women, and will provide employment as cooks to homeless people themselves.

(b) Fulfil the Supreme Court order to ensure that anganwadis cover all urban slum and street habitations, both authorised and unauthorised.

(c) All old people from the neighbourhood slum area should be permitted to share in the school mid-day meal of hot cooked meal in ICDS centres without any conditions, as practiced in the state of Tamil Nadu.

(d) Ensure the non-profit credentials of all centralised kitchens for mid-day meals and that they are not run by contractors based on the Supreme Court Order.

(e) Ensure that all children receive hot cooked mid-day meals in sufficient quantity and of good quality.

(f) Ensure that the cost of mid-day meals provided by the government is greater for urban areas (with a higher cost of living) and pegged to inflation (especially given the rising food costs).

(g) In an unauthorised slum, if there is no space for an anganwadi, a prefabricated structure could be build to function as anganwadi centre. In theory, if the slum is shifted, the building of the centre should be able to move with it.

(h) Create an ICDS anganwadi in slum areas for every 1000 population.

(i) Children of migrants should be permitted to receive the services of any ICDS centre with no requirement of any documentation. The mere presence of a child of the required age group should qualify her for ICDS services.

(j) Ensure that school authorities admit street children and those from homeless families without asking for any identity or address proof to ensure that they are not excluded from mid-day meals.

v) Residential care of children most in need

(a) For children of rural seasonal migrants, the village school should be converted into a community based temporary residential school, to enable the child to access food and education, without having to migrate every year with their guardians. The aged of the village who are often left behind in destitute conditions, may take care of the children in return for sharing the food in the community based hostels.

(b) For children who still migrate, it should be the duty of the education department of the host state to provide education in local language at work sites, and permit the child to access mid-day meals at the nearest government school.

(c) For children who live and work on the streets, the only way to secure their right to food (and with this their rights to education, health and protection) is to provide them alternatives to move decisively away from the streets and any kind of work. This is possible only through guarantees of comprehensive long-term care in open voluntary residential homes. Every city would need a large network of such schools. As stated already, this could be done by converging the Sarva Shiksha Abhiyan (a programme to bring every child to schools) and the Women and Child Department's night shelter programmes for hostels for street kids, and greatly enhancing allocations.

'Primitive' Tribal Groups

Constituting about eight per cent of the total population of India, the tribal people are among the most vulnerable groups in the country. Not only do they share with other disadvantaged groups the common travails of economic deprivation, they are also faced perennially with grave threats to their cultural integrity and socio-political freedoms, and their access and control over their natural environment and resources in ways that imperil critically their sustainable existence.

Due to faulty processes of declaration of forest lands in the past, the rights of the tribals over their traditional land holdings have gradually been extinguished. Insecurity of tenure and fear of eviction have led the tribal communities to feel emotionally as well as physically alienated from forests and forest lands. The condition of the tribals living in and around forests is becoming increasingly precarious and vulnerable due to displacement threats due to forest conservation initiatives etc.

The 2001 Census enumerated the total population of the country as 1027 million, out of which the population of Scheduled Tribes was 84.3 million, constituting 8.2% of the total population. The population of tribes had grown at the growth rate of 24.45% during the period 1991-2001. [Government of India 2005-06 : 39] India is by this count, home to more tribal people than any country in the world, exceeded only by the continent of Africa taken as a whole. It has been observed that not all of these communities are at the same level of development. In fact, there are certain communities which are at a much lower level of development even compared to other Scheduled Tribe communities. In the matter of devolution of funds for the development of Scheduled Tribes, the major share was taken by those communities who are more assertive and in a better position to demand their rights. As a consequence, the marginalised Scheduled Tribes have been systematically left out of the process of development.

Officially 'Primitive'

In order to ensure the development of these communities, certain groups were identified, for the first time in 1975-76 and thereafter in 1993, which are regarded as the poorest of poor amongst the STs and were called Primitive Tribal Groups (PTGs). The criteria fixed for their identification was the presence of pre-agricultural level of technology; very low level of literacy; and declining or stagnant population.

Seventy-five tribal communities were identified as PTGs spread over 17 States and one Union Territory (Annexure a). State Governments submit proposals for identification of PTGs in accordance with the prescribed criteria and their proposals are examined by the Ministry for Tribal Affairs in consultation with Planning Commission.

In fact even the usage of the word 'primitive' by the Government to define the most vulnerable tribal groups is highly debatable. The National Tribal Policy[150] proposes to use the alternative term Particularly Vulnerable Tribal Groups (PVTGs) instead of 'Primitive' Tribal Groups. However this report retains the word 'Primitive' but uses it in inverted commas to mark our disagreement with that usage.

The population of PTGs has increased marginally from 2.04 million in 1981 to 2.4 million in 1991.[151] The PTGs have been systematically identified since 1975-76 to 1993-94. No additional PTGs have been included based on the 1991 census. In its twenty eighth report, the Standing Committee on Labour and Welfare (2002)[152], notes down that the Ministry of Tribal Affairs, Government of India has requested the States and Union Territories with PTG population to undertake a baseline survey. Accordingly, a set of questionnaires and schedules have been circulated to collect information on population, literacy etc. along with other required information on the socio-economic status of each group so that plans and programmes can be formulated for their overall development. The results of this exercise are yet to be fully disclosed till date.

Continuous Negligence

Historically independent and relatively self-sufficient societies have succumbed to a variety of pressures, both external and internal, leading to a state of intense deprivation. Primitive Tribal Groups are characterised by low literacy rates, stagnant populations, lack of basic amenities, and virtually no viable economic options. The situation of children and women is particularly vulnerable since they are the last to gain access to basic services and decision-makers.

Scheduled Tribes are far more likely to be poor than the average Indian (Figure 1).

Figure 1: Population below poverty line in India and ST

	India	*STs*
Rural Areas	27.1	45.9
Urban areas	23.6	34.8

Source: National Sample Survey Organisation 1999-2000.

The poverty ratios for 'Primitive' Tribal Groups are not available separately; but it is certainly even worse than that of Schedule Tribes as a whole. This report will illustratively focus on the conditions of three of these acutely marginalised 'primitive' groups : Pahadi Korwas of Chhattisgarh, Saharias of Madhya Pradesh and Chenchus of Andhra Pradesh.

'Saharias' of central India are a major 'Primitive' Tribal Group who traverse difficult terrains in attempting to strike a balance between forests, across states and between mainstream and community life.

93 per cent of Saharia children are malnourished, with 15 per cent of the children being found to be 'severely malnourished'.[153] The percentage of children underweight, 'wasted' or 'stunted' are above 70 per cent. With such high rates of malnutrition among children, one cannot expect to see healthy adults. Anaemia is found in close to 87 per cent of adults with over half of them suffering from 'mild to

severe anaemia'. These figures are among the worst in the world.[154] An unpublished survey available with the Commissioners of the Supreme Court in the right to food case reveal that more than 95 per cent children, 39 per cent women and 29 per cent men, suffered from chronic grade III malnutrition, which makes them persistently vulnerable to sickness and death.[155]

The loss of their livestock due to the lack of water and food has further reduced their slender asset base and exposed them to greater risks. Although 26 per cent of Sahariyas possess 5-8 *bighas* (1 bigha = 0.4 acre) of land, 70 per cent of it is nonirrigated, stony and situated at mountainous slopes.[156] Unless these lands are developed properly, they cannot be put to any useful purpose. But the Government has not initiated any long-term plan for its development.

Unlike the central districts, the remote and densely forested northern and southern districts of the state Chhattisgarh remain poorly served by social infrastructure and demonstrate significantly worse levels of human development. It is in these areas where the highest concentration of tribal (including pahadi korwas) populations resides. Despite posing many challenges these are areas of acute destitution where targeted interventions could achieve substantial impacts on poverty reduction.[157]

It is ironical though, that while the government has launched an ambitious project to help the Pahadi Korwas, a 'Primitive' Tribal Group (PTG) in Chhattisgarh, simultaneous plans are afoot to uproot them from their homeland on the ground that tribals are destroying the forest and damage the eco-system. Living in abject poverty in mud houses in far-flung areas with no electricity, proper roads or safe drinking water, the tribals hardly present the face of the timber mafia that the forest department charges them with. The tribal people cut wood mostly for domestic purpose like building houses or lighting their *chulhas* (clay-burned stoves) and not for commercial exploitation. They depend on farming to sustain themselves.[158]

The Chenchus are an aboriginal tribe of the central hill

regions of Andhra Pradesh. Their traditional way of life has been based on hunting and gathering. In general, the Chenchu relationship to non-tribal people has been largely symbiotic. Some have continued to specialise in collecting forest products for sale to non-tribal people. The Chenchus are referred to as one of the Primitive Tribal Groups that are still dependent on forests and do not cultivate land but hunt for a living. They typify many PTGs who are living in the southern Indian hills.

Prof. Kodandaraman, Adviser to the Commissioners of the Supreme Court (CWP 196/2001), reports[159] based on a visit to the Nallamala forest areas of Mehboobnagar district in November 2007[160], that many of the Chenhus, in Appapur for example, live under the trees. Being a food gathering and forest dwelling community with unique way of life, Chenchus were provided with safeguards like the declaration of their area as 'Chenchu reserve' by the British and Nizam governments in the pre-Independence era. Even the latest Scheduled Tribes and Other Traditional Forest Dwellers (Recognition of Forest Rights) Act 2006 also recognized various individual and community rights for similar forest dwelling communities. None of these safeguards however protect the Chenchus who are constantly harassed by the police and the forest department.

Livelihoods in Peril

Developmental journalist, Sachin Kumar Jain, observes that if anybody visits any Saharia village[161] in Madhya Pradesh, it is impossible for him not to come across the news of a child death or maternal death because of starvation. [162] Even to a lay observer, it is clear that there is an extremely grave persisting nutritional emergency among the Sahariya tribal community.

A sombre situation of chronic mass destitution among the Sahariyas is also confirmed by the study by the official Centre for Tribal Development. It reports for the year 2002 an annual per capita income among Sahariyas of Rs. 2691, which is around seven rupees a day. Not surprisingly, more than half the Sahariya households are in chronic debt to private moneylenders.

The low availability of food grains to Sahariya families, as it is reported only 65 kilos per year i.e. 180 grams per day per person. For other items like salt, pulses, vegetables, spices etc., they had to manage within their meagre income which turns to be the sole reason of malnutrition amongst their children. The average age of the Sahariyas is 45 years which is one-fourth less than the national average.

In case of Chenchus, if rice is not available they are forced to eat tubers, leaves and fruits gathered from the forest. Most tribals prefer to depend upon their forests to satiate their hunger. But even their most basic access forest resources often falls into question in this era of forest conservation by environment protection lobbies. The Chenchus collect gum, honey and seeds. Despite their hard work, no family is able to earn more than Rs. 1000 a month. They walk long distances and stay in the forest .for days together.

For centuries, the Chenchus have been living in their forest which they consider as their mother goddess. Now, authorities are ready to evict them, destroy their livelihood, having made several promises shifting them from place to place. Homeless in their own habitat seeking shelter here and there deprived even of drinking water, with no access to hospitals when sick, a local Telugu newspaper[163] reports that 60 Chenchus have died in the last year and half most of them being children and women. Starvation deaths among Sahariyas are something which is much discussed in the public domain and excessively reported in the media.

The Right to Food Campaign in Chhattisgarh has brought to light the condition of three of the highly marginalised primitive tribal groups, namely, Baigas, Pahadi Korwas and Kamars. These groups suffer from the worst levels of malnutrition and morbidity. Most of these tribes are settled in thick forests and remote hilly areas. [164]

Most of the mainstreaming efforts by the state and other agencies have succeeded only in distancing the tribal people from their indigenous way of living, but unfortunately (if not willingly) failed to promise them a healthy life. When their non-tribal poor counterparts at least struggle hard to smoothen their hardship, uprooted tribals are just left pathless. Their natural living is on the verge of being illegalised and they do not have the energy or resource to sustain a 'modern' existence.

State and Schemes

1.Integrated Child Development Scheme (ICDS)

In 2006, Madhya Pradesh Right to Food Campaign team which was investigating the incidence of malnutrition deaths amongst Saharia in Patalgarh village, found that there was only a temporary Anganwadi in the village visited and the nearest anganwadi was situated some 17 kms. away. While, 70 children had been enrolled by the villagers in the Anganwadi, Supplementary Nutrition Programme (SNP) had been unavailable from January - June 2006.[165]

The 2006 Joint Commision of Enquiry (JCE) in Sheopur166, found that 850 ICDS centres were required but at the time of the investigation in only 647 had been sanctioned and amongst them only 587 were actually functioning.[167]

The greatest exclusion the Pahadi Korwas face too is in the ICDS programme. Out of their 500 odd habitations, only about 100 have *anganwadis.* Of the remaining some children from 150 odd hamlets were able to partially access ICDS facilities. Therefore children from 50 per cent of the Pahadi Korwa hamlets do not have any access to any of ICDS services.[168]

The outreach of ICDS to these groups is minimal, because:

(a) Villages exclusively inhabited by these groups have not been allocated any AWCs (e.g., in Achanakmar area of Bilaspur district, there are sufficient centres as per the population norm, but in a majority of the cases, the *anganwadis* are located in non-Baiga villages);

(b) They stay in hamlets which are far from the main village, where the *anganwadi* is typically located. In Beerupalli village in Andhra Pradesh, for instance, both the tribal and dalit hamlets were located at a far distance from the main village where the *anganwadis* was located.[169]

(c) Their own hamlet is often considered too small to open even a mini-*anganwadi*.[170]

The main reason for this degree of exclusion is related to their settlement pattern. Pahadi Korwa habitations are often on the edge or on top of the hills while the nearest main village lies in the valley. The distance and terrain makes it difficult for them to access the anganwadi. Despite Supreme Court orders, no preference has been given by the State Government to give a preference to Pahadi Korwa habitations while opening new centres. The common excuse is being that Pahadi Korwa habitations are too small (average size 40 households) to deserve an anganwadi.[171]

Other Primitive Tribal groups like Chenchus face similar tales of exclusion due to their remote settlement patterns.

2. *Mid-day Meals (MDM)*

A field visit by Harsh Mander, the Special Commissioner to the Supreme Court (CWP 196/2001) in Sahariya villages of Madhya Pradesh September 2004 found that children remained deprived of their daily food entitlements because the teacher came to school only twice a month. In some villages even if the school is functioning, children were given only a ladle each of *ghoogri* or dry wheat porridge each day. Some children took this dry food home as the only major meal for the entire family! Given the destitution of several 'Primitive' Tribal Groups, it is pathetic state of affairs that a large proportion of children who have no access to schools either due to their non-existence or unwillingness of children to attend mainstream education. Absence of schools would be justified by the State based on the physically isolated lifestyle of 'Primitive' Tribal Groups. The official alibi of the alleged unwillingness of tribal children to attend schools which merits careful interrogation.

A child-protection action research undertaken in tribal villages of Rajasthan[172] clearly elucidates the barriers which alienate tribal children within the mainstream schools. Urban-based curricula without any reference points to tribal history or culture, stigmatisation and racism against tribal students, timing of schools and teacher absenteeism are important hurdles. Tribal community members also were vary that after receiving an education (sometimes by staying in hostels) their children often did not identify themselves with their tribal community.[173]

3. *Targeted Public Distribution Scheme (TPDS)*

In conditions of stark and extreme impoverishment, an overwhelmingly large majority of Sahariya households surprisingly had Above Poverty Line (APL) cards. In other words, according to the government survey they were not classified as poor, and therefore not entitled to subsidised grain. Even for those with cards, ration shops often did not function; therefore most villagers were compelled to purchase wheat from the open market as Rs. 8 a kilogram.

This situation is despite the Supreme Court order of 2nd May, 2003 in Right to Food Case, which specifies that all Primitive Tribal Groups (PTGs) are entitled to an Antyodaya Card. There are also media reports which shows that fair price shops in Sahariya villages has been distributing rice to the Antyodaya Anna Yojana cardholders at twice the stipulated price (i.e. Rs. 6 per kilogram).

The Madhya Pradesh Right to Food Team found that in one of the Sahariya villages visited, only 70 Antyodaya Anna Yojana cards were issued last year despite the total population of the village being 580. However, even those villagers, who are fortunate enough to have a card, have not received rations for the past three months.

The administration has opened temporary Fair Price Shops at the village but according to the villagers it rarely opens. When the fact-finding team visited the village it found about 36 quintals of grain in the shop. When the issue was raised with the local administration, the very next day the ration was distributed.

In case of Pahadi Korwas, the level of exclusion has come down in last four years after the State Government implemented the SC order on Antyodaya cards for all 'Primitive' Tribal Groups. Pahadi Korwa Mahapanchayat was instrumental in aiding the process of card distribution. Almost 98 per cent of the surveyed families have received their ration cards at which they can get 35 kgs. of rice at Rs. 3 per kg. per month. The only discrepancy is in the case of around 1000 Pahadi Korwa joint families who got divided after their son's marriage and now have only one card instead of two.

Most Pahadi Korwas reported that they were able to access their 35 kgs. of rice every month at the stipulated rate. However they expressed one problem that due to the fair price shops (FPS) remaining open only for 2-3 days per month (in more than 50 per cent of cases), they had to face problems in arranging lump sum money at a short notice. However, most were still able to access their quota and the rice reached the shops in the first week of the month.[174]

4. National Rural Employment Guarantee Scheme (NREGA)

The Report of the Joint Commissioner of Enquiry found that some of the villagers have been registered and have also received their job cards but neither have they applied for work nor has work started in the village. The villagers had gone to meet the Panchayats Secretary, but he misled them by saying that there is no need for application and that the work would begin soon. The job cards were with the Panchayat Secretary, who makes all entries in the card and there were cases noted where the entries in the job card did not match the money reportedly received by the worker, which suggests leakages.[175]

The media reported that in a Chenchu village the forest department stopped a scheduled NREGA work that was supposed to take place.[176] The government had promised Chenchus work under NREGA and inaugurated road construction. However, as the forest department objected to digging, the work had to come to a halt. Although all of them found work for a month, only half of them were paid their wages and the others have not been paid.

In Chhattisgarh, only 20 per cent of the Pahadi Korwa households are estimated to have participated in NREGA works. The main reasons for low participation are twofold. Worksites are seldom close to Pahadi Korwa habitations. They have to come down from hills to work. Secondly, there are long delays in payment of wages (average delay of more than 2 months). Such uncertainty in timing of payment makes it difficult for the poorest of the poor like Pahadi Korwas to participate.

Recommendations

(i) Dry Rations

- Ensure the distribution of Antyodaya Anna Yojana (AAY) cards to every single family of all designated primitive tribal groups (PTGs) as per the Supreme Court order of 2nd May 2003.
- Enable tribal panchayats to run their own PDS shops, with grants of working capital from the tribal department.
- Introduce mobile ration shops in all the PTG areas, where ration dealers are unable to establish their shops, and ensure their regular distribution of food grains on fixed days coinciding with the weekly *haat* or tribal market.

(ii) Cooked Food

In primitive tribal group areas,

- Recruit local anganwadi workers and helpers from amongst the local PTG itself.
- Sanction mini-anganwadis exclusively for PTG hamlets irrespective of their size without any ceiling of minimum population.
- Ensure that anganwadis or at least mini-anganwadis are opened in every primitive tribal hamlet.

- Ensure that only hot cooked meals are served in anganwadis cooked by PTG women's groups, mahila mandals etc. Make arrangements for the provision of supplementation of key nutrients in pockets of high malnourishment.
- Provide additional foodgrain quotas to ensure that all old people from should be permitted to share in the school mid-day meal without any conditions.
- Ensure that all PTGs are served by tribal hostels dedicated for their children, with majority staff, non-negotiably of care givers, and - if available- teachers, from the PTG community, as there is much higher chance that the PTG children will feel accepted and secured with them. A campaign should be run with the assistance of the tribal panchayat and village leaders, youth and women's organisations, for full enrolment of all PTG children in these homes.

(iii) Livelihoods and Credit

- All PTG households should be given job cards under priority, and 2 members of the family entitled to get employment under NREGA.
- To prevent further indebtedness, all released bonded workers should also be permitted to draw their full entitlement of grain on credit from PDS shops every month. This should be adjusted against one-third of their daily wages once NREGA works are commenced.
- Joint forest protection committees should be constituted in all PTG areas, giving full rights over non-timber forest produce to these communities, and taking their active support to prevent timber mafias.
- A special task force should be created in all tribal districts to ensure time bound implementation of laws to restore land illegally appropriated from PTG members.
- Governments should abjure by law from further acquisition of land from tribal people who are designated to be 'primitive'.

(iv) Sentisization

- Change the school curriculum with reference to the richness of tribal culture to arrest the drop-out rate of PTG children.
- From PTGs, wherever first generation high school graduates are found, recruit them to give primary school instruction in the tribal dialect, and as care givers in tribal hostels.
- Ensure full implementation of the Panchayats (Extension to Tribal Areas) Act, 1993 (PESA) in PTG areas, which give control over forests and other commons to tribal communities.
- Adopt a single-window approach to make all social security schemes to reach out PTGs through the tribal panchayats.

Annexure (a)

a. List of Approved Primitive Tribal Groups

1. Andhra Pradesh	1. Bodo Gadaba
	2. Bondo Poraja
	3. Chenchu
	4. Dongaria Khonds
	5. Gutob Gadaba
	6. Khond Poroja
	7. Kolam
	8. Kondareddts
	9. Konda Savaras
	10. Kuttiya Kondhs
	11. Parangiperja
	12. Thoti
2. Bihar (including Jharkhand)	1. Asur
	2. Birhor
	3. Birjia
	4. Hill Kharia

State	Tribal Groups
	5. Korwa 6. Mal Pharia 7. Paharias 8. Sauria Pahariya 9. Savar
3. Gujarat	1. Kathodi 2. Kotwalia 3. Padhar 4. Siddi 5. Kolgha
4. Karnataka	1. Jenu Kuruba 2. Koraga
5. Kerala	1. Cholanaikayan (A section of Kattunayakan) 2. Kadar 3. Kattunayakan 4. Kurumbas 5. Koraga
6. Madhya Pradesh (including Chhattisgarh)	1. Abujh Maria 2. Baiga 3. Bharia 4. Hill Korwa 5. Kamar 6. Saharia 7. Birhor
7. Maharashtra	1. Katkaria (Kathodi) 2. Kolam 3. Maria Gond
8. Manipur	1. Maram Naga
9. Orissa	1. Birhor 2. Bondo

	3. Didayi
	4. Dongria-Khond
	5. Juang
	6. Kharia
	7. Kutia Khond
	8. Lanjia Saura
	9. Lodha
	10. Mankirdia
	11. Paudi Bhuyan
	12. Saura
	13. Chuktia Bhunjia
10. Rajasthan	1. Seharias
11. Tamil Nadu	1. Kattu Naickans
	2. Kotas
	3. Kurumbas
	4. Irulas
	5. Paniyans
	6. Todas
12. Tripura	1. Reangs
13. Uttar Pradesh	1. Buxas
	2. Rajis
14. West Bengal	1. Birhor
	2. Lodhas
	3. Totos
15. Andaman & Nicobar Islands	1. Great Andamanese
	2. Jarawas
	3. Onges
	4. Sentenelese
	5. Shompens

Most Discriminated Dalit Groups

The word *'dalit'* in Marathi literally means 'broken'. Popularised as an assertion of social anger and self-respect by the father of the Indian Constitution, Dr. B.R. Ambedkar, it reflects to this day the situation of millions of *dalits* within South Asia, who are systematically deprived of their civil, political, economic, social and cultural rights. The caste system, which has existed for more than 3000 years on the principle of social and occupational segregation based on notions of purity and pollution, lies at the root of this ugly reality.[177] Traditionally treated as 'untouchables', *dalits* occupy the lowest position in this abhorrent social system. Untouchability is the practice of imposing social disabilities on persons by reasons of their birth in certain castes, and involves avoidance of physical contact with persons and things because of beliefs relating to pollution.

It is important to state at the outset that the central problem and paramount aspiration of *dalits* has not only been for economic emancipation and improvement in conventional quality of life indices, but also for equality and dignity within the traditional social order which has denied them justice and self-respect for centuries. This is by no means to deny that the 'pollution line' and the 'poverty line' do very substantially overlap.[178]

Although untouchability is a feature of Brahminical Hinduism, it permeated even egalitarian religions such as Christianity and Islam when transplanted into Indian soil. For instance, the Helas of the Malwa and Nimar regions of Madhya Pradesh are manual scavengers, and no other Muslims are willing to share food with them or marry into their families. Similarly, the Pulaya Christians of Kerala, formerly untouchable Hindus, even after more than 80 years of conversion to Christianity, continue to be treated as untouchables even by the Syrian Christians.[179]

Life at the Margins

The constitutional abolition of untouchability implied

that caste Hindus could no longer be able to force *dalits* to perform any "polluting" occupations. But even today, degrading tasks like sweeping, scavenging and leather tanning continue to remain the monopoly of scheduled castes who are threatened with physical abuse and social boycotts. Barriers to education and other forms of employment have ensured that these occupations continue to be hereditary.

The injustice of social discrimination based on caste is part of a shameful and troubled historical legacy, which compels modern day challenge for the people of India, from the standpoint of equality and democracy. It is varied in its dimensions and has a vast geographical spread. This report restricts its scope to focus on barriers that *dalits* face in accessing food (and livelihoods), and three most oppressed dalit communities have been purposively selected for a more detailed analysis, the *Musahars, Madigas* and *Safai Karmacharis,* as they represent some of the most extreme hardships of *dalit* life in India.

Musahars

The word Musahar literally translates into 'rat-eater' which is a pointer towards the extreme destitution (and humiliation) experienced by this community. Musahars live in Eastern Uttar Pradesh and the East Champaran[180] district of Bihar (Figure 1). Of the 1.3 million Musahars in Bihar, less than 1 percent are literate[181].

Ninety-eight percent are landless labourers, who live in a stretch of fertile agricultural land but go without work for eight months in a year. Their unemployment has been aggravated by the mechanisation of agriculture, especially combined harvesters. They live in tiny huts made of leaf or thatch, in hamlets which are only allowed to be located at a great distance from all other communities.

Besides that there is a sort of identity crisis which adds to the derailing of their existence. Musahars as a community perform unskilled agricultural labour and in the 'brahmanical' caste hierarchy are considered to be *shudras.* Historically, 'untouchability' was not practiced against the *shudras* but with the consolidation of Brahmanical emphasis on the purity and pollution, 'untouchability' became prevalent against the *shudras* as well. *Musahars* consider themselves above other *dalits* like *chamars,* but this does not win them the favour of the dominant class (not necessarily upper-caste) as far as their landlessness is concerned.

For them other dalit communities are *'harijans'*, the term which they are sure does not denotes them, though the state lists them as Scheduled Castes (SCs). Other dalit communities however see the *Musahars* as below their rung. Both, the plight of landlessness and the non-identification with other *dalit* communities, alienate them equally from the dominant class as well as the oppressed class of the village.[182]

Madigas

Madiga[183] is a caste which is largely confined to the drought-prone Telangana and Rayalaseema and constitutes one of the largest *dalit* populations in Andhra Pradesh. The majority of Madigas are landless agricultural labourers but some continue their traditional occupations as leather tanners, cobblers and scavengers. Their hamlets with "mud-walled, one-roomed, mud-floored, thatched-roof huts"[184] are increasingly being pushed to the fringes of village settlements.

The extent of social discrimination meted out to the Madigas over centuries is appalling. They continue to be denied use of the village well, and are not allowed to walk on the roads, since even their shadow is considered to be polluting. The smoke from their funeral pyres is feared to contaminate and so they are forced to bury their dead. It is bizarre that even the sound waves of their voices are considered foul; and they have to cover their mouths with a pot when speaking to caste Hindus!

In the race for the benefits of reservation too, powerful *dalit* communities like the Malas have left them behind, and Madigas have only recently begun to assert their rights. The recent State wide agitation by the Madigas demanding separate safeguards for them in public employment, political office and educational institutions in proportion to their population in the overall category of Scheduled Castes, is a manifestation of the extent to which the community of the Madigas has been and feels neglected and ignored.

Manual Scavengers

Dalit manual scavengers or *safai karmacharis* have different caste names across the country[185], but they uniformly belong to the very bottom of the *dalit* sub-castes. Manual scavenging is largely a hereditary occupation reserved for *dalits. Dalit* manual scavengers are compelled to undertake their task, often being prevented from taking any other job. They are the worst victims of untouchability as they are considered unclean, impure and placed at the lowest level of the caste hierarchy. Even other *dalits* often consider them as untouchables. Manual scavengers, or *safai karmacharis,* are considered to be the most oppressed and disadvantaged of any community in India.

Their employers include both private individuals and government departments including the military, engineering services, the army and the railways[186]. After decades of denial and despite being a gross under-estimate,[187] in 2002-03 the Ministry for Social Justice and Empowerment finally admitted the existence of 6,76,000 manual scavengers in India and the presence of 92,00,000 dry latrines across 21 States and Union Territories. The irony is that although it is outlawed, dry community latrines continue to be maintained by large numbers of local city governments throughout the country, who employ manual scavengers for handling human shit.

Social discrimination against scavengers is rampant. Most live in segregated rural or urban colonies and are unable to make use of common resources. In many communities, in exchange for leftover food, scavengers are also expected to remove dead animal carcasses and deliver messages of death to the relatives of upper-caste neighbours. Their refusal to do so can result in physical abuse and ostracism from the community.

Systematically Denied

The economic trap that entangles the most discriminated amongst the *dalits* also curtails their socio-political mobility. It never allows them to move upwards in the caste hierarchy. Forced to stand in the end of the 'democratic' queue, starting with unequal income distribution to the denial of quality education and unavailability of healthcare; due to systematic denials and neglect, they are forced to stare at a bleak future.

Figure 1: Population below poverty line, 2004-5

	India 2004-5	*Scheduled Castes* 2004-5
Rural Areas	21.8	36.8
Urban areas	21.7	39.9

Source: India: NSSO 2004-5. Information on Scheduled Castes reportedby Minister of State for Social Justice and Empowerment, submitted in response to Lok Sabha question, April 28, 2008.

More *dalits* are below the poverty line than the national average (Figure 1). Surprisingly, this difference is even more acute in urban areas with almost two of every five *dalits* finding themselves below the poverty line.

The most discriminated amongst them are so poor that they often live in near starvation conditions. With no grain to store, *Musahar* homes often have two empty vessels as their only valuables. They are not even allowed inside other hamlets, unless summoned. There may be *pucca* or semi-*pucca* roads leading to other hamlets but the *Musahar* hamlets are invariably not connected.

Declining dependence on leather across rural society has further limited the livelihoods of the *Madigas* who are also politically deprived of programmes meant for the upliftment of other scheduled castes. Similarly, *safai karmacharis* across India *find* themselves deprived of most government amenities.

Economic Deprivations

Land ownership among *Musahars,* in particular, is negligible. Landlessness in Musahars case not only refers to the lack of agricultural land for cultivation but also land on which they have resided for generations. Even the implementation of the Land Ceiling Act proved futile as most the village land that was taken into state custody was redistributed amongst all other villagers, but not the *Musahars.*

Musahars have taken to working in the fields of dominant castes after. They are paid a pittance for their labour, but with the advent of modern agricultural techniques, even this option is no longer available. Many are therefore forced to work under appalling work conditions in brick kilns. Others migrate to towns and cities, leaving behind women, children and the aged.

In cities and towns too, *safai karmacharis* experience similar economic hardships due to irregularity in the payment of wages. Those working on contract are kept unpaid for several months. Those who joined the municipalities in the hope it would ultimately relieve them from indignity of manual scavenging later feel betrayed, for they not only lose their earlier work but now have no chance to go for any other work. In many places the municipal officials not only threaten the husbands of the women involved in scavenging but also do not give them any other opportunity of survival with dignity. No action is normally taken against the municipalities who have failed to comply. [188]

Distress migration is often the last resort for discriminated *Madigas,* who often move to nearby towns in search of employment. But with a very poor skill base, they often find only low end, low wage, unorganised, arduous and sometimes humiliating work. Most eke out their livelihood as rickshaw pullers, head load workers, cobblers and shoe shiners and construction workers. That has made these people into a vastly migrated community and now Madigas are present in all the parts of South India.

In the case of *Madigas,* the visible imbalance in accessing the benefits of reservations forms the basis for their economic insecurity. In Andhra Pradesh, there has now emerged conflict for Scheduled Caste entitlement between the two groups *Malas* and the *Madigas*.

Hunger and Starvation

Voiceless *Musahars* die silently, *safai karmacharis* painfully bear the burden of a distressing profession to feed their stomachs and *Madigas* migrate to distant lands in search of livelihoods and a dignified existence.

"We beat our hungry children to sleep" that is what a *Musahar* woman told to the people's tribunal on starvation in Eastern Uttar Pradesh. Other coping option to ensure food during off seasons is to avail loans from the local moneylender. Many *Musahars* are in debt for expenses incurred for marriages, deaths etc., and this further tie them in the vicious cycle of poverty. Starvation deaths of *Musahars* are now a popularly recognised concept among development journalists and mainstream media to routinely garner public sympathy.

Most, *safai karmacharis* want to change their livelihood option, but have few alternatives. Bezwada Wilson, the convener of SKA, says that if they are made food secure through other means, they would obviously leave this occupation. Few *safai kamdars* who are employed by government bodies like the Municipal Corporations or panchayats have little trade union support. Even in supposedly wealthier states like Haryana, Gujarat and Tamilnadu there are grievances about perennially late salaries. Most *safai kamdars* though, work in private homes for measly amounts of money such as Rs. 5 or 10 per month and waste food is provided as a bonus. They are subject to demeaning, humiliating practices such as begging for food every evening and accepting stale leftover food, sometimes not fit for dogs.[189] Majority of them, 76 percent are sinking in heavy debt.

30 percent of *Madigas* migrate each year in search of livelihood options[190]. But often they need to depend on moneylenders from whom they have to pay a minimum of

10 percent interest per month. These loans ultimately put them into an endless cycle of debt bondage.

Hunger as a way of life is not very uncommon in this country. But *dalits* have a disproportionate share of this extreme suffering. History reveals the ugly roots of this persisting inequality and the modern day offers little to change this course. Nutritional indicators such as body mass index, anaemia and child malnutrition, indicate that *dalits* are consistently worse off than caste Hindus.

Figure: Scheduled Castes Suffer from High-Levels of Malnourishment

	SC	*ST*	*OBC*	*Other*
Stunted Children under 3 years (percent)	44.1	44.3	39.2	31.1
Wasted children under 3 years (percent)	20.5	25.7	18.9	16.4
Underweight children under 3 years (percent)	52.2	56.7	46.4	37.3
Women whose Body Mass Index is below normal (percent)	39.5	46.6	32.6	26
Men whose Body Mass Index is below normal (percent)	33.7	38	27.7	21.9
Children age 6-35 months who are anaemic (percent)	82.3	85.1	79.7	74.4
Ever-married women age 15-49 years who are anaemic (percent)	58.8	69.2	55.2	52.1
Ever-married men age 15-49 years who are anaemic (percent)	26.5	39.7	22	21.3

Source: National Family Health Survey III.

State and Schemes

When the basic needs of a population are denied, the state is expected to intervene with remedial measures, mostly in the mode of welfare schemes. But, there can be three ways which (mis)lead eligible beneficiaries out of the purview of their rights to food. (i) Lack of awareness about the schemes themselves, (ii) an eligibility criteria with selection in the hands of local elites and (iii) tardy program implementation, all exclude the needy.

Another reason why most of the schemes fail to reach these groups, *Musahars, Madigas* and *safai karmacharis* is due to the exclusions that they have to face from both the sides, from dominant as well as other oppressed sections of the society. Policy design and local government machinery both determine the success of the food schemes in reaching *dalits.* From school teachers to panchayats presidents to electoral system where everyone and everything is ruled by caste, the reach of welfare schemes is filtered.

In Dogra village in Eastern Uttar Pradesh, where the starvation death of the, Nagina Musahar was reported in October 2004, the government immediately intervened, provided his widow with National Family Benefit Scheme (NFBS) and included many villagers in different schemes. But *dalit* communities across the country can scare afford to have such 'martyrs' to hunger simply to gain their rightful access to food schemes.

1. *Public Distribution System*

The targeted public distribution system (TPDS) which is designed with strict eligibility criteria subject to manipulation by local elites is often mired in problems of exclusion. *Dalits* invariably face the brunt of deprivation.

(Un)Fair Price Shops

- **Less Foodgrain :** In two of every five villages *dalits* regularly receive lesser quantities of foodgrains. In the Kushinagar district BPL card holders have reported that they get only. 17 Kgs. of food grains in a month. In Gopalganj District of Bihar, the situation is even worse as *dalits* have not been receiving any foodgrains for the few months.
- **Higher Prices :** In a quarter of villages, *dalit* are charged higher prices by the PDS dealer. *Musahars*

in Eastern districts of Uttar Pradesh routinely need to pay Rs. 5 or 10 more than the actual rates fixed by the Government to get their monthly quota of grain.

- **Dalit days** : PDS dealers in many villages service dominant castes throughout the week, while they arbitrarily designate "*dalit* days" once or twice a week with reduced hours.
- **Untouchable :** PDS dealers practice 'untouchability' in a quarter of villages, i.e. the dominant castes drops foodgrains from above into the cupped *dalit* hands below, so as to avoid "polluting" contact.
- **Unseeable :** In Bihar, dominant caste PDS dealers hang cloth screens in front of their shops before dealing with *Musahar* dalits.
- **Denied** : In Gorakhpur, 69 percent manual scavengers do not have a ration card.

Sources :

1. Rawat, Vidya Bhushan, Ram Bhuvan and Kirti Singh (2007) 'Status of Manual Scavengers in Gorakhpur, Uttar-Pradesh', http://www.countercurrents.org/dalitrawat250207. htm (last checked by author May 2008)
2. Personal observations made during the visit to Musahar dominated districts of Eastern Uttar Pradesh, in February 2008.

A study of a village in Andhra Pradesh, where a considerable majority of Madiga families live indicates that the PDS scheme does not necessarily address the food security problem comprehensively. Rice available from PDS outlets meets only part of their total food consumption.[191] Even if rice is available in the ration shop, unless Madiga households have money in hand to purchase it, it is as good as no rice. The PDS also plays marginal role in providing accessibility as the food grain made available through its outlets are not sufficient to meet the complete food requirements of the people. 15 to 20 Kgs. of rice provided per family per month, largely proves insufficient. Only rice is available while the staple food here is sorghum.

2. *Mid-day Meals*

Segregation encourages high drop-out rates among *dalits* [one of every three *dalit* children do not attend school (Figure 2)] and by implication teaches children that "untouchability" is both an acceptable and 'normal' practice. It also increases the drop-out rate amongst *dalit* children. In Punjab, 66 percent of children of *safai karmacharis* have dropped out from school due to caste abuse[192]. In its order dated 20 April, 2004, the Supreme Court specified that for the mid-day meal programme "In appointment of cooks and helpers, preference shall be given to Dalits, Scheduled Castes and Scheduled Tribes". This landmark order ensured that for a developing country like India, the 8,000 crore rupee programme embodied the twin objectives of not only feeding India's children but also nourishing their minds and freeing these of prejudice.

When a dalit cook does get hired despite the opposition, dominant caste parents threaten to withdraw their children from school, send home-packed lunch boxes or insist their children come home for lunch. Their children are forbidden to eat food prepared by the dalit cook. The pressure to dismiss the cook or shut down the mid-day meal program is insistent.

3. *National Rural Employment Guarantee Act (NREGA)*

On the verge of starvation, the most discriminated *dalits* like the *Musahars, Madigas* and scanvangers, have the greatest need for guaranteed employment with dignity. But unfortunately so far the evidence shows that the National Rural Employment Guarantee Act (NREGA) has failed to reach many *dalit* families, due to local level discrimination.

Though the *Musahars* in most of the villages of eastern Uttar Pradesh districts, had heard of the 100 days work programme, they are largely unaware of their rights. Many of them have job cards even though they have submitted photographs. Even in those *Musahar tolas* where cards had been issued, were kept with the village Pradhan for safe keeping! NREGA works are largely concentrated in the main villages. *Musahar tolas* are excluded as sites not for creating common infrastructure due to local politics, which are typically dominated by upper caste influences. In dominant castes areas, *Musahars* are sometimes not even allowed to enter or work on NREGA sites.[193]

4. *Integrated Child Development Scheme (ICDS)*

The Supreme Court of India, by order dated 13.12.2006, issued the following directions to the Union Government in relation to the Integrated Child Development Services (ICDS) Scheme :

(i) Government of India shall sanction and operationalize a minimum of 14 lakh AWCs in a phased and even manner starting forthwith and ending December 2008. In doing so, the Central Government shall identify SC and ST hamlets/ habitations for AWCs on a priority basis.

(ii) Government of India shall ensure that population norms for opening of AWCs must not be revised upward under any circumstances. While maintaining the upper limit of one AWC per 1000 population, the minimum limit for opening of a new AWC is a population of 300 may be kept in view. Further, rural communities and slum dwellers should be entitled to an "Anganwadi on demand" (not later than three months) from the date of demand in cases where a settlement has at least 40 children under six but no Anganwadi.

However, studies[194] indicate the long prevailing trends of exclusion of the most discriminated dalits even in pre-school education. *Madiga* children for example are excluded from being registered in ICDS anganwadi centres.

Arundhati Dhuru, Uttar Pradesh State Adviser to the Commissioners of the Supreme Court (CWP 196/2001), during a visit to the Gopalganj district of Bihar in March 2008, found that in the *anganwadis* in the *Musahar bastis* where the Anganwadi Workers (AWWs) belonged to other castes or other villages, the centres were usually closed. As a community with weak bargaining power, they have never even tried to pressurize the anganwadi worker to open the centre everyday. There are indeed many other *Musahar* hamlets, with no Anganwadis. Most of their children are therefore not registered as the nearest centres were in fact not in their accessible limits.

Recommendations

There are provisions for positive discrimination in favour of *dalit* groups under many anti-poverty and livelihoods. There are however large gaps in implementation, and needy dalit potential users of the programmes often fall through the cracks, or are blocked by continuing barriers of caste discrimination in ways that we have seen above. These barriers are most severe for the most oppressed and deprived dalit groups, and occur resolutely also in food schemes, many of which are theoretically universal in their coverage like MDMs, ICDS and NREGA.

Each of these programmes need to accommodate a clearly articulated policy of affirmative action favouring pro-active inclusion of *dalits* even in universal programmes like ICDS and MDM, and demand-led programmes like NREGA. The schemes, for instance, need to locate work-sites, and institutions like ICDS centres closer to *dalit* habitations; and to deploy a greater number of administrators - from state and district to local village and slum leveles - from *dalit* communities, especially those who suffer greatest discrimination.

We have noted that even dalits are not a homogenous group. We have observed that there are most discriminated communities even within the dalits, like the Musahars,

Madigas and safai karmacharis. The difficulty is that unlike so-called 'primitive tribes', most discriminated dalit communities have not been identified. It is important that these communities are identified on objective criteria, especially because of their enormous proneness to malnutrition, hunger and starvation.

The first criterion would be those communities in which the majority of members (more than 50 per cent) still engage in 'unclean occupations' like manual scavenging, disposal of human and animal carcasses, and tanning and leather work.

The second criterion would be those dalit communities in which at least 2 of the following criteria are fulfilled:

- more than 75 per cent households in rural areas do not own their homestead lands.
- more than 75 per cent in rural areas do not own agricultural land.
- more than 75 per. cent children under 3 years are underweight.
- more than 75 per cent have BMIs below 18.
- more than 75 per cent children are out of school.
- more than 10 per cent are in debt bondage.

This identification would of 'most discriminated against' dalit groups would be only for purposes of food, livelihood and social security schemes. It will be done by the respective state governments, in consultation with the Commissioners of the Supreme Court, as long as they are in position. After their offices lapse, the state governments would consult with National Commission for Scheduled Castes and Tribes, in finalising these assessment. For all dalit communities which are identified as 'most discriminated' against, by these criteria, every household should be entitled to AAY cards.

All settlements of these communities should be covered by ICDS centres in one year, and children should be given supplementary nutrition twice a day, instead of once.

NREGA works should be started in SC/ST hamlets in particular, and in the rural hamlets occupied by these 'most discriminated' against dalit communities every year, in order to facilitate the participation of SC/ST households in this programme, and incidentally also ensuring that benefits of the public works accrue to people of these communities.

The figures for job cards and employment should be disaggregated for SC ST, as well as for identified 'most discriminated against' dalit communities and PTGs, to enable review of adequate coverage of these groups, and the need for greater locational focus, and information and mobilisation campaigns among these communities.

A commission should be established by the Ministry of Rural Development, Government of India, on whether legislation is feasible and desirable to prevent large scale rural unemployment through in agricultural workers through regulation of mindless mechanisation of agriculture, especially through the use of combined harvesters. The Commission should include one Commissioner of the Supreme Court, and one Member of the Planning Commission.

There needs to be a renewed thrust to end manual scavenging, including deployment of municipal workers in open sewers, by strict enforcement of the law, and a special programme to train youth and women in these communities in computers and information technology, to enable their engagement in the modern economy.

There should be a country wide campaign to make the school a zero discrimination zone. Separate seating and feeding of dalit children should be gravely penalised. Supreme Court orders for hiring of *dalit* cooks in mid-day meals should be enforced strictly.

Bonded Labour

Introduction

A bonded worker is one who works against an advance which is to be repaid with interest through labour, is paid less than the statutory minimum wages, and lacks the freedom guaranteed by the Indian constitution to terminate or change one's employment or employer. Despite constitutional bans, unequivocal legal measures to outlaw bondage and forced labour, and the transformation of Indian society and economy since Independence, this repugnant system has endured across generations. The root causes of the stubborn survival of this oppressive mode of labour relations include the high instance of intense poverty, desperate chronic hunger, unemployment, debt, usury, failures of public sources of credit, landlessness, caste oppression, feudal agricultural relationships, denial by the state and continuance of the historical hierarchy of castes.

Legal Loopholes

Article 23 of the Constitution of India (1949) also bans all forms of trafficking in human beings and forced labour. However, the legislation Bonded Labour Act specifically abolishing bonded labour was passed by Parliament only in 1976.

The Bonded Labour Act 1976 Act defines 'bonded labour' as a service rendered under the 'bonded labour system'. This is a system of forced, or partly forced, labour under which the debtor enters into an agreement, oral or written, with the creditor. The 'advance' taken by the debtor or by any of his lineal ascendants and/or in consideration of any customary obligation (for belonging to particular caste or community), the debtor has to work him (her)self, or through a member of his/her family. This arrangement is either without wages or for nominal wages, where much of it is deducted against debt and interest. There is no freedom to engage in any other occupation or move about freely till the loan is repaid.

The Act cancelled all the liability to repay bonded debt and called for restoration of property of the bonded labourer. District Magistrates were entrusted with the responsibility to oversee the implementation under the act, and vigilance committees were constituted at local levels for identification and rehabilitation, along with specific provision for rehabilitation of rescued child bonded labourers.

The Supreme Court of India has, through its judgments taken a broad interpretation of the word 'force'.[195] It states that the word 'force' includes not just physical or legal force, but also force arising out of economic compulsions. This has caused some ambiguity particularly, in the case of certain sectors where market wages are normally below the legal minimum (as in agriculture).

The Report of the Central Committee in 1994[196] which was appointed to draw up a workable definition of Bonded Labour has concluded that all cases of payment of wages below minimum wage could not straightforwardly be brought under the Act. The issue of minimum wages is simply one measure (and by no means a necessary or sufficient measure) to judge whether the person is bonded or not.

However, the National Human Rights Commission (NHRC) Expert Group in 2001[197] concludes that all kinds of forced labour, not just debt bondage should be considered while identifying bonded labour. A number of other labour laws also explicitly or implicitly forbid the use of bonded and bonded child labourers - including the Child Labour (Prohibition and Regulation) Act; 1986[198], the Factories Act; 1948[199]; the Beedi and Cigar Workers (Conditions of Employment) Act; 1966[200], the Inter-State Migrant Workmen (Regulation of Employment and Conditions of Service) Act; 1979[201], Juvenile Justice (Care and Protection) Act; 2000.[202] While the legal framework is extensive, there exist several legal loopholes and weak enforcement mechanism, which are conveniently exploited by the employers.[203]

Disputed Claims

After a brief phase of relative official candour, and in some notable cases even official activism, during the 1970s and 80s, most governments have gone back into the most improbable denial. The Government of India has often taken refuge by only monitoring the traditional character of bonded labour and to avoid addressing the shameful facts of contemporary forms of debt bondage, which are described below. Despite stanch denials from the state, several independent studies, and civil society organizations, had shown empirical evidence of existence of bonded labour in India.

The International Labour Organisation (ILO)[204] in 2005 estimated that at least 12.3 million people worldwide were trapped in forced labour, out of which, 9.5 million live in Asia Pacific region especially in conditions of bondage in India, Nepal and Pakistan.

In the more recent past, however, the Minister of State for Labour and Employment, Oscar Fernandes in March 2008, has admitted that despite being banned by law nearly 32 years ago, bonded labour is still in practice in India.[205] He has, nevertheless, sought to imply that South India (with the exception of Karnataka) is bonded labour free.[206]

The government has released 1,855 such labourers from various states, and according to official data during April –. December 2007, 395 bonded labourers were reported, from the states of West Bengal, Uttar Pradesh and Bihar.

Circular Migration

Many traditional forms of agrarian relations have declined with diversification of economy and proliferation of occupations. Agricultural relations have metamorphosed in parts of the country from semi-feudal to semi-capitalist. However, bondage continues, not as a vestige of the past, but as a thriving contemporary form of labour exploitation and control, spreading to modern industries, the informal sector and the capitalist mode of agriculture including in states like Punjab. [207] Circular migration and short-term contracts characterise bonded labour in agriculture and industries.[208]

The contractual or migrant bonded labourers are the most vulnerable to exploitation. Employers prefer to hire migrant labour, as they are cheaper, more susceptible to exploitation and bondage than local labour.[209] Many economically buoyant states like Andhra Pradesh host large numbers of hapless workers in semi-bondage from impoverished states like Orissa, Chhattisgarh and Jharkhand, but significantly Andhra also exports migrant workers in similar conditions of semi-bondage to other states.

Migrant workers in all destinations are then subjected to oppressive and insecure work conditions, with nominal wages, and can be laid off at will. Many a times, a migrant worker is not paid the complete amount, often because usurious rates of interest have been applied to the initial amount if advance received by the worker. This forces him to come again in the next season. This ensures stable labour over four hundred thousand children work in cottonseed fields across India.

Ascribed Bondage

Bonded labourers are among the most marginalized, both socially and economically. Officially, 86.6 percent of bonded labourers are identified as belonging to Scheduled Castes and Scheduled Tribes.[210] Allocation of labour on the basis of caste is one of the fundamental precepts. *Dalits* as untouchables were provided with the most menial and *polluting* jobs. Most bonded labourers are low-caste, illiterate, and extremely poor. Even in the non-agricultural sector and in relation to tribals, forms of bondage draw on traditional hierarchical social and power relations. In the tribal areas, land alienation has resulted in increasing vulnerability to debt bondage. Further, displacement of tribals and increasing deforestation together create the need for credit and for seeking employment and livelihoods under bondage, often through migration. [211]

Child Bonded Labour

In 1996, Human Rights Watch had estimated that out of 3 lakhs child labourers in carpet industry, most are bonded.[212] There is a huge proportion of *dalits* and Muslims among children in bondage. In Orissa, they are usually known as '*buturu* ' and work as agricultural labour, domestic help or at *dhabas* (roadside eateries) or hotels in nearby towns. These children work for long hours, are often beaten up by their employers and miss out on schooling. They become impoverished, unhealthy and illiterate.

(Wo)man in Bondage

Gender distribution varies depending on the sector of activity. In Tamil Nadu it is estimated that 70 percent of women are involved in floriculture, 40 percent in beedi making, while men constitute an overwhelming majority of bonded labourers in almost all other sectors.[213] Women, however, are estimated to form an increasing numbers of migrants in bondage, as migration increasingly happens in family groups. Industries like quarry mining, brick making etc. increasing use women as labour.[214]

Even while husbands are bonded, women of the household are severely affected by it. It means more economic hardship for them. As there were no daily wages coming in to sustain the household, the responsibility of running the household put greater burden on women. Often, unable to meet the needs, they end up taking additional loans from the same employer for exigencies. Thus, such labour relationships put the family into a cycle of exploitative debt.

Women complain of verbal abuse, aggressive behaviour and sometimes even sexual exploitation by masters, employers or contractors. At a brick kiln in Andhra Pradesh it was reported that male workers were made to work as bonded labourers while young girls were sexually exploited on a daily basis, threatened at gunpoint.[215] Women face greater burden of caste discrimination too. They were called by their caste names, and not their individual name, which makes them feel humiliated.

Although older women are often spared of this ignominy, their age increases their vulnerability. As they can offer no hard labour, and help family in repayment, they are taken as a burden. To escape this, it was not uncommon to find that they too indulge in bonded labour to supplement the family income[216].

Released from Hell?

The Bonded Labour Act (1976) established institutional mechanisms in the form of Vigilance Committees at the district and sub-divisional levels. Vigilance Committees, under the chairmanship of District and Sub-Divisional Magistrates are to receive complains regarding bonded labourers. Executive Magistrates conduct summary trial of offences, to release the bonded labourers and to issue release certificates.

However, at most places Vigilance Committees are either non-functional or dominated by government officials and/ or political appointees. In Bargarh, Orissa, a study found that though the vigilance committee met regularly, it echoed government's argument about non-existence of bonded labour. When one of the members repeatedly demanded a fresh identification and release of bonded labourers, an NGO, known to take side with government was given the responsibility of conducting the survey. As a result, none of 1,200 bonded labourers who had filed a petition for release were identified as bonded labour. Similarly in Malkangiri, the vigilance committee, under political pressure has started to deny the existence of bonded labour[217].

A centrally sponsored scheme for rehabilitation of released bonded labourers was launched in 1978 where the assistance provided was shared on a 50 : 50 basis between centre and state. Centre released Rs. 10,000 per labourer. Expenditure incurred in 8th Five Year Plan amounted to Rs. 40.51 crore, while it Rs. 24.50 crores during the 9th Five Year Plan. During the 10th Five Year Plan (2002-07) Central Grants amounting to Rs. 97.28 crores was provided to various State Governments under the said scheme. The latest budget for 2008-9 has a provision of only Rs. 1.8 crores for the rehabilitation of bonded labourers indicating the low priority attributed.[218]

Even after release, issuing of certificates takes a long time and rehabilitation happens only in few cases. Prosecution of 'masters' have been almost completely ignored.

Many a times bonded labourers suffer more at the hands

of bureaucracy, than they did under their masters. It has been reported that out of 40 bonded labourers (including minors) from Madurai who were rescued from the states of Andhra Pradesh, Orissa and Uttar Pradesh, only 8 have been paid rehabilitation money of Rs. 20,000. The remaining thirty two labourers have received only an 'interim relief' of Rs. 1,000 each. The reasons for denial in release money were because they had not been issued release certificates from the district collector of the place where they were bonded. A man was denied assistance as his name was spelt wrongly in the release certificate. In a yet another case, the released labourer had to bribe a village administrative officer for releasing a cheque for Rs. 10,000. [219]

The greater problem in the implementation of the 1976 Act is that from the start, official activism in 'freeing' bonded labour extends at best to identifying a few, and releasing them, often with a lot of publicity, and 'rehabilitating' them with the release of a grant. But ever since the Act came into force, it is remarkable that almost never, in any part of the country, have employers of bonded labour been prosecuted or punished. It is therefore a 'painless' process, and on occasion, employers of bonded labour have been happy to participate, as bonded workers get 'dues' from the government rather than the employer, none answer the law, and 'freed' bonded workers can return to their employers after all the dust settles!

Hunger Trap

Their food security status is so fragile that a single failed crop, drought, or health emergency can disturb the delicate balance of surviving. Credit is not taken only for emergency situation but also for everyday life necessities. Most often, bondage is adopted as a coping mechanism from absolute hunger. Even the children surrendered to bondage indicate the extent of household food insecurity.

Their cash loans are sometimes extremely small. A few tens of rupees or a few kilograms of paddy, is sufficient to create a life of servitude. This bondage occurs because the poorest of the poor are largely uncovered by government food and livelihood schemes. In bondage, they often receive no wages. Much of their earnings are deducted against the advance.

Thus, bonded labour is the result of acute hunger, even though ironically through bondage, families try to ensure some buffer against hunger, albeit for short-term benefit. In the long run, bondage furthers food insecurity. Added to this is the exacting work and loss of freedom. More favourable options of livelihood and income generation are closed and wages are so low that they do not support savings or movement out of bondage. Food given to the person in bondage is ungenerous and usually at the minimum survival level. Most often, this food, meant for a person's meal is taken home to be shared by the family. Not only food is served in an undignified manner (instances of food thrown away at the bonded labour, or separate utensils, untouchability etc.), it is also monotonous, low quality (left over, stale, watery) and in insufficient quantities.

Chicken Feed

Those engaged in agriculture, most of them are given a meal or two; however, it is usually consists of inferior cereals. For example, in Andhra, bonded labourers are mostly given *taidal* and *korabua* (coarse cereals), and not paddy. As no or very little cash wage is paid, there is often not much food at home, and so the family shares much of what is given to the bonded labour member of the family. There were instances were food was stale, left over or even worms were found in the food.

Newer forms of bonded labour, for example migrant bonded labour face chronic food insecurity. Here, as the period of work is specified and an employer has no long term interest in keeping the bonded labour alive and active, their exploitation is greater. In far away cities, confronted, with unfamiliar people, language and with worksites on outskirts of human habitation, the problem is further aggravated. Migrant workers live in sub human conditions, often sleeping in open air or living in makeshift houses. They are continuously overworked and eat much less than what is required for such heavy manual labour. There diet is not only insufficient and monotonous, but also unhealthy and lacking in nutrition.

For migrants to brick kilns of Andhra Pradesh, weekly markets come up for migrant labour, selling the poorest quality of food, like broken rice or chicken feed, dried or rotting vegetables and discarded portions of meat. Not only are they are poorest in quality, the price charged is also exorbitant. Broken rice or chicken feed costs them Rs. 7-8 per kg., as against market price of Rs. 3-4. Their drinking water is same as that used for mixing clay for brick making. Also, the sanitation and toilet facilities are virtually non-existent leading to poor absorption of food.

Labourers are forced to work even when sick or injured, as employers do not want slackening production. However, if employers need to slow down for their own reasons, payments are stopped. Most of these labourers live under open sky or in makeshift arrangements, in absence of even the minimal amount of facility. There are numerous health hazards, from contaminated water, respiratory diseases and infections, occupational injuries and accidents and malnourishment due to lack of proper food. There is no availability of medical facilities, no insurance and no sick leaves with pay.

Recommendations

It is hunger that drives most people to bondage. The only way open to the country's most impoverished and disenfranchised people to feed their families and themselves is to sell away most cheaply not just their labour but also with it their dignity and their freedom. The country's Constitution and laws, the state, its food and development programmes, all fail them so profoundly that they are able to survive only through forms of slavery.

Yet it would be a grave mistake to believe that bondage at least ensures the food security of the bonded family. It is true that a bonded worker must be fed to be able to toil the many hours that his employer demands from him. But the food is without freedom, and therefore without dignity. It is often the cheapest and most monotonous food available. It also does not guarantee the survival of the family of the bonded worker. It rarely opens even future paths of freedom from want and indignity. It rarely leads to hope.

Acknowledge Bondage

1. No problem can be solved unless it is acknowledged. The central and state governments must resolutely end their stubborn denial, of the persistence of classical forms of adult and child bonded labour, and the emergence of dangerous and oppressive new forms, adapted to the globalised economy.
2. There must be a new national resolve to end this practice as utterly incompatible with India's claims of global economic leadership.
3. District Collectors should reconstitute vigilance committees under the Act at various levels, and collaborate with these to freshly survey truthfully the scale and forms of bonded labour.
4. Implement **Bonded Labour Act, 1976** with new vigour. A close cooperation between vigilance committees and civil society organizations is required.
5. In this round, stress should be on not just identification and release, but also enduring rehabilitation and above all criminal prosecution of the employers of bonded labour.

Distribute Grain

1. Once released, give **Antyodaya Anna Yojana (AAY) cards** to all bonded labourers.
2. Also, they could be given a special **pension for first six months** (equivalent to the NOAPS pension

prevalent at that point of time) to help them start afresh.

Prevent Fresh Bondage

1. All released bonded workers should be given **job cards under priority**, and 2 members of the family entitled to get employment under NREGA.
2. All released bonded workers should also be permitted to draw their full entitlement of **grain on credit** from PDS shops every month. This should be adjusted against one-third of their daily wages once NREGA works are commenced.
3. If they do not own their homesteads, they should be given first priority for free housing under the Indira Awaas Yojana.
4. All children (who may be themselves bonded or the children of released bonded workers) should get admission, if their parents choose, in SC/ST hostels. If they choose otherwise, they should be admitted to local schools, if necessary after organising residential bridge courses under SSA, and are also provided MDMS.

Recommendations for Bonded Migrant Workers

1. Registration norms for contractors under the Inter-State Migrant Workers Act must be rigorously followed.
2. Residential schools must be opened for children and elderly, in the 'sending areas' so that they can be taken care of and continue with schooling even when their parents migrate.
3. Registration of 'receiving' factories like brick kilns, stone quarries etc. under Factories Act.
4. Ensure payment of minimum wages.
5. Temporary anganwadi centres at the sites where migrants work, such as construction or brick kiln sites, must be opened to take care of children under six.

6. Transfer of entitlements, also across states (this will require proper registration and knowledge of people who are migrating, and would be taken care of by registration of factories and contractors). Also, it will need interstate cooperation. But if it is to work for people who are most powerless, it should involve the least paper work.

References

1 Discussions with Harsh Mander, based on his work with the survivors of these 3 disasters.

2 See the studies conducted by 'Guild of Service' for more details on status of widows in Varanasi and Vrindavan. For e.g. Guild of Service (2002) 'Status of Widows of Vrindavan and Varanasi : A Comparative Study', http://griefandrenewal.com/widows_study.htm (last checked by the author May 2008) and Guild of Service (2007) 'Spirituality, Poverty, Charity Bring Widows to Vrindavan'.

3 Tripathi. P.S. (2006), 'The living dead' Frontline Volume 23 - Issue 16 :: Aug. 12-25, 2006 4 Census 2001.

5 Based on Census 2001 figures almost 99 per cent of women in India are married by the age of 30, and therefore 30 is taken here, as the cut-off age for determining those who come in the 'single women' category.

6 This paragraph draws from Census 2001. The per centage distribution is similar to NSS 61st round.

7 The Khasi and Gharo tribes of Meghalaya, Nair and Mappilles communities in Kerala and the tribal groups of Minicoy Island in Lakshwadeep.

8 Chen. M. A. (1998), ibid.

9 Mander and Rai (2007), *Living with Hunger*, Centre for Equity Studies.

10 Chen. M. A. (1998), ibid.

11 Panda, P.K. (1997) *Female Headship, Poverty and Child Welfare: A Study of Rural Orissa, India,* Thiruvananthapuram : Centre for Development Studies.

12 Chen. M. A. (1998), ibid.

13 Available on website of Press Information Bureau, http://pib.nic.in/release/release.asp?relid=24579 (last checked by the author May 2008).

14 Dreze, J. (1990) *Widows in Rural India*, Discussion Paper No. 26, Development Economics Research Programme, London School of Economics.

15 Dreze, J. and P.V. Srinivasan (1997) 'Widowhood and poverty in rural India: some inferences from household level data' in M.A. Chen (ed.) *Widows in India: Social Neglect and Public Action*, New Delhi : Sage Publications.

16 Ministry of Women and Child Development's response to Lok Sabha Unstarred Question No. 4681 answered on 25.04.2008. This same response also stated "The Ministry of Women and Child Development has no proposal for the remarriage of young widows in the country." Contrary to newspaper reports quoting the Minister.

17 Calculations made by the Office of Commissioners to Supreme Court CWP 196/2001, based on data received from state governments.

18 BARC (2007), ibid.

19 For details on old age pensions in different states see the chapter "Burden of Age" in this report.

20 The current All India poverty line is around Rs. 360 per capita per month. Assuming a family of three, the poverty line for the family would be Rs. 1080. Rs. 500 is about 50% of this.

21 The total number of beneficiaries reported from all the States/UTs is 1,71,232 as against a numerical ceiling of 5,71,500.

22 Saxena, N.C. and H. Mander (2007) 'Seventh Report of the Commissioners', presented to the Supreme Court, CWP 196/2001.

23 Gopal K.S. (2007), op.cit.

24 On 2nd May, 2003, the Supreme Court directed that all households belonging to six "priority groups" would be entitled to Antyodaya cards. 'Widows and other single women with no regular support' was one of the groups identified.

25 Sujaya, CP (2000), National policy on older persons, *Seminar*, April.

26 Gopal, Meena (2006) 'Gender, Ageing and Social Security', *Economic and Political Weekly*, 41 (42), 4477-4486.

27 Gulati, Leela; and Irudaya Rajan, S. (1999). 'The Added Years: Elderly in India and Kerala',*Economic and Political Weekly*, 34(44), 46-51.

28 Moneer Alam and Mehtab Karim (2005), *Beyond the Current Demographic Scenario:* Changing Age Composition, Ageing and Growing Insecurities for the Aged in India and *Pakistan*: IUSSP International Population Conference, France.

29 S. Irudaya Rajan (2006), Population Ageing and Health in India, The Centre for Enquiry into Health and Allied Themes (CEHAT), Mumbai.

30 Chandrasekhar, C.P. Jayati Ghosh (2004) *The Market That Failed A Decade of Neoliberal. Economic Reforms in India*, LeftWord: New Delhi.

31 National Sample Survey Organisation (2006), *Morbidity, Health Care and the Condition of the Aged*: Report No. 507, NSS 60th round.

32 National Sample Survey Organisation (2006), *Morbidity, Health Care and the Condition of the Aged*: Report No. 507, NSS 60th round.

33 National Sample Survey Organisation (2006), *Morbidity, Health Care and the Condition of the Aged*: Report No. 507, NSS 60th round.

34 Chatterjee, Chandrima and Gunjan Sheoran(2007), *Vulnerable groups in India*, CEHAT, Mumbai.

35 Dandekar (1996) cited in S. Mahendra Dev et. al. (2001) *Social and Economic Security in India*, Institute of Human Development, New Delhi.

36 Agarwal (1990) cited in S Mahendra Dev et. al. (2001) *Social and Economic Security in India*, Institute of Human Development, New Delhi.

37 Pensions, Annapurna and NFBS.

38 The earlier criteria of 'destitute' was removed.

39 Mander, Harsh (2008) *Living with Hunger*, EPW.

40 Mander, Harsh (2008) *Living with Hunger*, EPW.

41 Mander, Harsh (2008) *Living with Hunger*, EPW.

42 Yeo Rebecca (2001) *Chronic Poverty and Disability,* Somerset : Action on Dsiability and Development.

43 Rao, Vidya, and Harsh Mander. (1996) An Agenda for Caring: Interventions for Marginalised Groups, NewDelhi: Voluntary Health Association of India.

44 The share of *households* estimated by NSSO to have a disabled member was 8.4 and 6.1 per cent in rural and urban areas respectively (though this share seems high given the number of disabled individuals and survey results on their household size),cited in O'Keefe Philip (2007) *People with Disabilities in India : From Communities to Outcomes,* India : The World Bank.

45 The difference in numbers between the NSSO and Census is because of the different methodology and definitions adopted for identifying disabled persons. NSSO uses only a representative sample whereas Census is the enumeration of entire population. Because of the different definitions adapted by Census and NSSO the estimates of different categories of disability also varies between the two sources.

46 The National Centre for the Promotion of Employment for Disabled people (NCPEDP) estimates that approximately 65 to 70 million people or 6 per cent of India's population are affected by disability. The Ministry of Social justice and Development, in its annual report 1999-2000, has given a figure of 43.99 million disabled persons in the country (Labour File, A monthly Journal of Labour and Economic affairs; Volume-7).

47 Yeo Rebecca (2001) *ibid.*

48 Mom Beverly Beckles (2004) *Poverty and Disability : Advocating to Eliminate Social Exclusion,* Trinidad and Tobago : National Centre for Persons with Disabilities In 1981 WHO studies estimated that on average 10% of national populations are disabled. However in 1992, this estimate was modified to 4 per cent for developing countries and 7 per cent for industrialised countries. Because of the different estimates also there is no agreement on which figures to use USAID use 10 per cent, DFID use 4-7 per cent.

49 Mom Beverly Beckles (2004) *ibid.*

50 Elwan Ann (1999) *Poverty and Disability : A Survey of the Literature,* Social Protection Unit : World Bank.

51 Elwan Ann (1999) *ibid.*

52 Thomas Phillipa (2005), *ibid.*

53 O'Keefe Philip (2007) *ibid.*

54 The differences by SC/OBC status are slight between PWD and non-PWD households but are of significance in terms of likely poverty rates.

55 O'Keefe Philip (2007) *ibid.*

56 Yeo Rebecca (2001) *ibid.*

57 O'Keefe Philip (2007) *ibid.*

58 O'Keefe Philip (2007) *ibid.*

59 O'Keefe Philip (2007) *ibid.*

60 O'Keefe Philip (2007) *ibid.*

61 O'Keefe Philip (2007) *ibid.*

62 O'Keefe Philip (2007) *ibid*

63 O'Keefe Philip (2007) *ibid.*

64 Mander, Harsh (2002) 'At the precipice of despair', *Frontline19(15)*

65 O'Keefe Philip (2007) *ibid.*

66 O'Keefe Philip (2007) *ibid.*

67 O'Keefe Philip (2007) *ibid.*

68 O'Keefe Philip (2007) *ibid.*

69 Mander Harsh, EPW 2008 *ibid.*

70 Mander Harsh, EPW 2008 *ibid.*

71 Mander Harsh, EPW 2008 *ibid.*

72 135 disabled respondents were interviewed across three villages each in Orissa, Rajasthan and Andhra Pradesh for the study.

73 Mander Harsh (2007), *Living with Hunger,*Centre for Eequity Studies : India

74 Uttar Pradesh and Tamil Nadu village survey, 2005 quoted in O'Keefe Philip (2007) *ibid.*

75 Yeo Rebecca (2001) *ibid.*

76 Yeo Rebecca (2001) *ibid.*

77 Grech Shaun (2006) 'Words for Numbers : Exploring the Cycle

of Poverty and Disability in Rural Guatemala', Research Report Submitted to University of London, Imperial College, London.

78 NHRC (2005) 'Disability Manual', India : NHRC.

79 The differences in awareness about the disability pension among all the four quartiles were not found too much but as the programme is usually targeted to the poor households with PWD, therefore, the 60 per cent awareness among the first two quartiles which are potential beneficiaries has impact on the overall performance of programme.

80 Mahendra Dev S. K. Subbarao, S. Galab, C Ravi (2007), 'Safety net programmes : Outreach and effectiveness', *Economic and Political Weekly* (September) : *3555-65.*

81 A visit by a team of office of the Commissioners of the Supreme Court (CWP 196/2001) in April 2008, to the two AWCs of Okhla Zakir Nagar Slum (Delhi) observed that both the AWCs in the slum are totally inaccessible to disabled persons, even it would be difficult for the non-disabled children to access those AWCs because of the type of the entrances the AWCs have. In one other visit to the Viklang Basti it was found the AWCs were too far from the slum instead of the fact that the habitation is mostly occupied by the disabled people who don't find time and energy to take their small children to the far AWCs.

82 Neenv Delhi Forces (2007)*ICDS in Delhi, A Reality Check,*Delhi: Neenv Delhi Forces.

83 Mander, Harsh and M. Kumaran, SOCIAL EXCLUSION IN ICDS : *Universalisation with Quality* and M. *Equity*, 2006, mimeo.

84 O'Keefe Philip (2007) *ibid.*

85 O'Keefe Philip (2007) *ibid.*

86 O'Keefe Philip (2007) *ibid.*

87 Sarva Shiksha Abhiyan (2006) 'Discovering New Paths in Inclusion : A Documentation of Home- Based Education Practices for CWSN in SSA ', India : SSA.

88 Talukdar Anju (2008) Brief Survey of Access to Food Rights by Disabled urban poor in Guwahati, Assam.

89 A meeting with Md. Alaudin, Secretary, Food and Civil Supplies Dept. Govt. of Assam, revealed that around 7,04,000 Antyodaya cards have been issued in Assam so far. It was

not possible to ascertain how many Antyodaya cards have been issued to persons with disabilities or their family members, as the cards were issued to various identified categories, but no separate record was kept of the number of cards issued under each head e.g. disability. Md. Alaudin expressed his inability to rectify the situation till there is a change in policy whereby the quota is increased and new cards can be issued and also mentioned that it would be difficult to issue cards to the shelterless who do not have any permanent address.

90 G Praveen Kumar (2006) 'NREGA and Inclusion of Disabled People', India : Chhattisgarh Disability Network.

91 G. Praveen Kumar (2006) *ibid.*

92 G. Praveen Kumar (2006) *ibid.*

93 *Annual Report 2006-07,* Ministry of Rural Development, New Delhi.

94 Letters of the Ministry of Housing and Urban Poverty Alleviation to the office of the Chief Commissioner for Disability.

95 Due to a variety of factors including inaccessibility and insensitivity of the classroom environment.

96 Zaidi, Annie. (2005) 'Homeless in Delhi', Frontline 22(01).

97 Lal, Neeta. (2007), 'On the streets where they live',

http://infochangeindia.org/20070701248/Children/Features/On-the-streets-where-they-live.html (last checked by the author May, 2008).

98 Tiwari, Poornima. (2007) 'Life on Streets', The Indian Journal of Pediatrics 74(3) : 283-286.

99 Census of India, 1991: 64. The term welfare institutions inserted by (United Nations 1999).

100 (2006), Pavement dwellers federation formed, Tamil Nadu, The Hindu, 12 September.

http://www.hindu.com/2006/09/12/stories/2006091204090600.htm

101 These choices are probably linked to preferred occupational choices and considerations of safety. Harsh Mander (2007), *Living Rough - Surviving City Streets,* Report of the Homeless Study done in Delhi, Chennai, Patna and Madurai, Centre for Equity Studies.

102 Lal, Neeta. (2007), 'On the streets where they live', ibid.

103 Mander, Harsh. (2007), *Living Rough - Surviving City Streets,* Centre for Equity Studies.

104 Laurie Goering (2008), 'India reviews wisdom of beggar haven', World, Chicago Tribune

http://www.chicagotribune.com/business/chi-beggars_goering_mar12,0,367079.story

105 Rani Sudha, (2008), 'Begging: A viable profession!', March 12, http://www.merinews.com/catFull.jsp?articleID=131968 (last checked by the author May 2008).

106 Pushkar Raj (2004), 'Criminalising poverty : Houseless and anti-beggary law in Delhi', PUCL

Bulletin, http://www.pucl.org/Topics/Industries-envirn-resettlement/2004/criminalise-poverty.htm (last checked by the author May 2008).

107 Mander, Harsh. (2007), *Living Rough - Surviving City Streets,* ibid.

108 Saxena, N.C. (2007), 'National Strategy for Urban Poor', Mid Term Evaluation Report of GoI - UNDP Project.

109 Planning Commission, Mid-term Appraisal, IX Plan, as quoted in 'National Strategy for Urban Poor' by Dr. N.C. Saxena.

110 Zaidi, Annie. (2005) 'Homeless in Delhi', *Frontline* 22(01)

111 Susan Loughhead, Onkar Mittal and Geof Wood (2001), *Urban Poverty India,* DFID India,

www.worldbank.org/html/fpd/**urban**/forum2000/papers/**india**.pdf (last checked by author May 2008).

112 Mander, Harsh. (2007), *Living Rough - Surviving City Streets,* ibid.

113 Mander, Harsh. (2007), *Living Rough - Surviving City Streets,* ibid.

114 Mander, Harsh. (2007), *Living Rough - Surviving City Streets,* ibid.

115 Benegal, Vivek., Kul Bhushan, Shekhar Seshadri and Mani Karott (1998), Drug Abuse Among Street Children in Bangalore,

www.nimhans.kar.nic.in/deaddiction/lit/Drug%20Abuse%20_Street%20Children_Bangalore.pdf.

(last checked by author May 2008). Monograph funded by CRY. It is a project in collaboration between the National Institute of Mental Health and Neurosciences, Bangalore and the Bangalore Forum for Street and Working Children.

116 Mander, Harsh. (2007), *Living Rough - Surviving City Streets*, ibid.

117 Most of the observations in this session draw from Mander, Harsh. (2007), *Living Rough - Surviving City Streets*, ibid.

118 Based on the personal conversation with the Madurai Meenakshi temple authorities and personal observations in Delhi Gurudwaras

119 Mander, Harsh. (2007), *Living Rough - Surviving City Streets*, ibid.

120 (2007), ICDS in Delhi : A Reality Check, Delhi FORCES (Neenv), http://www.righttofoodindia.org/ (last checked by the author May 2008)

121 In Chennai, in 2006 the Engal Chennai Pavement Dwellers Federation was founded.

122 Interestingly, provision of colour televisions to the poor is something promised by the present ruling party in its last election campaign.

123 Joint Director, Social Welfare Department, Government of Delhi (2008).

124 Workshop held at Indian Institute of Planning and Management (IIPM), Delhi on Jan 23, 2008.

125 For the purpose of its 49th Round Survey 'Slums in India'.

126 Many slum definitions also require some minimum settlement size for an area to be considered a slum, so that the slum constitutes a distinct precinct and is not a single dwelling. For example, the Indian census definition requires at least 300 people or 60 households living in a settlement cluster. The Challenge of Slums, Global report on human settlements, 2003, UNHABITAT.

127 UN- HABITAT(2000), The Challenge of Slums : Global Report on Human Settlements, UN.

128 Census 2001, Slum Population report, Government of India.

129 Saxena, N.C. (2007), 'National Strategy for Urban Poor', Mid Term Evaluation Report of GoI - UNDP Project.

130 Meghalaya is the only exception.

131 http://www.commoncauseindia.org/amended_memorandum.htm

132 Mander, Harsh. (2004) *The Ripped Chest*, Bangalore: Books for Change.

133 http://www.infochangeindia.org/UrbanIndiaItop.jsp?section_idv=24

134 NFHS – 3.

135 On 540 children aged 1-6 years and the relation of under-nutrition with age, sex, birth order, and type of family, literacy, and calorie intake were studied and analyzed. 57.4% (310) of the children were undernourished and less than 16% of the undernourished children were consuming not more than 90% of the recommended calorie intake and intake of calories decreases significantly as the nutrition status of the children deteriorates.

136 Rukmani R. (2002), Urban food security – Small town cry for attention, The Hindu, Novemebr 23, 2002.

137 Swaminathan M.S. (2002), The Food Security Atlas of Urban India, M.S. Swaminathan research foundation and World Food Programme, Chennai.

138 NSS Report (2004-05) No. 510: Public Distribution System and Other Sources of Household Consumption, Government of India.

139 Before 1996, PDS was universal, in that every household regardless of income was free to access it. The Targeted PDS (TPDS) controversially restricted access only to families designated to be BPL by governments.

140 CVC recommendations, as cited in Seventh Report (2007), Commissioners of the Supreme court in the case : PUCL v. UOI & Ors. Writ Petition (Civil) No. 196 of 2001.

141 Manikandan (2008) ,·Cuttack Pilot Study Report , Centre for Equity Studies : New Delhi.

142 Emergency food security network and FAO, *City level assessment and consultation on food and nutrition security in seven slum areas in Bhuj, India.*

143 As per official data from Dept. of Women and Child Development (2005), Govt. of India, there were 360 urban ICDS projects catering to about 90 million urban poor.

144 Supreme court Commissioners, (2007) seventh report : 28.11.2001 interim order : 'We direct the State Governments/ Union Territories to implement the Integrated Child Development Scheme (ICDS) in full and to ensure that every ICDS disbursing centre in the country shall provide as under: (a) Each child up to 6 years of age to get 300 calories and 8-10 grams of protein; (b) Each adolescent girl to get 500 calories and 20-25 grams of protein; (c) Each pregnant woman and each nursing mother to get 500 calories & 20-25 grams of protein; (d) Each malnourished child to get 600 calories and 16-20 grams of protein; (e) Have a disbursement centre in every settlement.' 29.04.2004 interim order : 'We ... direct that the sanctioned AWCs shall supply nutritious food/supplement to the children, adolescent girls and to pregnant and lactating women under the scheme for 300 days in a year'.

145 NIPCCD, ICDS evaluation, Ministry of women and child development, Government of India.

146 Mobile Creches (2004) Early Child Care Practices, New Delhi.

147 Manikandan (2008), Cuttack Pilot Study Report, ibid.

148 2003, cited in De Anuradha, Claire Noronha and Samson Meera, (2005), ibid.

149 Saxena, N.C. (2007), 'National Strategy for Urban Poor', Mid Term Evaluation Report of GoI - UNDP Project.

150 "The National Tribal Policy (A Policy for the Scheduled Tribes of India - Draft)" (2006), Ministry of Tribal Affairs, Government of India.

151 1981 and 1991 census figures respectively. The Ministry (Tribal Affairs) has indicated that it is yet to obtain the figures of 2001 Census from Registrar General of India.

152 Development of Primitive Tribal Groups, Twenty Eighth report, Standing Committee on Labour and Welfare (2002), Ministry of Tribal Affairs, New Delhi.

153 Jain, Sachin. (2005) 'Malnutrition Disaster in Madhya Pradesh', www.righttofoodindia.org/data/mp-malnutrition-samvad.doc (last checked by author May 2008).

154 Sen, Shonali. and S.Vivek (2003) 'Sheopur Report : Functioning of food and food-related schemes in Sheopur District, MP', http://www.righttofoodindia.org/data/sheopur.pdf, (last checked by author May 2008).

155 As quoted in Mander, Harsh. (2002) 'Denying Starvation', http://www.sccommissioners.org/pdfs/articles/denyingstarvation.pdf (last checked by author May 2008)

156 Jain, Sachin. (2006) 'Poverty, migration & national rural employment guarantee scheme a case study on Sahariya primitive tribal group in Madhya Pradesh',

http://www.righttofoodindia.org/links/field_reports.html (last checked by author May 2008).

157 'Preliminary Indigenous People Development Program', www.adb.org/Documents/**IndigenousPeoples**/ind/IPDP-SuppApp-Chhatt-Final.pdf (last checked by author May 2008).

158 Khatry, Rajendra. (2000) 'Missing the wood for the trees', http://www.indianexpress.com/india- news/ie/daily/20000704/ian04058.html (last checked by author May 2008).

159 All information on the Chenchus largely draws from Dr. Kodandaram's internal reports related to his Right to food work. Dr. Kodandaram is the Andhra Pradesh State Advisor to the Supreme Court Commissioners in Right to food case (CWP 196/2001).

160 ibid.

161 There are a total of 1159 villages.

162 Jain, Sachin. (2007), 'The forgotten Saharias of Sheopur', http://www.indiatogether.org/2007/feb/hlt-saharias.htm (last checked by author May 2008).

163 See VAARTA, 18th Feb, 2008 translated by Rama S. Melkote, as quoted in one of Dr. Kodandram's internal reports.

164 Garg, Samir. (2006) 'Grassroot Mobilisation for Children's Nutrition Rights', *Economic and Political Weekly* 41(34): 3694-700.

165 (2006), 'Unheard Whimpers, An Alert Note on Malnutrition Deaths in Patalgarh village of Sheopur district', Right to Food Campaign Madhya Pradesh Support Group,

http://www.mediaforrights.org/pdfs/reports/report1.pdf (last checked by author May 2008).

166 On 8th August, 2006 Dr. N.C. Saxena and the Special Commissioner Shri. Harsh Mander wrote to the Chief Secretary, GoMP informing him of their decision to constitute a Joint

Commission of Enquiry (JCE) to examine cases of starvation deaths reported and to look into the status of implementation of food-related schemes in the district. With this mandate, a JCE consisting experts visited Sheopur district on 5-6 October, 2006.

167 Shah, Mihir. (2006) 'Report of the Joint Commission of Enquiry',

http://www.mediaforrights.org/pdfs/reports/report3.pdf. (last checked by author May 2008).

It is a fact finding report produced on the incidence Of repeated deaths due to malnutrition in Sheopur District, Madhya Pradesh.

168 Based on the field survey done by Samir Garg, State Adviser to the Supreme Court Commissioners, Chhattisgarh.

169 Mander, Harsh and M. Kumaran. (2006) 'Social Exclusion in ICDS : A sociological whodunit?',

http://www.righttofoodindia.org/icds/icds_surveys.html (last checked by author May 2008).

170 Garg, Samir. (2006) 'Grassroot Mobilisation for Children's Nutrition Rights',ibid.

171 Based on the field survey done by Samir Garg, State Adviser to the Supreme Court Commissioners, Chhattisgarh.

172 Meharu, Charumitra. and Tegan Wong-Daugherty, (2004) 'BARE FOOT DEMOCRACY: Tribal youth speaking up through right-based participatory research'ibid.

173 ibid.

174 Based on the field survey done by Samir Garg, State Adviser to the Supreme Court Commissioners, Chhattisgarh.

175 Shah, Mihir. (2006) 'Report of the Joint Commission of Enquiry', ibid.

176 See VAARTA, 18th Feb. 2008 translated by Rama S. Melkote, as quoted in one of Dr. Kodandram's internal reports.

177 Not only is it integral to Hinduism, but is also practiced by Muslims, Sikhs and Christians. Indian society is accordingly divided into four hierarchical castes: Brahmins, Kshatriyas, Vaishyas and Shudras. The 'ati-shudras' or dalits, fall outside this fourfold hierarchy.

178 Mander, Harsh. (2004) *The Ripped Chest*, Bangalore: Books for Change.

179 Mander, Harsh. (2004) *The Ripped Chest*, ibid.

180 They are spread over Kushinagar, Gorakhpur, Deoria and Mahrajganj over an area of 11718 sq. kms.

181 Tewary, Amarnath. (2006) 'India's feisty untouchable woman', http://news.bbc.co.uk/1/hi/world/south_asia/4723680.stm (last checked by author May 2008).

182 Based on the personal observations made during the visit to Musahar dominated districts of Eastern Uttar Pradesh, in February, 2008.

183 The Madiga community is known as the Mang in Maharashtra, the Chakkaliya in Tamil Nadu and possibly the Matang in North India.

184 'Madiga', http://en.wikipedia.org/wiki/Madiga (last checked by author May 2008).

185 They go by many names in various parts of the country : han, hadi (in Bengal); balmiki, dhanuk (Uttar Pradesh); methar, bhangi (Assam); methar (Hyderabad); paki (coastal Andhra Pradesh); thotti (Tamilnadu); mira, lalbegi, chuhra, balashahi (Punjab); bhangi, balmiki, methar, chuhra (Delhi). Gita Ramaswamy, "India Stinking".

186 (2007) 'Hidden Apartheid - Caste Discrimination against India's "Untouchables"',

http://www.hrw.org/reports/2007/india0207/ (last checked by author May 2008). Hidden Apartheid was produced as a "shadow report" to the UN Committee on the Elimination of Racial Discrimination (CERD), in advance of its February 2007 consideration of a report by the Government of India. The report was produced by Centre for Human Rights and Global Justice & Human Rights Watch.

187 But the Government data is viewed as gross under-estimation as Safai Karmachari Andolan, claims through their survey that the total number of safai karmacharis would approximately be 13 lakhs.

188 Rawat, Vidya Bhushan. (2007) 'Is It Emancipation or Elimination of the Scavengers in Laar Town

(Deoria)' http://www.countercurrents.org/rawat251007.htm (last checked by author May 2008).

189 Thekaekara, Mari Marcel. (2007) 'The "Night Soil" Carriers', infochangeindia.org/index.php/200708296709/Agenda/Women-At-Work/-This-is-our-fate.html - 38k (last checked by author May 2008).

190 Deshingkar, Priya. and Daniel Start (2003) 'Seasonal Migration for Livelihoods in India : Coping, Accumulation and Exclusion', Working Paper 220, London : Overseas Development Institute.

191 Reddy, M. Thimma. 'Kollur Village Profile', www.cphp.uk.com/uploads/disseminations/R7828%20013%20Kollur%20Village%20Profile.pdf (last checked by author May 2008).

192 In a recent documentary film on Untouchability, "India Untouched", directed by Stalin, three girls explain to the director how they need to clean the premises and toilets of the school. When the director asks them why they are ought to clean toilets and not other caste students, a smart girl in that group replies that other children are from upper castes. The director again insists his question, "But why you have to do this?". The same girl replies with an unbearable smile, "You know the reason". In another instance in the same film, a mother says by weeping, "We send our children to school so that they need not do this for their livelihood, but the teachers ask them to do the same in schools". Her son was stopped from going to that school.

193 Based on the personal observations made during the visit to Musahar dominated districts of Eastern Uttar Pradesh, in February 2008.

194 Mander, Harsh and M. Kumaran (2006) 'Social Exclusion in ICDS: A sociological whodunit?', http://www.righttofoodindia.org/icds/icds_surveys.html (last checked by author May 2008).

195 The Asiad Workers' Case (1982) and the Bandhua Mukti Morcha Case (1984), Srivastav, Ravi S. (2005), Bonded Labour in India : its incidence and pattern, 2005. Working paper commissioned as an input to the ILO Director-General's second global report on forced labour, entitled *A global alliance against forced labour*, prepared for the 93rd session of the International Labour Conference, UN.

196 Srivastav, Ravi S. (2005), ibid.

197 Srivastav, Ravi S. (2005), ibid

198 The Child Labour (Prohibition and Regulation) Act; 1986 defines a child as "a person who has not completed their fourteenth year of age". It does not prohibit child labour per se, nor does it set a minimum age, hours and conditions of work for child labourers, while prohibiting the employment of children in twenty-five hazardous industries. The Act also envisages punishment for violation including for parents who induce their children to work in hazardous industries. However, implementation of the regulatory provisions of the act requires each state to formulate an act specific set of rules and regulations; the majority of states have not done so. Further, it gives tacit government approval to the use of child labour, when the child is a relative of the family, including in hazardous occupations or industries. The act is also inapplicable to government-sponsored schools or training programs.

199 The Factories Act 1948 strictly forbids the employment of children less than fourteen years old in factories, but applies only to factories employing ten or more people with the use of electric or other forms of generated power, or twenty or more people without the use of power.

200 It explicitly prohibits the sue of child labourers in beedi and cigar manufacture.

201 It requires establishments to register inter-state migrant workers employed. Contractors must be licensed and keep records of all migrant workers recruited. Migrant workers should be paid at the same rate as non-migrant workers, and regular inspections be carried to ensure compliance.

202 All cases related to children under the age of 14 are governed by the Juvenile Justice (Care and Protection of Children) Act, 2000, which is based on the principles of the United Nations Convention on the Rights of the Child (CRC), 1989. Section 26 of the Act pertains to procuring a child for hazardous employment, keeping him/her in bondage and withholding/ using those earnings is punishable.

203 The South Asian (2005), Indian Laws Against Bonded Labour, 15 March 2005.

http://www.thesouthasian.org/archives/2005/indian_laws_against_bonded_lab.html (last checked by the author May 2008).

204 International Labour Organization (2005), *'A Global Alliance Against Forced Labour'*, United Nation.

205 Government of India, 2008, Bonded Labour Released and Rehabilitated, Press Information Bureau, Rajya Sabha, 5th March. Minister of State for Labour and Employment Shri Oscar Fernandes (Independent Charge) in a written reply in the Rajya Sabha

http://pib.nic.in/release/rel_print_page1.asp?relid=36020 (last checked by author May 2008).

206 2008, 1,855 bonded labourers released : Minister, 6 March, http://www.nerve.in/news:253500133540 (last checked by author May 2008).

207 Brass, Tom (1995), *Unfree labour and agrarian change, A Different view,* Economic and Political Weekly, Jodhka, Suriendar S. (1994), *Agrarian changes and attached labour,* Economic and Political Weekly, Singh, Manjit (1995), *Capitalist Agriculture and Freedom of Labour,* Economic and Political Weekly.

208 Bremen, Jan (1996), *Foot loose labour,: Working in India's Informal Economy,* Cambridge University Press, Oslen, Wendy K. and Murthy, R.V. Ramana (2000), *Contract Labour and Bondage in Andhra Pradesh* (India), Journal of Social and Political Thought, Volume 1, Number 2.

209 Srivastava, Ravi S. and Sashikumar (2003), *An Overview of migration, its impacts and key issues,* Paper No. 2, Migration and Development and Pro-poor Policy Choices in Asia, DFID, London.

210 Ministry of Labour (200-01), Annual report, Government of India, *Annual Report 2000-2001,* p. 181. This figures appear to be based on both 1991 Report of the National Commission on Rural Labour and reports from thirteen states through March 31, 2000, of bonded laborers identified, freed, and rehabilitated.

211 For a review of labour migration in India and its impacts, see Srivastava (1998) ibid and Srivastava and Sasikumar (2003), ibid.

212 Human Rights Watch Children's Rights Project (1996), *The small hands of slavery, Bonded Child Labour in India,* Human Rights Watch/Asia.

213 Sugirtharaj and Sait (1995), Tamil Nadu Commissioners' Report, as cited in Srivastava Ravi (2005), ILO, ibid.

214 The Commission report says that women constitute 20 percent in the brickyards and 10 percent in the quarries.

215 2004, Orissa's migrant labourers : victims of sexual abuse, exploitation, 13 January, The Pioneer.

http://infochangeindia.org/200403303291/Human-Rights/News/Orissa-s-migrant-labourers-victims-of-sexual-abuse-exploitation.html (last checked by author May 2008).

216 Chakraborty, Bhaswati (2004), Gender issues in Bonded labour, A study of Ranga Reddy district, Andhra Pradesh, ILO, New Delhi

217 Analysing the effectiveness of the programmes for the eradication of bonded labour system, Abhay Xaxa, 2006, ibid.

218 GOI (2008), Notes on Demands for Grants, 2008-2009, Ministry of Labour and Employment

http://indiabudget.nic.in/ub2008-09/eb/sbe60.pdf (last checked by author May 2008).

219 Indian Express (2002), *Bonded to Bureaucracy*, Indian Express, April 19.

Summary of the First Report of the Commissioner

[Note : This first report was submitted by Dr. N.C. Saxena, who was the single Commissioner at that time.]

The First Report of the Commissioner (Dr. N.C. Saxena), presented on 12 October, 2002, focuses on the implementation of Supreme Court orders. The Report emphasizes that further steps need to be taken to make the Supreme Court orders effective. The Commissioner recommends employment, such as food-for-work programmes, as an important step towards food security and the elimination of hunger in India.

The Report presents a list ofindividuals and organizations nominated to assist the Commissioner in his work, as well as the role they are expected to perform. Clarifications related to the work of the Commissioner and assistants are provided.

A brief overview of some of the issues analysed in the first Report is presented below :

Request for Information

The Commissioner had sought information on compliance with the Supreme Court's orders and on the implementation of welfare schemes from all the states and union territories. The Commissioner expressed concern that many states have either not replied to these letters or given very general and formal replies, without providing much substantive information. In this context, the Commissioner requested the Court to direct the Chief Secretaries/Administrators of all the states/UTs to respond promptly and to provide full information to him.

Starvation Deaths

The Commissioner is very concerned that despite the endeavours of the Supreme Court, hunger-related deaths have been taking place. Several cases from different parts of the country are presented. The Commissioner stresses that it should be clarified that it is the duty of each respondent government to prevent such deaths. If starvation deaths are confirmed it will be assumed that the Court's orders have not been implemented. In such cases, the Chief Secretary/ Administrator of the State/UT's will be held responsible.

Offtake if Foodgrains and Related Problems

A study shows that the increase in offtake *of* foodgrains for all the welfare schemes between 2000-2001 and 2001-2002 is just 6 million tonnes. This shows that something is holding back real progress. The offtake by many states is very *low.* The list of beneficiaries of various schemes was not being publicly displayed, as directed by the Supreme Court. The Commissioner also reports that foodgrains were not reaching at fair price shops in time and that shopowners were distributing the grains only for three or four days a month.

Food for Work

In some states those working on the Food for Work programmes were not receiving their wages for months. This delay was caused by the non-availability of grain under Sampoorna Grameen Rozgar Yojana (SGRY). Such delays seriously hamper the government's efforts and cause unavoidable hardships to the needy. It therefore emphasized the need for immediate allocation of foodgrains under the Food for Work programme. The Government of India must take the necessary steps to ensure timely payment of wages. Moreover, the Commissioner reiterates the petitioner's claim for 20 million tonnes of free grain to states specifically for use in Food for Work programmes.

Mid-Day Meals

The Commissioner stresses the importance of mid-day meals in primary schools. However, he notes with concern that several states have not yet complied with the Court's order on this. Such states were requested to clarify the reasons for this delay.

Exports

The issue of export of foodgrains by the government is also mentioned with concern. It is pointed out that it is regrettable that the government subsidizes the sale of foodgrains to foreign countries while hunger-related deaths were taking place in the country.

Chief Secretaries/Administrators Responsibilities

The Commissioners emphasize the importance of a cooperative role of States and Union Territories in the fight against hunger. While reiterating that the Commissioner should not be viewed as a fault-finder, in case of persistent failure to comply with the orders of the Court the Chief Secretaries/Administrators would be held responsible [or contempt of Court.

.Summary of the Second Report of the Commissioner

[Note : This second report was submitted by Dr. N.C. Saxena, who was the single Commissioner at that time.]

The Second Report of the Commissioner (Dr. N.C. Saxena) was presented to the Supreme Court in February 2003. In it, emphasis is given to mid-day meals and to Sampoorna Grameen Rozgar Yojana (SGRY), the largest employment programme in India at the time of the Report. Moreover, the status of the implementation of other Supreme Court orders was also covered in this Report. A brief summary of these issues and the corresponding recommendations by the Commissioner are presented below :

Mid-Day Meals

The Report highlights the importance of introducing nutritious mid-day meals in primary schools. These meals are very effective in protecting children against hunger. Many states have shown a positive response by starting the programme with full or partial coverage. However, in Bihar,

Uttar Pradesh and Jharkhand the scheme has not been started at all. Considering the Importance of this programme, the Commissioner requests the Court to provide several directions. It is recommended that such states should be held accountable for total violation of Supreme Court orders and be directed to implement the programme immediately. Moreover, states that have started the scheme in a token way must be directed to extend the programme to the entire state. The Commissioner also recommends that an expert team be set up to prepare a budget for mid-day meals. States should also be directed to make an adequate budgetary provision and prepare guidelines for full implementation within 2 months. Finally, the Report stresses that states should continue to provide mid-day meals in drought affected areas during the summer holidays, and the Government of India should also be directed to provide free grain for this.

Sampoorna Grameen Rozgar Yojana (SGRY) and Relief Employment

Taking up the Sampoorna Grameen Rozgar Yojana (SGRY), the Commissioner shows great concern over its poor implementation in many states. Its poor performance is due to unutilised grain and a low utilisation of available funds under the scheme. Frequently, funds are not released on time. Other problems at the ground level are also pointed out. These include widespread cases of corruption, the use of machines which directly undermines the effectiveness of the scheme, excessive delays in receiving payments, reports that the grain component of wages is not reaching labourers. The Court is requested to direct respondents to utilise the entire allocation of funds and foodgrain in a timely manner and to ensure that there is complete transparency in the use of funds. It is also recommended that the Union of India should release foodgrains and funds on time. An order should be passed that when faced with serious financial constraints the entire wage may be paid in kind (foodgrains) only if the labourers so desire.

Issue of Ration Cards and Targeted Public Distribution System (TPDS)

The proper identification of those below the poverty line (BPL) is a prerequisite for the functioning of the TPDS.

Despite directions from the Court on the need to identify and issue cards to the Below Poverty Line (BPL) population, some states have not complied with these directions. Another concern is the total lack of transparency in the identification process. In some states, people are unaware of their entitlements and corruption is widespread. In order to avoid unfair exclusion of poor people from government schemes, the identification of BPL population is essential and cards must be issued immediately. The Commissioner requests the Court to direct all state governments, particularly the Government of Delhi, to issue ration cards immediately and to register complaints regarding BPL cards. Officers in charge should be held accountable for the non-distribution of cards. Moreover, it is recommended that all BPL cardholders should be allowed to purchase the allotted quota in instalments. Further, they should be allowed to buy the quota (in part or in full) for previous months as well. Migrant workers should also be entitled to draw grain on their BPL cards notwithstanding the fact that they have migrated out.

Pension and Annapurna Schemes

Pension schemes have been relatively successful programmes of central and state governments. These schemes reach the disabled, aged, destitute and widows, who are among the most vulnerable people in the country. Annapurna is a programme which provides 10 kgs. of grain free of cost to those who are eligible for a pension, but are not receiving it. However, despite being relatively successful, many deserving people are being left out of these schemes. The Commissioner therefore advises the Court to direct the Union of India, States and Union Territories to double the coverage of pension schemes and allocate resources accordingly. Moreover, it is also recommended that states should complete the identification of Annapurna beneficiaries within eight weeks of the date of the Report.

Verification of Reports on Starvation Deaths

The Commissioner stresses that it is imperative that drought relief is carried out on a massive scale if mass hunger and starvation are to be avoided. An earlier order of the Supreme Court established that the Chief Secretary would be held responsible for any starvation deaths that occur in a state. In accordance with this order, the Commissioners felt that it is important to verify whether the government has done its duty by implementing welfare schemes to reduce the chances of starvation deaths.

Access to Information

The Report raises Issues related to the lack of information about welfare schemes and poor awareness among beneficiaries of their entitlements. Public awareness is crucial for the success of the welfare programmes. The Commissioner requests the Court to consider directing all the States to pass the Right to Information Act in consultation with civil society groups at the earliest. Vital Information about the schemes should be displayed by the PRIs, especially by Gram Panchayats. Moreover, the Report also recommends that relevant records should be open to inspection. Members of the public should be able to obtain photocopies of documents related to development projects. The Commissioner also suggests that the Chief Secretary/Administrator of each State/Union Territory should review the schemes at least once a quarter and should send a quarterly monitoring report to the Commissioner.

Summary of the Third Report of the Commissioner

[Note : This third report was submitted by Dr. N.C. Saxena, who was the single Commissioner at that time.]

The Third Report of the Commissioner is presented with a sense of urgency. It reviews the two years since the Writ Petition (Civil) 196 of 2001 was submitted by the People's Union for Civil Liberties (Rajasthan). The Report emphasizes that there is still a catastrophic failure to protect the fundamental right to life enshrined in Article 21 of the Constitution and an overarching lack of State commitment to the prevention of hunger and starvation in India.

The Intervention of the Court is viewed as being potentially effective. Some useful orders have been passed and some positive steps have been taken by the respondents. Considering the massive problem of chronic hunger in the country, the Commissioners feel that these Initiatives have only made a small impact. Gigantic food stocks contrast with the fact that India remains one of the most undernourished countries in the world. The Commissioner is deeply concerned that the elimination of chronic hunger does not get the priority it deserves in policy planning and budget allocations. The routine violation of Supreme Court orders by the respondent governments is a symptom of this lack of commitment.

The need for further directions from the Supreme Court and for stronger monitoring mechanisms to enforce the Court's orders is stressed. The implementation of these orders varies substantially between different states and in worst cases like Bihar and Uttar Pradesh, there has been virtually no response from the governments.

A number of urgent issues are covered in the Third Report. The Report reiterates that the Court should not lose sight of the fundamental pleas presented in the original petition, such as the plea for the adoption of an "employment guarantee act" and for permanent social security arrangements for destitute households. The surge in foodgrain exports is also a matter of grave concern. Urban destitution is also mentioned as a problem which remains largely unresolved and which requires creative Initiatives.

Below is a brief overview of some of the main issues analysed in the Third Report and the Commissioner's recommendations to the Supreme Court.

The Employment Issue

It is pointed out that employment at a living wage is the best protection against hunger. The Report shows how central and state governments have demonstrated little commitment to rural employment in recent years. Employment generation under SGRY is extremely limited in the more deprived and hunger-ridden states. The Commissioner suggests that the Court direct all the States to utilise the funds available for SGRY. Moreover, arbitrary implementation of SGRY strengthens the case for considering an alternative approach based on the principle of "employment guarantee". The problem of labour being displaced in employment-oriented schemes by the use of excavators, trucks and tractors has been raised. Moreover, the Report stresses the need to revive and uphold the principle of open-ended employment (without "ceiling") in drought-affected areas.

Mid-Day Meals

The mid-day meals programme has made some progress. It is a serious matter that several states (notably Bihar, Jharkhand and Uttar Pradesh) were yet to introduce mid-day meals at the time of the Report. The Court is urged to consider ways of holding) these states accountable for this lapse and to request the state governments to submit affidavits explaining why mid-day meals are not being provided. Poor quality of meals being served in many of the complying States is also an important issue. Moreover, the Commissioner advises the Court to direct all state governments to continue providing mid-day meals during the summer vacations in drought-affected areas (and to consider doing the same in other areas as well) and to ensure that the basic facilities for the programme are provided.

Targeted Public Distribution System

Problems related to the Targeted Public Distribution System (TPDS) are also raised in this report. The Court is repeatedly directing governments to guarantee that households below the poverty line (BPL households) should obtain 35 kgs. of grain per month at subsidized prices. However, many factors are preventing this scheme from working properly. The Commissioner shows that the public distribution system is in a dismal condition. It has ceased to mean much to the poor in large parts of the country. In this context, the Report urges for radical reform of this system, based on a deep examination of its prevailing failures. Furthermore, the Court is also called to constitute, without delay, an expert committee to deal with this issue and related matters.

Below Poverty Line (BPL) Survey

The selection of Below Poverty Line (BPL) households is a complex issue. The BPL lists are unreliable. The Commissioner recommends that an expert committee be appointed to re-examine the methodology of the "BPL survey" and the larger question of targeting in the public distribution system. The Commissioners feel that in situations of drought and other calamities, relief should not be restricted to BPL households. Other households also tend to require support in such circumstances.

Integrated Child Development Scheme

The Report stresses that the provision of Integrated Child Development Scheme (ICDS) in every habitation, as directed by the Court, is not being properly observed and taken seriously. There seems to have been little action on this front. This scheme is essential to protect small children from undernutrition. The Government of India has been more interested in expanding the ICDS programme than in ensuring that it achieves results. In this context, the increase in the coverage of ICDS is recommended, taking into account that this scheme is not reaching enough children. Furthermore, ICDS should aim to give particular attention to children in the poorest families and to reach children aged under three.

Social Security for Destitute Households

The Report suggests the need for putting in place comprehensive and durable social security arrangements to protect destitute households from hunger. The extension of the Antyodaya Anna Yojana (AAY) programme, despite not being an adequate step on its own for this purpose, is presented as a potentially important component of the required social security system and a welcome step in this direction.

Other Schemes

As for the other schemes, such as the Annapurna, the National Old Age Pension Scheme (NOAPS), the National Family Benefit Scheme (NFBS), the National Maternity Benefit Scheme (NMBC) the Commissioner shows that there is not much to report. In most states, in spite of the intervention of the Court, there is little sign of improvement. Their implementation leaves much to be desired. Among the problems are poor coverage, under-funding, reduced commitment by the government and lack of information about the schemes.

Information Dissemination

To conclude, the Report draws the attention of the Court to the crucial role of information and public awareness for the success of the initiatives in the fight against hunger. There is a need for more systematic efforts to spread information at all levels and make sure that people are aware of their entitlements under food-related schemes. There is also a need for better monitoring system, stronger accountability, redressal and compensation mechanisms.

Summary of the Fourth Report of the Commissioners

India is one of the most undernourished countries in the world, a sad reality recently confirmed in the Human Development Report 2003. And the Fourth Report of the Commissioners to the Supreme Court, dated 14 August, 2003, places great emphasis on the fact that hunger amidst plenty is still a reality in India. The Report highlights that, in contrast with hunger and starvation that continues to haunt the country, the Food Corporation of India still holds 35 million tonnes of foodgrains, nearly 2 times more than the country requires to store in an average month, causing wastage of grains and absorbing enormous financial resources that could be used to assist poor people.

Although the Supreme Court's orders have led to substantial improvements in some aspects of the food system, the orders passed so far are not equal to the task of guaranteeing freedom from hunger and even these orders have been routinely violated. In this context, the Fourth Report stresses that, if the fundamental right to food is to become a reality, there is a need for bolder action.

A number of urgent issues related mainly with the implementation of earlier orders are covered in the Report. Below are some of those issues and the corresponding directions commended by the Commissioners.

Mid-Daymeals

The Commissioners advise the Court to reaffirm the calling for mid-day meals programmes to be introduced in all primary schools. The Court is also urged to clarify that the earlier direction permitting resource-poor states to introduce mid-day meals initially in just one-fourth of the districts is only a temporary measure; States have to be categorically directed to implement mid-day meals in the entire state within six months. The Commissioners also stressed on the need to make qualitative improvements in the meal served and on the need to tackle the issue of caste discrimination in the selection of cooks for the programme.

Integrated Child Development Scheme (ICDS)

Taking up the issue of ICDS or Anganwadis, the Report points out to the lack of attention given by most States to the plight of pre-school children from 6-months to 2 years with no satisfactory arrangement in feeding this extremely vulnerable group. The Commissioners stress that the order by the Court directing state governments to increase the coverage of ICDS has to be taken seriously. In this context, States should be directed to comply with the directions calling for an Anganwadi to be available in each habitation, and for the coverage of adolescent girls, pregnant and lactating women under this programme. Moreover, there is a need to direct states to ensure that all slums are within convenient reach of an Anganwadi and urban homeless children are also covered.

Antyodaya Anna Yojana (AAY)

Some considerations were also raised in relation to Antyodaya Anna Yojana (AAY) programme. Some guidelines issued by the Government of India suggest that AAY cardholders should be selected from the Below Poverty Line (BPL) list, in spite of conclusive evidence that the BPL list is unreliable. In this sense, the Report advice the Court to determine that the possession of BPL cards should not be an eligibility criterion for inclusion in the AAY programme. The Commissioners defend that anyone who is deemed vulnerable to hunger should be entitled to AAY card as a matter of right. Moreover, states should accelerate the issue of these cards.

Social Security Pensions

The Report reiterates the suggestion presented in the

Third Report that the coverage of social security pensions should be doubled.

Urban Destitution

Bold measures are needed to properly tackle the neglected problem of urban destitution. In this context, the Commissioners advise the Court to direct state governments and union territories to : carry out annual surveys of urban destitute persons; make arrangements to effectively protect them from hunger; ensure that relief kitchens are available within walking distance in all urban areas; ensure that all Indian citizens are eligible for a ration card, including the homeless. The Report also recommends the Court to direct the Government of India to supply free grain to state governments for the functioning of relief kitchens and also to NGOs that are willing to provide cooked meals to the urban destitutes.

Employment

In view of the fact that the enjoyment of the right to work is instrumental in securing the right to food, the Commissioners advise that some preliminary directions should be passed in this regard, such as the payment of minimum wages in employment programmes, the introduction of an employment guarantee scheme (Jaya Prakash Narayan Employment Guarantee Yojana) in at least 100 backward districts and the banning of the use of tractors and others labour-displacing machines on public employment programmes. The Court is also requested to direct the Government of India and the States to submit an affidavit outlining the steps taken to comply with the direction to double the creation of employment under the Sampoorna Grameen Rozgar Yojana (SGRY) scheme in May 2003 and direct states that are yet to comply with this order to do it by December 2003 at the latest. The Government of India should release the relevant resources (grain and cash) no later than four weeks from the order, to enable the states to plan and generate employment.

Restraint on Exports

The Commissioners raise a great concern to the fact that the energy shown by the Government of India in expolting food (one million tonnes of grains every month during the last 15 months) goes sharply in contrast with a continued passivity in dealing with endemic hunger at home. For this reason, the Commissioners advise the Court to direct the government to reconsider and restraint this policy of export of foodgrains, resorting to it only after fully and adequaltely meeting the food requirements of the people of the country.

Transparency and Monitoring

The Report points out that the right to food and the right to Information are interlinked and each is necessary to promote the other. The Commissioners stressed the danger of corruption in undermining the right to food, and called for promoting the right to information. The Report urges the Supreme Court to assert that all documents pertaining to food and employment schemes should be opened to public scrutiny and accessible for consultation by any individual at any time. These documents should be treated as public documents. The Commissioners also recommend that states should be directed to ensure prompt and wide dissemination of the directions of the Court.

Special Report (as a follow-up *to* fourth report)

The content in this section is largely drawn from a meeting convened by the Department of Women and Child Welfare at New Delhi on 25 November, 2003. The meeting was called to discuss the recommendations made by the Commissioners regarding the ICDS programme as well as analyze to what extent the Hon'ble Courts orders have been complied with.

5.1. It may be recalled that in an order dated 28 Novernber, 2001, the Hon'ble Court had directed all states to ensure that there is an Anganwadi centre in "every settlement". The intention of the order was to provide universal access to

ICDS. However, the Department of Women and Child Welfare has admitted in a recent meeting, that orders aimed at compliance with this directive have not been issued. Further, the Department maintains that due to financial constraints it is unable to cover "each child, pregnent & nursing mother and adolescent girl" under the scheme as directed by the Supreme Court. Requests made by the Department for enhanced financial allocations have been turned down.

5.2. The response of the department indicates that the Supreme Court Orders have been interpreted within the existing guidelines, rather than as directions that go beyond the same. This is the rationale used for not universalising the scheme either in terms of reaching every "settlement" or in terms of covering "each" beneficiary (child within the age group of 0-6, pregnant and nursing mother, adolescent girls).

5.3. The net result is that only 3.4 crore children are getting the benefit of supplementary nutrition under ICDS. This is nowhere near the number of children in the relevant age group (over 15 crore), or the numbers that are malnourished (8.5 crore), or even the numbers belonging to families below the poverty line (6 crores). The percentage of adolescent girls being covered is much less as the scheme for them has not been as per the information received from FCI as on 26.6.2003. Operationalised for all Anganwadi centres, the coverage of settlements is also not complete. At present for around 14 lakh habitations, there are only 6.05 lakh reporting Anganwadi centres. Thus the present coverage of the scheme is clearly insufficient to meet the needs of all those who require it.

We may add that 3.4 crore is the theoretical entitlement, actual coverage is much less, as the states do no provide sufficient funds to meet the cost of nutrition.

In the light of the above we advise the Honourable Court to :

A. Issue clarificatory orders that the term "settlement" as used in the Order dated 28 November, 2003 pertains to a cluster of households within a village. The order must not be Interpreted by the Department, as only operationalizing the present number of sanctioned ICDS projects.

B. Issue orders that the ICDS services be extended to every child, pregnant and lactating mother and adolescent girl, as directed in the order dated 28 November, 2003. The services must not be restricted to disadvantaged families or to a predetermined number identified and given to the states.

Index

A

Accelerated Irrigation,
 benefit programme, 57
Acknowledge bondage, 400
Ageing population, 299
Agricul tural Produce
 Marketing Committee, 67
Agriculture and Indian
 Economy, 57
Agriculture in Five Year Plans,
 61
Air India Statutory
 Coporation, 102
Andhra Pradesh,
 state of, 199
Anganwadis Centres, 229
Annapurna Scheme, 203
Antodaya Anna Yojana, 5, 200,
 202, 211, 216, 242,
 293, 296, 305
 limited quotas for, 325
Antodaya Scheme, 12
Applied Economic Research,
 National Council of, 72

B

Baiga Mahapanchayat,
 organisation of, 197
Bal Adhikar Suraksha
 Samiti, 152
Basic human rights,
 production of, 131
Below Poverty Line Scheme, 5,
 211, 230
Bhandarkar Oriental
 Research Institute, Pune,
 121

C

Centre for Development
 Studies, Kerala, 173
Centre Issue Price, 4
Chambal Fertilizer and
 Chemicals Ltd. 68
Chhatrapati Sivaji
 Maharaj Vastu
 Sangrahalaya, 121
Chief Secretaries, 229, 244, 251
Child bonded lebour, 394
City streets,
 hunger on, 341
Cluster Development
 Associations, 139
Constitution,
 Article of, 83
 Of India, 82
Council of Food and
 Agricultural organization,
 74
Credit,
 access to, 289
Criminal Procedure
 Code, 1973, 337
Crop production, 66

D

Dalit Adivasi Mahapanchayat, 181
Dalit groups,
  discrimination of, 376
Deccan Development Society, 43
Declaration of Human Rights, 97
Delhi University, 6
Democracy in America, 110
Department of Food and Public Distribution, 214
Deputi Collector, 151
Directive Principle of state policy, 82
Distribution Grain, 400
Dorabji Tata Collection, 121
Dorabji Tata Trust, 116, 124, 148
Dry land agriculture, 140

E

Economic
  impacts of, 51
  deprivations, 381
  social rights of, 93
Education programme, 152
Employment
  Assurance Scheme, 201
  guarantee, 298
  opportunities, 7

F

Farmer,
  debt relief for, 56
  National Commmission on, 63
Food Act,
  Right to, 75, 78, 79
Food and Public Distribution, Department of, 3, 42
Food Commissioners,
  right to, 78
Food Corporation of India, 85, 119, 213
Food schemes,
  access to, 290
Food security,
  and Ecology Security of, 128
  absorption, 29-30
  and Agriculture Organisation, 85
  challenge, 27
  hunger malnutrition and, 1
  of United Nations, 97
  Mission, 29
  various aspects of, 28

G

Gandhi, Mahatma, 29
Geographic Background, 155
Global Hunger Index, 13
Government of India, 12, 46
Grace, W.G., 123
Gram Panchayat, 132, 205
Gram Sudhar Samiti, 108, 109, 114, 142, 151, 158
  programme management at, 176
Gram Swaraj, 144
Gross,
  capital formation, 59
  domestic product, 57
Group empowerment,
  training on, 187
Group information, 178

H

Hanumant Rao Committee,
    145
Hariyali Kishan Bazars, 60
HDFC Bank, 72
Healtcare, 178
    facilities of, 311
Home delivery,
    percentage of, 262
Human Development Report,
    2
Human Rights,
    Act, 1993, 93
    European Court of, 89
    Universal declaration of,
    84
Hunger,
    and starvation, 382
    concept of, 22
    pans of, 45
    trap, 397

I

ICICI Bank, 72
Indian Constition, 81
Indore Milk Union, 141
Ineffective State
    Pansions, 323
Infant Martality Rate, 37
Informal jobs, 338
Information Act,
    Right to, 183
Insuffiect calories, 320
Integrated Child Development
    Scheme, 17, 227, 228, 387
Integrated Child Development
    Service, 204, 236
International Labour
    Organisation, 393

J

JRD Tata Centre for
    Ecotechnology, 125

K

Kisan Credit Cards, 72

L

Lady Meherbai Tata, 127
Latin America, 16
Legal restriction, 67
Livelihood and employment
    access to, 288
Livestock support, 141

M

Mahila Adhikari Manch,
    members of, 181
Management of natural
    resources, 117
Media advocacy,
    workshop on, 192
Mid-day Meal Scheme, 17, 117,
    201, 202, 220, 224, 240
    contractor's quality, 353
Minimum Support Prices, 4
Ministry of Consumer
    Affairs and Food and
    Public Distribution, 214
Mission,
    man with a, 121
Municiple Corporation, 343

N

National
    ariculture extension
    system, 57
    Calamity contingency
    Fund, 33
    Council of Women, 122

Family Health survey, 17
Family Benefit Scheme, 204, 293
Food security, 31
Food security act, 13
Food security mission, 2, 57
Horticulture mission, 29
Human Rights Commission's 82, 101
Institute of Advanced studies, 125
Maternity Benifit Scheme, 204, 244
Old Age Pension Scheme, 203
Rural Employment Guarantee Scheme, 294, 370
Social Assistance Programme, 226

Nehru Gram Bharati
 University, Kotwa, 151

Nehru Jawher Lal, 63

O

Old age security,
 recommendations, 307

Old age homes alternatives, 312

Olympics,
 India into, 121

Oriental Insurance Company, 141

Other welfare programmes, 345

P

Participatory Rural Appraisals, 146

Pension Scheme, 291

People,
 number of, 10
 Union for Civil Liberties, 102

Planning Commision, 1

Political impact, 52

Poverty,
 degree of, 300

Primary information,
 selected village of, 164

Prime Minister, 11, 31

Primitive Travel Groups, 243, 293

Programme functionaries,
 meeting with, 177

Programme
 Coordinator of, 172
 Director of, 172
 supervisor of, 172

Property rights, 287

Pseuda foods,
 consumpsion of, 321

Public
 distribution scheme, 13
 distribution system, 24, 42, 243, 293, 345, 384

Punjab Agriculture University, 67

Punjab Agro Industries corporation, 63

R

Rajiv Gandhi Drinking Water Mission, 30

Rajiv Gandhi Wateshed Mission, 108

Rashtriya Krishi Vikas Yojana, 29, 57

Recommendations,
summry of, 267
Registrar General of India, 246
Responsibilities,
allocation of, 172
Right to food,
Blockwise information of, 156
globalisation and, 86
internation law, 100
judicial production of, 101
legal foundation of, 81-82
meaning of, 98
village selected of, 159
Rights to Information Act, 149

S
Sampurna Gramin Rozgar Yojana, 201, 213, 238, 423
Schooling,
barred of, 317
Self Help Group-Bank Linkage, 138
Sen, Amartya, 18, 72
Sexena, N.C. 218, 219
Social capital,
growth of, 111
Social security pensions, 276, 431
South Asia, 39
South Korea, 66
Special feeding arrangement, 278
Srivastava, P.N., 1
Starvation deaths, 420
State and Schemes, 383
State of food insecurity, 1
Street Children, 336
Sub-Saharan Africa, 7, 26
Subsidised food grains, 274
Supplementary Nutrition, Programme, 12, 17
Supreme Court, 7, 28, 40, 80, 81, 83, 101, 183
commission of, 42
orders of, 198
Surrounding insecurities, 348
Swabhiman Kala Natya Samiti, 183
Swadhar scheme, 290, 297
Swarna Jayanti Shahari Rojgar Yojana, 354

T
Targeted Public Distribution System, 5, 201, 369, 428
Tata Agriculture Rural Training Centre, 116
Tata Communications, 119
Tata Institute of Social Science, 216, 127
Tata Memorial Hospital, 127
Tribal region,
food security issues, 48

U
U N Millennium Summit, 84
Understanding food security, 21
World Food Programme, 6
Union of India, 93, 198, 205, 215, 266
United States, 12, 19, 20
Urban homeless, 334
public help for, 343
Urban slum dwellers, 346

V
Vajpayee, Atal Bihari, 11

Vivekanand Viklang Ashram
Sidhi, 149
Volunteers,
capacity building of, 178

W

Wadhwa, D.P. 256, 266
Watershed development, 145
Wheat
economic cost of, 5
Work programme, food for, 211
World Food Summit, 21, 28, 84, 97
Plan of Action, 74, 97
World food system,
functioning of, 27
World
Bank, 19, 20, 90
food Programmes, 96
food Council, 96
food day, 96
Writ Petition, 198

Z

Zero hunger,
programme, 12,
towards of, 11